# Manatee Insanity

## THE FLORIDA HISTORY AND CULTURE SERIES

UNIVERSITY PRESS OF FLORIDA

Florida A&M University, Tallahassee

Florida Atlantic University, Boca Raton

Florida Gulf Coast University, Ft. Myers

Florida International University, Miami

Florida State University, Tallahassee

New College of Florida, Sarasota

University of Central Florida, Orlando

University of Florida, Gainesville

University of North Florida, Jacksonville

University of South Florida, Tampa

University of West Florida, Pensacola

# Manatee Insanity

## Inside the War over Florida's
## Most Famous Endangered Species

**Craig Pittman**

**Foreword by Raymond Arsenault and Gary R. Mormino**

University Press of Florida

Gainesville \ Tallahassee \ Tampa \ Boca Raton

Pensacola \ Orlando \ Miami \ Jacksonville \ Ft. Myers \ Sarasota

First cloth printing, 2010
First paperback printing, 2022

27  26  25  24  23  22    6  5  4  3  2  1

Library of Congress Cataloging-in-Publication Data
Pittman, Craig.
Manatee insanity : inside the war over Florida's most famous endangered species /
Craig Pittman ; foreword by Raymond Arsenault and Gary R. Mormino.
p. cm.
Includes bibliographical references and index.
ISBN 978-0-8130-3462-1 (cloth) | ISBN 978-0-8130-6884-8 (pbk.)
1. Manatees—Conservation—Florida. 2. Florida—Environmental conditions.
3. Wetland ecology—Florida. I. Title.
QL737.S63P58 2010
333.95'95509759—dc22    2009047420

The University Press of Florida is the scholarly publishing agency for the State
University System of Florida, comprising Florida A&M University, Florida Atlantic
University, Florida Gulf Coast University, Florida International University, Florida
State University, New College of Florida, University of Central Florida, University
of Florida, University of North Florida, University of South Florida, and University
of West Florida.

University Press of Florida
2046 NE Waldo Road
Suite 2100
Gainesville, FL 32609
http://upress.ufl.edu

For SRP and CMP, who once told me
manatees are cooler than video games

# Contents

# Foreword

*MANATEE INSANITY: Inside the War over Florida's Most Famous Endangered Species* is the latest volume in a series devoted to the study of Florida history and culture. During the past half-century, the burgeoning population and increased national and international visibility of Florida have sparked a great deal of popular interest in the state's past, present, and future. As the favorite destination of countless tourists and as the new home for millions of retirees and transplants, modern Florida has become a demographic, political, and cultural bellwether. Florida has also emerged as a popular subject and setting for scholars and writers. The Florida History and Culture series provides an attractive and accessible format for Florida-related books. From killer hurricanes to disputed elections, from tales of the Everglades to profiles of Sunbelt cities, the topics covered by the more than forty books published so far represent a broad spectrum of regional history and culture.

The University Press of Florida is committed to the creation of an eclectic but carefully crafted set of books that will provide the field of Florida studies with a new focus and that will encourage Florida researchers and writers to consider the broader implications and context of their work. The series includes standard academic monographs as well as works of synthesis, memoirs, and anthologies. And while the series features books of historical interest, authors researching Florida's environment, politics, literature, and popular or material culture are encouraged to submit their manuscripts as well. Each book offers a distinct personality and voice, but the ultimate goal of the series is to foster a sense of community and collaboration among Florida scholars.

*Manatee Insanity* represents Craig Pittman's second contribution to the Florida History and Culture series. His first book, *Paving Paradise: Florida's Vanishing Wetlands and the Failure of No Net Loss*, written with coauthor Matthew Waite, addressed one of modern Florida's critical environmental challenges. Now, in his latest work of investigative journalism, Pittman returns to the endangered waters of Florida with a different focus. The manatee, known to scientists as *Trichechus manatus latirostris*, has long been one of Florida's most beloved and vulnerable animals. But Pittman is the first environmental writer to explore the complex history, culture, and science of the controversies and concerns surrounding this remarkable creature. With more than a touch of whimsy, but also with an abiding interest in the uncertain fate of this unique species of Florida fauna, Pittman follows the manatee through time and space, detailing interaction with a variety of human actors, from environmentalists to legislative policy makers to powerboat owners.

Pittman, like all good environmental historians, takes the long view, tracing the manatee's saga across several centuries. But most of the book deals with the thirty-five years since the passage of the federal Endangered Species Act. Afforded official protection as an endangered species, the manatee has drawn unprecedented attention in recent decades—in popular culture, in environmental conferences, in scientific journals, and even on license plates. But all of this attention has not eliminated the slow-moving mammal's vulnerability to speeding powerboats, which have killed more than five thousand Florida manatees since 1974.

Pittman's account of the continuing effort to preserve the manatee's place in Florida's overcrowded and fragile ecosystem is both fascinating and poignant. Written with verve and brimming with insights, *Manatee Insanity* is destined to be a classic. Like its protagonist, this book invites reflection and wonder about the natural world; indeed, for manatee lovers it will surely be the next best thing to sliding into the water and actually sidling up to one of Florida's gentle giants.

Raymond Arsenault and Gary R. Mormino
*Series Editors*

# Preface to Paperback Edition

SEVEN YEARS AFTER THIS BOOK was first published, the U.S. Fish and Wildlife Service made the subtitle incorrect—but confirmed that the title is as accurate as ever.

Right after celebrating "Manatee Appreciation Day" on its social media accounts in March 2017, the feds announced the decision to drop manatees from the endangered list. Manatees would be reclassified as threatened.

The agency made that change despite a record number of manatees killed by boaters in 2016—more than 100.

Scientists like Buddy Powell objected to the change. Crowds at an Orlando public hearing opposed the move. Emails, letters, and petitions of protest arrived from 87,000 people across the nation. Those all failed to change the agency's mind.

"While it is not out of the woods, we believe the manatee is no longer on the brink of extinction," Larry Williams, head of the agency's Vero Beach office, told reporters that day. "This is truly a success story."

Normally the criteria for taking a species down a peg on the list of imperiled species is that the threats have diminished. Instead, Williams cited Runge's latest computer model, which showed that manatees faced no risk of ever going extinct.

The feds also acknowledged, though, that the status change was driven by a lawsuit filed by a libertarian organization called the Pacific Legal Foundation.

The foundation represented a group called Save Crystal River, which opposed new rules requiring boaters there to slow down during the summer as well as winter.

Internal agency documents uncovered by a recent lawsuit showed that the decision was also part of the fallout from electing as president a critic of the Endangered Species Act. After Donald Trump took office, the agency's Atlanta office set what it called a Wildly Important Goal—a WIG, for short—to take 30 species a year off the endangered list or lower them to threatened. Manatees were in the first 30.

As if this turnabout was too much, four months later Snooty died. The South Florida Museum held a celebration of Snooty's 69th birthday that drew 4,000. A day later the popular attraction got stuck in an access panel that had been left ajar and could not resurface. The community mourned, and a petition went around to replace the Confederate monument in downtown Bradenton with one of Snooty.

Then, in the winter of 2020, lots more manatees began dying.

The die-off, while startling, was hardly unexpected. For years, pollution flowing into the Indian River Lagoon had been fueling algae blooms that killed tens of thousands of acres of seagrass. When winter came, the manatees sought refuge in the warmth of the shallow lagoon but had nothing to eat.

"They literally had to choose between dying of cold stress or dying of starvation," Pat Rose said, his voice shaking.

By the end of 2021, more than 1,000 manatees had died, many from malnutrition. Several congressmen called for returning them to the endangered list, but the federal wildlife agency has yet to take that step.

The feds did agree to an experiment: giving the starving manatees some supplemental food. In December 2021, biologists began dropping lettuce into a small square of PVC pipe floating in the lagoon. A month later, in January 2022, the first whiskery snout appeared to nibble at the makeshift salad bar. Soon there were hundreds more.

Then something astounding occurred: as biologists provided the manatees with about 3,000 pounds of Florida-grown lettuce a day for two months, the taxpayers didn't have to pay a dime. Contributions from around the globe covered the cost. Donations totaling more than $150,000 poured in from about 1,000 people in Canada, Mexico, Japan, and Great Britain—proof that manatees remain Florida's most popular species, whether they're endangered or not.

# List of Abbreviations

| | |
|---|---|
| ABATE | A Brotherhood against Totalitarian Enactment |
| CCA | Coastal Conservation Association |
| DEP | Department of Environmental Protection |
| DERM | Department of Environmental Resource Management |
| DNR | Florida Department of Natural Resources |
| EIS | Environmental Impact Statement |
| FDLE | Florida Department of Law Enforcement |
| FMRI | Florida Marine Research Institute |
| FWC | Florida Fish and Wildlife Conservation Commission |
| FWS | U.S. Fish and Wildlife Service |
| IUCN | International Union for Conservation of Nature |
| MMPA | Marine Mammal Protection Act |
| MTAC | Manatee Technical Advisory Committee |
| OMB | Office of Management and Budget |
| PEER | Public Employees for Environmental Responsibility |
| TVA | Tennessee Valley Authority |

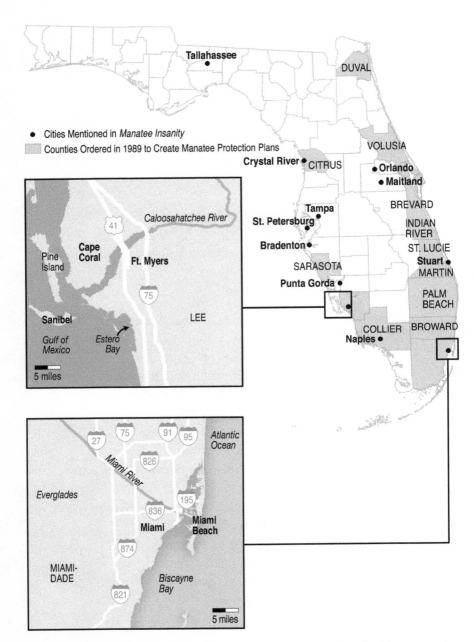

Tallahassee

DUVAL

VOLUSIA

Crystal River ● CITRUS

● Orlando
● Maitland

BREVARD

Tampa
St. Petersburg ●

INDIAN
RIVER

Bradenton ●

ST. LUCIE

SARASOTA

Stuart ●
MARTIN

Punta Gorda ●

PALM
BEACH

COLLIER   BROWARD
Naples ●

Caloosahatchee River

(41)

Cape
Coral

Ft. Myers

Pine
Island

(75)

Sanibel

LEE

Gulf of
Mexico

Estero
Bay

5 miles

(27) (75) (91) (95)   Atlantic
Ocean

(826)

Miami River

Everglades

(195)

(836)
Miami

Miami
Beach

(874)

MIAMI-
DADE

Biscayne
Bay

(821)

5 miles

Sites of important events in the history of manatee protection, including the thirteen counties that were required to draw up manatee protection plans. Dana Oppenheim, Spectrum Design Studio.

# Prologue

## The Sirens' Song

AS THE SUN DIPPED LOW over the Gulf of Mexico on December 2, 2002, a chill wind rippled across the Caloosahatchee River. Gusts swirled through the streets of downtown Fort Myers, past the city's riverfront convention center.

Near the convention center's doors, a crowd of about three thousand people milled around, waiting for showtime. Some in the crowd waved signs that proclaimed "Don't Tread On Me!" "Don't Give Up the Ship!" and "Save Our Jobs!" One man, dressed from head to toe in red, white, and blue, toted a large white cross labeled "Property Rights."

There were skinny teenagers and white-haired retirees, scruffy sailors in tattered jeans, businessmen in sharply creased khakis, even one blond-haired woman in black leather pants, clacking around on impossibly high heels.

What brought them together on this cool evening was a white-hot anger. They were angry about new rules that they believed would hamper their livelihoods and lifestyles, rules designed to protect a homely marine mammal that had been classified as endangered for thirty-five years. One man in the crowd, a burly dock builder from Cape Coral named Mike McCartney, summed up the crowd's feelings with a homemade T-shirt: "Stop the Manatee Insanity!"

Three local television stations parked their satellite trucks out front and dispatched roving reporters to interview people in the crowd. One of the people they interviewed was the blond woman in the leather pants. She turned out to be a local real estate agent named Kimberly D'Agostino, who would later complain, "This creature is infringing on *my* habitat."

Just before 6 p.m., the doors were at last unlocked and the crowd surged through the lobby. They shoved their way past busts of inventor Thomas Edison, poet Paul Laurence Dunbar, and other luminaries of enlightenment and education who once lived in the region. Nobody stopped to admire the statuary. They poured straight into the cavernous meeting hall like a river of boiling-hot lava.

At the back of the hall was a movable partition. The government officials who had set up this meeting had underestimated the turnout, so they had to keep moving the partition back, back, back. Finally the partition was all the way back, and still the people kept pouring in, filling every chair and then lining the walls.

Up front, at a table draped in black, on a stage with a black backdrop, sat Dave Hankla of the U.S. Fish and Wildlife Service (FWS). Hankla, a slim and somewhat aloof bureaucrat with a blond Alfalfa haircut, was wearing a gray polo shirt with his agency's flying-duck logo on the chest, khaki slacks, and a carefully composed poker face.

The open doors let the winter chill inside, and in his short sleeves, Hankla shivered. No one in the audience noticed. As far as the crowd was concerned, he might as well have been wearing a brown shirt and a Hitler mustache. This was his meeting, but it was definitely not his audience. One of the signs now being waved at Hankla by the crowd said, "United We Stand Against FWS."

The TV reporters finished doing their live reports from inside the meeting hall and turned off their bright lights. Then the meeting began. Hankla spoke into the microphone in a dry, reedy voice, using words like "promulgate" and "incidental take." He talked for nearly half an hour about the law, about speeding boats causing "watercraft deaths" among manatees, and then about what seemed to the federal government to be a clear correlation between the number of docks and the number of boats. He tried to explain why his agency wanted to limit the building of new docks as a way of limiting the number of motorboats that could go out and maim and kill a species that was supposed to be protected by two of the strongest federal laws on the books.

Dave Hankla listened with a poker face as three thousand people screamed at him. Photo courtesy of the *St. Petersburg Times*.

"This is *not* a blanket denial of permits in Southwest Florida," he said, a statement that elicited a buzz of disagreement and even some derisive laughter.

When Hankla finished talking, a public hearing on the new regulations was supposed to begin. The first speaker to grab the microphone was a bluff and blustery state representative named Lindsay Harrington. Like D'Agostino, Harrington made his living selling real estate. He had silver hair and a thick mustache. A heavyset man, he sometimes suffered from gout, giving him a bit of a limp, but it didn't slow him down much.

Harrington didn't really want to talk to Hankla. Although the mike stand had been set up so speakers would face the stage, Harrington turned it around so he could address the crowd.

"Many of us," he bellowed, "believe this goes TOO DAMN FAR!"

The crowd roared back its agreement, a ferocious rumble that sounded like an audience of ancient Romans turning thumbs-down on a fallen gladiator.

Up front, Hankla's expression did not change. But toward the back of the auditorium, watching with an expression of horror, stood forty-six-year-old Cynthia Frisch. Frisch had a patrician profile that gave her a passing resemblance to John Singer Sargent's famous painting of Madame X, but at that moment she felt more like the figure in Edvard Munch's *The Scream*.

Frisch really loved manatees. One night, while out on a dinner date in Naples, she spotted four manatees swimming near a dock. Like someone in a trance, she walked into the water with all her clothes on, wading right up to the manatees. They swam all around her legs. It was one of the most glorious nights of her life. Her date freaked out and faded away, but her joy at communing so closely with her favorite animal remained fresh in her memory years later.

Yet despite Frisch's overwhelming love for manatees, all of the uproar in Fort Myers—the hearing, the protesters, the shouting, the anger—was her doing. Frisch had intended to help manatees, never expecting to stir up so much hate. After all, as she later explained, "If there's an animal that's a symbol of peace other than the dove, it's the manatee."

Normally, Frisch was a voluble talker, her features becoming increasingly animated as her words tumbled out in a quickening stream. But that night in Fort Myers, as Frisch listened to the parade of speakers who followed Representative Harrington, each of them complaining that this effort to protect manatees was bad for Florida, bad for America, bad for both the economy and the environment, all she could say was, "Oh, my God!"

•

The manatee might seem an unlikely cause for so much *Sturm und Drang*. It has a body like a dumpling, a tail like a spoon, and the myopic squint of Mr. Magoo. One writer compared it to "a colossal yam with flippers."

The manatee's vaguely feminine shape led ancient sailors to confuse it with the fabled mermaid—although the first time Christopher Columbus saw one, he complained that mermaids weren't nearly as attractive as he had been led to believe.

It might be more accurate call them the hippies of the animal kingdom: staunch vegetarians, nonviolent, but with a powerful sex drive. They even greet each other with something like a kiss.

Manatees have been classified as endangered since the first endangered species list came out. But they aren't like the other wildlife on the endangered list. Most endangered creatures are about as easy to spot as J. D. Salinger. To catch even a glimpse of a Florida panther would require an arduous hunt through a thick and swampy wilderness, and even then you'd need a pack of hounds and an experienced tracker to find one.

But at the end of the twentieth century, as Florida became the fourth-most-populous state in the nation, manatees were comparatively easy to find. They were as likely to surface by a suburbanite's dock as to hide in the Everglades' mosquito-infested mangroves.

"They are, literally, in our backyard," said Bob Bonde, a federal biologist who has been studying manatees since the late 1970s.

As with the duckbill platypus, the manatee's absurd features—whiskers even on the females! nipples in the armpits! flippers with fingernails!—seem to serve no purpose other than to prove that God has a sense of humor. Yet their combination of curious looks and easy accessibility has made manatees one of Florida's natural tourist attractions. There are at least two documented cases where manatees swam up near elderly visitors at Homosassa Springs Wildlife State Park, and the delighted tourists looked down and said, "Ahhhhhhhh!"—and, to their dismay, saw their false teeth fall out and plop into the water.

The image of the manatee is even more widespread than the animal itself. Manatees adorn everything from license plates to postcards, postage stamps, and calendars. They have starred on late-night television shows and in murder mystery novels. A whole industry has grown up around them involving tour boat operators, dive shop proprietors, and the purveyors of cheesy knick-knacks.

Besides their oddity and ubiquity, the other big reason for the manatees' popular appeal has been their vulnerability. They have no natural enemy but man.

Like dolphins and whales, manatees are mammals, warm-blooded creatures that nurse their young. They spend their lives submerged in the water, but stick their gray snouts out about every five minutes to breathe. That's when they are easiest for humans to spot—or to hit with a boat. Since 1974, when biologists began keeping track, more than five thousand manatees have been killed by boats.

Although their bones are as brittle as china plates, manatees are surprisingly resilient. Their skin is like ripstop nylon, making it tough to tear through, and their blood coagulates quickly, so their wounds heal fast. Many manatees have been hit by boats and, though wounded, have survived—although sometimes they needed a little help.

The Lowry Park Zoo in Tampa holds the usual collection of tigers and elephants and monkeys. But one of the most popular exhibits is a big water tank full of gray behemoths swimming in what looks like enough shredded lettuce to stock every salad bar in America. Flocks of children press their noses against the glass, their faces a mixture of awe and morbid fascination. The kids chatter with excitement as the manatees silently glide by, showing off backs and sides and tails cut deep with scars. The Lowry Park tank is actually a waterlogged hospital, a humane place for the manatees to recover from injuries inflicted by humans.

At least two-thirds of all manatees in Florida, and perhaps more, carry scars from being hit by boats. Many have been clobbered repeatedly. When manatee biologists talk about such things, they usually bring up the one that had scars from being hit forty-nine times.

The fiftieth collision proved to be fatal.

•

In a cluttered classroom on the second floor of a brick school building in St. Petersburg, a dozen three-year-olds sit in a circle around their teacher. Their legs have been folded in what they have learned to call "crisscross applesauce." The teacher, a willowy redhead with deep laugh lines around her eyes and mouth, slowly reads them a book about manatees, her voice soothing and calm.

In the book, a mama manatee tries to keep its baby away from a motorboat, but the calf is curious and strays toward the whirling propeller.

One child in the circle, a pretty girl in a pink dress and braids, suddenly blurts out, "Once, when we were getting off our boat, we saw a picture with a manatee on it."

"There were manatees there!" says a serious boy with white-blond hair. He too had seen those dockside warning signs posted for boaters.

"That's right, and be careful," agrees the teacher, ready to get back to the book.

A curly haired boy catches on, his dark eyes growing wider as he makes the connection between the warning sign and what the teacher has been reading. He tells the girl: "A speedboat could hurt them."

The pink-dress girl shakes her head.

"*My* boat doesn't hurt them," she insists firmly.

This is the crux of manatee politics: Everybody loves to see a manatee swim by, but nobody wants to admit to any responsibility for hurting one. And if no one is responsible, then why should there be rules to limit or change human behavior?

After all, Florida has long enjoyed a reputation for being a place with few rules to limit the pursuit of pleasure and profit, a place where the first state flag bore the slogan "Let Us Alone." Many residents still feel that way, especially when they're out on their boats.

More than a million people own boats in Florida. It's part of the state's image: the Donzis pounding through the surf, the flats boats cruising to their fishing spots, the water-skiers waving to the camera. Organizations that claim to speak for all of the state's boaters have demanded to know why the government would impose special rules to slow down the boats to protect an animal that seems to be populous enough that it gets in everyone's way.

Or as one state legislator put it: "How many manatees are enough?"

•

For a decade, as the environmental reporter for Florida's largest paper, the *St. Petersburg Times*, I covered the seemingly endless battles over the state's best-known endangered species.

I sat through interminable government hearings, rode with the officers trying to enforce the speed zones, flew with biologists trying to count manatees from overhead, went boating with a leader of the biggest pro-boater group, repeatedly watched biologists dissecting dead manatees. One winter day I even snorkeled alongside a manatee, the only one of a small herd that wasn't scared off by my flailing around. Afterward the tour boat operator gave me a videotape of the encounter. I remain grateful he didn't mail a copy to *America's Funniest Videos*.

As I covered Florida's war over the manatee—which the *New York Times* called "one of the fiercest fights over an endangered species since loggers in the Pacific Northwest strung mock spotted owls on the grills of their trucks"— I repeatedly heard scientists refer to manatees as "sirenians." For the species known as *Trichechus manatus latirostris*, this is the order name. The story goes that, because manatees and their relatives the dugongs resembled mermaids, taxonomists classified them as the order Sirenia.

But that word always bothered me. As anyone with a passing acquaintance with Greek mythology could tell you, mermaids are not Sirens. Mermaids are alluring creatures with the head and torso of a woman and the tail of a fish. From Hans Christian Andersen's "The Little Mermaid" to the movie *Splash* to the costumed swimmers at the Weeki Wachee Springs tourist attraction, the popular image of mermaids is a benign one. As Shakespeare wrote in *A Midsummer Night's Dream*:

> Once I sat upon a promontory,
> And heard a mermaid on a dolphin's back
> Uttering such dulcet and harmonious breath
> That the rude sea grew civil at her song
> And certain stars shot madly from their spheres,
> To hear the sea-maid's music.

The Sirens, however, were anything but beautiful, and definitely not benign. They were creatures with the head of a woman and the body of a bird. Their music was not intended to calm the rude sea. Their songs seduced mariners to leave their safe channels so their ships crashed on the rocks and the sailors drowned. I always imagined them sounding like the Wilson sisters from the rock group Heart singing "Crazy On You"—the voices twining together in a way that was not exactly pleasant, yet remained strangely compelling.

The poet Homer tells how Odysseus, to get his ship past the singing Sirens, jammed wax in his crew's ears so they wouldn't be distracted from seeing the world the way it really was. Then he lashed himself to the mast, so he could listen to the Sirens without being able to reach the wheel.

The taxonomists' confusion over Sirens versus mermaids is actually an apt metaphor for the situation with manatees. Fans of manatees (fanatees?) see them as misunderstood mermaids who want nothing more than to live in harmony with man. The people who regard them as a threat see manatees as Sirens, a sailor's worst nightmare, an agent of disaster.

Both sides have played the siren themselves, singing songs that sounded good but led to destructive actions. Both sides have at times misinterpreted science to produce results that fit their preconceived notions. Both sides have lashed themselves to an ideal image—one that they say speaks of freedom and heritage and wilderness—that should unite them, but instead has led to bitter conflict.

The fact is, manatees are not what they appear to be. Although they seem vulnerable, they are remarkably tough animals, able to absorb exceptional pain and injury and still keep going. Their status seems precarious, yet they have proven to be highly adaptable, finding a way to survive in a world where the habitat of man continues to intrude into their own.

But there are limits to how much punishment they can absorb, and how much they can adapt to a world where they are frequently treated as a living speed bump. Science has shown that their future is far from assured. Whether manatees survive has already proven to be a major test of whether the state and federal laws that are supposed to protect such species are to be based on science or on politics.

Ironically, the first time Lindsay Harrington's predecessors in the Florida Legislature turned to the subject of manatees, it was to offer them more legal protection than they had ever had before. The irony cranks up to 11 when you learn the legislature took this action at the instigation of an avid boater—who also happened to be Miami's first big real estate broker.

# Sweet Water, Dirty Water

IN THE 1980S, Miami had a reputation as a glittering, cosmopolitan city. Its sizzling style and casual violence were celebrated in a trendsetting TV show called *Miami Vice* as well as a bloody gangster movie called *Scarface*.

As both the TV show and movie implied, Miami's booming economy got a big boost from the multimillion-dollar cocaine trade. The drug dealers depended on souped-up speedboats smuggling in contraband from South America, with law enforcement officers sometimes being paid to turn a blind eye.

People around the world saw those images. They could see Miami was a place where garish opulence existed side by side with heartbreaking poverty. They could see it had a polyglot populace that was not so much a melting pot as a bubbling cauldron of political, racial, and religious tension. And yet, despite those obvious drawbacks, millions of them wanted to live there too. After all, Miami was the city on the edge of the future, the new Casablanca, Magic City.

It was also a remarkably young city. A century before *Miami Vice*, Miami didn't exist.

In fact, in the 1880s there wasn't even much of a settlement there, just a handful of hardy souls who had carved out a spot among the thick tropical hammocks along the Miami River. The river, which one pioneer described as "a beautiful clear-water stream," got its name from a Seminole Indian word that meant "sweet water."

On the south side of the river, where it flowed into Biscayne Bay, lived a storekeeper named William Brickell who told wild stories about his past. He claimed to have practiced law in California. He boasted that he had tried his hand at mining in Australia. He claimed to have served as an adviser to the Mikado in Japan. Now he was eking out a living in an American jungle. Brickell had built a two-story house among the wild palms for his wife and seven children, and then turned one room into a trading post.

Among Brickell's best customers were the Seminoles. They paddled up to his wharf in cypress canoes bringing venison, alligator hides, sweet potatoes, and egret plumes to trade. Sometimes they also brought one of their favorite delicacies, manatee meat. In exchange, they wanted flour and other recently discovered necessities, such as alarm clocks and hand-powered sewing machines.

On the north side of the river stood Fort Dallas. The fort been a busy spot during the war with the Seminoles, but now it was abandoned. Soon it would become the home of an ambitious widow from Cleveland named Julia Tuttle.

Back then, one early settler wrote, "this country was an absolute wilderness, with the nearest railroad 400 miles away, and in the whole country . . . there was no road, no horse, no wagon, and only 11 voters. Our nearest town was Key West 150 miles away and our only transportation was by boat."

But that was all about to change. The 1880s marked the first influx of what Floridians today call "snowbirds." The settlers called them "swells" because they seemed to wash ashore with every tide. The swells were drawn to South Florida by the warm winters, as well as the chance to catch tarpon and kingfish, to enjoy sailing on the bay, or to hunt the vast array of wild game.

"Panthers were still to be found, wild turkeys were plentiful, deer numerous, alligators and crocodiles of huge size filled every river and lagoon, green turtle swarmed on the southern beaches and shoal-water feeding grounds, and the cumbersome manatee was common," one settler wrote.

While the tourists might shoot the wildlife for sport, the pioneers saw it all as food—especially manatee, which they could capture using nets, or kill with a harpoon or a gun. One veteran of the Seminole Wars who had sampled some sea cow described it as quite a taste sensation: "The fattest, juiciest Tennessee beef is by no means equal to it and I doubt if there is anything in the animal kingdom that is so utterly delicious."

Those pioneers knew how to stretch a prime cut of meat for as long as possible. When the women cooked dinner—usually outdoors, over an open fire—

they might whip up some "Gypsy Stew," which one settler described as made from "whatever was at hand. The meat base was usually wild hog, gopher (tortoise) or manatee."

In late 1884, a swell named Frederick Streeter Morse stepped off the boat at Brickell's wharf for a winter visit. Morse, twenty-four, hailed from Boston, then widely regarded as a hub of urbane sophistication. At the time, Boston held more people than all of Florida. Morse's ancestors had put down roots in Boston in 1630, and in the two centuries since, the family had prospered. But Morse's father, a well-to-do merchant, died when Morse was just three, leaving the boy to be raised by his mother.

Despite Morse's wealth and breeding, the slender young man with the bushy mustache had a friendly manner and a quick wit. He was, a later acquaintance said, "a great boy for the blarney." Another described him as "a bright, talkative young fellow, full of jest."

Morse had traveled to Florida because he suffered from some unspecified ailment, possibly tuberculosis, which led doctors to advise him to avoid Boston's brutal winters. Florida was warm all right, but as Morse stood on the dock he faced what was surely the most forbidding environment he had ever seen. Another visitor a decade later described landing at the same spot and finding only "a fair-sized clearing with a few flowers and fruit trees and, of course, the coconuts (palms). Beyond that was dense jungle, merging further back into pine forest almost as wild." Add to that the swarms of bloodthirsty mosquitoes, not to mention sharks, gators, and other predators waiting to chomp on the unwary traveler, and you've got a landscape as different from Boston as can be.

Still, the area had its attractions. Biscayne Bay itself amazed visitors accustomed to the opacity of northern seawater. Wrote another swell of that era: "No sea-lover could look unmoved on the blue rollers of the Gulf Stream and crystal clear waters of the reef, of every delicate shade of blue and green, and tinged with every color of the spectrum from the fantastically rich growths on the bottom." Anyone sailing along "feels himself afloat on a sort of liquid light, rather than water, so limpid and brilliant it is." And in contrast to the industrial North, "the air had never a smudge of man's making."

Morse lodged at Brickell's trading post that winter. It was a good place to meet the locals and learn the lay of the land. He breathed in the clean air and looked at the limpid sea and decided he liked it. He spent a second winter there, and when he went back North in the spring of 1886, he bought a boat and sailed south to stay. The swell had become a settler.

Morse could see the sort of future a place like this could offer a young man with money, connections, and a good line of blarney. He went into real estate.

He sank all of his savings into buying land. He corresponded with anyone interested in buying some of it. He familiarized himself with the whole region. Despite his supposedly delicate health, he even hiked the treacherous coastline with one of the "barefoot mailmen" who carried letters and packages along a 120-mile route from the settlements to the north, walking or swimming the whole way.

Morse hired a man to clear his land for development. The unmarried real estate mogul then built a house he called his "bachelor shack," and with the help of his hired man he built a road from there to the bayshore. He cultivated tomatoes and other crops he could sell up North for a profit, especially in the winter—and then used his experience as a selling point for potential customers.

Now when boats landed at Brickell's dock with a new group of swells, Morse showed up to meet them. He would offer to show them around, meanwhile pitching the various properties available. No longer was he a pale Boston Brahmin in a stiff collar and button shoes. Visitors saw "a smiling, bare-headed, suntanned man in blue jeans and a shirt open-throated to the February breeze."

"'Just in time for breakfast,' was his genial greeting," one tourist reported. "'Ever taste a good ripe papaya?' He led us to his little 'bachelor shack' close by. 'After that we'll say how-do to the people around here, then take a little sail down the Bay to a place for you to stay.'"

Living in a land with few roads, Morse quickly became an avid sailor. It was a common pursuit. When several sailing enthusiasts founded the Biscayne Bay Yacht Club—still in existence today as the oldest continuous organization in Miami—Morse was one of the club's fourteen charter members.

To celebrate Washington's Birthday in 1887, another recent northern transplant, an ex-newspaperman turned children's book author named Kirk Munroe, organized a sailing race on Biscayne Bay. Morse, in his sharpie *Amy,* was one of the regatta's fifteen competitors. He lost to Brickell, who piloted a sloop made in Staten Island.

After the race, all the contestants and spectators, about fifty people in all, enjoyed a hearty meal of fish chowder at the area's newest (and only) hotel, the Peacock Inn.

The Peacock Inn was in Coconut Grove, a somewhat larger settlement about six miles south of Brickell's store. The inn—really just a two-story house with an extra guest room—had become a center of pioneer society in South Florida. It was a place where "both natives and swells gathered to discuss and debate every topic from fish and the weather to world affairs," noted one historian. "Afternoon tea at the inn became a daily ritual and dinner was a bountiful, ceremonious but unhurried affair. The crux of such evenings was the spirited, animated gusto of earnest conversation on a variety of subjects, whether cultural or mundane, as the townspeople gathered on the cool outdoor veranda." Morse, being "a great boy for the blarney," must have been a frequent participant in these discussions, as was the lanky and sociable Kirk Munroe.

Because there were so few settlers, and they had so little access to store-bought supplies, they usually shared whatever bounty they came across, particularly when the catch of the day was a manatee. In September 1891, Munroe—on the verge of being voted the most popular author of boys' adventure books in the country—wrote an indignant letter to the editor of the *New York Times*. He wanted to complain about a story that said a manatee on display in that city was the first to be captured alive, and that manatees lived only in fresh water. Munroe, who lived in Coconut Grove, wrote that he had frequently sighted manatees "disporting in the breakers" in salty Biscayne Bay, where they fed on the ample sea grass beds.

"Only three months ago two of my neighbors discovered a herd of five and killed one," Munroe wrote. "It was of such a size to supply our settlement of 100 souls with meat for three days."

Munroe went on to note that one of his friends, Captain John Zellers of Indian River, made a good living capturing manatees that were exhibited at Philadelphia's centennial celebration and P. T. Barnum's shows. Zellers, according to Munroe, was so skilled at capturing the creatures in his nets that he had been nicknamed "Manatee." He "has exhibited others of his own account at the seaside resorts from Cape May to St. Augustine. His captures have all been made on the St. Lucie, the Loxahatchee, and the Indian Rivers, but always in salt or brackish waters."

An expert manatee-hunter like Zellers could make a handsome profit off the public's appetite for novelty. A *New York Times* report on a twelve-foot-long manatee from Indian River brought to New York for exhibit in 1879 noted that it "is so rare as to be an object of interest to those well-versed in natural history." The story estimated that manatee to be worth ten thousand dollars, but the usual price for a live manatee was closer to one hundred.

Dead manatees could double a hunter's earnings. "The profits of manatee hunting are large," a publication called *Forest and Stream* reported in 1880. "The skeleton, if properly cleaned, will readily bring $100, and the skin a like sum if taken off whole, being in demand by scientists for museums all over the world."

Scientists were so eager to get manatee specimens because they feared that soon there would be none. A relative, the Steller's sea cow, had been hunted to extinction just twenty-seven years after being discovered in the Bering Sea. Surely the manatee faced a similar fate. Before long, *Forest and Stream* predicted, as civilization encroached further into the wilderness along the rivers where manatees were found, there wouldn't be any left to capture. "Then it will surely happen that the peace-loving manatee will be driven away and they will become but a legend or old man's tale," the magazine warned.

Some scientists speculated that the manatee population that had once seemed to be thriving was already in decline. "It is undoubtedly a fact that the American Manatees are much less abundant in many regions than they were at the time of the discovery of America," Frederick W. True, a scientist with the Smithsonian Institution, wrote in a government survey of the nation's fisheries published in 1884, the year Morse first arrived in South Florida. "They have withdrawn before the advances of civilization. . . . Putting all the facts together, it seems evident that not many centuries will pass before Manatees will be extremely rare, especially in our own country. More specimens should be accumulated in our museums . . . and its wanton destruction should cease."

Some of Florida's settlers had also noticed an apparent decline in the population. One Indian River resident reported that in 1880, when he first built a home there, "he often saw them from the door of his little house at The Narrows passing up and down the river and occasionally he saw them at play when they would roll up, one behind the other, like the coils of a great sea serpent." But he didn't see any more after 1887, he told a curious biologist eight years later.

Even the tourists took up the refrain. An 1889 *New York Times* piece about what travelers might see in Jacksonville noted that a small, barnacle-covered manatee was on display for visitors, then added that such creatures "were now very scarce."

In 1892, a publisher put out a book for young readers called *Sea-side and Way-side* by a writer and anti-liquor activist named Julia McNair Wright. Wright was best known for a popular guide to domestic bliss, *The Complete Home*. In her new book she became the first writer to portray manatees as something other than a scientific curiosity or a source of food. In a chapter titled "A Real Live Mermaid," Wright informed her readers that manatees were "as amiable, mild, gentle, playful, kindly a creature as ever drew breath."

She then mangled several facts about them. She mistakenly claimed they lived only in herds, migrated from the Caribbean, and were commonly found in what she called "the Santa Lucia River" in Florida. Then she predicted that because manatees were being "recklessly slaughtered" by hunters, "the manatee, like the buffalo of the Western plains, is likely soon to be extinct."

Wright was not the only children's book author warning readers about the future of manatees. In 1892, Coconut Grove's own Kirk Munroe produced a book called *Canoemates*, which charted the adventures of a pair of boys named Sumner and Worth as they paddle across the wilder parts of South Florida. Along the way they encounter cowboys and Seminoles and soldiers, not to mention panthers and other wild creatures. In one chapter, titled "One of the Rarest Animals in the World," Munroe's heroes suddenly are startled by "a huge black object" that rears up and nearly capsizes their craft:

"It must have been a whale," said Sumner. "No," answered Lieutenant Carey; "but it was the next thing to it. It was a manatee or sea cow. . . . I wish you boys might have a good look at him, though, for the manatee is one of the rarest animals in the world. It is warm-blooded and amphibious, lives on water grasses and other aquatic plants, grows to be twelve or fifteen feet long, weighs nearly a ton, and is one of the most timid and harmless of creatures. It is the only living representative of its family on this continent, all the other members being extinct. The Indians hunt it for its meat, which is said to be very good eating, and for its bones, which are as fine-grained and as hard as ivory. In general appearance it is not unlike a seal. It can strike a powerful blow with its great flat tail, but is otherwise unarmed and incapable of injuring an enemy. Several have been caught in nets and shipped North for exhibition, but none of them has lived more than a few weeks in captivity."

"What made that fellow go for us if he isn't a fighter?" asked Worth.

"He didn't," laughed the Lieutenant. "He was probably asleep, and is wondering why we went for him. I can assure you that he was vastly more scared than we were."

A year later, the Florida Legislature stepped in to help out "one of the rarest animals in the world." Leading the charge: Munroe's friend, Fred Morse.

By 1893, Morse, like many a Florida real estate mogul since, had gone into politics, another good career choice for someone handy with the blarney. He was elected as Dade County's delegate to the Florida House of Representatives. At the time, the legislature met every two years in Tallahassee, where—just like today—the lawmakers' votes often demonstrated their allegiance to powerful interests and not to what might most benefit their constituents.

The legislature that year was dominated by the state's railroad barons. The populist movement was making a push to regulate the industry, so railroad lobbyists—then known as "corporation agents"—were busy in every hotel, boardinghouse, saloon, and poker room in the city convincing lawmakers to bury the measure. They succeeded.

Amid all the arm-twisting, a few other issues arose. The lawmakers prohibited raffles, regulated the length of rifles, and passed the state's first water laws—the so-called ditch and drain laws authorizing counties to "build drains, ditches or water courses upon petition of two or more landowners." Floridians would be paying for that mistake for more than a century.

The legislature also imposed some new regulations on fishing. The fishing regulations won the backing of Governor Henry Mitchell, a Tampa newspaper editor whom relatives described as "a great big man [who] had bad teeth" and was "very, very ugly." He called for protecting the state's fisheries from outsiders, who were making money off Florida's marine resources. "The fish business is very profitable and rapidly increasing," Mitchell told the lawmakers.

At Mitchell's urging, the legislature passed laws that required non-U.S. citizens to get a fishing license; prohibited non-citizens from exporting their catch out of state; prohibited the harvest of oysters except for home consumption from May 1 to October 1; and restricted the types of fishing nets that could be used.

On the first day of the session, April 4, 1893, Representative Morse proposed his own measure to protect the state's marine life: House Bill 295, "an act to protect the manatee or sea cow."

Morse's bill encountered no opposition. It passed the House unanimously on May 27, and the Senate followed suit on June 1. Five days later, Governor Mitchell signed it into law.

The new law said hunters could no longer kill or capture as many manatees as they wanted, not without first getting permission from their county com-

Fred Morse was "a great boy for the blarney," so of course he went into politics. Photo courtesy of Florida Photographic Collection, State Archives of Florida.

mission. Anyone caught hunting manatees without a county permit faced a fine of five hundred dollars—or worse, up to three months in jail.

Not just anyone could get a permit, either. "Whenever the County Commission of any county shall be satisfied that the interest of science will be subserved, and that the application for a permit to kill or capture a manatee or sea-cow in that county is for a scientific purpose and should be granted," the new law said, "they may grant to such a person making the application a special permit."

In other words, manatees weren't for eating anymore. They were just for studying.

Adding to the regulatory protection, the law said no one could get a blanket permit to catch ten or twenty manatees at a time. Instead, the law required a hunter to get a separate permit for each manatee to be captured or killed.

What prompted Morse to sponsor such a measure? Unfortunately, his reasoning is not spelled out in the legislative record or anywhere else in the state's archives. But as a sailor, Morse had surely seen manatees in Biscayne Bay just as Kirk Munroe had. It's possible that as a northern transplant he found them as fascinating as the denture-dropping tourists a century later.

As a cultured Boston native, he enjoyed a good read. By the time he died he had amassed an impressive library. So he may have seen the many articles and books predicting the species' imminent demise.

Morse's manatee bill could have been influenced by his friendship with Kirk Munroe, who was not only a writer but also an early environmental activist. Munroe and his wife, Mary—a highly educated and opinionated woman— helped found the Florida Audubon Society a few years later.

The Munroes were extremely concerned about how the rising demand for egret plumes for use in ladies' hats was rapidly wiping out South Florida's bird rookeries. Mrs. Munroe, who relished taking part in the Peacock Inn debates, had a reputation as what some people today might call a radical eco-nazi. On visits to New York, she would trail society women through the streets and then pounce, demanding to know where they got the feathers on their hats. On at least one occasion she reached up and snatched the feathers out. She also played a crucial role in getting state leaders to establish a state park that later became the nucleus of Everglades National Park.

In November 1891, just two months after Kirk Munroe wrote to the *New York Times* about how one manatee could feed one hundred people for three days, the author lamented in a magazine piece that "Florida is overrun by . . . what are inelegantly but truly named 'bird butchers,' 'fish hogs,' and 'skin hunters.'" And as his writing in *Canoemates* proved, Munroe believed that the manatee's days were numbered.

It's easy to picture Representative Morse relaxing in a rocking chair on the veranda of the Peacock Inn, perhaps after another yacht club regatta, and chatting with the Munroes about the plight of the poor, defenseless manatee. He would of course promise the couple—his most famous, most vocal, and most influential constituents—that he would do something about the problem just as soon as he got to Tallahassee. The Munroes might have even written the language of the bill for him.

Another possibility is that Morse intended the law as a protectionist measure. As someone who was acquainted with everyone in the region, he probably knew Captain Zellers as well as Kirk Munroe did. His new law would weed out the amateur manatee-hunters who were killing just for sport and leave the netting to professionals like Captain Zellers who had established local political connections.

There is another intriguing possibility. On March 17, 1893—less than a month before Morse filed his bill—the local paper, the *Tropical Sun*, ran a small notice on its front page announcing a new local business:

> A company has an application for a charter, the purpose being to propa-
> gate sea cows or manatees in the waters of Dade County. The farm will
> be in Card Sound, just south of Biscayne Bay, and will embrace about
> 100,000 acres of water, the bottom of which is covered with the grass so
> greedily devoured by manatees. The industry will be very profitable; the
> animals, when fully grown, weigh up to 1,500 pounds; the flesh is supe-
> rior to beef and the hides are equal to walrus skins.

Could Morse's bill have been aimed at quashing this budding business venture before the manatee ranchers blocked off the boaters' access to Card Sound?

The *Sun* story did not name the proprietors of this proposed manatee farm. One historian later speculated that one partner might have been the newspaper's own editor, described as "Guy Metcalf, the unfrocked schoolmaster, gold coast lothario, roving news gatherer, associate of side-show operators and carpetbaggers." Whether because of Fred Morse's law or the logistical difficulty of rounding up a whole herd of sea cows, the manatee-farming proposal never got past the talking stage.

Whatever Morse's motives, his manatee law made people sit up and take notice. Three years after it passed, the *New York Times* ran a story on a nine-foot-long female manatee named Betsy that had been caught at the mouth of the St. Lucie River and then carted north for display in Central Park. The paper took care to note that "the Florida species is nearly extinct, and there is a state fine of $500 for their capture or destruction." But the captor, the paper wrote, "has a license to secure them for scientific purposes, and he has captured five altogether."

The law apparently even had a deterrent effect on some would-be consumers of manatee meat. In 1896, the same year the *Times* ran its story on the Central Park manatee, the *Miami Metropolis* noted that a South Florida visitor had spotted two large manatees in a canal and "said he easily could have got one of them . . . had he not remembered there was a heavy fine for killing a manatee."

More than twenty years after Morse's law took effect, famed botanist David Fairchild contended that it had prevented many a senseless manatee death:

"Tourists have always had an insane desire to shoot the entirely helpless animals, but with a check of $500 laid on the act, few care to pay the price for the sport."

However, when wealthy playboy-turned-biologist Charles Cory toured South Florida soon after Morse's law went into effect, he documented that the Seminoles were still harpooning manatees, and not for scientific purposes. He even went after a manatee himself, apparently with no legal consequences. It would not be the last time a law aimed at offering ironclad protection for manatees would suffer from inconsistent enforcement.

In 1894, Morse was interviewed by a St. Augustine newspaper reporter for a story later reprinted in the *Tropical Sun*. In the story, he did not plug his new pro-manatee law or mention anything else he and his colleagues in the legislature had done. Instead, he turned the article into a real estate sales pitch.

"In the Biscayne Bay region lie undeveloped thousands of acres of rich muck lands for gardening, spruce pine lands, such as are selected for the pineapple plantations of Lake Worth and Indian River, and pine lands adapted to the growth of the lime, lemon and all tropical fruits," he told the reporter. "A man having five or ten acres under careful cultivation should have a considerable income in return."

Around this time Morse landed the largest real estate client of his life, a man whose vision would change the face of Florida.

•

Standard Oil tycoon Henry Flagler was building a railroad line down the state's east coast and constructing a fancy new hotel at every stop. Everywhere he extended his railroad—St. Augustine, then Daytona, then Palm Beach—he transformed a sleepy village into a booming resort.

Julia Tuttle, the ambitious widow now living at Fort Dallas, pestered Flagler for years to extend the line to her little settlement on the Miami River. Flagler repeatedly brushed her off. He was busy, not only with his railroad and hotel businesses but with a nasty divorce from his second wife. Ultimately he needed the legislature to pass a special law just so he could be free to marry a third time.

Then, in December 1894, a hard freeze hit Florida, wiping out citrus crops throughout the areas where Flagler's railroad lines ran. Temperatures fell to fourteen degrees at Jacksonville. In Palm Beach, ice formed a layer an eighth of an inch thick on a fountain in front of Flagler's Royal Poinciana hotel.

Such a cold snap meant bad business for a man promoting his Florida resorts as a warm place for the swells to spend the winter. What made it worse
was that Flagler raked in most of his profits not from the hotels but from railroad freight charges. If the freeze doomed the fledgling Florida citrus industry, Flagler's freight cars would rattle back north empty, and soon his railroad
empire would wither.

Flagler dispatched an assistant to check the conditions at Mrs. Tuttle's settlement. The assistant returned carrying a sprig of orange blossoms to show it
had not been affected by the freeze. Flagler quickly decided to build a new
line down to Mrs. Tuttle's little clearing in the wilderness. It didn't hurt that
she and the shopkeeper Brickell had offered to give Flagler half of their land.
In exchange, Flagler promised to build roads and bridges throughout the area,
enabling Tuttle and Brickell to develop and sell the other half.

In 1896, just four months after Flagler's new railroad line arrived, Fred
Morse presided over one of the initial meetings to discuss declaring their growing village a city. Subsequently a group of about four hundred black and white
residents gathered at a pool room called The Lobby and voted to incorporate.
The racially mixed crowd elected a mayor and council, with Morse selected as
the first city council president. Morse was not the only Flagler employee to win
a city post. Flagler had so many employees among the ranks of the new city's
leaders that there was talk of naming the place "Flagler." The tycoon declined
the honor, so the new city became Miami.

The arrival of Flagler's railroad wrought tremendous changes in Miami, and
not just because the train brought thousands of tourists, along with, as one
writer put it, "speculators, tradesmen, merchants, and laborers." To build the
railroad along the coast from Palm Beach to Miami required dredging and
filling the roadbed along the old barefoot mailmen's route, thus destroying
mangrove wetlands, altering inlets, wiping out sea grass beds, and changing
the natural flow of water.

Flagler's plans included not just a railroad and a hotel, the Royal Palm, built
at what had been Fort Dallas. Flagler also owned a steamship line to carry passengers beyond Miami to Key West. But the steamships needed a deeper port
than the Miami River could provide. That meant he had to dredge a nine-foot-
deep channel through the mouth of the river out into the bay. The dredging left
behind big piles of spoil which Biscayne Bay Yacht Club members complained
ruined their sailing.

Flagler also built the city's first sewer system, with the outfall dumping sewage straight into the river. Within a decade the tons of sewage tainted the "sweet water," causing serious health problems for Miami's residents.

Morse didn't complain about Flagler's changes. He stayed busy the rest of his life running Flagler's Model Land Co., developing and selling home lots to the new arrivals pouring in via the rail line. He became a Mason and an Elk and a Knight of Pythias and a mainstay of the local Episcopal church. Miami became so civilized that Morse even moved his elderly mother down from Boston to live with him.

Other pioneers didn't fare as well. Mrs. Tuttle died two years after Flagler's arrival without seeing the booming development or big money she had long envisioned. Meanwhile, the dredging for the port left Brickell's store cut off from river traffic for a time, until he was able to sell the spoil for road construction. He eventually saw a profit from land dealings, but didn't live long to enjoy it. He died ten years after Mrs. Tuttle.

Morse himself died in 1920 at age sixty-one, prosperous but still unmarried and apparently childless, still living with his mother. He left behind a city on the cusp of a major real estate boom, soon to be followed by a bust that prefigured the Great Depression.

In 1930, ten years after Morse's death, Miami's population hit 110,000. One of the other charter members of the Biscayne Bay Yacht Club bemoaned the sorry state of the big city, compared to the unspoiled beauty of the wilderness settlement: "Now locomotive, factory, and power-house chimneys pour out their wasteful and defiling soot . . . we have the bitter reek of burning peat from the ground fires in the drained Everglade lands. Meanwhile the sea itself is badly polluted with tar and sludge pumped out of the oil-boats' ballast tanks as they enter the Gulf of Mexico through the Straits, so that it is sometimes impossible to step on the beach without miring yourself in clinging filth."

As for the wildlife, he wrote, "the big game is all gone, the brilliant birds are a half-forgotten memory, most of the shoal-water food fishes . . . are rarities, the delicious green turtle is only a tradition, the manatee is dying out."

Or was it?

•

Fast-forward nearly twenty years, to the winter of 1949.

Five days a week, thirty-three-year-old Joseph Curtis Moore Jr. toiled happily at his regular job near Homestead. But when the weather turned cold, he would get up early on weekend mornings and drive an hour north to Miami. Once there, he spent hours peering down at the murky Miami River, searching for manatees.

Joe Moore was one of the first biologists to work at Everglades National Park. Because he wanted his three daughters to share his enjoyment of the wild, "he would often bring animals home to us—just to experience—and then return them to the wild," recalled one of his daughters, Melliny Lamberson. "We had a raccoon, a mink, flying squirrels, alligators."

Moore himself became fascinated by animals at an early age. He was born at the start of World War I and grew up in Washington, D.C. When he got a chance, he spent time wandering through the Smithsonian, the city library, and especially the National Zoo.

When Moore was a boy, his choice of diversions was generally limited to anything where the admission was free. He "came from a very large, poor family and lived through the Depression chopping wood all winter to stay warm," his daughter said.

When Moore was nine, his discerning mother somehow scraped together the money to buy him six volumes of Ernest Thompson Seton's animal stories. After that, his course in life was set.

While Moore was a student at the University of Kentucky, in what little free time he enjoyed between his classes and the two jobs he worked to pay his bills, he would wander in the woods sketching any wildlife he saw. But Moore wasn't the stereotypical science geek, the ninety-eight-pound weakling with Coke-bottle glasses. Thanks to all that wood he chopped, he was a lean and muscular fellow. While at the university, he won a Golden Gloves boxing tournament.

He fell for a fellow botany student, Evelyn Lannert, and they wed in 1940. A year later, Moore headed south to the University of Florida to earn his master's degree, but World War II intervened. He saw action as a naval officer during the D-Day invasion. Back home, he completed his grad work and landed a job at Florida's new national park, the successor to the one Kirk Munroe's wife helped to start.

Everglades National Park, opened in 1947, offered an inquisitive scientist like Moore a wide variety of species to study. Soon after he arrived in May 1949, he began cranking out papers about everything from glossy ibises to long-tailed weasels. But one species in particular intrigued him. He was, he wrote later, "greatly attracted by the mystery surrounding the life and habits of the manatee."

After all, no less an authority than Harvard's noted biologist Grover Allen had listed the Florida manatee among the species on the brink of disappearing in his book *Extinct and Vanishing Mammals of the Western Hemisphere* in 1942.

But Moore's new boss at Everglades National Park, superintendent Daniel Beard, thought otherwise. During World War II, Beard had led a committee of federal biologists in writing a book on American animal species that mankind's carelessness and greed had pushed to the point of extinction. However Beard's book, called *Fading Trails*—published the same year as Allen's—contended that "the fat, homely manatee is not doomed in United States waters. It can continue to lead its entirely innocuous existence if present laws are kept on the books and enforced." Just a month prior to Moore's arrival, the *Miami Herald* ran a story headlined "Sea Cows Making a Comeback," which quoted Beard as saying he had "seen several specimens" in the park.

So who was right, Allen or Beard? Were manatees dying out, or staging a revival? With Beard's encouragement, Moore set out to find the answer.

Moore logged hours on end in a boat, searching the countless coves around the park's soggy southern tip. He leafed through the park's patrol logs for sightings by the rangers. He dug through the *Miami Herald*'s files for stories. He diligently wrote letters to people all over Florida asking about manatees.

He got reports back from Fort Lauderdale, West Palm Beach, Stuart and St. Augustine on the state's east coast, and then along the Gulf of Mexico at Fort Myers, Charlotte Harbor, even rural Gulf County up in the state's Panhandle. A former county official in Cedar Key, in the state's Big Bend area, wrote that he had "rigidly enforced" the 1893 law against killing manatees without a permit, "and the manatee became very plentiful."

Despite Fred Morse's law, though, Joe Moore learned that plenty of Floridians still ate manatee meat. The report from Gulf County was about a manatee that had been butchered by hungry fishermen. He heard about a Daytona Beach fish-camp owner who had harpooned one on the Halifax River. Old-timers in the Everglades told him that Cow Pen Key got its name because young manatees were captured and penned up there to be fattened up for a feast. The number of manatees in the Everglades, Moore observed, "appear[s] to be inversely proportional to their accessibility to the fishing villages of Chokoloskee and Flamingo."

Of course, as another Florida naturalist noted in the 1940s, "eight hundred pounds of meat as good and tender as veal is a temptation to man in any day

Joe Moore frequently brought the Everglades' wildlife home to show his kids.
Photo courtesy of Melliny Lamberson.

or generation." As a result, "most crackers find it hard to refrain from taking one into camp when the opportunity offers."

But there were more intriguing reports from, of all places, downtown Miami. Moore learned that Navy officers patrolling the coast in airships during World War II had spotted up to thirty a day while soaring over Biscayne Bay. A former city inspector told Moore that in 1943, when workers dynamited rocks in the Miami River to deepen Flagler's shipping channel, about a hundred manatee carcasses had piled up.

Moore began making inquiries around Miami. "Bridge-rail fishermen and bridge tenders told me that the best time and place to see manatees was on a cold morning at the Miami Avenue bridge," he wrote.

Beginning in November 1949, Joe Moore started making his weekend drives up to the city to check the river. He only went when the weather was cold, which guaranteed his solitude. "I was alone, because it was still early morning, and most of the inhabitants of Miami—a city in the grip of a cold snap—were still shivering in bed," he wrote years later.

Moore knew that manatees tend to be sensitive to cold weather. In 1895 a biologist with the wonderful name of Outram Bangs had reported that the big freeze of the year before that swept Florida—the same one that prompted Flagler to extend his railroad to Miami—had killed manatees in the Indian River. Moore's correspondents had alerted him that in the winter, manatees often congregated at a place called Blue Spring, where the water bubbling up from underground stayed seventy-two degrees year-round. Manatees had been riding out cold snaps in the warmth of Blue Spring since at least the turn of the century.

Still, the Miami River seemed an unlikely place to spot this wild creature. The "beautiful clear-water stream" was now the heart of a major metropolitan area, as well as the center of its shipping industry. The waterway was used by everything from fishing dories to submarines, one writer noted, and along the shoreline "for miles there are nothing but fish wharves, boat yards, and the general foreshore of commerce and trade. The water is indescribably polluted."

A big reason for the water's murkiness: despite the city's growth, Flagler's original sewage disposal program was still in use. By the end of 1949, forty-one sewer pipes flowed into the bay, and twenty-nine more emptied their waste into the river.

Moore discovered that there was one pipe in particular that attracted the manatees, a six-by-six outfall under the Miami Avenue bridge. This wasn't a sewer pipe. This pipe belonged to the local power plant. It discharged water after it had been heated up to produce steam to drive the plant's turbines.

Whenever the air temperature dipped below fifty degrees at night, Moore wrote, the next morning he would find a group of manatees crowded into the warm current from the power plant pipe. In the search for manatees, he had hit the jackpot. Despite the chill in the air, he spent hours watching the Miami River manatees surface to breathe, then drop beneath the waves again. He made careful notes about everything he saw.

One of the first things Moore noticed about the Miami River manatees were odd markings on their hides. "They displayed prominent scars, great notches in their tails, and distinctive arrangements of lesser scars and notches," he wrote. "Many of these wounds had been inflicted in series, evidently by whirling propellers of boats."

One manatee in particular caught his attention. Its tail was so "unbelievably mangled," he wrote years later, that when he first saw it emerge from the water it looked like the hand of a sea monster.

"A later tally revealed that four-fifths of the dozens of manatees that I came to know individually had their tails scarred, notched, or sliced," Moore wrote. "In many cases this was done by boat propellers."

It didn't take much of a leap of logic for him to figure out where the scars came from. Motorboats had by then become a common sight in Florida's waterways.

The first outboard boat motor predated Fred Morse's arrival in South Florida in the 1880s. But the idea really took off after a third-grade dropout named Ole Evinrude took a rowboat to buy ice cream for his fiancée, Bess. On the way back from the store, Evinrude's ice cream melted. A self-taught machinist, Evinrude decided there had to be a way to hook up an engine and a propeller to a boat to make it go faster. He produced his first one, a five-horsepower model, in 1907. To this day, outboard motors still follow Evinrude's basic blueprint.

Just as the invention of the automobile was soon followed by the first auto race, so did the invention of the motorboat lead to the first motorboat races. By the 1920s, Miami had become the center of motorboat racing in America. In fact, America's most famous boat racer, the five-foot, six-inch speed demon Gar Wood—nine-time winner of the most prestigious prize in racing—bought a twenty-room mansion on Fisher Island, next to the main Port of Miami channel. In 1931, while zooming through a Miami Beach race course, Wood became the first boater to break 100 miles per hour, and a year later he set a new record of more than 111 miles per hour.

"With her throttles wide open under Wood's hands, the *Miss America* was just a streak to the spectators in the yards of millionaires' homes lining the beautiful watercourse," the *Miami Herald* reported.

By the 1940s, Florida's proliferation of fast-moving motorboats had begun forcefully intersecting with its slow-moving manatees. In Beard's book *Fading Trails*, the future superintendent of Everglades National Park became the first writer to report what resulted: "Often, the animals are wounded or killed by boat propellers." The hide of one "battered and oil-besmeared old fellow" seen in the Miami River, Beard wrote, "is criss-crossed with scars from propeller blades."

Just six months after Moore started working for Beard in 1949, the Audubon Society's magazine published a story about manatees that opened with the author riding on an unnamed Florida waterway with a state game warden who—to the writer's amazement—"was steering the speeding patrol boat by means of his bare, almost prehensile toes."

Suddenly the patrol boat lurched as if it was about to go airborne. The writer looked back to see something large and dark in their wake.

"Them blasted sea cows," the game warden drawled to the magazine writer. "I'll break a wheel on one o' them yet."

Figuring out that the manatees' prop scars came from boats did not require the deductive skills of Sherlock Holmes. But then Moore had a flash of inspiration about how to make use of those scars, and what he did next would change the course of marine mammal biology.

Moore sketched an outline of a manatee's body on a template and printed out several copies. Then, as he watched the manatees swimming in the Miami River, he sketched on the outline where each manatee had its scars. By noting how each manatee had been injured, he could use the scars to identify them as individuals.

Before Moore came along, scientists had no way to differentiate among manatees in the wild. To human eyes, manatees looked alike. Now Moore had figured out a way to tell them apart. Their scars were like fingerprints—if fingerprints were carved with a buzz saw.

Over the next six years, using his sketches, Moore was able to pick out fifty-seven different manatees huddled beneath the bridge on cold days. By spotting which manatee was which, he could monitor their behavior, their breathing, their reproduction, everything he could see on a frosty morning.

Moore's studies of the Miami River manatees lasted only until 1955, when he left Everglades National Park for a job with the American Museum of Natural History in New York. In the Big Apple he was no longer a biologist who could pick up any critter he encountered and bring it home. Instead he became just "a man in a suit," his daughter said.

Joe Moore published only four papers on his manatee studies, and it was only in the last one, published in December 1956, that he mentioned his

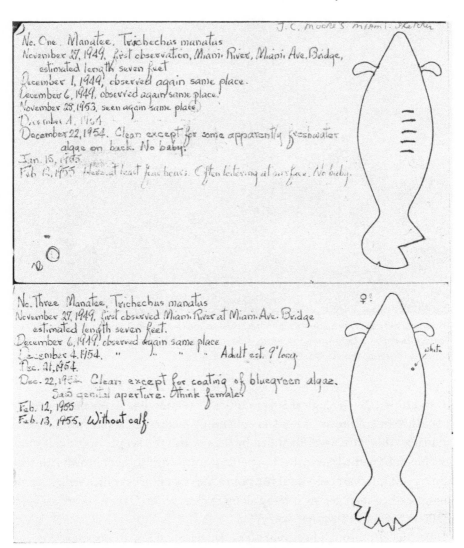

Moore figured out that if he made sketches of the scars, he could tell the manatees apart.
From the collection of Dan Odell, used with the permission of Melliny Lamberson.

prop scar sketches. He went on, both in New York and later as curator of
mammals for the Field Museum of Natural History in Chicago, to produce
well-regarded studies of beaked whales and other mammals. But his discovery of how to use the manatees' scars remains his lasting legacy. Fifty years
later, state and federal wildlife biologists are still using prop-scar patterns to
identify manatees for study.

Biologists still use scars to identify manatees, just as Joe Moore did. They named this manatee Popeye because a boat ripped open its side, exposing the muscles under the skin. Photo courtesy of Sirenia Project, U.S. Geological Service.

In a tiny U.S. Geological Survey office in Gainesville, homemade wooden bookshelves hold rows of binders containing pictures of about two thousand manatees that have been identified by their scars. The keeper of the collection is a biologist named Cathy Beck, a petite woman with straight brown hair who seems painfully earnest—until you notice the poster on her office wall. It shows an unscathed manatee swimming along in clear water. Over its head is a voice balloon asking, "What, me worry?"

Beck clicks through her computer's database, calling up photos of Popeye, a manatee with a slash so deep on one side that all its muscles were exposed; Phalanges, with a shredded tail that resembled waving fingers; and Whatamess, named for the complex cross-hatch of wounds on its back.

"I've seen animals that you just can't believe are still alive," Beck says.

Beck and her colleagues have documented manatees that have suffered more than a dozen boat-related injuries. One they spotted had been hit almost once a year since it was a calf. It wound up with a broken rib sticking out of its side, yet somehow survived.

Each time they were hit, the manatees almost certainly felt terrible pain, Beck and her colleagues concluded. The injuries to female manatees probably curtailed their ability to reproduce, too.

"The incidence of wounding by boats in Florida manatees is probably unparalleled in any marine mammal population in the world," Beck and two other biologists wrote in 2001.

Yet this collection of photos forms the most complete portrait of any marine mammal species in the world, allowing scientists to study every aspect of manatee life. Still, Beck says, "It's a horrible way to get our information."

Climb a ladder to the highest shelf in Beck's office, and you'll find the earliest pictures in the collection: black-and-white snapshots taken in the late 1960s around a sleepy little Gulf Coast town called Crystal River. Many of the pictures were shot by a wiry teenager who, like Fred Morse, just happened to be an avid boater.

## When Woodie Met Buddy

BUDDY POWELL LOVED NOTHING BETTER than spending all day aboard his boat, roaming the hidden coves and gin-clear springs of Crystal River.

His given name was James A. Powell Jr., but nobody called him that. His dad was known as Jimmy and his mother was called Kitty, so he became just plain Buddy.

Buddy Powell had straight brown chestnut hair that sometimes drooped down over his forehead, falling over serious brown eyes. Until he was ten, he and his family lived in tourist-crazy, snowbird-packed Pinellas County, in a town called Clearwater.

But then his parents decided Clearwater was getting too crowded—a somewhat ironic decision, since Jimmy Powell made his living selling real estate. When it came time to move, the Powells looked northward, to Citrus County.

Since the 1950s, the Powell family had owned a cottage there, in the town of Crystal River. They spent nearly every weekend and summer vacation at the cottage. They relished the peace and quiet it offered, not to mention the fact that the river lived up to its name. Crystal River's water was a lot clearer than Clearwater's water.

In the early 1900s, Crystal River had been the site of a mill that manufactured cedar pencil slats for the Dixon Pencil Co., but the mill closed. By the end of the 1950s, most of the residents eked out a living either as farmers or as commercial fishermen, netting for mullet and catching blue crabs and stone crabs. The county's entire population totaled about eighty-seven hundred people.

Unlike Pinellas County, Citrus County's coastline had no beaches to draw tourists. Instead the coast consisted of an intricate maze of mangrove islands dotting a vast salt marsh. The marsh gradually deepened into the Gulf of Mexico.

By the time the Powells moved there in the mid-1960s, Crystal River was seeing the first trickle of retirees and snowbirds. They were part of an influx of newcomers that would quadruple Citrus County's population to thirty-five thousand by the mid-1970s.

The two hotels on the waterfront, Kings Bay Lodge and Port Paradise, catered mainly to visiting anglers who would hire the locals to guide them to the best places to fish for bass, redfish, and spotted sea trout. Most of the other out-of-town visitors were divers interested in exploring the region's underwater glories, particularly the springs in Kings Bay where 600 million gallons of water a day gurgled up from deep underground to feed Crystal River's current. Back then, the flow from the main spring was so strong it was almost impossible to swim down into it. But there weren't enough visiting divers to support more than one dive shop, a place called Aqua Peer.

The Powells bought a house on one of the new canals that developers were beginning to dredge out of the marshlands to create new waterfront property around Kings Bay. The house was near a place called Three Sisters Spring, a place so wild it was like stepping into a Tarzan movie. Buddy Powell liked to put on a mask and snorkel and swim over there to see what he could see.

Powell spent every second he could exploring the river, the bay, and the islands. He would be out there on the misty mornings, when wisps of steam would hang in the cool air above the warmth of the spring-fed flow, and in the evenings when the water's rippling surface reflected the scarlet glow of the sunset.

When Powell was young, his parents let him use a rowboat to ferry his grandmother around Crystal River. When his grandmother died, she left him some money. His parents used the bequest to buy him his own motorboat, a Boston Whaler. Having his own speedy motorboat greatly expanded the area the boy could explore on his own. He went everywhere and drank it all in.

There was only one thing that bothered Powell, one thing in the river that made him nervous. It started when he was about five or six, on a morning when he and his father were in a boat together fishing for bass. Suddenly his father leaned over and said, in an urgent whisper, "Stay still."

The boy peered over the side and saw, swimming just beneath their boat, "a monster of gigantic proportions, its ghostly gray shape slowly and silently gliding between the cathedrals of water weeds," Powell wrote years later. "I'm not sure I was breathing."

Powell's father explained that the monster was a manatee, also known as a sea cow. "He also said that, though he loved to fish, he had only seen a few in his life," Powell wrote.

When the family bought their house in Crystal River, Buddy decided to learn more about these mysterious creatures. He put on a snorkel and fins and, on spotting another manatee, slipped into the water near it, thinking he might sneak up on it and see what he could find out.

"It turned to look at me, and I must've come out of the water like a Polaris missile and he went the opposite way just as fast," Powell said.

One day in 1967, when he was thirteen and cruising along in his Boston Whaler, Buddy spotted a man sitting in a small Sears johnboat, staring intently at the water. The man had a lean and athletic build, a mustache, and long, dark hair that curled down around his sharp face. He didn't look like anyone else in buzz-cut, conservative Crystal River. And what he was doing didn't make any sense to the boy boater.

"He wasn't fishing," Powell recalled. "He wasn't diving. He was clearly out of place. I wondered, 'Why is he on my river?' I wanted to know what the hell was he doing there."

Even odder was the name on what Powell derisively dubbed a "bathtub boat": *Trichechus*. What could that mean? Was it even in English?

With a shrug, Powell zoomed on by without stopping. But the next time he went out in his Whaler, there was the guy in the johnboat again. And the next time. And the next. Powell studied the mysterious stranger for about a month. Finally, his curiosity overcame his shyness. He pulled alongside and asked the man if he needed help.

"No," the stranger replied in an accent clearly different from the typical Florida drawl.

When the man explained what he was doing, Buddy Powell was stunned.

The stranger's name was Daniel Stanwood "Woodie" Hartman. He was from New England, and he was working on his doctoral thesis at Cornell University. He said he was in Crystal River to study manatees.

The only problem was that, like Buddy Powell, he was a little afraid of them.

Hartman is a pivotal character in the history of both manatee science and manatee protection—and yet his background gave no indication that this might be in his future. His father had been a professor at a small liberal arts college in Maine, but in English, not biology. The professor died when Hartman was four. Hartman's mother took him with her to live with her parents in Cambridge, Massachusetts. An interior decorator, she became involved in an affair with an Italian count with impeccable taste. That led to the couple moving to Washington, D.C., to open a business together. But the count's wife refused to divorce him, so he returned to Italy. Hartman, meanwhile, attended a series of prestigious prep schools. Looking back, Hartman says he wasn't a standout student in any subject.

"I didn't question anything," he explained.

His summers were what shaped his future. He spent all his vacation time at his grandparents' cabin on Lake Parlin in Maine's North Woods. There he was free to do on land what Buddy Powell would later do on the water: explore.

"Left to my own devices, by default really, I spent my days looking for frogs and crayfish and salamanders, birds' nests, otter and muskrat signs, stuff like that," he recalled.

Like Joe Moore, Hartman fell under the spell of Ernest Thompson Seton's tales of noble animals who suffered from the cruelty of humans. Then, when he was eight, his godmother's husband—an avid birdwatcher—gave him a different kind of a book. It was one of Roger Tory Peterson's field guides for birds. Hartman quickly succumbed to what he called "the lure of listing." Now his days in the woods had a purpose: looking for new species he could add to the list of birds he had spotted and identified.

"My adolescence happened to coincide with the publication of the Peterson Field Guide series, eventually covering every subject relating to natural history," Hartman said. "With each new publication, I would buy the book and immerse myself in its subject matter, whether wildflowers, astronomy, geology, insects, animal tracks. . . . As my scope broadened, I started questing for and listing flowers, mammals, reptiles and amphibians. I was hooked."

Hartman earned a biology degree from Williams College, then went for a graduate degree in wildlife management at Cornell. He decided that for his doctoral thesis he absolutely had to go to Africa.

"He was at the time very naive," said Jim Layne, his thesis adviser. "He had this idea he wanted to do something for conservation. Something that would have some benefit to conservation. . . . Woodie just isn't too practical."

Hartman lined up some grants to pay for a trip to Kenya, where he planned to trap and study small mammals. He didn't stay long.

"My funding collapsed, and the Africans were stealing my traps," Hartman said. "So I hitched a ride back to America and went to see my adviser."

Layne had recently taken a job as the director of research at the Archbold Biological Station, near Lake Placid in central Florida. Instead of venturing off to some exotic (and expensive) overseas locale, Layne told Hartman to try doing his fieldwork in the United States. Still longing for a trip to someplace tropical, Hartman asked Layne for suggestions on a project he could pursue in Florida.

"He said two subjects leaped to mind," Hartman recalled. "One was feral hogs." Ever since a few swine escaped from Spanish explorers in the 1500s, Florida has been plagued with rampaging herds of feral hogs, nasty beasts with sharp tusks. Hartman found that subject less than appealing.

But he liked Layne's other suggestion: manatees. Layne told him that, prior to Joe Moore's observations in the Miami River, there had been no published studies of manatees congregating in warm water during the winter months. If Hartman could find another place where they congregated during the winter, he could scrutinize this poorly understood species and perhaps uncover their secrets.

Hartman didn't take long to think about the logistics of the switch from Africa to Florida before saying yes.

"He was a free spirit," Layne said. "In those days I guess you would've classified Woodie as a hippie."

Without further ado, Hartman cranked up his pickup truck and drove across Florida on a reconnaissance mission. He checked out several places that seemed likely to fit what he was looking for, including Blue Spring.

Then he tried Crystal River, where the bubbling springs kept the water a constant seventy-four degrees, even in the coldest weather. When he walked into Aqua Peer, he saw big black-and-white photos of manatees lining the walls. Aqua Peer's owner, Tom McQuarrie, told Hartman the manatees flocked to Crystal River every winter.

Hartman figured this would be the perfect place to do his study. He wrote up a proposal to Layne for a study of Crystal River's manatees. He asked Joe

Woodie Hartman spent hours on the water in Crystal River searching for manatees. Photo courtesy of Buddy Powell.

Moore to review it. Layne and Moore both agreed he had the makings of a good fieldwork project.

So Hartman married his girlfriend and they moved south, renting what he described as "a little place close to the water." His new wife liked the idea of spending the winter in Florida. The newlyweds arrived in the fall of 1967, full of anticipation for their Florida adventure.

Then came the disappointment. Months passed, and Hartman didn't see a single manatee. Where were they? Weren't they supposed to be showing up in droves?

Meanwhile the couple got a cool reception from the other people in town.

"We were liberals from the North who didn't go to church, so the town gave us a wide berth," Hartman said.

Finally, when the temperature dipped low enough, the manatees swam into Crystal River, seeking the warmth of the spring. Hartman was elated. It was time to put his plan into action.

His study proposal called for him to do something no other scientist had ever done: don a mask and snorkel and climb into the water with the manatees, observing the creatures in their element. When he spotted a few noses pop up above the surface, he eased off the bow of his boat and swam toward his study subjects—and immediately regretted it.

"The first time I ever got in the water with them, it just happened to be a mating herd," Hartman said.

Most of the time, manatees are docile and shy. The exception: when they're mating. As Hartman learned firsthand, male manatees have an exceptionally strong sex drive. A dozen or more males may gang up on a female and chase her for some distance. As Hartman would later document, hot-to-trot male manatees aren't too discriminating. If no receptive female is available, male manatees will engage in homosexual behavior. There has even been one report of an extremely determined male manatee attempting to impregnate a dead female even as a biologist was winching the carcass out of the water.

"It's something you don't talk about when you're speaking to elementary school classes about manatees," Hartman said.

In short, nothing, not even death, will stop a male manatee that's ready to rut, and woe to anyone or anything who gets in between the fleeing female and her horny, half-ton suitors.

"Suddenly I was upon them, or rather they were upon me," he wrote later, "looming forth some 20 feet away, spectral gray leviathans, colossi, ridiculously imposing. . . . One was heading directly for me. Scientific inquiry be hanged! I swallowed my pride and rocketed back into the boat. I was safe, a confessed coward."

This left one problem, though. "I agonized over how I was going to study them if I was too scared to get in the water with them," Hartman said.

He bought a glass-bottomed bucket and tried peering at them through its lens, but it was no good. The only way to earn his Ph.D. was to climb back into the water.

Once he had tamped down his panic, Hartman settled into a pattern of running his johnboat out to the spring or into the river every day to stare down at the water and hunt for the manatees. If he found any, he would quietly slip into the river near them and spend three hours or so snorkeling nearby. He took photos with an underwater camera—a Kodak Brownie in a homemade underwater housing he had borrowed from Tom McQuarrie at Aqua Peer— and made notes in pencil on a waterproof pad.

Hartman quickly realized he was under a handicap. He needed a guide who knew the local waterways, someone who could help him interview local fishermen, perhaps someone with a faster boat—say, a Boston Whaler.

One day when Powell stopped to razz him about sitting around staring into the water, Hartman asked his teenage tormentor if they could cut a deal.

"It didn't take long for us to discover that we had little in common, but we could work out an arrangement whereby he could help satiate my curiosity about manatees, and I would teach him how to navigate through the local waters," Powell wrote later.

As a result, every morning before school, every afternoon after school, and on the summer days when school was out, Buddy Powell would zoom out to assist Hartman in studying the manatees. With his Whaler, they could travel farther. They could get to where the manatees were much more quickly. There were other benefits. Hartman taught Powell how to shoot pictures with the underwater camera, freeing the grad student to concentrate on taking notes.

Powell's parents were excited about seeing their son help with a scientific study, although it took them a while to warm up to the long-haired Yankee he was hanging out with. Eventually they came around, even paying for gas for the boat. But the new Mrs. Hartman grew somewhat annoyed at the way the teenage boy kept monopolizing her husband's time. When the couple later divorced, Powell wondered if he was to blame (according to Hartman, he was not).

Over the next two years, Hartman and his assistant kept tabs on about sixty manatees, getting so close to them that, more than once, a female grasped Powell's mask to give him a whiskery kiss.

The more Hartman watched the manatees, the more he learned about their behavior—and the lower his opinion became of the other people using the bay and the river. He saw bored fishermen hook manatees intentionally and play them back and forth for sport. He saw other divers poking them, grabbing them, chasing them, even trying to ride them. He heard tales about someone attacking a manatee with a garden rake, leaving the head of the rake embedded in the animal's back as it swam away.

He also saw visiting anglers who were dumbfounded to see this big monster swim past.

"I have seen stunned fisherman actually drop their rods and scan their minds' eyes for rational explanations—muskrats, beavers, otters, porpoises, whales, even divers," he wrote later. "One teenager was heard to insist, 'Mullet don't grow that big, Pa.'"

Nearly every day, Hartman saw dredges at work somewhere on the bay or along one of its new canals, scooping up fill to create land where none existed. The dredges were not only eliminating manatee habitat but also stirring up the silt so much that it turned the clear water cloudy.

He also discovered that nearly every manatee he saw carried scars on its back or tail from being hit by passing boats. Of course that made it easier for him to pick out which one was which, just as Joe Moore had done.

Hartman gave many of the Crystal River manatees names that, to his ear, sounded redolent of the Old South: Flora Merry Lee, Pearly Mae, Creola, Lavaliere, Gallatin, Piety, Sadie. Because he spent so much time with them, he became quite attached to them, particularly Lavaliere, the one he later described as "quite a flirt."

Having gotten acquainted with the manatees from below the water's surface, Hartman persuaded the Florida Board of Conservation to lend him a plane so he could look for them from above. Although he disliked flying, Hartman strapped on a football helmet and climbed on board with a pilot nicknamed Grizzly Bear to survey Citrus County's waterways from the air.

And then, just like in Africa, the money ran out. Hartman wondered if he could get some help from the National Geographic Society, founded in 1888 to create "a society for the increase and diffusion of geographic knowledge." The society sponsored expeditions, financed research, and published an extremely popular yellow-bordered magazine. The magazine had pioneered underwater color photography, probably a good omen for a project like his. Although his professors tried to discourage him from even trying, Hartman figured he should give the magazine a shot. It turned out that the mysterious manatee still held the power to fascinate scientists.

"I sent *National Geographic* a very bad contact sheet of pictures, most of them just of parts of manatees," Hartman said. "I got a very nice letter back from the head of science and exploration who said he was personally very interested in funding my research. I asked for five grand. I should've asked for fifty."

An editor's note in the August 1968 issue of the magazine touted Hartman's work as "the first intensive study of manatees in their natural habitat." Then,

Buddy Powell provided Hartman with a faster boat and a local guide, and in return learned to swim with the animals he once feared. Photo courtesy of Buddy Powell.

pointing out that Hartman had been aided by a grant from the society, the note segued into an advertisement for readers to sign up as a society member. Accompanying the note was a photo of Hartman swimming with a manatee. The photo is credited to "J.A. Powell Jr."

The five thousand dollars from the National Geographic Society "was a saving grace for me," Hartman said. Thanks to the grant—and to his wife's taking a job at a local convenience store—his work on his thesis could continue.

Although the grant did not require it, Hartman then wrote a story about his work for *National Geographic*. The magazine sent a professional photographer down to Crystal River to snap better underwater photos of Sadie and the other manatees. Hartman's story ran in the magazine's September 1969 issue, headlined "Florida's Manatees, Mermaids in Peril."

Sandwiched among stories on "The Coming Revolution in Transportation" and "The Friendly Irish," Hartman's piece offered readers in living rooms and barbershops across America a first-person look at the manatees of Crystal River. The piece also featured some startling photos of his research subjects, shot both from underwater and from the air, often with a diver nearby. Included was one small photo depicting what the cutline called "ugly scars, carved by a speedboat's slashing propeller. . . . The animals often loll just beneath the surface, invisible to boatmen, and many bear marks of similar encounters."

By the time the story appeared, Hartman was no longer in Crystal River. He had gone back to Maine to work on his dissertation. But the magazine piece hit home with a select audience: television nature show producers.

In late 1970, crews from two of the shows turned up in Crystal River at the same time. One was the venerable *Mutual of Omaha's Wild Kingdom*, with its avuncular host Marlin Perkins, the director of the St. Louis Zoo. The other was the quirkier, and far more impassioned, *Undersea World of Jacques Cousteau.*

Cousteau first gained fame in 1943, when he was a lieutenant in the French navy, as co-inventor of the aqualung diving apparatus—better known today by the acronym SCUBA, for "self-contained underwater breathing apparatus." His invention freed divers from the clunky suits and helmets that had limited their movements underwater. Now they could swim as freely as the fish.

Cousteau then wrote a best-selling book about his achievements, set a world free-diving record, and helped develop underwater television filming. He had already won three Oscars for his documentaries before he began producing hour-long programs for TV in 1966. His deal with the American Broadcasting Corporation called for him to produce four shows a year for four years. It became so popular that the *Undersea World* ran for nine years on ABC, and then continued on public television.

With his thick accent and his frequent descriptions of various species as "cheeky," Cousteau was an easy figure to spoof (as any viewer of the *Spongebob Squarepants* cartoons can attest). Yet he was a master showman who knew how to dazzle an audience with never-before-seen images of marine exploration. He was at times prone to making wild statements—vowing to find the lost city of Atlantis, or predicting the rise of a species of gilled man-fish—which the press dutifully reported because he was Cousteau, the man who regularly produced astonishing inventions and amazing movies. Who knew what other miracles he might have up his sleeve?

Thanks to Cousteau, "audiences came face to face with sharks, whales, dolphins, sea turtles, walruses, penguins, and giant octopuses," a writer once noted. "They had their eyes opened to the man-made pollution that was fouling the oceans thousands of miles from land. And they grew accustomed to the highly personal, Gallic-flavored English of the ubiquitous captain, whose deeply lined face, dazzling smile, and red woolen watch cap made him one of the most recognizable figures on television."

Cousteau had become an avowed ecologist after seeing a picture of the Earth snapped by the astronauts during the 1969 moon landing. In his programs he frequently criticized mankind's abuse of nature.

In this battle of the TV shows, Cousteau's crew had one major advantage over Perkins's *Wild Kingdom*. They had had the foresight to hire as their scientific consultant a newly minted Cornell Ph.D. named Daniel "Woodie" Hartman.

"I was the only person studying manatees at the time," Hartman said. "They had no other choice for scientific consultant."

Philippe Cousteau (*left*) spent weeks in Crystal River with Woodie Hartman (*right*), trying to get footage of manatees for *The Undersea World of Jacques Cousteau*. Photo courtesy of *St. Petersburg Times*.

Cousteau's production company flew Hartman to Los Angeles to meet with the famous explorer and his son, Philippe. Then as winter set in, they brought him back down to Crystal River. There was no script, no plan. They just needed to shoot enough underwater footage of manatees to make an hour-long TV program. When the manatees showed up, they would start.

While they waited for the manatees, the crew drank wine at Philippe Cousteau's Port Paradise bungalow—a lot of wine, plenty for everyone, even for the teenager who kept hanging around.

"I was underage, and there was a lot of wine," Buddy Powell said years later, smiling at the memory. "I remember the crew having to take me home and explain to my parents what happened. If it had been anybody else, I would've been in trouble." The fact that it was Cousteau made it all right.

Time passed. No manatees. That year the weather was abnormally warm. The stars of the show didn't need the spring to survive. Instead the manatees stayed in the murkier parts of the river where shooting underwater proved problematic.

Still, Cousteau's crewmen did not let the winter go to waste. They managed to get some footage at Blue Spring of vacationers in fast boats roaring past manatees, divers chasing the manatees, even a few swimmers trying to ride on the manatees' backs.

But what Cousteau and his crew really needed were up-close images of undisturbed manatees. The best place to obtain those was Crystal River. So if no manatees would show up in Crystal River on their own, then Cousteau's crew would just have to go and get one—even if they had to go all the way to Miami to do it.

In 1969, a twelve-hundred-pound male manatee somehow wandered into a thirty-three-inch sewer pipe under a highway in North Miami and got stuck. After being rescued, the manatee, now named "Sewer Sam," went to live at the Miami Seaquarium. By early 1971, Seaquarium veterinarian Jesse White figured Sewer Sam was ready to return to the wild. Cousteau offered to handle the job—as long as his film crew could cart Sam across the state and release the manatee in Crystal River.

It was a risky move. Nobody had ever attempted to release back into the wild a manatee that had been held so long in captivity. If Sewer Sam died, Cousteau would be blamed. It would be a disaster for his reputation.

While Cousteau's crew was picking up Sewer Sam, Cousteau gave a Miami reporter an interview that didn't mention anything about what could go wrong while hauling a manatee across the state. Instead, he focused on the big picture, explaining to the reporter that the problem with manatees was that they weren't cute or sleek or dangerous enough to appeal to the public.

"It is not a glamorous predator like the shark, not touching and funny like the porpoise," he said. "People look at a sea cow and either it's not doing anything or it is eating—one or the other."

Cousteau explained that he was determined to use his program to stimulate popular interest in manatees and their future.

"If we can get people interested in the animal, that's enough," he said. "If we can get them to love a form of life, the people will find a way to protect it. . . . Eventually it all rests on man's ability to control himself. Nothing more or less will save the sea cow."

Of course, being Cousteau, he followed that up with an outlandish suggestion: "There is a lot of talk these days about food from the sea. Well, the sea cow is the only animal in the flesh—just like the cows that live on the land. . . . Perhaps it could be exploited in the same way that we now manufacture beef on the land." Fortunately, in the show, he didn't mention anything about raising herds of manatees for a modern version of "Gypsy Stew."

After Cousteau's crew loaded Sewer Sam into a crate, they flew the manatee six hundred miles across the state, with the Seaquarium's vet along to make sure nothing bad happened on the two-hour trip. Sam then spent two weeks swimming in an enclosure Cousteau's crew had built in Three Sisters Spring, getting acclimated to a world that was very different from the Miami canals it was used to.

Then the crew attached a radio tracking device to Sam's flipper and turned the manatee loose into the river. For several days Sam hung back. Finally the Miami manatee moved into the main part of the river and joined three or four other manatees swimming nearby.

When Cousteau got the news that Sam had at last joined some other manatees, the camera caught him looking as relieved as a man who has bet his mortgage payment on a spin of the roulette wheel and won.

Using the rehabilitated manatee's journey as a hook for the show proved to be a masterstroke. Thanks to the Sewer Sam saga, viewers now had a storyline to follow, a character to root for. And now Cousteau was not merely an observer of manatee behavior, but a champion of manatee conservation.

Titled "Forgotten Mermaids," the manatee episode of *The Undersea World of Jacques Cousteau* aired at 8 p.m. on Monday, January 24, 1972. In those days there were only three commercial broadcast networks—no cable, no satellite channels. Airing opposite the Cousteau show that night, one network showed an old Bing Crosby movie that might appeal to older folks, while the other featured an edgy comedy show aimed at the younger generation, *Rowan and Martin's Laugh-In*. So Cousteau faced very little competition for Middle America's TV time.

Every Cousteau special constituted "event" television for many families who considered them to be educational TV, guaranteeing high ratings. A review in the *New York Times* the day the show aired hailed "Forgotten Mermaids" as "one of the best hours in the series."

The script was credited to a writer with the improbable name of Bud Wiser. The show was narrated by *Twilight Zone* host Rod Serling, who always sounded like he had a chunk of irony caught in his throat. The program began with Serling telling the same anecdote Hartman used to lead off his *National Geographic* piece: how Christopher Columbus had spotted "mermaids" that weren't as attractive as he had expected.

Then, as images of gray manatees swam by on the screen, Serling told viewers, "These are living legends, elusive, shadowy creatures that once gave substance to a myth. These are manatees. . . . From Columbus' time to our own, no animal on earth has been so misunderstood, so little known. The manatee holds little appeal for man. It defies conventional images of grace and beauty. It offers no promise of pleasure or profit. It is neglected and ignored."

Serling told the viewers that Cousteau and his crew would launch a mission "which they hope will draw man's attention to the plight of an ancient animal, held sacred by primitive man, now considered without use or purpose."

Early in the show, Cousteau was shown boarding a helicopter to fly along the St. Johns River headed for Blue Spring. The countryside that unspooled below him was filled with junked cars, smokestacks, and dredge-and-fill development. The only thing missing was a teary-eyed Indian chief.

"Below me everywhere lies evidence that the manatee's world is rapidly shrinking," Cousteau growled in a voice-over. Man had left behind "monuments to his carelessness," he told viewers, adding, "Chaotic development has already drained and destroyed much of the manatee's natural homeland."

Then came the scenes of divers harassing manatees at Blue Spring, and boats roaring past. Serling, his voice dripping with scorn, told viewers: "Almost all the waterways in Florida have become speedways for a growing armada of pleasure boats." As a result, he said, the propeller had become "the peaceful manatee's single most unnatural enemy."

As a boat roared straight over a clearly visible manatee, Cousteau's voice took over the story: "Those not fatally wounded are mutilated and scarred. In man's race for excitement, the manatees have become unintentional victims."

The Bud Wiser script offered no interviews with the boaters themselves, no opposing viewpoints—just Cousteau and Serling, tag-teaming against oblivious mankind in the name of saving a species. Perhaps the manatee served no useful purpose for man, Cousteau told his viewers, but that didn't give humans the right to run it over for fun. He asked: "Does not the manatee, as much as any other creature, have a right to life?"

Later, during the part of the show covering the release of Sewer Sam, there was a brief scene featuring Hartman, sitting on a dock with his shirt off, chatting with a group clustered around Cousteau. As if to emphasize their common cause of helping manatees, Hartman and Cousteau both wore red stocking caps. Hartman recounted the story of the manatee with the garden rake embedded in its back.

"A garrr-den rehk!" Cousteau repeated, his disgust palpable.

Toward the end of the show, as Cousteau's crew splashed loudly to encourage Sewer Sam to leave Three Sisters Spring and move out into the river, the camera lingered briefly over a brown-haired young man, identified by Serling's voice-over as "young Buddy Powell of Crystal River." There was no mention of his work with Hartman, just a comment that the kid was helping Cousteau.

By the time the show aired in January 1972, everyone involved in it had moved on. Sewer Sam had disappeared from Crystal River, never to be seen again. Cousteau was busy planning a lengthy and perilous voyage to the Antarctic. Hartman had returned to his grandparents' cabin in Maine to work on turning his dissertation into a book. Even Buddy Powell had left, headed for college at Stetson University in Lakeland. He watched the show with a group of students in a college dorm, and "I didn't let on to anyone it was me."

Powell and his college buddies were among an estimated forty million people across the United States who watched *The Undersea World of Jacques Cousteau*. Millions more saw it in reruns, as well as when it aired in more than a hundred countries around the world.

Suddenly, lots of people were aware that Florida was home to a strange creature called a manatee, and that it was being slaughtered by careless boaters and harassed by divers.

"That was definitely the catalyst" for everything that has happened with manatees since then, Powell said years later. "It really galvanized a lot of interest."

After the show aired, "no one ever stopped me in the street for an autograph," Hartman said. But now, thanks to his *National Geographic* story and the TV show, Hartman was a minor celebrity. An environmental group, the Friends of the Earth, offered him a grant to go back to do further studies. When he arrived back in Crystal River in 1973, though, he didn't live like a big TV star.

"I rented a flophouse," Hartman said. "I ran out of money because they were slow getting the grant money to me. I had to take out some loans to complete my research."

Hartman wanted to find every place in the state where manatees congregated. He hoped to get an idea of the extent of their population as well as a rough count of their abundance. He posted signs at boat ramps and beaches asking people to call him with information about manatees. He interviewed countless fishermen and waterfront homeowners. And as before, he took to the skies to survey the waterways.

His major expenditure was a Piper Cub, purchased for eight thousand dollars, which he christened "Grand Funk Airplane." He made a deal with a Crystal River pilot named Lee Weaver, who was also an aerial photographer.

"If he would fly me so many hours, I would give him the plane at the end," Hartman said. "We flew that plane all over."

But Hartman frequently suffered from airsickness, especially with the way Weaver liked to flip the plane upside down and let go of the stick while he snapped photos. So this time Hartman let his assistants do most of the flying— Powell again, along with a local marine science teacher named Pat Purcell, and another man named Gary Huffman. For six weeks in the summer of 1973, Grand Funk Airplane crisscrossed Florida and even strayed into Georgia.

There was "a lot of regurgitation" on those flights, Purcell recalled, because Weaver "loved to fly so low the marsh grasses would make the wheels on the Piper Cub turn."

Hartman and his helpers toted up all the animals they saw, then tried to account for the ones they couldn't see because of murky water or poor weather. Hartman told a reporter that he and his assistants had calculated there must be "only from 800 to 1,300 manatees left."

Years later, though, Hartman said that was at best a "guesstimate," and Powell conceded that their calculations were "just full of errors."

And then Hartman left again. He went home to Maine and wrote his book. Published in 1979, *Ecology and Behavior of the Manatee (Trichechus manatus) in Florida* remained for decades the authoritative work on the subject. But that was it.

Instead of parlaying his celebrity into a university or government research job, Hartman turned his back on all of it. Instead he spent twenty years as a professional tour guide for rich adventurers who wanted to see exotic locales around the world.

But before he left Crystal River, Hartman made a suggestion for the benefit of manatees that would eventually make that community erupt with anger— and would lead to a battle that would foreshadow the war that would come twenty years later.

3

# Selling the Sea Cows

BUDDY POWELL COULDN'T BELIEVE IT. The meeting at the Crystal River High School gym had been a disaster, full of yelling people who wouldn't listen. They just kept jumping up and down on the bleachers, shouting him down, accusing him of trying to kill their business.

Then, when the meeting was over, he walked out to find all four tires on his truck were flat.

Powell, now twenty-five, no longer looked much like the slender teenager who had been Woodie Hartman's assistant. The Boy Wonder Biologist had grown into a short, wiry guy with long, stringy hair and a scraggly brown beard. He still had that same intense focus to his eyes, though. Powell had gotten a degree in biology and gone to work for the U.S. Fish and Wildlife Service, hired to study manatees. Among other projects, he had helped with the first project to attach a radio tag to a manatee and then track where it went.

Powell found a pay phone and called his boss, then a tow truck. While Powell waited, he asked some people he knew to stick around with him. He didn't want to be stranded outside the high school by himself on this dark December night in 1978.

Later, at the garage, Powell found out that all four of his tires had been punctured by something sharp—probably a knife. What had happened to him was no accident. Someone at the meeting had it in for him.

"I wasn't really scared," Powell recalled two decades later. "It was just their way of getting across the message that they weren't happy."

But he got that message loud and clear every time he went out on a boat to cruise the waterways he had loved since childhood: "There were lots of threats, lots of cursing at me on the water."

What had Powell done to so anger the residents of his hometown? He had advocated putting limits on boating and diving in King's Bay, in order to protect manatees.

"I was saying, 'Give the manatee a sanctuary and you're going to have more of them. This is the best way to ensure the manatees are going to remain in the bay,'" he said.

Powell's mentor, Woodie Hartman, had first proposed a manatee refuge in Crystal River back while he was working with Cousteau's crew to film "Forgotten Mermaids." His suggestion angered the boaters and fishing guides, who were convinced he intended to drive them out of business.

"It is true that I am for a manatee refuge on the river, but the rumors of the consequences are not true," Hartman told a reporter for the *Citrus County Chronicle* in January 1971. All he was suggesting, he said, was to limit boat speeds to twenty miles per hour on the river between October and March, when the largest numbers of manatees were congregated there. He also suggested closing off what he called "minimal" areas to all boating.

That should be sufficient to ensure that "danger to the manatees from propeller blades would be minimized," Hartman said. Still, he acknowledged, "I don't think residents will go along with the idea."

Sure enough, local officials quickly dismissed his proposal.

But once America saw the Cousteau TV special, manatees became a big business in Crystal River. Not long after it aired, a second dive shop opened in town, run by a man who advertised that he could show tourists the famous Crystal River manatees—for the right price. Soon he was followed by others making the same offer. People began pouring in, eager to pay to see a real live sea cow.

"We started having these dive shops come in and commercialize the manatee situation," said Pat Purcell, the biology teacher who worked with Hartman.

The people flocking to Crystal River to see manatees were curious about them, but not particularly well informed. In Cousteau's TV show, the crew had fed the manatees a few water hyacinths. The tourists started cruising around Crystal River "dragging the hyacinths behind boats and trying to stuff the water hyacinths in the mouths of the manatees," Purcell recalled. "It was ridiculous."

Despite what the tourists thought, many locals still regarded manatees as a cross between a navigational hazard and Sunday dinner.

"There were still people poaching manatees back then," Purcell said. "You'd find manatees killed and strips taken off their backs for food. Divers had been known to stab them with knives."

Five months after the Cousteau show aired, Hartman came back to Crystal River to give a speech to a meeting of the Nature Conservancy at the Port Paradise hotel. He called for new restrictions to protect manatees. He said county officials should slow all boats to five miles per hour in Kings Bay and parts of the river, and he said they should forbid scuba diving or snorkeling in Kings Bay between October and April.

"Divers are a constant source of harassment to the manatees," Hartman said. He called it "a moral issue rather than an economic or political one."

But economics and politics, not morality, drove the opposition to his proposals. The notion that the government might impose limits on human behavior to benefit wildlife didn't sit well with either the manatees-are-business crowd or the more tradition-minded natives.

The newly opened dive shops opposed anything that might restrict their customers' access to either the manatees or the springs where the manatees congregated. The marina operators objected to any restrictions that might limit where or how fast boaters could go. The local fishing guides opposed anything that might require them to slow down or to stay out of any waterway. And then there were the developers, who opposed any limits on what they could do with waterfront property.

Since the opponents controlled the Citrus County economy, local government officials paid more attention to them than to Mr. TV Star with the Ph.D. Despite backing from the Friends of the Earth, Hartman's proposal never got off the ground.

Hartman's young protégé ran into the same opposition six years later, when he supported an effort by state officials to limit boat speeds in Kings Bay and create a refuge there. People complained that those pointy-headed bureaucrats wanted to shut down boating and diving in the entire bay, even if it drove the whole town into the poorhouse. Weren't the needs of the working folks more important than the needs of a bunch of clumsy animals that weren't smart enough to get out of the way? After all, one boater grumbled to a reporter, "Manatees don't pay taxes."

"The county commissioners said it'll never happen here—it'll have a negative impact on the economy," Powell said.

Not even Powell's status as a local boy persuaded the opponents of his good intentions. It just made him the target of more personal insults.

"A friend of mine was at a bar talking to a marina operator when this scraggly dog walks up," Powell recalled. "My friend says, 'Is that your dog?' And the marina operator says, 'Yeah, his name is BP—Buddy Powell.' My friend asks 'Why Buddy Powell?' And the marina guy says, 'Because it's short, scraggly, and nobody wants it.'"

Yet there were a few people in Crystal River who agreed with Powell, people who weren't dive shop operators or marina owners or fishing guides. They had developed a fondness for the flavor these homely animals brought to life in Florida, not the flavor they brought to the dinner table.

All these manatee fans needed was a catalyst. It arrived in 1979, when a developer announced plans to build homes on several islands in Kings Bay.

As soon as Powell heard about the development plan, he knew it was bad news. "There's no place left like Crystal River," he told a reporter. "If development runs rampant like it has in South Florida, you can kiss Crystal River goodbye."

Powell's agency imposed some small, seasonal manatee sanctuaries in Kings Bay, but that wouldn't halt the development. Powell asked one of his more experienced colleagues what to do. The colleague alerted a national group called The Nature Conservancy, which purchased environmentally sensitive land to preserve it.

Nature Conservancy officials announced they would try to raise $425,000 to buy the islands from the developer—but they wanted local residents to contribute. That's where Bob and Pearl Dick stepped in.

Bob Dick had made his fortune running a chemical company in Michigan. Then he and his wife decided they didn't want to live in dirty Detroit anymore. They were particularly sick of the pollution they saw in Lake Erie.

When they moved to Crystal River in 1973, they vowed to do everything they could to keep it from becoming a filthy mess like their old home. Yet it seemed to already be happening. They were seeing fewer and fewer fish. They worried about an explosion of algae in local canals. They noticed that the sandy bottom of the river had become thick with weeds.

As a leader of Concerned Citizens of Citrus County, Bob Dick became a persistent critic of the city's sewer system, which dumped its treated effluent into the river. He proposed a moratorium on all development in Crystal River until the sewer system could be upgraded—a proposal that was about as popular as Buddy Powell's manatee sanctuary plan.

Meanwhile, Pearl Dick became Crystal River's most prominent manatee activist, someone who used the popularity of manatees for something other than private profit.

"We were all fond of the manatees," she said years later. But when she heard about the plans to develop the islands, "that's when we really hopped on it."

The Nature Conservancy sent her T-shirts printed with the image of a manatee. She sold them around town for ten dollars each to raise money for buying the islands. Every Friday she would sell the shirts outside the Winn-Dixie grocery store, and every Saturday she would move her operation to the Publix grocery store. Many shoppers would stop to buy a shirt or at least chat with her about how the fund-raising drive was going—but not the town's business leaders.

"We couldn't get the business people behind us," she recalled. "It was all the little people working together to get the money."

Over two years Pearl Dick sold twenty-five thousand dollars' worth of T-shirts. Her husband's organization helped out too. One of its members, an artist named Helen Spivey, took the fund-raising on as a personal cause.

Spivey was the daughter of a wealthy Orlando businessman who lost everything when Florida's 1920s land boom went bust. Her family wound up living in a cabin they built in the woods of Central Florida. That's where she discovered how much she enjoyed communing with nature. Now she was married to a retired Navy chief petty officer everyone called Bear. The couple had moved to Crystal River in the early 1970s and quickly became alarmed about the degradation of the area's waterways.

One day Spivey saw one of Hartman's signs asking residents to call him to report manatee sightings. She started keeping an eye out for manatees. Their odd looks and aquatic grace captured her interest. When the Concerned Citizens held an auction to raise money for the refuge, Spivey not only helped raise money but also contributed a painting she had made of swimming manatees.

Spivey and the Dicks had plenty of help from outside Crystal River. Leading a statewide fund drive for The Nature Conservancy was Nathaniel P. Reed, who had been assistant secretary of the interior under President Nixon. Tall and lean with an aquiline nose, Reed was an aristocratic figure whose profile often reminded people of a particularly aggressive wading bird. In the 1960s Reed had helped the famous *River of Grass* author Marjory Stoneman Douglas block the construction of a jetport in the Everglades.

Reed charged into the effort to preserve Kings Bay with a similar zeal. He told reporters that the islands in Kings Bay were "a critical habitat for Florida's unique and most glamorous animal"—probably the only time anyone ever called manatees "glamorous."

Soon, though, the drive for the sanctuary did pick up some glamour straight from Hollywood: a celebrity endorsement from Burt Reynolds. Once a Florida State University football star, Reynolds had become a popular leading man in television and movies in the 1970s. He was not known for taking bold environmental stances, but now he cut a commercial for The Nature Conservancy urging people across the state to donate to the Kings Bay fund drive.

Then the state's biggest utility stepped in too. Florida Power and Light owned several power plants around the state where manatees congregated in cool weather. In fact, it had owned the one on the Miami River where Joe Moore had done his studies. The company had become the target of criticism from environmental activists for the pollution from its smokestacks and the radiation risk from its Miami nuclear plant. The utility mounted a counteroffensive by promoting its aid to manatees. Now the company began selling pictures of manatees, donating the proceeds to the Kings Bay fund drive.

By 1982, the drive had raised enough money. The Nature Conservancy bought the islands, then handed them over to the federal government. The U.S. Fish and Wildlife Service declared the area to be the Crystal River National Wildlife Refuge on August 17, 1983.

How much had the fund-raising drive changed attitudes in Crystal River? On November 15, 1984, the local chamber of commerce sponsored Citrus County's first Manatee Festival. The festival—a fund-raiser for the chamber, not for manatees—featured a concert by southern rock legend Greg Allman.

The festival kicked off with the dedication of several life-size manatee sculptures by artist Don Mayo, which were placed in front of Crystal River's welcome sign. From now on, manatees would be part and parcel of the town's identity.

•

Fifteen years later, in 1999, Buddy Powell was the head of manatee research for the state's marine science lab in St. Petersburg. He got an idea, one that blended the past with the present and repaid an old favor.

He called up Woodie Hartman, now retired to Maine, and offered him a job. Come back to Florida, Powell told Hartman. Write an update on the status of manatees.

Like Rip Van Winkle awakening after a twenty-year hibernation, Hartman's return to Florida showed him that the world he once knew had changed dramatically. Nowhere had it changed as much as Crystal River, where the city's official motto was now "Where man and manatee play."

"At Crystal River, the manatee had evolved from the unpublicized drawing card of a single dive shop into a fully fledged marketing tool," Hartman said.

Everywhere he looked, the city that once disdained its sea cows now celebrated them—on billboards, on park benches, even on the badges of its police officers. A dozen dive shops catered to the manatee-mad tourists, who numbered one hundred thousand a year. One woman, featured in a documentary that year, said swimming with Crystal River's manatees was "the greatest experience of my life."

Some of the marina operators who had lodged the loudest objections to the sanctuary now had some of the biggest operations, all aimed at customers who wanted to see a manatee in the wild. For them the sea cow had become a cash cow.

They were not alone. The hotels and restaurants and gift shops profited too. Tourists could choose from a wide variety of manatee-themed souvenirs to take home: manatee wine bottle stoppers, manatee cocktail napkins, manatee salt and pepper shakers, manatee clocks, manatee wind chimes, even a brand of cayenne pepper sauce called Manatee Madness. Scattered around Crystal River were a dozen more businesses unrelated to diving or sightseeing that had inserted a reference to manatees into the name of their muffler shop or beauty salon in the hopes of attracting customers.

"Today, if we did not have the manatees around, this would be a sleepy little burg that would not have the economic base we have now," Mary Craven, the tourism coordinator for Citrus County, told the *St. Petersburg Times*. "A lot of people came here and bought their businesses here because of manatees."

One study put the value of manatee-related tourism in Crystal River at seven million dollars a year. Some people called Citrus County a poster child for how the rest of the state could protect manatees while still enjoying a good economy.

Manatees had not only made Crystal River popular and prosperous. They had put the place on the map. Every time Craven attended meetings with officials from Walt Disney World and other theme parks, she said, "I'll say I'm from Citrus County and they look at me. Then I say 'Crystal River' and they say, 'Oh, manatees.'"

The annual Manatee Festival, held in late January or early February, drew some sixty thousand people. They joined in the wine-and-cheese tasting, strolled around the arts and crafts show, danced to the live music from Lee Greenwood and other big-name stars. Kids could enjoy the pony rides, the face-painting, the bouncy moonwalk. Plenty of families took the free tour boat rides out to oooh and ahhh at all the manatees crowded into the warm springs.

To Hartman, the transformation was stunning. "The manatee," he wrote in his report, "has risen from obscurity to icon in less than a generation. It is now as much a signature of Florida as the alligator or the cabbage palm."

Just as Powell had once predicted, thanks to the refuge there were now far more manatees to see in Kings Bay—more than three hundred of them. Although Sewer Sam had disappeared, there were still a few of the original herd he and Hartman had studied. Sadie, for instance, despite being injured by a boat, continued producing calves.

The sanctuary had expanded to cover twenty islands, and both the state and the federal government had been trying to buy Three Sisters Spring to add it as well. Outside the sanctuary was a mosaic of slow-speed zones, no-wake zones, and no-entry zones where no boats or divers could disturb manatees at all. To enforce the rules, rangers patrolled the waterways, as did volunteers in kayaks who called themselves Manatee Watch.

There were other changes as well. Helen Spivey, the artist, had served two terms on the city council and then was elected to a term in the legislature. Repeated problems with the sewer plant had led to a moratorium on development until it could be fixed, just as Bob Dick had wanted. The revamped plant now sent its effluent to a hayfield to be spread as fertilizer, instead of being dumped in the river.

And yet—despite the popularity of manatees, despite the rules that were supposed to protect them, despite the rangers and volunteers—there were still problems.

While there were more manatees in Citrus County's waters than ever before, there were also more boats. From 2000 to 2005, boat registrations in Citrus County increased by 37 percent, to 16,739.

And despite all the protections, manatees were still being hit by boats. Between 1990 and 2007, forty-eight manatees died in Citrus County from being run over.

In 1999, the year Hartman visited, three manatees were killed by boats in Citrus waters—one in February, one in October, one in November. The first was a male, the other two females. One of the females, found floating in Crystal River on the shore of one of the islands in the refuge, had suffered not only propeller wounds but also broken ribs and a collapsed lung. The other, found in a canal just off the river, had also suffered deep propeller wounds, broken ribs, and a torn lung. That manatee also happened to be pregnant, so one boat killed two animals.

Then there were the divers. Federal rules had made it illegal to touch manatees anywhere else in the United States—except for Crystal River, where the practice had been grandfathered in. Now every diver who swam in Kings Bay wanted to pat a manatee on the head like a dog, or scratch it on the back, or just swim along beside one. But some people went beyond that.

Crystal River City Council member Susan Kirk, who lived near one of the sanctuaries, told a reporter that she could stand on her sea wall most any day "and I'll see 10 or 15 divers come off a dive boat and chase the manatees into my corner. That's harassment." If she yelled at the divers to stop, she said, the response was usually a string of profanities.

In 2006, two former volunteers with Manatee Watch, Steve Kingery and Tracy Colson, shot video of snorkelers chasing, feeding, even riding on manatees, and then posted it on the Internet site YouTube. They said they gave up their volunteer kayak work out of frustration. Simply telling people to stop violating the rules wasn't enough to stop repeated violations. The pair spent three months compiling graphic evidence of what was going on and made it so public that no one in authority could ignore it.

One scene Colson recorded showed a baby manatee swimming out of the sanctuary and blundering into a group of snorkelers and their tour guide. As the baby tried to dive away from the humans and get back to its mother, the divers grabbed it and lifted it to the surface. Then the tour guide tugged it around to position it for the tourists' cameras.

The YouTube video embarrassed the town and upset the dive shops and tour operators. It also prompted federal officials to consider even tighter restrictions on human contact with the manatees.

"People are not following the rules, and those folks are putting the whole thing in jeopardy. They could ruin it for everyone," refuge manager Jim Kraus told a reporter.

But tour operators complained that only a few people were causing the most problems, which was no reason to shut down everyone.

"We have enough rules," said tour guide Marty Senetra of Bird's Underwater Manatee Tours, one of the most popular of Crystal River's tour operations. "We need enforcement."

Beyond what was happening to the manatees, there had been a steady decline in conditions in Kings Bay and Crystal River. The flow of the main spring, once strong enough to push swimmers back, had been greatly reduced. The culprit: the steady increase in pumping drinking water out of the underground aquifer to slake the thirst of the growing populace.

"Now you hold up a handful of sand and it barely is strong enough to blow the sand off your hand," Purcell said.

Meanwhile the water, once clear as crystal, turned murky. Wetlands that once filtered out pollution had been filled in by developers, allowing pesticides and other pollutants to run unimpeded into the river every time a hard rain fell. And while the sewer plant no longer dumped its effluent in the river, septic tanks and poorly maintained sewer lines still leaked into the water.

The steady boat traffic stirred up pollution-laden sediment, further limiting visibility. Meanwhile, a particularly nasty microscopic bacteria called *Lyngbya* spread throughout the bay, causing what one government report called "habitat destruction, navigational and recreational use impairment, odor and aesthetic problems."

That Crystal River's manatees were still in trouble, and their habitat in such decline, is astonishing not just because of their popularity and importance to the local economy. It's also astonishing because manatees and their habitat by this time were supposed to be protected by some of the strongest laws on the books—including one that Hartman himself helped to pass.

But as with Fred Morse's manatee protection bill in 1893, when it came time to put those laws into action, everyone's best intentions fell far short of actually protecting manatees.

# 4

## Making the List

AS HE WAITED HIS TURN, Woodie Hartman tried to contain his nervousness. He was used to being outdoors, not inside a cavernous hall of marble and dark wood. He was used to wearing a wet suit and a snorkel, not a coat and tie. He was used to swimming with manatees, not testifying before Congress.

Yet here he was, along with experts on sea otters and whales and polar bears, to tell a congressional subcommittee why there should be a federal law to safeguard marine mammals.

Decades later, his most vivid memory of that September 1971 hearing was that of being "awed by the authoritative atmosphere." He was so nervous he remembered "investing the committee members with supernatural powers. It was quite a scene, for me anyway."

Hartman was scheduled to be the next-to-last witness of the day, so he had a long time to wait and think about his presentation. He had good reason to be nervous. If the subcommittee chairman, John Dingell, resembled any divine being, it might be the Old Testament God who dumped all the plagues on Egypt. A tough-talking Michigan congressman, Dingell had been elected sixteen years earlier to fill his father's House seat, then hung onto the post like a bulldog with a bone. He was known for holding hearings where he put witnesses through the wringer.

At last Dingell called Hartman's name, and the uneasy scientist took his seat in front of the microphone.

"My name is Daniel Hartman," he said, leaving out his nickname. "I am here to testify on behalf of a rare and little known group of mammals called Sirenians. The group is represented in the United States by a single species, the Florida manatee or sea cow."

At the turn of the century, Hartman told Dingell's committee, "the Florida manatee was on the threshold of extinction. . . . Manatee steaks were, and still are, considered a delicacy."

He mentioned Fred Morse's law, but then added that it was "rarely enforced. The law, furthermore, has little relevance today. It was originally designed to protect manatees from poachers, but poaching is no longer a serious threat."

Instead, Hartman told the committee, manatees were being threatened by herbicides dumped into the state's waterways, by dredging that destroyed their habitat and turned the water murky, and by industrial effluents that polluted rivers and streams.

"Still more hazardous to their survival, indeed the chief source of manatee mortality," he said, "are the whirling propellers of speeding power craft which overtake the animals unaware at the surface.

"To adequately protect the manatee, therefore, new legislation must be enacted, legislation that is directed toward pollution abatement and reduction of boat speeds in manatee habitat."

Struggling to keep his voice even, Hartman told the congressmen about his research. Then Congressman Dingell ordered the lights turned out. It was time for Hartman's slide show.

Hartman started off with some pictures of Crystal River and a couple of manatees swimming—and then he got to what he called "one of the major threats to their survival."

Click went the slide projector. "Here is a little bull lying on the bottom," Hartman said. "You can see where a propeller has run down the center of his back."

The next slide clicked into place. "Again, an adult bull," Hartman said. "Once more the pattern of wounds inflicted by a propeller."

Then one more slide, a picture of Sadie and her mutilated fluke: "Here is a cow with a calf to her left. Note how a propeller has cut off half her tail."

Of the seventy or so animals he had studied in Crystal River, Hartman told the congressmen, almost all "had at least one set of propeller scars on them."

The slide show did the trick. The congressmen were convinced.

●

That Congress would even consider such a law would have seemed absurd only forty years before.

Federal law said little then regarding wild animals. The job of protecting wildlife had been left primarily up to the states—and with the occasional exception of lawmakers like Fred Morse, state legislators usually cared more about hunting and fishing regulations than about protecting animals for their own sake.

The first federal law concerning wild animals, the Lacey Act, was passed in 1900, and it was concerned with helping the states do their job. The Lacey Act aimed to put a stop to the trade in bird plumes that had so outraged Kirk and Mary Munroe and other Audubon members.

Although several states (though not Florida, not yet) had banned the sale of the plumes taken from their native birds, canny plume hunters got around the ban by shipping the feathers to states where the birds were not native. Then they could legally sell them. So a Republican congressman from Iowa named John Lacey proposed a law that would give the state laws the federal government's backing. The Lacey Act prohibited interstate commerce in animals and birds killed in violation of state law, and required the Agriculture Department to ensure the preservation and restoration of certain species—but only of game animals.

Those in the feather trade fought back by trying to get the state laws repealed. For instance, the Millinery Association lobbied for New York lawmakers to overturn that state's ban. The association brought witnesses to Albany to testify that enforcement of the law would throw thousands of people out of work. The industry's effort failed to sway the legislature—and the threat of massive unemployment failed to materialize. Instead, the milliners switched to using lace, silk, and ribbons.

The Lacey Act slowed, but did not stop, the slaughter of birds. Fourteen years after it passed, the last passenger pigeon—a species once so abundant in the Midwest that its flocks eclipsed the sky—died in a Cincinnati zoo.

Gradually, though, the idea began to take hold in some quarters that animals deserved to be spared from extinction simply because they existed. In
1936, pioneering conservationist Aldo Leopold published a short article called
"Threatened Species" in which he argued that such creatures as the ivory-billed
woodpecker and the grizzly bear should be preserved, not for their value to
man, but because they filled a place in a natural system. It was a revolutionary
idea, and one that did not catch on for some time.

In 1940, Congress did pass a law banning the hunting of bald eagles—not
because the eagle filled an important place in nature, but because it was the
national symbol. Still, it was a step beyond valuing only game animals.

Leopold's theme of valuing all species was picked up and expanded upon in
the 1942 book Daniel Beard helped write, *Fading Trails*. Beard and his coau-
thors wrote that their purpose in producing the book was "to show how certain
forms of wildlife have approached the brink of extinction. . . . All forms of
animal life, whether they be game species, fur bearers, predators, or what, are
valuable in nature's enduring battle for perfection. Each form of life does its bit
to help maintain the elusive 'balance' between all living things."

Yet another twenty years would pass before the federal government that employed Beard would take action to protect those species named in the book—
the sea otter, the California condor, the whooping crane, the American crocodile, and of course the manatee.

Rachel Carson's 1962 best-seller *Silent Spring* set the stage by warning readers of the perils of pesticides, herbicides, and insecticides. Carson painted a
vivid picture of the end result of pollution: songbirds falling out of the trees,
dead, and humans poisoned as well.

Federal biologists were not as concerned about songbirds as they were about
the whooping crane, a magnificent bird with a distinctive bugling call. Its flocks
had dwindled down to a mere thirty or so. The Interior Department's Bureau
of Sport Fisheries and Wildlife—later to become the U.S. Fish and Wildlife
Service—persuaded a friendly congressman to squeeze $350,000 into the fed-
eral budget for an endangered wildlife research program that would benefit the
whooper and other species.

But what other creatures beside the whooper needed help? In 1963, nine of
the bureau's biologists sat down to figure that out. The Committee on Rare and
Endangered Wildlife Species produced its first draft by August 1964. Called the
"Redbook," this first draft included sixty-three species: thirty-six birds, fifteen

mammals, six fish, and five reptiles and amphibians. The committee mailed out the draft to other biologists across the country and got an earful about all the species they had missed.

One creature not included in the Redbook: the manatee. Its absence rankled the bureau's regional director in Atlanta, a stocky white-haired man named Walter A. Gresh. He made it his business to rectify the oversight.

Government is honeycombed with men and women like Walter Gresh, people who toil in obscurity, their names unknown to the general public. As with spies in wartime, their very anonymity gives them the cover they need to quietly change the course of history.

A Pennsylvania native, Gresh earned a degree in forestry and for a time worked in the Arkansas timber business. But Gresh was more interested in animals than trees. He became a state game official in Pennsylvania and West Virginia before joining the federal wildlife agency in 1939. Twenty-five years later, at sixty-two, Gresh was closing in on retirement, but he had hardly slowed down.

Gresh fired off a memo to Washington demanding to know why the Redbook had failed to mention Florida's sea cow. The answer came from Lansing Parker, the associate director of the bureau, who was overseeing its endangered species work. In a September 1965 memo to Gresh, Parker explained that in picking which animals to put on the Redbook list, "we were dealing mainly with species where land acquisition would be necessary for their preservation. This is not to say that the acquisition of land for the benefit of the manatee may not be essential, but we do not have the facts at the present time."

Rather than spending federal money buying waterfront land, Parker wrote, "one of the most effective methods of preserving the manatee would be through a system of public education . . . so that due regard would be given to it by persons using power boats to avoid injuring or disturbing the animal."

Still, Parker conceded that Gresh might have a point. He told Gresh to check with Florida officials about listing the manatee as endangered. He also suggested Gresh pass along any other recommendations "for protecting this unique mammal."

Gresh put in a call to the executive director of what was then known as the Florida Game and Fresh Water Fish Commission, a politically savvy bureaucrat named Ozro Earle Frye Jr., who took his time responding, much to Gresh's annoyance.

Earle Frye was no Aldo Leopold. The former Navy pilot had been hired as

Walter Gresh pushed hard for the manatee to be put on the first federal list of endangered species. Photo courtesy of the U.S. Fish and Wildlife Service.

the Florida game commission's first field biologist in 1946. His boss immediately shipped him off to Charlotte County to boost the bobwhite quail population around the commission chairman's ranch. Frye invented a quail feeder that would attract the birds. He tested the first one in his own backyard, and the second went to the chairman's ranch. Luckily for Frye, it worked.

After that success, Frye rose steadily through the ranks. When Gresh began nagging him about manatees, Frye had just been named to the executive director's post, a job he would go on to hold for twelve years, longer than any of his eight predecessors.

Frye spoke often of his fondness for barbecued armadillo, but he was no backwoods bumpkin. He had earned a master's degree in wildlife management at the University of Florida, and would go on to earn a Ph.D. and serve as president of the Florida Academy of Sciences.

As for manatees, one of Frye's grad school classmates had been none other than Joe Moore. Frye had contributed to one of Moore's earliest published studies, a census of all the mammal species to be found in one Florida county—one of them, of course, being the manatee.

So when Frye wrote back to Gresh on September 20, 1965, he first made a point of recommending Moore's manatee papers.

"If you or your staff are not familiar with these," he added dryly, "I will be happy to give you the references."

Then Frye gave Gresh what he really wanted: his opinion.

"Our general feeling about the manatee is that it appears to be holding its own in Florida," Frye wrote. "In fact, it is probably more abundant now than it was a few years ago, principally because it has been under complete protection for several years." Frye cited no figures or sources to go with that contention.

He also made no mention of boats. Instead, Frye told Gresh that the biggest problem facing the manatee was the same one facing all of Florida's fish and waterfowl: their habitat was "being destroyed by dredge and fill operations, silting, drainage, and other activities of man."

In short, Frye wrote, "I very definitely think that the manatee should be considered an endangered species, but again must emphasize that it is being endangered because of the destruction of habitat—not because of direct destruction of the manatee."

When Gresh passed Frye's letter along to his superiors in Washington, he underlined the first part of that last sentence about manatees being endangered by the loss of habitat. Next to it Gresh scribbled: "Amounts to the same thing."

The clearly irritated Gresh also wrote a memo to bureau director John Gottschalk dated October 6, 1965: "I have finally been able to get out of Earle Frye in writing agreement that manatees should be considered in the list. Although Earle insists on qualifying his statement, I feel that the animal itself, or its habitat, when endangered, should be listed."

Gresh's recommendation worked its way through the committee overseeing the Redbook list. The members did not just take Gresh and Frye's word for whether manatees were endangered. No, the committee consulted with an expert—but not Joe Moore.

Instead, they called Craig Phillips.

Phillips had designed and built the National Aquarium in Washington and now served as its head curator. Although the National Aquarium possessed no manatees, Phillips probably knew more about them than anyone else in the country except Joe Moore. And unlike Moore, Phillips had actually plunged into the water with one.

In fact, Phillips had even eaten a manatee, one that had been killed by scientists to study its brain. No sense letting all that delicious meat go to waste.

"It tasted very good," he said years later. "It tasted like beef, but it looked like pork."

Phillips grew up in Florida, the son of St. Petersburg's longtime municipal publicist, whose job entailed churning out reams of "feature stories" for northern newspapers about how warm the Tampa Bay area remained during the bleakest winter.

As a boy, Phillips enjoyed prowling St. Petersburg's shorelines and wooded areas. He collected snakes, lizards, even bats—at one point he had fifty of them flying around the house.

Phillips taught himself to identify and sketch a wide variety of plants and animals. At age eleven he became the local paper's nature columnist. Later, while serving in the South Pacific during World War II, he sent his parents a twenty-page letter about the insects and sea life around New Guinea. Not until the last line did he bring up the war, noting laconically, "We were under aerial fire today."

Eventually, Phillips became the first curator of the Miami Seaquarium, the facility that would later rescue Sewer Sam. Phillips had seldom seen manatees around St. Petersburg when he was growing up. But during his years at the Seaquarium he captured several to put on display. The fate of one in particular, a female he captured in the Miami River, haunted him for years afterward.

He named her Cleopatra "because she was so beautiful," Phillips wrote in *The Captive Sea*, published in 1964, a year before Gresh began campaigning to put manatees on the Redbook list.

"Her body was fresh and glistening as she emerged from the river and her breath came forth in a languid sigh. . . . She was in the net, the most beautiful sea cow I had ever seen," Phillips wrote in his memoir.

To his delight, Cleopatra turned out to be pregnant. Five months after being captured, the manatee gave birth at the Seaquarium to a female calf.

A month later, Phillips got a call from the Coral Gables Police Department that an orphaned calf was swimming around one of the department's patrol boats. Nearby the police had spotted the corpse of its mother, apparently killed by a speeding boat.

Phillips and his wife, Fanny, headed out to capture the orphan. But when Phillips grabbed the calf by its flippers to pull it out of the water, "the manatee instantly turned a half-somersault and pulled me into the canal head-first. . . . With a crash of foam I plunged downward into the dark water, still maintaining my grip on the creature's wrists. He may have turned the tables on me, I remember thinking, but he's not going to get loose from me as long as I can hold my breath! . . . Finally I managed to pull him against me and locked my arms around his chest, meanwhile shouting to Fanny for assistance."

Together they managed to drag the calf to the shore. When they carted the orphan back to the Seaquarium, Cleopatra adopted the male newcomer too, allowing the new calf to nurse under its flipper just like the female calf nursing on the other side.

A month later, Phillips left on a family vacation. On his return, he discovered the female calf was dead. Cleopatra and the male calf died soon afterward. He was heartbroken.

An animal autopsy, known as a necropsy, explained what happened, Phillips wrote. It was like something out of Rachel Carson's nightmares.

"During my absence from the Seaquarium and strictly against my orders, one of the maintenance personnel had sprayed the area adjacent to the manatee tank with DDT and Chlordane in an effort to kill mosquitoes, and airborne oil droplets containing these deadly poisons had settled on the water surface," he wrote. "The chemicals were gradually absorbed by the manatees, who could not tolerate them. . . . Eventually we did obtain some more manatees, but the untimely death of our family remains one of the saddest events of my experience, as Cleo and the babies will always be, to me, irreplaceable."

Decades later, Phillips said that the fact that the federal biologists would call him for advice on manatees was not surprising, since the only real studies that had been done on the species at that point were Joe Moore's.

"Apparently there weren't a lot of manatee experts around back then," Phillips said. "I didn't have a hell of a lot of competition."

Like Frye, though, Phillips cautioned the Committee on Rare and Endangered Wildlife about making unsupported assumptions regarding the status of the manatee. In particular, he warned them against jumping to conclusions about how many, or how few, manatees there might be.

"According to Craig Phillips . . . the manatee may actually be more abundant than is believed at present, due to the fact that it is one of the most difficult of all totally aquatic mammals to observe in the wild," the committee wrote in its

Craig Phillips warned the Fish and Wildlife Service that manatees were "one of the most difficult of all totally aquatic mammals to observe in the wild." Photo courtesy of the *St. Petersburg Times*.

January 1966 report—an analysis that decades later would prove to be particularly prescient.

But the committee contended that such scientific ignorance was actually a sign of how badly manatees needed federal protection.

"It is, however, considered herein to be endangered because of the lack of reliable estimates as to its numbers in Florida, and because of its reduced range," the committee wrote, noting that manatees had once been found from Texas to North Carolina.

Under "reasons for decline," the committee conceded, "There is no evidence of recent decline."

But then the report contended that at some point in the past there had probably been a decline in the number of manatees because of "hunting for flesh, oil, and skins; wanton slaughter for 'sport'; silting of coastal feeding grounds; freezing weather inducing pneumonia; crocodiles and sharks, possibly taking a few very young animals; injuries received from keels and propellers of power boats."

And what could be done about all that? The committee had a few vague ideas: "Continue legal protection; establish sanctuary areas; impound certain areas and experimentally stock."

With that unsigned two-page report, Gresh got his wish. The committee added manatees to the list of endangered species.

There was no attempt to determine the size of the population, no call for further scientific studies, no mention of beefing up the number of game officers to enforce Fred Morse's law (and no explanation of how to "experimentally stock" the species). It was just put on the list and that was that.

The first official endangered species list was published in the *Federal Register* on March 17, 1967. Besides manatees, the list covered seventy-seven other mammals, birds, amphibians, fish, and reptiles, including such Florida species as the Florida panther, the Key deer, the alligator, the dusky seaside sparrow, and the Everglades kite.

"An informed public will act to help reduce the dangers facing these rare animals," President Lyndon Johnson's interior secretary, Stewart Udall, predicted in announcing that first list.

Over the next four decades, a lot changed on the endangered species list. Alligators bounced back enough to be taken off the list in 1987. Others didn't fare as well. The last dusky seaside sparrow died in captivity at Disney World in 1990.

Meanwhile, lots of other species were added to the list, including plants and insects, which had not been eligible for consideration in 1967. As of 2008 more than twelve hundred species of flora and fauna were classified as endangered under federal law.

One thing didn't change. Year after year, decade after decade, manatees remained on the list, forever teetering on the brink of extinction, forever in need of rescuing—even though the laws designed to help them got tougher and tougher.

•

The list that Secretary Udall unveiled was drawn up under the Endangered Species Preservation Act of 1966. That law, as Lansing Parker had warned Walter Gresh, concerned habitat and little else.

The law gave the Interior Department fifteen million dollars to buy up land to help preserve the species on the list. But the law did little beyond that to protect the animals on the list from other threats. It ordered the Departments of Interior, Agriculture, and Defense to protect threatened species "insofar as is practicable and consistent," and told Interior to "encourage" other federal agencies to do the same "where practicable."

In other words, protecting the listed species was largely voluntary, and thus the protection was usually nonexistent. (Even the protection of habitat didn't get started until 1968, when the government finally got around to purchasing twenty-three hundred acres in the Keys for the Key deer.)

But an increased concern about the environment was now sweeping the country—with good reason. Polluted lakes suffered massive fishkills. An Ohio river caught fire. In some cities the smog was so thick, men had to change their shirts twice a day. Fed up, activists organized the first Earth Day demonstration in 1970. Twenty million people—a tenth of the American public—hit the streets to protest.

By then a Republican moderate named Richard Nixon had won election to the White House. While not that interested in the environment, Nixon saw an opportunity to latch onto a popular issue to boost his poll numbers. Nixon created the Environmental Protection Agency and the White House Council on Environmental Quality. He signed into law the Clean Air Act and the National Environmental Policy Act.

On the staff of Nixon's Council on Environmental Quality was a scientist named Lee M. Talbot. He was much more in sympathy with the Earth Day activists than his boss in the Oval Office. Talbot had worked as an ecologist for the United Nations and for the International Union for Conservation of Nature (IUCN), a Switzerland-based alliance of private environmental groups.

While Talbot worked for the IUCN, in 1960, he helped the organization compile a card file of species from around the world that appeared headed for extinction, giving him a keen interest in saving species that were in trouble. Later, as head ecologist at the Smithsonian Institution, Talbot had testified on behalf of the 1966 Endangered Species Preservation Act—but what he wanted was something far stronger, something without loopholes.

An ex-Marine, Talbot enjoyed mountain climbing, scuba diving, skiing, and auto racing. He was not a man to shrink from a challenge. Now, with his White House job, he was in a position to do something about changing the law. Like Walter Gresh, he would work behind the scenes, out of the limelight, to change history.

When he arrived at his White House job, "I had kind of an agenda," he explained years later.

Talbot was particularly concerned about whales. Some species were being hunted to extinction, just to be made into cosmetics, margarine, and pet food. When the Interior Department tried to add them to the endangered list in 1970, the department's lawyers said the law wouldn't allow it because no one could prove they were threatened throughout their entire range—in other words, all of the world's oceans. To Talbot, what was happening with the whales was symbolic of the fate of all marine species. But the public wouldn't get all that worked up over, say, a cod.

"They have trouble relating to a cod," Talbot explained, "so I thought, well, people can relate to a whale."

The whales weren't alone. The papers and television were full of stories about bloody fur seal hunts, and about dolphins being drowned in tuna nets. Thanks to the surging public outrage, Talbot got a green light from the White House to work up a bill to save the whales.

Talbot's bill marked a departure from every previous federal wildlife measure. He called for a complete moratorium on killing, capturing, maiming, or even harassing all marine mammals. Only people with a permit could harvest polar bears, seals, dolphins, whales, and manatees. It was like Fred Morse's law, but extended nationwide, and expanded to other species.

But Talbot went further than Morse had ever dreamed. To get a permit, the applicant would have to prove that his or her activities would not jeopardize the future of the species. For the first time, the burden of proof would be on those who would exploit the resource, instead of the scientists.

Watching over all of this permitting and protection activity would be a board of experts, the U.S. Marine Mammal Commission, that would deliver an annual report to Congress and make recommendations to other federal agencies. If the other agencies chose to ignore the commission's recommendations, they would have to explain to Congress why—and all those reports and letters would be available to the public to review, too.

When Talbot's marine mammal bill went to the Office of Management and Budget (OMB), some of his more radical provisions were sliced out before it was sent along to Congress. Talbot knew this might be a sign of problems in the future, since OMB's weaker version was probably the one that the National Marine Fisheries Service and U.S. Fish and Wildlife Service wanted.

Rather than pick a fight with the other agencies, Talbot chose to make an end run around them, even though it meant crossing party lines. He got in touch with Congressman Dingell's committee counsel, Frank Potter. Soon thereafter the Democratic congressman introduced a marine mammal bill that sounded a lot like Talbot's original version.

The Michigan congressman might seem an unlikely ally to a tree-hugger like Talbot. After all, Dingell was an avid trophy hunter and gun collector. He was a lawyer, not a biologist. His biggest campaign contributor was the American automobile industry, hardly the most environmentally friendly business in the world.

But before law school, Dingell had spent five summers working as a park ranger, an experience he never forgot. Over the years he sponsored or co-sponsored a host of key environmental legislation, including the Clean Water Act. As chairman of the House Committee on Merchant Marine and Fisheries, Dingell could offer marine mammal advocates a bully pulpit to warn the country about what was happening to the whales and polar bears. His staff lined up experts like Hartman to testify during four days of hearings, setting up the rationale for the bill.

The bill clearly struck a chord with voters concerned about seals, whales, and dolphins. At one of the September 1971 public hearings—held at the height of the controversy over the Vietnam War—a Massachusetts congressman announced that no other issue he had ever seen in his twenty-four years in office had generated as much mail from the voting public.

In December, Dingell's committee issued a report recommending Congress pass a tough new law protecting marine mammals:

Recent history indicates that man's impact upon marine mammals has ranged from what might be termed malign neglect to virtual genocide. These animals, including whales, porpoises, seals, sea otters, polar bears, manatees and others . . . have been shot, blown up, clubbed to death, run down by boats, poisoned, and exposed to a multitude of other indignities, all in the interests of profit or recreation, with little or no consideration of the potential impact of these activities on the animal populations involved.

The committee report talked about whale hunting and dolphin netting, and then turned its attention to another threat:

Still another problem to which marine mammals may be inadvertently exposed is the operation of high-speed boats. Manatees and sea otters have been crippled and killed by motorboats and at present the Federal government is essentially powerless to force these boats to slow down or to curtail their operations.

But the committee stopped short of endorsing all of Hartman's recommendations for protecting manatees from the hazards that had put the species on the endangered list:

These hazards are principally a) the operation of powerboats in areas where the manatees are found, and b) the excessive use of herbicides in areas draining into these waters, which in turn destroys the habitat and food supply of the manatees.

While the new law "would provide the Secretary of the Interior with adequate authority to regulate or even to forbid the use of powerboats in waters where manatees are found," the committee shied away from giving the government too much power—for instance "to forbid the use of herbicides."

Still, the committee said, "The definition of taking . . . includes the concept of harassment, and it is intended that this term be construed sufficiently broadly to allow the regulation of excessive or wanton use of these chemical compounds, as well as the operation of powerboats."

The bill passed Congress and was signed by Nixon on December 21, 1972. Most men would be satisfied with such a triumph, but Talbot was just warming up.

Talbot viewed the Marine Mammal Protection Act (MMPA) as just a "wedge," a tryout for his grandest scheme of all. With help from Dingell's aide,

Potter, and an Interior Department undersecretary named Nathaniel Reed—the same Nat Reed who ten years later would lead the campaign to buy the islands in Kings Bay—Talbot set to work rewriting the law governing all endangered species.

•

Once or twice a week, Talbot would meet with Reed and one or two of Reed's assistants at Reed's favorite Chinese restaurant off Constitution Avenue. Over egg rolls and moo goo gai pan, they would hammer out the language of their new bill. They believed their cause to be a righteous one.

"We had the fervor of youth and a sense of high ethical standards for how man should treat his fellow creatures on spaceship Earth," Reed said years later.

The endangered species law on the books was full of what Talbot called "weasel-words, such as 'insofar as possible or practicable.'" They effectively rendered the law meaningless.

In February 1972, at Talbot's urging, Nixon called for a stronger law to protect endangered species, contending that "even the most recent act to protect endangered species . . . simply does not provide the kind of management tools needed to act early enough to save a vanishing species."

The Fish and Wildlife Service came up with a proposal, but Talbot deemed it too weak, still littered with those weasel-word phrases he detested. Working together, Talbot, Reed, and Potter rewrote it.

"We targeted everything that was too weak," Talbot said, and struck it out. They also banished the word "practicable" from their version, so that federal agencies would have no excuse for not protecting endangered flora and fauna.

And they created a new category called "threatened." Not quite as dire as "endangered," it would offer protection for species before extinction loomed too closely on the horizon.

They hadn't forgotten habitat, either. Their new law said the government was supposed to conserve and protect "the ecosystems upon which endangered and threatened species of wildlife depend"—in effect ordering every federal agency to preserve every piece of land or water where listed species live, a sweeping command unlike anything that came before.

"We were in uncharted waters," Reed said, admitting the trio had no idea just how far-reaching their proposal would be. Nevertheless, he said, their strong words came from a strong belief that opposed "ending a life that evolved on earth, in some cases before we did, just to satisfy ourselves."

The most crucial part of Talbot's new law was in Section 7, which told federal agencies that they could no longer pay lip service to protecting endangered species while conducting business as usual. Instead, the law said "not that they will do it at their discretion, or that they will use their best efforts, but that they will just do it," Potter said.

Federal agencies about to undertake activities that might affect an endangered or threatened species—building dams and highways, dredging ship channels, leasing offshore property for oil drilling, issuing permits for development in wetlands—would now be required to consult with the Fish and Wildlife Service or the National Marine Fisheries Service. They would have to get a formal opinion from those agencies that their actions were not putting the species' future in jeopardy.

Yet in debating the measure, Congress paid absolutely no attention to Section 7 and its potential to disrupt both government and business activities. The politicians were too caught up in trying to top one another at being the most sensitive to the plight of the poor endangered animals. They didn't even understand what animals might be involved.

"They weren't thinking of dung beetles," Lynn Greenwalt, the cautious bureaucrat then at the head of the Fish and Wildlife Service, grumbled years later. "They were thinking of huge grizzly bears and bald eagles and stately monarchs of the air."

The bill Talbot, Potter, and Reed had written, sponsored by Dingell, sailed through both the House and Senate with little opposition. When Nixon signed the Endangered Species Act of 1973, he too seemed oblivious to the potential for controversy.

"Nothing is more priceless and more worthy of preservation than the rich array of animal life with which our country has been blessed," Nixon said grandly.

Thanks to the idealistic Talbot, Reed, and Potter, a pair of federal agencies— the U.S. Fish and Wildlife Service and the National Marine Fisheries Service— had been handed two powerful weapons to use in combating the forces wiping species from the planet—weapons they had not really asked for and were extremely reluctant to use. As Talbot had feared, it turned out to be far easier to pass the MMPA and the Endangered Species Act than to get hidebound bureaucrats to carry it out.

"It's hard to change the ways of a bureaucracy," Talbot explained. "They're used to doing things one way."

This was no gradual change, either. The new laws Talbot and his cohorts had thrust upon the agencies, he said, were "almost 180 degrees from the way the business had been done up to that time."

The National Marine Fisheries Service was used to promoting fishing, not regulating it. For fifteen years after the MMPA passed, it still shied away from curtailing any industry practices. It even avoided doing any research on declining fishing stocks that might lead to restrictions.

"The absence of information was a license to fish," explained a former National Marine Fisheries Services official.

But then Alaskan salmon fishermen sued the agency for allowing Japanese salmon fishermen to use drift nets that killed thousands of dolphins. That 1987 suit, which ended Japanese drift-net fishing in U.S. waters, stunned agency officials and led to the change in policy Talbot had sought. Now the burden of proof would not be on the scientists and regulators to show that an industry was causing harm to a protected species. Instead, the court decision said, the industry must bear the burden of proving that it would not harm a protected marine mammal.

Enforcement of the MMPA's ban on killing or harassing the animals fared no better. Five years passed before federal agents charged anyone with violating the law—and although it was a Florida case, it had nothing to do with boats running over manatees.

The man the agents arrested, a retired Navy veteran named James C. Smith, had been spotted putting along in a nineteen-foot motorboat off St. Petersburg Beach and firing a gun into a school of porpoises, killing one of them. Unfortunately for Smith, he pulled the trigger in full view of the captain of a passing charter boat and the boat's seventy passengers. After his arrest, Smith agreed to plead guilty in exchange for a sentence of two years of probation, a fine of five thousand dollars that he didn't have to pay if he stayed out of trouble, and the forfeiture of his boat. He also agreed to undergo psychiatric counseling.

The U.S. Fish and Wildlife Service was just as hesitant to use its new powers as the Marine Fisheries Commission. Greenwalt, the agency's head, had a background in managing wildlife refuges, not issuing permits or regulating industry. He was the son of a longtime refuge manager, the son-in-law of another, and had spent most of his career in that same system.

Greenwalt believed that the quickest way to lose his new powers over endangered species was for anyone in Congress to find out that he had them, so he refused to use them. It was as if Clark Kent had decided to keep his glasses on and stay away from telephone booths for fear someone might spot his Superman cape.

"The Fish and Wildlife Service has never been known to be a pioneering or aggressive organization," Talbot said.

The fact that the agency remained cautious about using its powers even when it had the backing of the White House Council on Environmental Quality, the top management of the Interior Department, and the chairman of the key House committee overseeing wildlife issues "says a lot about the people in the Fish and Wildlife Service," he said.

As with the MMPA, it took a lawsuit to flush out the truth.

•

The Tennessee Valley Authority (TVA) had decided to build a seventy-eight-million-dollar dam on the Little Tennessee River. The Tellico dam was widely viewed as a boondoggle designed only to promote land speculation, not actual need. Undeterred by the criticism, TVA officials predicted the dam and reservoir would spur the creation of a sparkling model city of fifty thousand people.

Opponents of the dam had repeatedly struck out trying to block Tellico's construction because of its effect on the farmers and others whose property would be inundated. But then a scientist discovered that the dam threatened to wipe out the only known habitat of a tiny fish called the snail darter. Dam opponents seized on the darter in a last-ditch attempt to stop the dam.

A University of Tennessee law professor with the memorable name of Zygmunt J. B. Plater—son of a onetime Polish diplomat—teamed up with one of his students, Hiram G. Hill Jr. Together they petitioned the wildlife service to add the snail darter to the endangered list on an emergency basis. Initially, facing political pressure from Tennessee's congressional delegation, federal wildlife service officials resisted listing the darter, until finally Nat Reed himself signed the petition. Reed said Plater and Hill's case "put me in this incredibly difficult position" with the congressmen.

Once Plater and Hill had the darter listed, they sued to stop the dam—not really to save the darter, Plater later explained, but to save hundreds of family farms and other aspects of human habitat.

"By the early 1970s, 69 dams impounding 2,500 linear miles of river had been built in the region, and the last place left with high quality, big river habitat was that last 33 miles of the Little Tennessee," Plater wrote years later. "Thus, by its existence as an endangered species in this last un-dammed place, the snail darter was a vivid ecological and legal indicator of the fact that this was the last such high-quality, un-dammed place remaining for the interests of human society as well as for small fish."

Plater, representing a coalition of farmers, sportsmen, environmentalists, biologists, and parts of the Cherokee Nation, fought the case all the way to the U.S. Supreme Court. During oral arguments, U.S. Attorney General Griffin Bell, representing the TVA, pulled from his pocket a test tube containing one of the two-and-a-half-inch darters and waved it around. He wanted to show how silly it would be to stop a nearly completed public works project just to save a little fish.

But then one of the justices asked Bell if the law said some species are entitled to more protection than others. No, Bell replied, the law said that all species deserve equal protection—an answer that would prove fatal to his case.

In June 1978, the Supreme Court ruled by a vote of six to three that under the Endangered Species Act, protecting the snail darter's habitat was more important than the TVA's desire to build another dam. After all, the justices noted, Congress's expressed intent in the law had been "to halt and reverse the trend toward species extinction, whatever the cost."

Appalled at the implications of the TVA case, Congress promptly reversed itself. It passed legislation that exempted the Tellico dam from the Endangered Species Act, no matter what that meant for the snail darter. President Jimmy Carter signed it into law, then called Plater to mumble an apology.

In 1979, the TVA completed the dam and flooded the valley where the snail darter swam, thus destroying its habitat and, presumably, its future existence.

A year later, though, the same scientist who had first discovered the snail darter near the dam site stumbled across more of them swimming in another river sixty miles away. Apparently the little fish weren't quite as endangered as everyone thought. By 1984 the Fish and Wildlife Service had lowered the darter's status from "endangered" to "threatened."

As for the vast and sparkling model city that the Tellico dam was supposed to stimulate, it never materialized. The only thing ever built on the property was a retirement home called Tellico Village. As writers Charles C. Mann and Mark L. Plummer note in their book *Noah's Choice: The Future of Endangered Species*, the tax revenue that Tellico Village generates is far, far less than what the dam cost the federal taxpayers.

•

While the snail darter controversy raged through Congress and the courts, the Fish and Wildlife Service continued dragging its feet about dealing with the problem of manatee protection. Unlike the darter, the manatee was supposed to be covered by not just one but both of Talbot's laws, and it enjoyed far greater public popularity.

But in 1978—six years after the MMPA passed, and five years after the Endangered Species Act became law—manatees were still being clobbered by boats. Eighty-four manatees died that year, twenty-one of them killed by boat collisions.

The man Talbot had handpicked as the director of the new Marine Mammal Commission took a dim view of the agency's sluggishness. John Twiss was a New York native whose work for the National Science Foundation had sent him to explore both the Arctic and Antarctic. His letters to Greenwalt about manatees carried a markedly chilly tone.

Twiss wrote in March 1978 that the commission was already concerned about what was happening—or not happening—with regard to manatees. The agency had failed to put anyone in charge of the manatee effort, Twiss pointed out, and the committee of experts that was supposed to be drawing up a plan for saving the species hadn't met for two years. And why, he asked, had the agency still not proposed *any* regulations for slowing down boats?

While the perils facing manatees were known long before the Endangered Species Act and the MMPA were passed, Twiss wrote, "it appears that little or no affirmative action has been taken by the service to resolve the problems under those statutes."

Five months later, Twiss fired off another sharply worded letter to Greenwalt, warning him that unless the agency took "decisive action" in the near future, "the commission believes that this species may well become extinct in this country in the foreseeable future."

Twiss was particularly critical of the agency's failure to investigate any boat-related manatee deaths, much less prosecute anyone: "We are concerned that the service's enforcement efforts are inadequate for protecting this seriously endangered species from human activities which apparently are a major source of mortality."

He recommended that Greenwalt figure out a way for his officers to "actively police human activities that are detrimental to manatees." But Greenwalt complained that his agents found it too difficult to enforce the law because they couldn't prove that "by merely exceeding a set speed, a boat is harassing manatees."

Twiss let his irritation show in his reply. "As I know you are aware," he snapped back, "substantial evidence . . . has been accumulated showing that power boats do kill and injure manatees."

Proving beyond a shadow of a doubt that a speeding boat will kill a manatee might be impossible, Twiss told Greenwalt, "but we are dealing with probabilities and common sense argues that the slower a vessel is moving in areas where manatees are concentrated, the better the chances of a manatee getting out of its way and the better the chances of the boat operator's detecting and avoiding the animal."

Still the wildlife agency dragged its feet. Finally, in November 1978, Twiss went over Greenwalt's head, sending a letter to Assistant Interior Secretary Robert Herbst. All of the wildlife service's marine mammal programs should be subjected to "an intensive review," he wrote, starting with manatees.

"The manatee is in danger of becoming extinct in Florida waters," Twiss told Herbst bluntly, yet "the weak presentation by Department of the Interior representatives charged with management . . . suggested that problems exist which are frustrating the resolution of issues associated with the protection and recovery of this species."

Still, one of the big issues had finally been resolved. For six years Florida officials had been insisting they had no authority to enforce the new federal laws—only the handful of federal wildlife officers assigned to Florida could do it. Finally, the Fish and Wildlife Service deputized some Florida Marine Patrol officers to chase down speeding boats too.

Even better, the Florida Legislature had passed a new law called the Manatee Sanctuary Act. This noble-sounding law declared the manatee to be the state's official marine mammal. Killing or even harming a manatee, whether on purpose or by negligence, would be a crime, and anyone who hit one with a boat could see that boat permanently confiscated. The law also ordered state officials to impose boating speed limits in crucial areas "to protect the manatees or sea cows from harmful collisions with motorboats."

The new law had failed to pass on the first try, in 1977. A year later it sailed through, aided by the potent testimony of a painfully earnest Audubon Society employee named Patrick Rose.

Rose was tall and gap-toothed, with the flat, deliberate speech patterns of a native midwesterner. He grew up in Independence, Missouri, the tenth of eleven children born to a car salesman and a clothes designer.

When Rose was six, one of his brothers took him fishing in a nearby lake. The two boys hiked along a railroad track to get there. Rose loved it so much he couldn't wait to go back.

"I knew I could go back and fish again by following the railroad tracks to the lake," he recalled fifty years later. "I got my line, hooks, and worms together and set out down the tracks."

But before he got far from home he tripped on a railroad tie. When he fell, one of the hooks went through his hand. The boy ran home crying. To avoid getting in trouble for sneaking off, he told his parents he had fallen on a stray hook in the yard. After a doctor removed the hook, the family searched the yard for any more hooks while the would-be angler wallowed in his guilt.

Despite that early misadventure, Rose still loved fishing and anything to do with water. In the fourth grade he stumbled across a *Weekly Reader* story about manatees that called them sea cows. He remembers being baffled about how cows could live under water.

By college he had learned to use Cousteau's SCUBA invention. During breaks in his studies at the University of Missouri he would visit a brother in Florida, scuba diving or snorkeling in the springs and rivers to see what he could find.

Rose even went diving in Kings Bay around the same time Cousteau's crew was filming there. Although Rose never saw the star explorer, he saw something more startling. As he swam through a murky part of the bay, he spotted something starkly white amid the darkness. It was a healed-up prop cut.

"The first part of a manatee I ever saw was a scar," he said.

Soon after he earned his master's in biology, Rose got married and, in 1976, convinced his wife to drive to Florida. They had three hundred dollars to their name. His wife got a job at National Cash Register, while Rose landed at the Florida Audubon Society, first as a volunteer, then as a paid employee bringing in fifty dollars a week. The couple ate a lot of tuna, peanut butter, and out-of-date hot dogs, "which I found out later isn't too good for you," Rose said.

Then Florida Power and Light, the utility that owned the power plant where Joe Moore had done his studies, gave Florida Audubon a grant to study the influence that power plants had on manatees. Rose traveled to ten different power plants, snapping photos wherever he went and producing the study the utility wanted.

Now he was ready to tell the legislature what he had found—and, like Woodie Hartman testifying before Congress, he brought along photos that proved most persuasive to the lawmakers.

"I showed pictures of manatees being hit by boats," Rose explained. "There was one where—it was a series. It didn't show it for sure, but it showed manatees being approached by a boat and the boat going right over top of them, in a relatively shallow area of the Orange River. . . . And of course I showed them pictures of manatees with scars." After Rose's slide show, the measure passed.

To Twiss and his bosses at the Marine Mammal Commission, Rose seemed like just the energetic go-getter who could take charge of the federal manatee program. At Twiss's urging, the commission awarded a grant to the Fish and Wildlife Service to hire Rose, assigning him to coordinate federal manatee protection efforts—but while he was still working for Florida Audubon too. Rose immediately set to work writing the long-delayed plan for the species' recovery.

Meanwhile, though, things didn't work out quite so well for the manatees. Although the legislature passed the Manatee Sanctuary Act, it included a loophole big enough to fit a cruise ship through. Any new state rules to protect manatees must refrain from "unduly interfering with the rights of fishers, boaters and water skiers using the areas for recreational and commercial purposes."

So manatees continued dying. Twenty-four were killed by boats in 1979, sixteen in 1980, and then came a big jump to sixty-four in 1981.

As the carnage continued, Florida's most famous resident became determined to do something to stop it. For help, he turned to the state's best-known politician—a man who was undergoing a crisis of his own, thanks to a woman in a bikini.

## 5

Barnacle Brains and Parrotheads

BOB GRAHAM HAD A PROBLEM, and it was right there in *Sports Illustrated* for all the world to see.

Graham was a buttoned-down Democrat with a Harvard law degree. He had hair as shiny as patent leather and cheeks as round as Alvin the Chipmunk's. Graham grew up on a dairy farm in South Florida, the youngest son of onetime gubernatorial candidate Ernest "Cap" Graham and half brother to the *Washington Post*'s late publisher Phil Graham (Katherine's husband). Although Graham's family made a fortune developing Cap Graham's pastureland into the suburban town of Miami Lakes, Graham's record in the legislature had been solidly progressive on environmental issues.

But ever since Graham won election as governor in 1978, his environmental allies had been grumbling about him. They said he was running with a different crowd these days.

"I can't even get in to talk to him, and I run the biggest conservation organization in Florida," complained Johnny Jones, executive director of the Florida Wildlife Federation. "As a governor, he ain't got it. People say he has gotten more conservative, more right-wing, so he can run for President, and to do that he has to pacify those people who don't like environmentalists—the sugarcane league, agribusiness, the biggies."

Graham might have ignored Jones's complaints, except they showed up in the February 9, 1981, issue of *Sports Illustrated*.

*Sports Illustrated* had never been known for tackling environmental issues. It generally published stories about athletes and their teams, period. On this occasion, though, the magazine ran a story headlined "There's Trouble in Paradise," in which reporters Robert H. Boyle and Rose Mary Mechem nailed Florida's politicians and business leaders for destroying everything that made the state special.

Developers were wiping out mangroves, they reported. The winding Kissimmee River had been turned into a polluted ditch. The Everglades was dying. From the Panhandle to the Keys, the story said, out-of-control growth had Mother Nature on the ropes.

"The sad fact is that Florida is going down the tube," the reporters wrote. "Indeed, in no state is the environment being wrecked faster and on a larger scale."

According to the story, Jones and other sportsmen blamed Graham for taking the side of "the despoilers."

As Graham's top environmental aide read the story, he chuckled to himself. Estus Whitfield knew that Jones's complaints were valid. In his first two years in the governor's office, Graham had focused on education and the death penalty, not the environment. Whitfield figured that Jones—a plain-talking plumber who had a keen grasp of how the government had fouled up the flow of the Everglades—had somehow spurred the magazine to do this story, knowing it would get Graham's attention.

Whitfield carried the magazine to his boss, warning him it contained bad news. He watched as Graham read it, and years later still vividly recalled how the governor's face got redder and redder.

"The thing that's emblazoned on my mind is Graham's reaction," Whitfield said. "He immediately started saying, 'We need to do something here.'"

The governor and his aide recognized that this could be a public-relations disaster, both for Florida and for Graham. To make matters worse, the story had been published in the magazine's most popular issue of the year.

Every winter, the magazine produced its "swimsuit issue," full of color photos of attractive female models in barely there bathing suits—and that's the issue where Graham was being blasted. There was a tenuous tie-in between the story and pictures: the swimsuit photos had been shot on Florida beaches.

The picture of a nearly nude Christie Brinkley on the cover, promising even more daring photos inside, guaranteed that this particular issue would circulate far and wide. Eventually some of the buyers might get past the bikini pictures and read the story about Florida, and take in Johnny Jones's comments about Graham.

Just in case anyone in Florida's capital had missed the magazine story, the *Tallahassee Democrat* reprinted it in its entirety on February 11, 1981. The story started on A1 and jumped inside, filling an entire page—and this time there were no pictures of bikini-clad women to distract the readers.

How could any politician recover from this kind of horrible press?

The governor's own fourteen-year-old daughter showed him the way. Suzanne Graham asked her dad to take her to a concert by a musician that she liked. She said his name was Jimmy Buffett.

"Who's Jimmy Buffett?" asked Graham, never the hippest guy in the room. But he agreed to go.

When that February 17, 1981, concert was over, as Graham walked out of the Florida State University field house with his overjoyed daughter, he was on his way to turning things around, thanks to the singer he'd never heard of.

•

Florida's most famous troubadour was born in Mississippi on Christmas Eve 1946. Jimmy Buffett grew up in Mobile, Alabama, an hour's drive from his future home state. At an early age he fell under the spell of tales told by his grandfather, an old salt who had run away to sea as a boy and wound up captain of his own vessel.

Instead of shipping out as a cabin boy on a barkentine, Buffett earned a degree in journalism from the University of Southern Mississippi. He chose that college because of its proximity to New Orleans. He could frequently drive over on weekends to play his guitar in various Crescent City dives.

After graduation, Buffett put his j-school degree to work briefly as a reporter for *Billboard* magazine, covering the Nashville music scene. He left journalism behind when he landed his own recording contract.

The music Buffett played had a country-rock feel with a bit of folk mixed in. His singing was only so-so, his guitar-playing merely serviceable, his melodies somewhat interchangeable. His great strength was his songwriting. He was as adept at evoking longing and regret as he was at coaxing a laugh. He would litter his lyrics with puns and pop-culture references, then slip in some melancholy insight into human nature.

Buffett was no overnight success. In the early 1970s, he was flat broke and bunking in Miami with country singer Jerry Jeff Walker. A scheduled gig in

Coconut Grove fell through. On a whim, the pair decided to drive down to Key West in Walker's 1947 Packard. They headed south through the Everglades, then hopped from island to island on a series of bridges that had been built atop the bed of the railroad Henry Flagler had built to connect Miami to Key West.

Buffett discovered he felt at home in the laid-back little town at the end of Highway A1A. He relocated to Key West, dividing his time between a fifty-foot sailboat and local watering holes like Sloppy Joe's and The Green Parrot.

Living in the Keys helped Buffett find his musical niche. He wrote songs about those tattered souls wandering among Florida's beaches, boats, and barrooms. His albums became a musical version of his grandfather's sea tales, chronicling the lives and loves of drug smugglers, stranded sailors, luckless fishermen, lost tourists, and aging rowdies. With his shaggy blond hair and bushy mustache, Buffett even looked like a down-at-the-heels buccaneer.

His sixth album, *Changes in Attitudes, Changes in Latitudes*, released in 1977, brought him his first top-ten hit, "Margaritaville," an ode to suntans, tattoos, and drowning memories of a soured romance in a succession of blender drinks. He had other hits—the raucous "Cheeseburger in Paradise," for instance—but by 1981 his music wasn't being played as much on the radio. Critics paid his records little attention, sniffing that he "had a tendency to sail the same obvious waters, coasting on familiar musical currents."

Buffett didn't care. He had built a loyal following among a group of die-hard fans who called themselves "Parrotheads." They flocked to wherever Buffett played, turning the parking lots and performing halls into a makeshift Margaritaville. He sold out venues across the country, and even his hitless records went gold.

The loyalty of the Hawaiian-shirt crowd made Buffett a rich man. Thanks to the Parrotheads he acquired a home in Palm Beach, a house outside Aspen, Colorado, and a ketch moored in Martha's Vineyard. When he wasn't on the road, Buffett would pal around with celebrities like writer Hunter S. Thompson and comedian John Belushi—people who, like Buffett, had a reputation for fueling their good times with various chemical substances.

At the end of January 1981 Buffett released a new album called *Coconut Telegraph*. Accompanied by his Coral Reefer Band, he hit the road to promote it, with his first scheduled stops in Florida. That February night in Tallahassee, with the governor and governor's daughter in the audience, Buffett played a song from his new album that would prove to be extremely popular among the Parrotheads. It was called "Growing Older But Not Up," and one verse in particular caught Governor Graham's attention:

Sometimes I see me as an old manatee
Heading south as the waters grow colder
He tries to steer clear of the humdrum so near
It cuts prop scars deep in his shoulders
That's how it flows right to the end
His body's still flexible but
That barnacle brain don't bend.

After the concert ended, Graham took his daughter backstage to meet Buffett—one of the perks of being the state's chief executive is a permanent backstage pass. The visit had been arranged by Graham's senior aide, Ron Book.

As Book and Graham's daughter looked on, the governor and the singer began chatting about the new song that mentioned manatees.

"I told him how much I liked that song," Graham said, recounting the story two decades later. "It struck me, because we're thinking about what can we do to protect the manatee, a peculiar Florida endangered species. And Jimmy said, 'Well, I'm interested in that.'"

Did Johnny Jones's criticism in *Sports Illustrated*, published only days before the Buffett concert, motivate Graham to take the next fateful step?

Neither Book nor Whitfield believe it did. The magazine story made only a passing mention of manatees, but focused more on the Everglades, the two aides point out. The story "did jar Graham," Whitfield said—but it pushed him to become more active about saving the River of Grass, not manatees, he said.

For his part, Graham said he didn't remember seeing the magazine. He said he couldn't even recall who posed on the cover or how she was dressed (or not).

"I must have sublimated it," he said.

On the other hand, Graham could not remember any other reason for him being so interested in manatees that night, and neither could his two aides.

For whatever reason, Buffett and Graham then went a step beyond simply agreeing that they were interested in manatees. They agreed that manatees needed help.

"I volunteered my services to be involved at that point in an awareness campaign of the plight of the manatee in Florida," Buffett testified years later. "And I made the governor aware of my intentions and offering of my services."

Just like Buddy Powell, Buffett had first encountered manatees when one swam near his boat. His first thought: "Whoa! What's that?" But over the years he had come to view manatees as a symbol of his adopted home state.

"To me, the manatee represents what we all like about Florida—kind of cruising in warm, clear water and not bothering anybody," the singer explained.

But even as a casual observer, Buffett had noticed how many had been hurt or killed by speeding boats.

"What we're seeing now is an increase in irresponsible boat operators," he said in a 1981 TV interview. "In this state, you don't have to have a license to drive a boat. . . . In the state of Florida you can put down your money and buy a 500-horsepower boat and hit the Intracoastal. You've got a thousand people a day moving to Florida, and they're buying boats—you've got more boats than manatees. I think that's the reason our kill rate is up so much—people running boats without knowing anything about operating boats."

During their backstage chat, the thirty-five-year-old tropical troubadour made it clear to Graham that he wanted to be more than just a famous face cutting a few public-service commercials. He said, "I don't just want to be a token celebrity. I want to be involved."

Graham suggested forming some sort of committee that would encourage boaters to slow down and watch out for manatees. At that point, Graham recalled later, "it took about three milliseconds to decide he should be the chairman of this new effort."

Then Graham took his daughter home, leaving it up to his aide to figure out how to turn that nebulous idea into a reality. Buffett, meanwhile, headed off to his next concert.

"Jimmy never thought we would follow that up," Ron Book said. "He thought Graham was just saying nice things to him."

But a few weeks after the backstage encounter with Buffett, Book scheduled a meeting with the singer at the fanciest hotel in Palm Beach. He took along a manatee biologist too: Pat Rose of the U.S. Fish and Wildlife Service. They met Buffett at The Breakers, an oceanfront hotel built by Henry Flagler the same year he extended a rail line to Miami.

At the meeting, Buffett, Book, and Rose hashed out ideas on what they could do for manatees. Buffett agreed to star in a series of public-service announcements telling boaters to slow down and avoid manatees. If needed, he said, he would put on a benefit concert to pay for a manatee awareness campaign. He also said he could travel around to the state's college campuses with Rose to show a movie about manatees.

Buffett and Book talked about raising money for a manatee awareness campaign by selling T-shirts featuring the lines from "Growing Older But Not Up," with Buffett's signature to make it more attractive for the Parrotheads. Buffett suggested something more substantial: posting signs at boat ramps, dive shops, fuel docks, and marinas warning boaters to avoid manatees. He also said he would try to work in a manatee reference on his next album.

And finally, according to Book's notes of the meeting, Buffett agreed to "serve on [the] board of a non-profit Protect the Manatee organization." Buffett suggested putting Rose on the board, as well.

At that point, Rose, who was also still an Audubon employee, had a brainstorm. To really attract donors, he said, this new manatee protection organization would need to obtain tax-exempt status from the Internal Revenue Service. Getting the IRS to grant tax-exempt status wasn't easy, and it might delay starting this new manatee effort. So Rose suggested putting the new organization under the umbrella of the venerable Florida Audubon Society, so that it would automatically be tax-exempt.

That was fine with Buffett. He made it clear that his goal was a nimble organization that wouldn't get bogged down in red tape. He wanted "an independent organization free of government control or agency control or anything, basically a grassroots organization," he testified years later.

Except, of course, it wasn't free of government control—the governor controlled it. A month after the backstage meeting with Buffett, Graham told the press he was creating a Save the Manatee Committee. He would appoint all eleven of the committee members, and he was pleased to announce that none other than the famous Jimmy Buffett would serve as chairman.

"You can't but help like a manatee," Buffett told reporters at the March 1981 announcement. "And their only predators are people who aren't aware of the problem."

In addition to Buffett and Rose, the original members of the Save the Manatee Committee included the head of the state Department of Natural Resources; the president of Kirk Munroe's Florida Audubon Society; Nat Reed, who was busy raising money for The Nature Conservancy to buy the islands in Kings Bay; and a representative of the Outboard Marine Corporation.

No one objected to Graham's appointing to the manatee protection committee a representative from the industry that made the manatee's biggest threat. That's exactly what Buffett wanted, something inclusive, where every-one worked together for a solution to the problem.

"What was great about the whole thing that I considered at the time was, it was the first effort by which we were gathering people from the government, from the private sector, from environmental organizations . . . to collectively do something for the manatees," the singer testified later.

At the committee's inaugural meeting in May in Tallahassee, Graham showed up attired in his usual business suit with a tie covered in tiny Florida silhouettes. He stood with Buffett, who wore a white sport coat and no tie, and gave the singer his own A1A road sign as a reward for promoting Florida tour-ism with his songs. Ron Book had also arranged for Graham to host a luncheon for Buffett, and invited a bunch of starstruck lawmakers, state officials, and reporters. They all had to have their picture taken with the King of the Par-rotheads.

Buffett's comments to the press that day sounded like a direct response to the *Sports Illustrated* story. He told the reporters that by setting up a committee to save manatees, Graham was taking "a positive step to do something to save a little piece of Florida from looking like another piece of concrete, like a lot of it already does."

But then, to Graham's dismay, the whole press conference got off track.

"I thought this was going to be a total love-in," Graham said years later. "We were saving this unique animal, one of the icons of Florida."

Instead, the Tallahassee press corps focused on the contrast between Buf-fett's hedonistic image and Graham's more straitlaced one. One reporter, re-minding the governor of his law-and-order reputation, asked how he could square his opposition to drug abuse with Buffett's lyrics about using drugs.

Graham knew he had to get out of this situation somehow without insulting his new friend or making himself look ridiculous.

"Rule number one in a situation like that is to give an answer that doesn't allow for any follow-ups," he explained years later.

So the governor told the reporters that in his view, rather than glorifying drug use, Buffett's songs "point out the problems, the distress, the human trag-edy of the use of drugs."

It was, Graham admitted later, "a totally dingbat response—but it accom-plished the objective."

Nobody asked Graham anything else about Buffett and his music. Clearly, the governor listened to a different stereo system than the rest of the world.

However, that wasn't the end of it, because then the reporters trotted over to ask Buffett what he thought about Graham's comments.

"Buffett was momentarily stumped when he was told later about the governor's characterization of his work," a wire service report noted dryly.

Buffett tried to explain that his lyrics about smoking pot or snorting cocaine were only "a kind of escapism. . . . I'm in it for the humor of it." The reporters prodded him to say more on the subject. But Buffett, as an ex-reporter, could see where this was leading, so he simply shut the whole discussion down.

"I'm only concerned with the manatee," he told the press gaggle. "As far as anything else is concerned, I'm politically neutral."

Over the next twenty years, though, Buffett and Graham would repeatedly join forces for political reasons. Buffett campaigned for Graham over and over, pushing his reelection as governor, his race for the U.S. Senate seat, even his

Jimmy Buffett (*left*) gained respectibility by working with Bob Graham (*right*), while the buttoned-down Graham appeared slightly less tightly wound. They spoofed each other's images during the Capital Press Skits. Photo courtesy of Florida Photographic Collection, State Archives of Florida.

ill-fated bid for the presidency. He also campaigned for other Democratic candidates.

Their styles seemed so radically different that once, at the annual Capital Press Skits (a Tallahassee version of Washington's Gridiron dinner), they even spoofed themselves. Buffett dressed up in a suit like Graham's, Graham donned a Hawaiian shirt, and together they mangled one of Buffett's hits.

Yet what made them different also made their partnership work. Katharine Hepburn once observed that what made famed dance duo Fred Astaire and Ginger Rogers click as a team was that "he gives her class, and she gives him sex." In this case, the pairing with Graham made Buffett seem respectable, while hooking up with Buffett made Graham seem hip—or at least less tightly wound.

•

On the day of the Save the Manatee Committee's first meeting, the reporters spent so much time focused on the clashing styles of the governor and the singer that they missed a crucial part of the story. They failed to notice the strange nature of the organization that Graham had just created.

He had set up the Save the Manatee Committee to be a quasi-governmental body, with some of its members being actual government officials. But the committee had no power to regulate boat speeds. It couldn't set up manatee sanctuaries. It could only recommend those actions to other state agencies.

Yet the Save the Manatee Committee was also an environmental advocacy group, set up as an affiliate of the venerable Audubon Society. The manatee committee would pay Florida Audubon 10 percent of its revenue for office rent and other services, such as accounting.

Because of its Audubon connection, the Save the Manatee Committee did not set up shop in Tallahassee. Instead, Audubon provided housing for the new organization near Orlando, at first in its own state headquarters, then later in the corner of a drab office building in suburban Maitland, two miles away.

Over the next several years, Buffett staged concerts that raised thousands of dollars for the manatee cause. He authorized the use of his likeness for T-shirt sales that raised even more money. He spent so much time talking to officials in Tallahassee about manatees that he bought a home in north Florida, near the Suwannee River.

Meanwhile, the committee Buffett chaired used the funds he raised to post

After Jimmy Buffett (*left*) offered to spearhead a committee to protect the manatee, federal biologist Pat Rose (*right*) suggested putting it under the umbrella of the Florida Audubon Society. Photo courtesy of Pat Rose and the Save the Manatee Club.

the educational signs he had suggested in waterways around the state, warning boaters they should slow down for manatees.

Letters poured in from Parrotheads and manatee fans from around the world, offering to contribute to the cause. Buffett's committee created a new entity, made up of people who had donated money. They called it the Save the Manatee Club.

Then, in 1984, Buffett came up with a revolutionary idea for bringing in money using the manatees instead of his famous face. In exchange for donating fifteen dollars—only ten dollars for school groups—people could "adopt" a manatee of their own. The donors wouldn't actually get a manatee, just a certificate that said they had adopted this particular marine mammal, which was given a name. The certificate would come with a photo and a history of that particular manatee's activities during the past ten years.

A week after Buffett announced the Adopt-A-Manatee program, more than a thousand people had already written in to claim a critter of their own. About two hundred of them asked about using their adoption as a Christmas gift for a family member or friend.

A story in *Reader's Digest* brought an even bigger surge of new donors. The money started flowing into the committee's coffers in waves big enough to make a surfer smile.

Buffett had come up with a brilliant marketing ploy, one that raised consciousness as well as money. By adopting an individual manatee, one with a name of its own, people would feel a sense of responsibility toward the animal. The adoptions transformed the abstract issue of manatee protection into a personal cause for thousands of people all around the globe. In 1990, for instance, an elementary school class in Arizona wrote letters to Citrus County officials demanding to know why they weren't doing enough to protect Lucille, the Crystal River manatee that the class had adopted.

By the time the Adopt-A-Manatee program had started, the vice-chairman of the committee, Pat Rose, was running its day-to-day activities as a state employee. Rose had left both Audubon and the U.S. Fish and Wildlife Service. He had been hired to launch Florida's own manatee program under the state Department of Natural Resources, starting virtually from scratch. Rose needed to lighten his load, so the Save the Manatee Committee agreed to let him hire an executive director.

Rose took out an ad, but he already knew the person he wanted for the job— a woman who had no background in either biology or business management. She didn't know much about Florida either.

Judith Delaney hailed from the Bronx, but she didn't sound like the typical brash Noo Yawker. She was a reserved woman with chestnut brown hair and a degree in art history. Her mother had been a secretary, her father a sewing-machine repairman. Her dad died when she was eleven, leaving her nothing to remember him by except a simple painting he had made of a farm.

She grew up watching starlings in a backyard tree. She was fascinated by how the birds interacted. When she moved to Fort Lauderdale in the early 1980s, landing a job as a telephone solicitor, she looked for an apartment that would offer her another soothing natural view. She found one overlooking the north fork of the Middle River.

One day, she said, "I was going out on the dock and twelve manatees swam by. Then a fast-moving boat came by, going upriver."

She phoned the Florida Marine Patrol to report the boater. The marine patrol's laconic response: sorry, ma'am, can't do anything. That made her mad enough to drop her usual reserve.

"And I said, 'You're going to hear from me,'" she said. "So I started a petition . . . trying to get that area declared a sanctuary."

But no one took her seriously. She went to talk to a county advisory board on boating issues. At the meeting, she said, "they told me, 'If you see a fast-moving boat, throw a tomato at it.'"

Instead of stocking up on produce, she began volunteering with the Audubon Society, trying to promote the cause of manatee protection. She called the state's new manatee coordinator to ask him to send a speaker down for a meeting, but she got no response. She called him again. Rose was busy with his new job, but the woman just kept pestering him.

"She had dogged me about getting speakers for a manatee education event in Broward County," Rose said. Her persistence persuaded him to hire her for the executive director's job: "I figured if somebody is bugging *me* about protecting manatees, that was someone I wanted on my side."

Delaney, who later married a construction worker and became Judith Vallee, had her job interview with Rose at an outdoor café by a Hobe Sound canal. While they talked, a manatee swam by—a good omen, Vallee thought.

She started her new job in early 1985. She hung her father's painting in her new office as her sole personal decoration, and ate a tuna fish sandwich at her desk every day for lunch. She answered the phones, handled the "adoptions," and, despite her strong aversion to public speaking, even helped out with lobbying the legislature.

Some of the older, more experienced lobbyists looked down their noses at the tongue-tied amateur stumbling around in their arena. One who always seemed to Vallee to be standoffish was Audubon's veteran lobbyist, Charles

Lee. Lee got his start as an environmental advocate when he was a teenage fisherman in Miami. He would persuade his mother to drive him to meetings so he could push for the creation of Biscayne National Park. He had pioneered the field of environmental lobbying in Florida. For years he had been the only green lobbyist in Tallahassee, playing the lonely role of David battling the Goliath-like hordes of lobbyists for development, agriculture, mining, utilities, and manufacturing.

One day in the capitol's marble hallway, though, Lee sidled up to Vallee and made a crucial suggestion. Lee told her, "You know what you should do? You should get a manatee license plate."

In 1986, to raise money for a memorial to the astronauts who died in the explosion of the space shuttle *Challenger*, the Florida Legislature had approved the sale of a special *Challenger* license plate. Specialty plates were virtually unheard-of then, but the *Challenger* plate proved to be a huge success. They went on sale in 1987 and in the first year raked in five million dollars.

Vallee could see what Lee's proposal might do to raise money for manatee causes. She took the idea to Rose, and together they approached one of the most influential public-relations men in Florida, Bud Chiles. The son of U.S. Senator Lawton Chiles, the PR man persuaded some of his clients—politicians running for reelection—to sponsor the measure. Buffett flew in from a concert tour to testify about what a good idea it was.

Then a surprise glitch popped up from an unexpected quarter: Pat Rose.

Rose told Vallee that instead of funneling money to Buffett's committee, the license plate sales should help pay for something else. He wanted the money to go toward the state's fledgling manatee research and education efforts. But the plate should still carry the phrase "Save the Manatee," as if the motorists buying it were still supporting Buffett's favorite cause.

Rose's request put Vallee in a tough spot. On the one hand, he was talking about taking away a sure source of funding for her organization. Yet how could she oppose the man who had hired her? Weren't they both interested only in helping manatees?

That's why, in a move that she would later come to regret, Vallee went along with it. She signed an agreement to let the state use the phrase "Save the Manatee" on the new license plate, yet relinquished any claim to the revenue from its sales.

"So she gave up what history shows was a tremendous amount of money," Rose said years later, a bit ruefully.

From when they first went on sale in 1990 until 2007, the "Save the Manatee" plates brought in thirty-four million dollars. Not a dime went to the organization with that name. Yet a misconception spread statewide that Vallee's organization didn't need contributions because it was collecting all that license plate money.

"It's been *so* confusing," she said.

One of the first people to get a new "Save the Manatee" tag was Buffett. Someone came up with the brilliant idea of making his a vanity plate, with his name spelled out on it. The only problem was, vanity plates are limited to six letters and the singer's last name contains seven. So his manatee plate said "Buffet"—a dining suggestion the early settlers would have appreciated.

Only later did Vallee and Rose regret switching who got the license plate money. At the time, they thought the Save the Manatee Committee would do fine without it. By 1992 the organization had thirty thousand members— nearly as many as Florida Audubon's thirty-two thousand—and its fund-raising efforts brought in seven hundred thousand dollars a year. Manatees were as politically popular as motherhood and apple pie, and everyone wanted to show their support for the cause.

"People were clamoring to get on the bandwagon," Vallee said.

With the Save the Manatee Committee working so closely with state and federal officials, the prospects of saving the species seemed brighter than ever. Adding to the sense of a team pulling together was another group that Rose had set up in 1981, the Manatee Technical Advisory Council (MTAC). The MTAC, mostly made up of manatee scientists but also including the occasional legislator or activist, offered state officials its expert advice on how best to spend the money pouring in from the "Save the Manatee" plate sales.

To top it all off, the assistant director of fisheries for the U.S. Fish and Wildlife Service told the Marine Mammal Commission that the recovery plan that Rose had written was "probably . . . [the] best recovery plan" ever prepared.

One of Rose's bosses at the state Department of Natural Resources bragged to the commission that all the cooperation among the parties involved made it "the classic example of how to do environmental and ecological management anywhere."

Actually, though, trouble was bubbling just below the surface. When the breakup came, it turned out to be as nasty as any high-profile divorce.

## 6

## The Breakup

JIMMY BUFFETT NEVER RECORDED a protest song. He didn't perform at Woodstock or march on Washington. Yet in April 1992 he led a picket line during one of the odder protests in Florida history.

His hair thinning, his upper lip now bare of the rogue's mustache that was once his trademark, Buffett marched back and forth in front of Audubon's suburban Orlando headquarters with a sign declaring "Audubon is for the birds!" With him marched a group of supporters toting signs that said things like "Please Release Me, Let Me Grow!"

What got the normally laid-back singer so upset? The president of Florida Audubon, a grandfatherly marine biologist named Bernie Yokel, had launched what Buffett termed "a hostile takeover" of the Save the Manatee Club.

Yokel started by suspending Judith Vallee.

"Bernie came here and accused me of insubordination," Vallee recalled. Yokel brought in another Audubon official to take over and keep an eye on Vallee. According to Vallee, Yokel told the man, "Sit with her, at her desk, and if she tries to use the phone, unplug it!"

Yokel contended he was trying to quell a mutiny.

"If you got some sort of a rebellion going on, you've got to act to protect the assets of the corporation," Yokel said.

Not only were the leaders rebelling against Audubon, he said, but they had begun keeping some pretty suspicious company. He pointed out that the Save the Manatee Committee included a boating-industry executive.

He didn't mention that the committee members were selected and appointed by the governor. Instead, he blamed Buffett.

"It appears to me, Jimmy may have fallen into the company of one of the manatee's enemies," Yokel told reporters.

Really, though, the fight wasn't over manatees or motorboats. When the dispute landed in court—the way all disputes in the United States tend to—the truth came out.

•

As far back as 1987, the Save the Manatee Committee had been talking about splitting off from Florida Audubon. At first the Audubon board saw no problem with that. It even approved a resolution supporting such a split—someday.

In the meantime, though, Audubon's staff had noticed something about the manatee group's finances. Its supporters, be they fans of manatees or Margaritaville, contributed a lot of money. As long as the committee remained a part of Florida Audubon, those contributions showed up on Florida Audubon's books.

According to Yokel, Audubon couldn't use the Save the Manatee money for its own expenses. Without the manatee money in its coffers, though, Florida Audubon's financial status wouldn't seem as sound. As a result, its ability to attract grants would suffer. And if the Save the Manatee Committee became an independent entity, an Audubon staffer pointed out, Audubon would face stiff competition for donations, which would cut into its funding even further.

Then, in 1989, came the first sign of real trouble. The man who had suggested putting the Save the Manatee effort under Audubon, Pat Rose, paid a call on Bernie Yokel to ask for help.

Since leaving the U.S. Fish and Wildlife Service for the Florida Department of Natural Resources in 1984, Rose had been keeping busy. Working out of the state's marine science laboratory on St. Petersburg's waterfront, he had launched the state's fledgling research efforts, funded by the license plate sales he had steered away from the Save the Manatee Committee. And he and his staff had their hands full reviewing permits for waterfront development and dock facilities.

When Rose would object to various projects, he would usually draw fire from politically connected developers. Soon word of Rose's obstructionism would reach the ears of the secretary of the Department of Natural Resources, Elton Gissendanner.

Gissendanner had been a veterinarian and former mayor of North Miami. He had landed his job at the DNR, not because of his experience, but because he was a longtime Bob Graham supporter. Yet he didn't yield readily to political arm-twisting, Rose said.

"People would come in and put pressure on Gissendanner and he wouldn't roll over," Rose recalled. "He would call me up and say, 'Pat, what the hell are you doing? Everybody else is okay with this project.' And I would say, 'No, not everybody.' And then we'd go through what the problems were." And in the end, Rose said, Gissendanner would back him up.

But in 1987, Gissendanner resigned in disgrace. A drug smuggler nabbed by the agency's Florida Marine Patrol accused him of taking a hundred-thousand-dollar bribe to make the charges go away. Ultimately, Gissendanner pleaded guilty to obstruction of justice and drew a sentence of eighteen months behind bars.

Criminal indictments were becoming a habit for the DNR. Gissendanner's predecessor, Harmon Shields, had been sentenced to five years for trying to collect $235,000 in kickbacks for manipulating state land purchases.

The Gissendanner scandal didn't stick to Bob Graham, who had already concluded his second term as governor. Graham won election to the U.S. Senate—in part because he had worked hard to revive his reputation as a good steward of the environment in the wake of the *Sports Illustrated* story.

To replace him in the governor's mansion, the voters chose another Bob, a Democrat-turned-Republican named Bob Martinez. He had been a teachers union official. His party-switch helped him win election as mayor of Tampa, then mount a successful statewide campaign for governor. A bitterly divisive Democratic primary left that party in tatters, making it easier for Martinez to become the first Hispanic ever to be elected as the state's chief executive.

Martinez aspired to follow in Graham's footsteps as an environmental steward. But he lacked Graham's political skills and he had no experience with the rough-and-tumble of Tallahassee. Nowhere was that more evident than in what happened when he tried to pick a new DNR chief.

Rather than maintain the tradition of using the DNR post as a patronage plum, Martinez appointed a committee headed by Nat Reed to screen the applicants and pick the most qualified as finalists. But Florida's system of government makes the governor just one vote among what was at the time a seven-member cabinet—and the other six were Democrats who resented Martinez as a turncoat.

Reed's search committee did its work and sent a list of highly qualified nominees over to the cabinet for the final selection. But then one of the cabinet members, Insurance Commissioner Bill Gunter, tossed in a ringer: Tom Gardner, a Gunter protégé who was then a deputy to Secretary of State George Firestone. Gunter had even taken the precaution of getting the Florida Department of Law Enforcement (FDLE) to run the necessary criminal background check on Gardner—without letting the governor know.

When the cabinet voted, Gardner got the nod on a five-to-two vote, leaving Martinez flushed and angry, and Reed muttering about "old-time Florida politics." Afterward, a reporter asked Gunter why he kept the FDLE check a secret from the governor.

"We wanted to win," Gunter replied.

But what had the Democrats won, other than a chance to make Martinez look clueless? The man they had forced on Martinez had even fewer qualifications than Gissendanner for the DNR job. At least Gissendanner, as a veterinarian, had worked with animals before being put in charge of Florida's parks, beaches, marine patrol, and state lands program.

When the forty-year-old Gardner was tapped to lead the DNR, he hadn't held a single job outside state government since graduating from Florida State University nearly twenty years before. He had worked for the state's welfare agency and, since 1981, for the secretary of state, which runs elections and maintains corporate records, as well as overseeing the state's archives and museums.

But Gardner had never spent a day working for any of the state's environmental agencies, and he had never before exhibited any interest in environmental issues. Reed's committee had interviewed him. They found him singularly unimpressive.

Gardner did hold one unique distinction among the applicants: he was the only one with a federal gun-dealer license. He owned about twenty shotguns, rifles, and pistols, including what he described as a "Dirty Harry model .44-magnum with a 6-inch barrel—they don't make those anymore."

But he wasn't a hunter, he told reporters, explaining, "I think animals are too pretty to shoot."

Gardner turned out to have some peculiar ideas about how to run the DNR.

For instance, he proposed allowing private companies to build for-profit tennis and volleyball courts, equestrian centers, shooting ranges, softball fields, swimming pools, and marinas in the state's parks and preserves. Gardner acknowledged that even his own staff protested his plans.

"They say it's not natural," he told reporters.

Then there was the time a powerful ranching company, Lykes Brothers, fenced off a waterway called Fisheating Creek that flowed through its property, even though local residents used it for fishing, boating, and the occasional baptism.

Gardner flew down to Glades County to check out the situation personally —but he let Lykes Brothers pick up his tab for his plane ride, lodging, and food. Shortly afterward he announced his department could not spare the resources to battle the Lykes Brothers in court. (The attorney general's office took on the crusade, ultimately winning back public access.)

When top jobs came open at the DNR, Gardner did not fill them with qualified applicants. Instead, he hired current and former state legislators who had no more experience with natural resource issues than he did. For instance, in 1988 he hired Representative Virginia "Ginger" Bass, a Pensacola Democrat, to fill the post of deputy assistant executive director, shortly after she cast a vote to create the seventy-one-thousand-dollar-a-year position. Two years later he also hired the Republican minority leader in the House, Dale Patchett of Vero Beach, to fill a similar job.

Gardner may have hoped their connections would boost his own political juice. Instead, the opposite occurred.

When he hired Democratic state senator Tom Brown, who was still in office, it turned out to be a colossal blunder. In the special election to replace him, the voters picked a Republican, eroding the Democrats' control of the state senate.

Meanwhile, Patchett's past indiscretions as a legislator—accepting all-expenses-paid trips from utility lobbyists—led to misdemeanor charges, an ethics commission investigation, and lots of unfavorable headlines for the scandal-plagued DNR.

Gardner's methods for dealing with manatees further boosted his reputation as someone more interested in politics than environmental protection.

At a resort outside Everglades City, manatees were being slaughtered by boats roaring along a canal leading to the Gulf of Mexico. Initially, Rose and his DNR scientists proposed creating a speed zone that would require the boats to slow down. But the resort owner complained that that would put him out of business, because boaters would not want to take so long to get out of the canal to go fishing.

Gardner's Solomonic solution: cut the canal in half, with one side for the power boats and the other side for the manatees.

"I'm not sure how the manatees were supposed to know which was their side," Audubon's Charles Lee remarked.

Gardner also proposed dredging deeper navigational channels in waterways throughout the state. That way, he said, boaters would stay out of the shallow areas where they might hit manatees. He apparently did not consider what damage to the waterways might result from such widespread human alteration.

Unlike Gissendanner, Gardner paid close attention to what waterfront developers and the boating industry wanted—and they wanted Pat Rose gone.

When a biologist named Pam McVety became Rose's boss at the DNR in 1988, she said, Gardner "told me to get in there and fix this. Pat is too out of control. . . . I was told to watch out for Pat. Pat had become a lightning rod for the manatee issue. But I found him to be very reasonable and very creative."

Although McVety did her best to protect Rose from political heat, she said, "we had a lot of people angry with us who were used to getting their way."

At one point in late 1988, Gardner announced to reporters that he was fed up with the way Rose was doing his job. Gardner was so fed up, in fact, that he intended to take over the manatee protection program personally.

According to the agency's spokesman, Gardner had become convinced that Rose and his St. Petersburg science staff were "unfairly" using manatee protection as an excuse to block developers from building boat docks, marinas, and other coastal structures.

"He said he will no longer allow the marine mammal section to be solely responsible for stopping something through their review," the spokesman told a reporter. "The concern is that the manatee program should not be used as an environmental backstop."

Instead, Gardner wrote in a memo to the staff, the DNR should focus on enlisting boater support for manatee protection—and also start an extensive captive breeding program. Gardner's memo did not address how the DNR would go about rounding up manatees for breeding, where the breeding would occur, who would oversee the calves, and where they would be released into the wild.

Fortunately, Gardner's attention soon wandered onto some other topic, so Rose's staff could get back to doing their jobs. Still, in a February 1989 memo to a Republican legislator, Nat Reed complained that the DNR's manatee program remained "uncoordinated, under-prioritized, under-funded, under-manned—a disgrace. I don't know what it will take to shake this state up and provoke the necessary actions needed to protect the manatee."

The political interference and the DNR's lack of resources so frustrated Rose that he turned to Yokel for advice.

"In your life, you have people you trust and you put on a pedestal," Rose said. "Bernie was somebody I considered a mentor. He was somebody I looked up to and admired."

Exactly what happened next remains in dispute twenty years later.

Yokel says Rose suggested that the committee should hire him as a full-time employee—but with the same forty-thousand-dollar annual salary he was earning at the DNR. That was far more than Judith Vallee or any other Save the Manatee employee was earning at the time. So Yokel turned him down.

"It was clearly a financial decision," Yokel said. "The decision was easy. There wasn't room for that kind of expenditure, with all the overhead that goes with it."

According to Yokel, Rose then threatened him. Unless he got what he wanted, he would split the Save the Manatee Committee off from Audubon.

"He made it clear he would work for a separation if we wouldn't do that," Yokel said. "There was a certain leverage applied there."

Still Yokel refused to hire him—and it wasn't just because of the money.

"I did not want to work with the man," Yokel said in 2008. "He's difficult to work with. The survival of the manatee has enough problems without complicating it by working with a difficult person."

Rose remembers everything differently. He remembers confiding in Yokel as a trusted mentor, or at least as someone he thought of then as a friend. He remembers pouring out his tale of woe, then asking, "What would you think if I wanted to leave the agency and work for Save the Manatee? I could work as a biologist, or as a government relations person, or reviewing permitting. Is that something you think might work out?"

According to Rose, Yokel didn't say yes or no. Instead, Yokel urged him to write a letter outlining why he should be hired by Save the Manatee as a full-time employee—a proposal he says went nowhere, for reasons he then did not understand.

He disputes Yokel's story regarding a salary demand and a threat to split from Audubon. Those things never happened, Rose contends.

One thing they both agree on: Save the Manatee and Audubon did begin negotiations about changing their relationship, negotiations that would drag on for three years.

In the meantime, Rose did change jobs—but within the DNR. He moved to Tallahassee to take a newly created post overseeing the Office of Protected Species Management. To make the move, Rose said, he agreed to skip a 30 percent pay raise he could have had if he had stayed at the St. Petersburg lab.

When he started working in Tallahassee, Rose said, conditions at the DNR improved. Now that Rose could build a personal relationship with Gardner, he and McVety were able to persuade Gardner to support their efforts.

"He grew to trust me instead of listening to what others were saying," Rose said. "Within a year we put forward the most aggressive protection package ever attempted on behalf of manatees and accomplished more in a few short years than has ever been accomplished."

They also angered more people than ever before.

•

At a spring 1989 meeting of the governor and cabinet, the new secretary of state, Jim Smith, said he was concerned about the rising number of manatees being killed by boats.

"While we're giving this subject an awful lot of lip service, the fact is, the death rate is going up," Smith said.

Somehow, Smith said, the state would have to make boaters slow down. "If we want to protect this species," he said, "we're going to have to be willing to do some tough things."

Smith was concerned about the increasing number of boating accidents killing humans, too. For three years in a row, Florida's boating fatality rate was more than double the national average.

At Smith's suggestion, Martinez and the cabinet told the DNR to recommend some specific actions that would protect both man and manatee.

This was exactly the opening Rose had been hoping for. Throughout the summer, McVety and Rose met with boaters, anglers, fishing guides, divers, water-skiers, as well as environmental activists, to talk about what new regulations might be necessary.

On October 24, 1989, they presented Martinez and his cabinet with the plan they had drawn up, titled "Recommendations to Improve Boating Safety and Manatee Protection for Florida Waterways." Despite the title's emphasis on boating safety, the heart of the plan was aimed at protecting manatees.

McVety and Rose had targeted thirteen of the state's coastal counties: Miami-Dade, Broward, Palm Beach, Martin, Indian River, St. Lucie, Brevard, Volusia, and Duval on the east coast, and Collier, Lee, Sarasota, and Citrus on the west coast. Ten of those thirteen counties were places where 80 percent of all boat-related manatee fatalities occurred. The other three were important travel, feeding, and resting areas for manatees.

The plan required those thirteen counties to draw up blueprints detailing where docks, marinas, and boat ramps could be built to avoid any impact on manatees and their habitat. The plan imposed a staggered set of deadlines for completion of those plans, with the final four counties required to submit their maps by June 1993.

Martinez and his cabinet liked what they heard: a statewide plan for action that still let local officials make land-use decisions. Citrus County had already started working on its manatee protection plan, so they told the other twelve to get started.

The target was broader than just the thirteen counties, Martinez explained years later. "We were hopeful that other counties would follow suit," he said.

The governor and cabinet also approved the plan's other recommendations: asking lawmakers to set a statewide boating speed limit of thirty-five miles per hour in marked channels and twenty miles per hour at night, and asking the legislature to require all boaters to pass a licensing test just like the one drivers must pass before getting on the road.

Last but not least, they adopted a new rule for existing marinas in the thirteen counties. In any county that did not have an approved manatee protection plan, state policy would limit marina expansions to just one additional powerboat slip for every hundred feet of shoreline at marinas with more than five boat slips.

Several boating-industry officials complained that all these new regulations were unnecessary. Manatees weren't really disappearing, so they didn't really need that much protection.

"The dinosaur is extinct," grumbled Jim Robinson, executive director of the Marine Industries Association of Florida. "The manatee is not extinct."

The plan won cabinet approval so easily, McVety said, because "at that point we hadn't riled everybody up. It was almost an intellectual exercise: 'Here's the animal and everybody thinks they're cute.'"

But then came the hard work of implementing the plan.

"Pat and I were on the road constantly," recalled McVety. They traveled to the counties where the new regulations faced public hearings—hearings that often turned rowdy because, she said, "the marine manufacturers would bring these busloads of their workers and they were drunk."

Sometimes, McVety said, they had to get Florida Marine Patrol officers to escort them out of a meeting past a phalanx of hecklers. Once she couldn't get *into* a courthouse because so many angry boaters were circling the block towing their boats.

Frequently, county employees would forget to leave the air-conditioning turned on for the nighttime hearings. As the temperature rose, tempers flared. Yet McVety and Rose would stick it out, no matter how sweaty they got, no matter how many people lined up to yell at them.

"It'd be midnight, 1 a.m., and I'd come out with a major migraine," McVety said.

Boaters made it clear that they strongly opposed the proposed speed limits—or in fact any limits at all.

"Below 30 mph, high-performance boats are very heavy in the rear, you can't see over the bow, you use more fuel, and it's no fun to run," Terry Jorgensen, owner of Boat Show Marina in De Land, complained to a reporter at one hearing.

Often, local government officials were more sympathetic to local boaters and businessmen than they were toward some ugly animal that offered no obvious boost to their tax base.

"Look, you've got to put things in perspective," an Indian River County commissioner told Rose at a 1990 forum on boat speeds. "Unfortunately, there is a process called evolution. Darwin wrote about that—species come and go."

Faced with such opposition, Rose often responded in kind, McVety said.

"He was passionate," McVety said. "He also was very articulate when it came to debating a point of science, and his logic was sharp and pretty intellectual for most, I suspect. He did like to have the last word, as did the opponents."

Those heated exchanges could quickly turn into the worst kind of one-upmanship. McVety said there seemed to be "lots of testosterone floating around in the air."

Rose's iron determination to set limits on boater behavior won him few converts. When he conducted a public hearing in Brevard County, "speaker after speaker got up to express his opposition," one of those opponents wrote years later. Although it was a public hearing, Rose "didn't really listen to what the public said" and instead "wrote it off as emotion."

Looking back on Rose's role in the conflict years later, McVety said, she realized that "opponents may have found him to be arrogant because of all he knew and his ability to articulate it. Some of the opponents were pretty aggressive and harsh in their attacks on the program. Some just couldn't comprehend that they had to share the waters with an animal."

Opponents from the boating industry often contended that Rose's program of manatee protection was just an excuse. They said he was really trying to block developments that environmental activists didn't like.

Rose, in an interview with the *Orlando Sentinel*, all but confirmed that accusation. "It should be obvious to anyone by now that this is about a lot more than just saving one creature," he told the reporter. "People in Florida are going to have to face it: You're going to have to put a lid on growth. And if this creature is the vehicle to do that, then so be it."

The boating industry's chief lobbyist, Wade Hopping, told the *Sentinel* that Rose had slipped up. Promoting that kind of anti-growth agenda would backfire, he predicted. The day would soon come when manatees would lose their public support.

"You watch," Hopping said. "The pendulum will swing back the other way."

•

By far the strongest opposition to the new speed limits surfaced in Volusia County, a place where speedy sports had long been a way of life. Volusia was home to both the nationally known Daytona Speedway and the wildly popular racing association NASCAR.

Volusia County officials wanted to set a top boating speed limit of forty-five miles per hour on the Intracoastal Waterway and the St. Johns River. Rose and McVety insisted that was far too fast, while boaters insisted it was still too slow.

Ultimately the county council gave in to the state's demands—all but one member. He was the owner of an automotive supply store, Big John's Auto, who had legally changed his name to Big John to match his business signs. Big John insisted that boats roaring along at forty-five miles per hour didn't hurt any manatees.

"The boats don't kill manatees, only irresponsible (boaters) do," a reporter quoted him as saying, substituting a milder word for the vulgar one that Big John tended to use more frequently.

But the battle wasn't over. Opponents of the new speed limits gathered ten thousand signatures on a petition to overturn them. Leading the drive was a fish-camp owner named Rick Rawlins.

Rawlins's heavyset frame and balding pate made him resemble 1940s actor Sydney Greenstreet. For more than thirty years, Rawlins and his brother Ron had owned the Highlands Park Fish Camp on the banks of the Norris Dead River. Their fish camp lay about three miles from Lake Woodruff National Wildlife Refuge, a twenty-thousand-acre wilderness.

The DNR wanted boaters to slow down to twenty-five miles per hour on the river, a speed that Rawlins contended was overly restrictive. He compared it to "saying all traffic from here to Orlando must go 25. It's unenforceable, it's unreasonable, and it's totally ridiculous."

Even worse, the DNR insisted on a speed limit of five to seven miles per hour around his fish camp. Rawlins grimly predicted anglers would be so frustrated at being forced to slow down that they would abandon his fish camp, driving him out of business within a year. (It was still operating in 2009.)

Rawlins launched a group called Citizens for Responsible Boating. At its meetings, he would blast the DNR and the Save the Manatee staff as "government elitists" and "weirdos." He complained that he was a victim of "extreme enviro-nazi-ism," because to regulators like Rose "businesses don't matter, people don't matter. Manatees matter."

Privately, the Save the Manatee staff referred to his C.R.B. group as "Crabs," but Rawlins's rhetoric began attracting mayors and city commissioners from various towns throughout Volusia, giving his group more clout. At one gathering at a seafood restaurant, Rawlins even paraphrased Winston Churchill: "We will fight you on the boat ramps. We will fight you on the rivers. I promise you, I will never give up."

The controversy grew so nasty that at one public hearing, Rawlins threatened to harpoon every manatee he saw. Meanwhile, one Volusia council member who supported the speed limits, an attorney named Clay Henderson, reported getting death threats.

"It was kind of a muffled voice," Henderson said. "It sounded male but you couldn't really tell. He said, 'Don't go out in a boat by yourself. We're looking for you.'"

While Volusia was the most contentious, similar skirmishes erupted all across the state as boating interests fought successfully to turn back the tide of regulation. Only four counties—Citrus, Collier, Miami-Dade, and Duval—took all the required steps in drawing up their manatee protection plans for waterfront development. A decade later, those same four would remain the only ones approved out of the thirteen that Martinez and the cabinet had singled out.

•

Even bigger battles were occurring in Tallahassee, where the $3.5-billion-a-year boating industry could usually count on a sympathetic reception from contribution-hungry state legislators.

In the state capital, where the free-spending lobbyist has always reigned supreme, boaters had on their side one of the most effective lobbyists of all. The National Marine Manufacturers Association, the Chicago-based trade group that represents every company making products for recreational boaters, had hired a wizard named Wade Hopping.

Hopping grew up in Ohio, the son of a bar owner whose establishment boasted the first television set in Dayton. The father ditched the family when Hopping was eleven. Hopping's mother frequently disappeared for days, too, leaving her son to fend for himself. He fell in with a bunch of other boys also lacking in parental restraint.

"We probably violated the law a hundred times, but it's not like we were hoods or anything," Hopping recalled.

He went to college against his high school counselor's advice, then barely made it through law school. Now Hopping wore the white hair and beard of a wise man, augmented by a résumé that included a short stint as a Florida Supreme Court justice in the 1960s. He possessed a folksy manner that helped camouflage his encyclopedic knowledge of how to manipulate state government for his clients' benefit.

When a legislator helped out, Hopping would tell his clients that—in addition to sending thank-you letters—company officials should personally present a contribution to the candidate during his or her next campaign. Such a show of gratitude would help to win future favors.

Hopping had been lobbying in Tallahassee for more than two decades, beginning back when Republicans like him were in the minority. Although he made his living off what government did, he firmly believed that "government's like kudzu. You have to prune it back every year."

Over the years, Hopping had represented nuclear plants, sugar growers, and mining companies. Most of his clients were developers looking for loopholes that would let them build what they wanted wherever they could.

At the marine manufacturers' behest, Hopping took on the one-slip-per-hundred-feet policy. But he insisted it wasn't an attack on the poor, pitiful manatees.

"We've never fought the idea of protecting the rascals," Hopping said. But then he asked, innocently, "What does the number of boat slips have to do with protecting manatees?"

With Hopping working for the boat makers, the legislation Rose and McVety's plan had proposed ran into a brick wall. The bills calling for a state-wide speed limit and for licensing boaters, two measures designed to save the lives of boat owners, never made it out of committee. Another measure would have pumped nearly $3 million a year into manatee research and protection by adding a surcharge on boat registrations. That one barely scraped by, but at a sharply reduced amount of $750,000.

Meanwhile, top DNR officials began to pressure McVety and Rose to compromise with boating interests, or even better, just give them whatever they wanted.

"I would get all the hardcore scientific data, and tell them, 'Okay, we've met with the county commissioners,' and then be told, 'Oh no, you're not going to do that. I got a call from so-and-so and you're going to back off,'" McVety recalled.

Yet the Save the Manatee Committee had begun to stake out positions that went beyond what Rose and McVety wanted. For instance, while Hopping tried to do away with any regulations on marinas, Judith Vallee called for state officials to block any new marina construction whatsoever in the thirteen counties until they had come up with their manatee protection plans. Rose and McVety were being squeezed between the two extremes.

To keep an eye on the creation of the county protection plans and speed zones, Vallee hired Save the Manatee's first staff biologist. She was a bubbly brunette named Patti Thompson who decorated her office cubicle with tabloid headlines like "Gentle Sea Cows Attack Boozing Boaters!"

Thompson, like Hopping, was an Ohio native. She had followed a golf-pro boyfriend to Florida. When they split up, she enrolled in marine biology courses at the University of Central Florida. She planned to study whales until the first time she spotted a manatee "and I thought, Whoa! . . . It changed my course."

Even though Rose still sat on the Save the Manatee board, Thompson began to regard him as too cautious, too willing to cut a deal to keep the rule-making process moving forward.

"We were always at odds about how things should be dealt with," she said. Although for the most part Save the Manatee supported the DNR's positions, she said, "sometimes I thought: 'This could be better.' The rules started looking like a compromise between the angry hordes and what was best for manatee protection."

•

When Governor Martinez ran for reelection in 1990, his work on behalf of manatees did little to win him votes. Instead, voters focused on how he had backed an unpopular tax and then backed down and agreed to rescind it.

He lost to the Democratic nominee, former U.S. Senator Lawton Chiles. A fourth-generation Florida native from Lakeland, the slow-talking Chiles had invented a clever campaign gimmick to earn publicity during his first Senate race. He hiked the length of Florida, from the Panhandle to the Keys, in 1970. That stunt earned him the nickname "Walkin' Lawton," and the first in a string of election victories.

But Chiles had retired from politics in 1988 to deal with a crushing depression he called "the blacks." He blamed his condition on his inability to cut the federal deficit. Two years later, in 1990, Chiles came roaring back onto the scene, aided by a prescription for the antidepressant Prozac, to wallop Martinez. Four years later he won a tight race for reelection, beating an inexperienced Republican upstart named Jeb Bush—aided by an endorsement from Jimmy Buffett.

During his two terms, Chiles set a new mark for quirkiness among Florida politicians, already a fairly quirky breed. He often showed up late for meetings because he had spent his morning in the woods hunting turkeys. He marked his second inauguration by standing on the dais with a homemade potato gun and, to the dismay of the well-dressed politicos in attendance, firing spuds toward the governor's mansion.

Although a progressive on social issues such as health care for uninsured children, Chiles lagged behind Graham and Martinez on environmental issues. For instance, he saw no problem with building a new prison in the middle of a twenty-thousand-acre state preserve called Tate's Hell Swamp. After all, he argued, just look at the name. Wouldn't Hell be the perfect place for prisoners?

Chiles tried to appoint to the game commission a hunting buddy who had been convicted of violating game laws in Louisiana and had been investigated repeatedly by Florida game officials.

As for manatees, despite getting electoral assistance from Buffett, and despite his son's work with the license plates, Chiles simply wasn't interested in them.

"He let other people set the policies and dictate the direction of the department," Rose said. "It was doubly sad because we expected so much."

Gardner resigned from the DNR in 1991 under a cloud, just like his two predecessors, thanks to an investigation into mismanagement of the Florida Marine Patrol (although, unlike them, he was not charged with a crime). The list of potential replacements included Nat Reed. Instead, Chiles picked one of Gardner's deputies, the former legislator once known as Virginia Bass.

On paper her selection seemed like a politically astute move. The twice-divorced Bass was now on her third husband, and he happened to be Speaker of the House T. K. Wetherell. By picking Mrs. Wetherell, the governor had guaranteed that the DNR's budget would always get a favorable reception in one house of the legislature.

But Wetherell and her deputy, former representative Dale Patchett, viewed everything in a political light. The DNR—already an agency rife with problems and scandals—became a highly politicized place to work, Rose said.

"It became like pulling teeth to do anything," Rose said. "You had to move mountains just to fill a sandbox."

Politics even affected personnel decisions. McVety came back from lunch one day to discover her replacement sitting at her desk. She was shuffled into a policy job that took her out of the front lines. When she asked why, McVety said, "I was told we were too aggressive. . . . There was a lot of anger about Pat. But Pat did what I asked him to do."

Now Hopping's push to do away with the one-slip-per-hundred-feet policy finally bore fruit.

"I was ordered to stop enforcing it," Rose said.

Although the DNR had published ads notifying the public that the policy was going to be turned into an actual rule, the rule never did go into effect.

"It was advertised more than once but never actually approved," Rose said. "It became known as the 'non-rule rule.'"

Wetherell and her deputies now insisted that Rose had to resign his long-time position on the Save the Manatee board because it constituted a conflict of interest. Instead, Rose wrote to the state Ethics Commission and got an opinion saying he had no conflict. That just made his bosses even angrier, he said.

Ratcheting up the stress level even higher, Rose could not count on any help from the committee on which he served. Instead, it was now fighting for its very existence.

•

Save the Manatee had become too successful. Despite past assurances of future independence, Audubon's board now did not want to let Buffett's committee go its own way.

"Those were the instructions I got: don't let this slip away. Keep it together," Yokel recalled.

From the Audubon board's perspective, Yokel said, the Save the Manatee Committee "was something that had grown up in Florida Audubon. It was going pretty well. It had a lot of public support. It didn't make sense to change. It didn't make sense for the manatees, for Save the Manatee or for Florida Audubon."

Once again, there are two views of what happened. According to Rose, "we had three years of what turned out to be bad-faith negotiations. We finally agreed to be a subsidiary of Florida Audubon, just so we could move on. And they were so greedy they wouldn't even accept that."

But Yokel contends it was the Save the Manatee folks who negotiated in bad faith. Three times he and Buffett sat down to negotiate a deal, Yokel said.

"Each time we reached agreement," Yokel said. "Each time I think he had a conversation with Rose. Each time he notified us that it was off."

All through the talks, Rose said, "we tried to keep it out of the press and keep it from becoming a public fight."

But in February 1992, the negotiations broke down for good. That's when Judith Vallee notified the press that the Save the Manatee Committee planned to go independent. That's when Yokel suspended, then fired her.

"They said the reason for the takeover was Bernie thought we were incapable of protecting the manatees without them," Vallee said.

Yokel changed the locks on the door, took over the bank account, and seized control of the organization's mailing list. Seizing the mailing list might have seemed a canny move. Without it, Buffett could not appeal to the club's thirty thousand members for help. But it so angered Buffett that he called a press conference in Tallahassee to announce he was suing Audubon.

"They're in effect trying to put us out of business," Buffett told the Tallahassee press corps. "They're trying to run our organization. Nobody has given them this power; they're acting illegally."

Now that everything was out in the open, Yokel didn't back down from the fight.

"All this time, Jimmy has been threatening a media storm," Yokel told reporters, then reached for a pun. "Unfortunately, it's the manatee that's going to be *buffeted* by this whole thing. If we're going to save that manatee, we're going to have to stay together." After all, he said, "this is the best damn program I have ever seen for protecting an endangered species."

The quarrel between the two groups sparked headlines in more than just the Florida papers. The *Washington Post*, CNN, and even *People* magazine all carried stories, putting the dispute on display for the world to see.

Allegations flew back and forth as each side accused the other of putting money ahead of manatees. Audubon officials accused Buffett of doing little to aid the organization after his first flush of enthusiasm in 1981. They contended that "the Audubon Society found itself struggling to keep the effort alive" without him.

They predicted that this fight would damage the entire conservation movement.

"I think they've done a lot of harm to the manatee, they've done harm to Save The Manatee program, and they've probably done some harm to all environmental programs," Florida Audubon's board chairman, Allen Clark, told CNN.

Buffett accused Audubon officials of selling out the environment by cutting deals with corporate polluters such as phosphate miners. Developers sponsored cocktail parties at Audubon events, he pointed out. A development company executive even sat on Audubon's board.

"I'm very leery of Audubon's whole philosophical viewpoint," Buffett told the *Miami Herald*. "They've made so many compromises. I just don't trust them any more."

Buffett hired two attorneys, a jolly ex-snake wrangler named Thom Rumberger and a more serious junior associate named Dan Gerber. They painted Audubon as fat and stodgy. Documents they introduced into evidence showed that in 1990 Florida Audubon spent just 28 percent of its $1.4 million income on its conservation programs, while nearly all of the manatee club's income—roughly $500,000—went to manatee work.

While the battle raged, the remaining employees of the Save the Manatee Committee struggled to keep their morale up. But they could think of little else besides Audubon's power play.

"They were very reluctant to fire the staff, but we were under real duress," Patti Thompson said. "People work here because they believe in the cause, then to see this. On my answering machine at home I'd put a new message on every day: 'Day thirty-five, Save the Manatee Club held hostage!'"

Under the circumstances, the work suffered. A teacher from Gulf Breeze Middle School, near Pensacola, wrote in to complain that although six classes had sent in money to adopt a manatee, no one ever sent them any photos or updates on their animal. She blamed "the Audubon Society kidnappers."

Seeing the two groups duking it out in the media and in court dismayed grassroots activists. "I've had at least two people tell me they are going to resign from Florida Audubon," the vice-president of the Orange County chapter of Audubon said. "One person said he didn't care what the problem was . . . but he didn't want his money spent in court."

People with no love for Buffett's group saw in the turmoil a chance to advance their own agenda. The *Fort Lauderdale Sun-Sentinel* reported that a Broward County planner working on that county's manatee protection plan had told his boss he had been threatened by a marine-industry executive. In a memo, the planner said the industry executive had "accused him of being insensitive to boaters" and warned him "that the director of the state Save the Manatee Club was fired because she refused to compromise." The executive denied making those threats, the paper noted.

To make matters worse, in court both Yokel and Rose—who was still working for the DNR—testified about the 1989 conversation they had about Rose quitting the DNR and going to work for Save the Manatee. Audubon's attorney contended that Rose's actions were all part of a pattern by Save the Manatee officials to make money off the endangered manatees.

"It was horrible," Rose recalled. "They basically tried to make each one of the Save the Manatee Committee board members out to be a greedy, bloodsucking fool."

But money is the fuel every environmental group needs. In May, Buffett launched a rival group, the Manatee Protection League, and staged a concert in Fort Lauderdale that raised about sixty-five thousand dollars for the new organization. Later, the singer testified he had never taken a dime from Save the Manatee, not even to reimburse his travel expenses.

"I did it because it's something that I wanted to do for the state of Florida and to do something to make the manatee representative of the preservation of our lifestyle," he testified. "If somebody had told me back in those days that yes, Jim, you can do this, but at a certain point you will become . . . a tool of the Florida Audubon Society, and we'll take over the running of your money and your hiring and firing policy, I would never have entered into such an agreement like that whatsoever."

In the end, Rose held the key to winning the first round of the court case. He had kept a trove of documents on the formation of the Save the Manatee Committee, contradicting Audubon's assertions.

As a result, Seminole County Circuit Judge C. Vernon Mize Jr. ruled that the Save the Manatee Committee should get its $640,000 budget, thirty-thousand-member mailing list, and trademark logos back from Florida Audubon while both sides prepared for trial. Rose's documents had persuaded him that Audubon functioned more like a paid contractor handling administrative duties than an overseer with the power to hire and fire employees like Vallee.

Yet the victory came with a price. An *Orlando Sentinel* story on the ruling noted: "Last week, several influential advocates were unable to attend key hearings on speed limits in Volusia and Indian River counties because they were in court battling each other."

Months passed, and the case remained unresolved. Audubon got a new board chairman, a Miami resident named Karsten Rist. A German immigrant with a thick accent, Rist suggested in February 1993 that the two groups ought to compromise. Clay Henderson, the Volusia County council member, volunteered to help craft a settlement.

The agreement Henderson worked out called for an autonomous Save the Manatee Club that would be independent from Audubon. The two organizations would form a joint group called Toward Education and Advocacy for the Manatee (TEAM). The Save the Manatee Club would spend ten thousand dollars annually for three years on it, as well as giving Florida Audubon another ten thousand dollars a year to help lobby the government. Patti Thompson joked that the payments were actually a form of alimony.

A month later the two groups met at Wekiwa Springs State Park for what the *Sentinel* described as "a cross between a civilized divorce proceeding and a parents' reluctant farewell to a child-turned-adult." When Buffett called for a vote on the settlement, only one Audubon board member offered a nay—Yokel.

"I think it's nice that the humans can finally settle this matter," Buffett quipped afterward.

In all the news coverage of the lawsuit, though, the reporters once again missed the big story. The Save the Manatee Club hadn't just split off from the Florida Audubon Society. It had also declared its independence from the state government.

Governor Chiles selected one last board of directors—including Rose, again. But after their terms expired there would be no more gubernatorial appointees. Instead, the Save the Manatee Club would pick its own leaders, and set its own course.

With its newfound autonomy, "the Save the Manatee Club started having its own opinion about things," Thompson said. "It was helpful to start having people on the board who were not appointed by the governor. People who thought for themselves, and thought not enough was being done."

After all, as the news stories on the fight repeatedly reminded everyone, there were only twelve hundred manatees left in Florida. Now, as the Save the Manatee Club cranked up its fund-raising machinery, that number became a steady refrain: please help, please give, because there are only twelve hundred manatees.

Every time Thompson heard one of her co-workers say that phrase, though, "I would wince," she said.

She knew where the number came from—a state program that harkened back to Hartman's original aerial survey. She knew what was wrong with it, too. And she wondered how long it would take before that phrase would, as she put it, "come back to bite us in the butt."

## Flying Blind

LENISA TIPTON STUCK HER HEAD out of the airplane window. Icy air blasted into the cockpit of the tiny Cessna, stuttering along at seventy-five miles per hour as it circled the looming smokestacks of Tampa Electric Company's Big Bend power plant.

Tipton waggled her cinnamon fingernails at the small gray smudges in the water 350 feet below. She was adding them up. After a couple of minutes, Tipton, twenty-seven, sat back in her seat and closed the window.

"Oh, that hurt," she said, rubbing her numbed face. "But I got so many more animals that way."

Then she asked the pilot to go around again.

Throughout the 1990s, a team of biologists like Tipton took to the skies over Florida nearly every winter to see how many manatees they could see. Like Joe Moore and Woodie Hartman, they were taking advantage of the manatees' tendency to congregate during cold weather. When the mercury dipped low enough, manatees would gather where the water was still warm—at springs, power plants, and deep canals—making them easier to find. So if the air temperature dropped below fifty degrees for three days in a row, conditions seemed right for what scientists had dubbed a "synoptic survey."

Tipton, a California native, was working for the Florida Marine Research Institute, the state marine science lab that had occupied a spot on St. Petersburg's waterfront since the 1940s. On this February day in 1999, she was among

sixty biologists soaring over Florida's waterways adding up all the manatees they could see. She alone was responsible for counting all the manatees
throughout the Tampa Bay region. To do the job required four hours of flying,
as she ranged four hundred miles from Tarpon Springs in northern Pinellas
County all the way down to Manatee County in the south.

Tipton met pilot Rich Castle, twenty-nine, at about 9:30 a.m. They rendez-
voused in the offices of a charter flight company called Bay Air at the small
municipal airport across the street from the marine lab. Because Castle had
taken his earliest flights back when he was a teenager, very little about his
charter clients ever surprised him. But when Castle saw the loops traced out on
Tipton's charts for the day, the route she was supposed to cover while counting
manatees, his eyes widened.

The pilot looked up at Tipton and, without a trace of a smile, asked her,
"Were you drinking when you traced this out?"

Actually, she explained, these were routes that had been covered for years,
every time there was a synoptic survey. She herself had flown this twisty route
with another pilot a month earlier. She didn't mention it to Castle, but that had
been her very first synoptic survey. This would be her second.

Castle and Tipton took off twenty minutes later, with Tipton sucking on
a succession of Brach's Starlight peppermints to counteract airsickness. As
the plane soared over St. Petersburg's wealthier neighborhoods, the Cessna's
shadow darted across big backyard pools. They saw not one manatee amid the
waterfront seawalls.

Then they headed for the St. Petersburg end of the Gandy Bridge over Tampa Bay. Florida Power operated a small backup power plant on Weedon Island,
near an archaeological dig that had turned up artifacts of a prehistoric civilization. The plant only ran part time. When it was producing power—say on
a very cold day, when lots of homeowners ran their heaters—it discharged a
steady stream of warm water into Tampa Bay. Still, Tipton figured they would
strike out there too.

Castle tilted the plane sharply and began to circle, and Tipton peered
down.

"Oh my God!" she yelped. "They're everywhere!"

Some of the manatees were feeding on sea grass a little ways out from the
plant, but most of them were resting, piled on top of each other like a litter of
newborn puppies.

They circled the plant, then went around again, with Tipton leaning out the window as far as she dared. After a third circuit, Castle asked if that go-round had been satisfactory.

"That was wonderful," Tipton said. "Can we do it, like, six more times?" So they did.

After they crossed Tampa Bay, they found even more manatees gathered in the warm water around the Tampa Electric Company plant in downtown Tampa. Castle dropped the plane down to about 150 feet below the tops of the smokestacks. He joked that this was a technique not taught in flight school: "Okay, you go below the towers and below the smoke, totally uncoordinated, and have the lady stick her head out the window."

Tipton's dizzying flight carried echoes of Woodie Hartman's football-helmeted adventures in "Grand Funk Airplane," but with a few significant differences:

- Hartman did his survey in the summertime, when the manatees were spread out and harder to spot, instead of in the winter, when they congregated at warm spots.
- He did his counts with just one airplane, over a long period of time, instead of trying to cover the state all at once with a squadron of volunteers in planes and helicopters.
- And Tipton's flight, unlike Hartman's, originated with a political aim, not a scientific one.

•

When Hartman, Buddy Powell, and Pat Purcell flew around Florida counting manatees, the aerial survey "was the only way we could come up with an estimate of manatee abundance," Hartman explained years later.

But Hartman knew that his 1973 survey was missing a lot of animals in the murky water. He tried to create a formula to factor in the manatees they had failed to spot. The resulting number was at best a "guesstimate," Hartman said. Powell said their calculations were "just full of errors."

In 1976, a new team tried a new method for a manatee census. One of Powell's colleagues at the U.S. Fish and Wildlife Service, Blair Irvine, came up with a plan to send a team of biologists into the skies over the course of a few days during the winter.

Years later, Irvine said he proposed it out of frustration and ignorance. "We knew we had this endangered animal that we didn't know much of anything about," he said. Nobody even knew how many there were: "People were saying,

'Oh there are as few as two hundred,' and others were saying, 'No there were two thousand or so.'" As a result, "we wanted to take a quick and dirty snapshot of the population, and I mean quick and dirty, and get what a ballpark population might be."

Irvine's plan required circling power plants over and over while counting however many manatees appeared to be visible. He considered sheer persistence the key to coming up with something like an accurate count.

"If you don't lose your lunch—and I've been on both ends of that—you might come up with something," he said.

Irvine managed to get nine planes into the skies at various times between the end of January and the start of February 1976. Among those doing the counting were two veterans of the Hartman survey: Powell and Pat Purcell. The count this time: 780 manatees.

If he had used Hartman's fudge-factor formula, Irvine noted later, that number would double to 1,560. However, Irvine held some serious doubts about that formula, because he couldn't figure out how Hartman had applied it to produce his published estimates.

Still, Irvine conceded that Hartman had a point about missed manatees. Counting manatees from the air, even when they're gathered at a warm-water site, was a tricky business. Irvine had discovered that flying back over a site two hours after the first go-round could produce a count that doubled the first one. The twofold difference, he wrote, "suggests either manatees were moving in and out of the survey area or, more probably, that only those close to the surface were being counted."

Nevertheless, nine years later, a group of biologists sat down and reviewed the results of all the aerial surveys, both the statewide ones and several regional aerial headcounts. Based on those shaky figures, they came up with a rough estimate of the statewide manatee population: twelve hundred.

For years that estimate remained the one usually cited by both state officials and the Save the Manatee Committee, which meant it was endlessly repeated by newspaper and television reporters. During public hearings on the new speed zones and manatee protection plans, every time someone would ask how many manatees there were, the answer would be, "About twelve hundred."

But people in the boating industry didn't buy that number. "Something's wrong. It just doesn't compute," said Frank Herhold, vice-president of the state's Marine Industry Association.

Boating-industry officials contended the number had to be much, much higher. Some said there could be as many as five thousand. So they lobbied the DNR to conduct a new aerial survey.

"This has been a high priority item for the Marine Industry Association of Florida for three years," John Lowe, an industry lobbyist, told a reporter in 1991. "The numbers game has been frustrating. I think they're going to probably find that there are a lot more than the 1,000, 1,200, 1,500 they toss around."

Finally the DNR agreed. Pat Rose even hired an expert to run the aerial circus. He picked a scientist named Bruce Ackerman, who had a triangular face topped by a mop of hair, a wispy mustache, and a somewhat unusual background for a biologist.

Ackerman grew up in Maryland in a family known for producing engineers. However, his passion turned out not to be blueprints and buildings, but backpacking with the Boy Scouts. By the time he finished his bachelor's degree at the Massachusetts Institute of Technology, he had hiked the whole Appalachian Trail. Ackerman was also a devoted bird-watcher. He had camped in the Everglades and the Keys, just to add birds to his life list.

But Ackerman had come to the conclusion he could not get paid for birding. As he earned a master's from Utah State and a doctorate from the University of Idaho, he developed a skill that used his training in math as well as in biology.

"My specialty was in a subfield of statistics relative to counting things when you know you're going to miss some," he explained with a wry smile.

He worked primarily with animals of the West—mountain lions, deer, elk, moose. Like Florida, Idaho has a lot of phosphate mines. That gave Ackerman the experience Rose was looking for.

"They were going to shave off the tops of the mountains, which was going to mess up the migration of the deer, elk, and moose," Ackerman said. "That's when they realized they needed a better procedure to count deer. So at Idaho, I studied how to count."

Although he had no experience with manatees, the problems posed by counting deer in the mountains appeared similar, he said.

"To count deer, you fly around in a copter and count as many as you can in a specific area, and then you make a statistical correction for what you're going to miss," Ackerman said. "Some are standing up, some are lying down, some are under trees. That's not a very different problem from manatees."

But counting deer around a mountaintop proved to be a lot easier than counting manatees across a whole state.

The first aerial survey of manatees that he led in January 1991 was, Ackerman said, "a logistical nightmare. There were twenty teams—sixteen in aircraft, four in copters, fifteen different agencies involved." Altogether it was "kind of a patchwork."

Marine-industry lobbyist Wade Hopping said he was glad the scientists had finally counted all the manatees.

"I'm certainly curious about what they get," he told the *Orlando Sentinel*. "We ought to be dealing with facts here. And I don't think we are."

However, the weather didn't turn as cold as Ackerman had hoped. The conditions for an accurate count were off. Still, when Ackerman added all the figures together, the statewide tally turned out to be 1,268 manatees—about what the state and environmental activists had been saying all along.

Immediately the marine industry demanded a recount.

"The results were a problem for all sides, because we really had hoped to count more animals, and of course Wade and crew thought there were a lot more animals than were counted," recalled Pam McVety, still Rose's boss at that point.

A month later, Ackerman's volunteers tried it again, and this time they came up with a higher number: 1,465 manatees.

Rose told reporters he hoped no one would regard the new figure as a sign the population had suddenly gained an extra two hundred manatees. His hopes were quickly dashed. State legislators began getting letters saying, "What do we need manatee legislation for? We've got more than ever."

Ackerman's crew flew another count in 1992, coming up with 1,844 this time—400 more than the year before, thanks to cooler weather and greater experience among those doing the counting.

But in 1993, the temperature did not drop low enough for conditions to meet what Ackerman believed to be ideal for counting. Why burn up all that expensive fuel and get untrustworthy results? So the scientists did no synoptic survey that year. The same thing happened in 1994, too.

Now there were howls of outrage from people who "had the perception of a government cover-up going on," Ackerman said. Since each count had found more manatees than the one before it, "the perception was that there could be more."

As a result, Rose said, "there was pressure being put on by the marine industry association." The industry persuaded the legislature to mandate that the state's scientists fly a synoptic survey every single winter, no matter what.

Thanks to that mandate, in January 1995, Ackerman's squadron took to the skies again—and counted just 1,456 manatees, a drop to below even the 1991 total. Fortunately a second cold snap hit in February, and this time they counted 1,823.

Obviously the 400-manatee jump didn't result from a baby boom. Instead, it was proof that variable weather conditions were a big factor in the aerial survey results.

The basic problem with the aerial counts is that they depend on catching manatees at the surface, where they can be easily spotted, explained Bob Bonde, a federal biologist who took part in dozens of aerial surveys over the years. Most of the manatees remain submerged, and thus virtually invisible, even when the planes circle over repeatedly.

"It's almost like flying over New York City on a busy day and seeing how many people are in the streets and using that to estimate how many people are in the city, without seeing how many are inside the buildings," Bonde said.

Even when biologists are positive they know where a manatee might be, spotting one can be difficult because of the murkiness of the marine environment, Bonde said. Over the years, using satellite tracking devices similar to the radio tracker that Cousteau's crew put on Sewer Sam, Bonde and his colleagues have been able to follow individual manatees through the honeycomb of waterways along Florida's Atlantic coast.

Thanks to the tag, "you know it's in the canal behind a house and so you go up and knock on the door," Bonde said. "And the guy who answers says, 'No we don't have any manatees here. I've been here thirty years and I've never seen one.' Then you take them back there and show it to them."

The synoptic aerial surveys carried other risks as well, particularly when the counting was being done by people who had not done it before. One big risk: double-counting the same manatees, inflating the final tally. Leaning out of a circling plane and trying to keep track of which manatees had been counted on all the previous circuits was "like counting kernels of popcorn when they're popping in a bowl," Bonde said.

•

After every count, Ackerman would take all the reports from around the state and retire to his cubbyhole of an office at the marine science lab, where a grimy window overlooked a dock. A sign on his wall commanded: "GET OVER IT!!! I choose to be happy today. Focus on happiness. Make good use of Today!"

He would play classical music and compare the maps that all the biologists involved in the count had turned in, trying to make sure one crew didn't count the same manatees that another crew had already counted.

Over the years, Ackerman kept trying to figure out a way to estimate how many manatees they had missed—the same way he calculated the missed deer in Idaho—but in a way that would be far more reliable than Hartman's seat-of-the-pants math. But there were just too many variables to account for: Was it really cold for several days before the count? Or did it just turn cold that day? Was it sunny or cloudy? Was it sunny in one place and cloudy in another? Did the temperatures vary too much between Duval County on the state's northeast coast and Collier County on the southwest coast? Too many things could change. Too many things could go wrong.

Perhaps, some scientists thought, it would be better to simply feed the numbers into a computer program and use math to arrive at the answer. A University of Florida graduate student named Miriam Marmontel tried that route in the mid-1990s. Working from an estimated statewide population of two thousand—slightly more than any of Ackerman's surveys had found—she used a computer program called VORTEX to calculate the future of the species.

After Marmontel handed in her doctoral thesis, her faculty adviser trumpeted her findings to the *Orlando Sentinel*. The fact that her adviser, a professor named Stephen Humphrey, happened to be the co-chairman of the newly liberated Save the Manatee Club gave the announcement an added dose of credibility.

"Is the manatee endangered?" asked the March 1994 *Sentinel* story. "The controversial question sprang from findings announced last week by researchers from the University of Florida. . . . Manatees are not in imminent danger of extinction, the authors concluded, contradicting the conventional wisdom regarding Florida's most identifiable endangered species."

Humphrey told the paper that "my wife is mad as hell at me for releasing this information," but added, "I don't think the environmental community does itself a service when every issue is a crisis."

The only problem was, the story was wrong. Marmontel was "fairly upset" by the news coverage of her study, said Patti Thompson. Marmontel wrote a rebuttal for the Save the Manatee Club's newsletter headlined "Florida Manatees Are Still Endangered."

"A scenario with an initial population size of 2,000 and population parameters calculated from the 16 years of data resulted in a gradually declining population, a probability of persistence of 44 percent in 1,000 years, and a mean final population size equivalent to only 10 percent of the original value (or about 200)," Marmontel wrote. "A chance of persistence of less than 50 percent in 1,000 years is very low for a large mammal like the manatee."

If humans could stop destroying the manatees' habitat, she wrote, the future might look brighter.

"However," she added, "given the high incidence of boat-related mortality and rapid growth in boat traffic and coastal development, the prognosis is not good."

•

While Marmontel dealt with the fallout from misinterpretations of her calculations, the state's biologists were trying to figure out better methods for counting manatees—say, using a blimp instead of an airplane.

"The surveys from the planes on the coldest day of the year with the window open, flying in a tight circle, was not anybody's idea of fun," Pam McVety explained. With a blimp, "the fuel usage would have been lower, and the ability of the dirigible to stay in one position would make the counting easier and more accurate."

They tried a few tests using advertising blimps—the Metropolitan Life Insurance blimp with the cartoon Snoopy on the side, and the SeaWorld blimp painted like Shamu the killer whale. The blimps worked superbly, Ackerman said. Unlike the airplanes, they held steady and didn't make the biologists nauseous.

The only problem: Those big blimps were usually unavailable unless there was a big golf tournament or a pro football game going on in the neighborhood. Their true purpose was to serve as big billboards, not platforms for scientific research.

Then, in 1996, one of the state marine lab's scientists, a slender, balding man named Brad Weigle, formed a corporation, took out a home equity loan, and bought an experimental two-man blimp made by a factory going out of business. Weigle intended to convince state officials to hire his blimp for counting manatees, then branch out to counting other animals as well.

Weigle hired a pilot who had flown the Shamu blimp for SeaWorld, and they conducted some preliminary tests that showed the two-man blimp ought to work. Weigle and his crew moored the newly christened "Ecoblimp" at the municipal airport in St. Petersburg, intending to show it off to reporters at a press conference scheduled for mid-morning on May 1.

About 2 a.m., a St. Petersburg resident named John Forziano was having a beer, listening to the Grateful Dead and warming up a plate of nachos in his tenth-floor apartment in a building called the Coronet. Louis Meile, a carpenter who lived four stories down, had just stopped by to talk to him.

Ten minutes into their chat, the whole building shook as if it had been hit by a meteor.

Gusting winds had caught the eighty-one-foot Ecoblimp, pulling it free from its moorings. The wind carried it seven blocks and then smashed it into the side of the Coronet.

"It bounced all the way down the face of the building," Meile told a reporter afterward. "It was baboom baboom, bam bam bam, and then, CRASH!"

"That was the sound of Weigle's dream hitting the sidewalk," the *St. Petersburg Times* reported.

The Ecoblimp sustained a huge gash in its side. Its pilot's gondola had been destroyed. It never flew again. Synoptic surveys continued being conducted by nauseous biologists leaning out of circling planes.

Even if Weigle's blimp had worked, it would not have solved what McVety viewed as the synoptic survey's biggest flaws.

"The numbers counted only showed you where some of the animals were on the coldest day of the year. Period," she wrote in an e-mail to a reporter years later. "It actually told you very little about the stability of the population or the ability of the population to increase. It didn't address what was happening to their food sources, which were being destroyed because of pollution and boats prop-dredging grass areas. It didn't tell you about the gene pool and whether it was still large enough to ensure a healthy population. It didn't address what was happening to the young animals and a whole lot more."

Ackerman himself, writing in 1995, conceded that "the greatest value of the surveys may be as a snapshot of the whole state population at once," but "the results are not statistical estimates of population size and will probably not provide estimates of population-size trends."

The difficulty of providing an accurate census underscored the point the National Aquarium's Craig Phillips had made to federal biologists thirty years before: Don't classify manatees as endangered based on what you think their numbers might be. They're too hard to count. Thanks to Phillips, the federal biologists had still classified the species as endangered, but based on "the lack of reliable estimates . . . and because of its reduced range."

However, Phillips's warning had gotten lost over time. With the escalating fights over Pat Rose's manatee protection regulations, the synoptic survey results took on an importance far beyond their actual scientific value. Every announcement about the synoptic survey findings had to be filtered through a political prism, where high numbers and low numbers meant different things to each side.

"Manatees have been so politicized lately, so polar and controversial," Ackerman said. "It's political. It's not at all logical."

Every winter when Ackerman announced his survey results, he cautioned reporters that the numbers should not be treated as anything more than an estimate of the minimum number of manatees. Nevertheless, the press dutifully reported the fluctuating results as if they were announcing the latest stock market numbers: Manatees up two points in light trading!

Then the manatee's advocates—not only the Save the Manatee Club but also other environmental groups who touted their love for the homely creatures—would invariably discuss Ackerman's numbers prefaced by the word "only," as in "only twelve hundred manatees left."

Every time Patti Thompson heard her co-workers use that word "only," she would try to warn them about how shaky the synoptic survey results were. Nobody paid attention, she said.

The state's annual announcement about the number of manatees counted, combined with the repetition of the word "only," led the general public to think of their endangered status as being pegged to how many—or how few—there were.

Then, in January 1996, Ackerman's critter counters hit the jackpot. Thanks to almost perfect weather conditions, they counted a record 2,274 manatees, A month later, another round of counting produced an even higher number: 2,639.

"We always thought there were more out there than we counted," an ecstatic Ackerman told reporters.

Rather than satisfying the boating interests, the higher numbers instead produced even greater skepticism among opponents of the new boating regulations.

"It just shows that they're not as endangered as they said," complained Rick Rawlins, the Volusia County fish-camp owner running Citizens for Responsible Boating. "They say they have better methods of counting, but it's a manu-factured crisis."

Ackerman himself, buoyed by the higher count, put forward a proposition that startled manatee advocates: "Two years ago people assumed the popula-tion was declining. I'm putting forward the case it's increasing."

Wade Hopping completely agreed with him. The lobbyist said this higher figure meant that it was time to decide if manatees really needed all those pro-tective speed zones.

"It should be an indication to re-evaluate where we are," he said. "The good news is the species is doing well, and now we need to help the boaters do well."

Less than a month after that record-setting February 1996 survey, though, another set of numbers came out that undercut Ackerman's optimism.

This set of numbers was compiled by a group of biologists who worked out of a nondescript building tucked into the back corner of the Eckerd College campus in St. Petersburg—a place where the otherwise spotty landscaping fea-tured what seemed like the thickest, lushest stand of banana trees in the state.

## Growing Bananas with Curious George

FLORIDA'S LARGEST ESTUARY, Tampa Bay, is a shallow bowl about twelve feet deep. Its four hundred square miles of water is still ringed by some marshes and mangroves, but mostly the perimeter has been covered by the asphalt sprawl of three cities—Tampa, St. Petersburg, and Clearwater—as well as a clutch of smaller towns like Safety Harbor and Apollo Beach. From the air, the bay itself looks murky and brown, like a giant puddle left by the last hard rain. But it contains more than two hundred species of fish, including snook, redfish, and spotted sea trout.

Bob Smith loved Tampa Bay. He lived in a landlocked suburb called Brandon, a onetime Hillsborough County cattle pasture that had been turned into a textbook example of mall-and-sprawl. Every chance he got, Smith would hitch up his trailer and haul his twenty-one-foot mullet boat to the nearest ramp so he could go fishing.

Smith was in his fifties, a burly, bearded man with a veteran angler's ruddy complexion. Although he worked for a telecommunications company, he knew the bay's every curve.

Smith's father had been a commercial fisherman in the days when Tampa Bay yielded a dependable supply of seafood. He taught young Bob all of the bay's secrets. He showed the boy the thick beds of sea grasses where young fish hide. He pointed out the deep holes, gouged out by developers dredging up fill for the marshes, many of them now full of fish. He warned the boy about the dead spots where pollution had taken its toll.

On a sunny spring Saturday, Bob Smith went fishing with his brother, his uncle, and a friend from his church. Smith and his brother Rick were aboard Smith's own boat, the *Miss Dee*. His uncle, Charles "Sonny Buck" Battles, rode with Smith's friend, Pete Zuazo, in Pete's boat. They set out about 8 a.m. on March 24, 2001, intending to head back to shore around 2 p.m.

As the time drew near to point their bows toward home, the fishermen decided to try one last spot. The two boats headed toward an area of the bay that old-time anglers always called "the middle grounds," a shallow expanse of sea grass beds near the end of the main runway of MacDill Air Force Base. Smith knew the middle grounds would be thick with sardines, the kind of fish that attracts other, larger fish. The men had caught trout there before. Smith figured they might get lucky again.

Suddenly, another boat cut across near them, roaring through the shallows. It was a cabin cruiser, about twenty-four feet long, and looked to be going maybe twenty-five miles per hour.

Smith kept his eye on the boater, convinced the man was about to run into some serious trouble. Not only was the water too shallow for his boat, but it was particularly murky in that spot. One of the bay's deepest holes, dug up years before to extend the air base's runway, was nearby. Now the military was trying to atone for past environmental sins by filling it in. The dredged material had been stirred up, and now it floated, suspended, in the water, making that part of the bay particularly opaque.

Sure enough, as Smith watched, the speeding boat banged into something and then began churning the bay bottom, its propeller producing sandy clouds in the water. Then the boater pushed the throttle higher and turned the wheel. The cabin cruiser veered away, bound for a deeper part of the bay.

Smith steered the *Miss Dee* closer to the spot where the boater had turned. He could see something in the water. At first he thought it was a tarp, the kind the Coast Guard puts out to contain spills. When he got closer, though, he realized it was a spreading red stain.

The speeding boat had hit a manatee. The propeller had sliced huge hunks of flesh from its hide. The animal was bleeding profusely. The cuts were deep enough to puncture the lungs.

"I could hear the air rushing in and out," Smith said.

Pete Zuazo grabbed his cell phone, but he wasn't sure who to call. He dialed the state troopers, the county sheriff, everybody he could think of, to no avail.

By then the manatee had drifted into deeper water. Smith, his brother Rick, and their uncle jumped into the water to offer the injured animal some comfort. They could see it wouldn't last long.

"Nobody should die alone," Smith explained.

They patted the wounded manatee on its side and told it to hold on. "It was pitiful," Smith said. "She would dive and come back up. She seemed responsive to the touching."

They spent about fifteen minutes treading water and talking to the manatee, Smith said, and then "she finally rolled over on her back. I knew she wasn't going to make it."

After the dying manatee sank for the last time, they did not see it again. They spent some time looking, too. Finally Smith and his fishing buddies gave up. They didn't feel much like fishing anymore, so they headed for shore.

On the way back, they encountered a boat from the state wildlife agency. They told the officer on board where to find the carcass they had just left. He went straight to the middle grounds but couldn't locate the body.

A day later, the dead manatee floated back up to the surface in another part of the bay, near a place called Picnic Island. A passing boater spotted it and reported it. The same wildlife officer from the day before recovered the body and towed it to a boat ramp. There, employees of the Florida Fish and Wildlife Conservation Commission hauled it out and loaded it onto a truck.

The truck drove to a low, fenced-in building tucked into a seldom-seen section of the Eckerd College campus. The sign outside the building said "Florida Marine Mammal Pathology Laboratory." That's where the dead manatee landed in the capable hands of Tom Pitchford.

Pitchford stood six foot one. He was still as lean as he was in college, when he worked as a lifeguard. He had a face as narrow as a corner, with dancing blue eyes and tousled hair that was starting to go gray. He rarely wore socks or raised his voice.

Pitchford spent nearly all his waking hours thinking about manatees. He had tried to swim like them. He had tracked down places where they hide. He had rescued scores of hurt ones. He had hauled in hundreds more that were dead.

He even met his wife, Meg, while rescuing a manatee. They both wound up covered with mud, yet somehow, love bloomed. They got married and had three kids without ever getting around to a honeymoon. They were too busy studying manatees.

Pitchford's fingers were long and slender, the fingers of a concert pianist. Instead of using them to play a piano, though, Pitchford poked them into dead animals.

Every time a manatee turned up dead, state employees collected the carcass and brought it to the path lab. Then Pitchford and his colleagues could cut the animal open and figure out what killed it, a process known as a necropsy. If this were a TV show, the title would be *C.S.I.: Sea Cow.*

"If you can't understand why they're dying, you're really working in the dark about how to save them," Pitchford explained. "It's an unprecedented effort to document every animal dead in a species. Every animal that dies in an entire species."

Pitchford ran the lab, a job he was given by none other than Buddy Powell during the time when Powell ran the state manatee research program. In a degrees-of-separation game for manatee biologists, the line would go like this: Joe Moore to Woodie Hartman to Buddy Powell to Tom Pitchford.

Over the years, Pitchford and his path lab staff had seen plenty of manatees that had been clobbered by boats. They had also seen them squished by canal locks, stunned by chilly water, tangled in fishing line. Very little surprised them. Once the lab's most senior biologist, the white-haired Sentiel "Butch" Rommel, nearly drowned inside a whale carcass. Survive that experience, and nothing else really comes close to topping it.

Everyone at the lab had so-gruesome-it's-funny stories about their work. On one memorable occasion, a British television crew happened to be on hand when a badly decomposed manatee carcass arrived at the lab.

With the camera rolling, the reporter described, in her most proper strawberries-at-Wimbledon accent, how unbearably awful the stench was, and how the body was so full of gas that it was hissing.

Just then Butch Rommel made his first incision. There was a loud BANG! The heart exploded from the body and shot past the reporter's head.

"Whoa!" she yelled, jumping sideways.

Running the path lab would be depressing, Pitchford said, except that the staff frequently gets called in to help save manatees that are sick or injured. Then they scramble for their trucks, even on nights and weekends. Pitchford's job was like running a coroner's office and a paramedic unit at the same time.

"If you can participate in a rescue and keep even one manatee from being the next carcass on the table, it's worthwhile," he said.

In Pitchford's office, books and papers were stacked everywhere. Post-It notes climbed the door like ivy. On the floor was a Tinkertoy set he borrowed from his kids so he and Rommel could work out a forensic puzzle. Leaning against his desk was the bottom half of a boat motor, another piece of the puzzle.

From his office window, Pitchford could see some of the lush banana trees that grew around the lab. The trees grew so well because the staff fertilized them with what they took out of the stomachs of the dead manatees. The rest went to a rendering plant in Tampa to be turned into animal fat for manufacturing lipstick, soaps, paint, and varnish.

The staff had dubbed the fruit from its trees "Manabananas."

"They're good!" Pitchford said with a laugh. Then, in a more serious tone, he added, "You try to make something positive out of the fact that we get so many dead manatees a year. I mean, it's 200,000 pounds of manatee a year."

Sometimes, when Pitchford sat in his office chatting with a visitor, he could seem a bit distracted, his eyes wandering over to the many plaques on his wall. But when he put on his rubber boots and apron, grabbed a skinning knife, and straddled a fresh carcass on the lab's steel examining table, he was completely focused. Every few minutes the lab's bug zapper would emit a purple flash and go ZZZZZZZZZZZZT! Yet not even that bit of B-movie creepiness could throw him off.

In the lab, above the board where the staff kept all the statistics from recent necropsies, hung a ceramic manatee angel, ascending. Although Pitchford thought most manatee-related art seemed like kitsch, this piece had caught his fancy. The only other decoration in the lab: a full-size manatee skeleton mounted on the wall.

Once, as a present for a friend, Pitchford created his own manatee art. He whittled an intricately detailed miniature manatee, then showed it to his friend.

"He loved it, but I said it's not finished," Pitchford recalled. "Then I put some healed propeller cuts on the back. He said, 'I wish you hadn't done that.'"

While examining the dead manatee that Bob Smith had seen killed, Pitchford and Rommel found that it had suffered sixteen propeller cuts that sliced deep into its back, tearing holes in its lungs. They found eight similar cuts on its fluke. The cuts on its back looked like a massive zipper had passed over the animal.

Pitchford and Rommel also found bone shards. The boat hit the manatee so hard that it didn't just break the animal's ribs, it shattered them like glass.

There was a thatch of sea grass in the manatee's mouth, showing it had been killed while feeding. Then they reached into its uterus and pulled out a well-developed fetus. This female manatee had been pregnant. The boater with the cabin cruiser had killed not one manatee but two.

While Pitchford and other colleagues worked on the necropsy, another biologist flipped quickly through a binder full of manatee photos, looking for a match. Blond-haired Kristin Fick, a mild-mannered, matter-of-fact woman originally from New Jersey, knew that this particular manatee seemed familiar, but she couldn't figure out why. The book would likely hold the answer.

Each photo in the book Fick held showed a manatee with a scar from being hit by a boat. The photos were the culmination of Joe Moore's discovery about using scars to identify manatees. It was a bound counterpart to the computerized collection Cathy Beck compiled in Gainesville for the U.S. Geological Survey's Sirenia Project. Both were part of the photo-identification project first launched by Buddy Powell, using pictures of the manatees that he and Woodie Hartman had studied in Crystal River.

When at last Fick spotted the picture that matched the dead animal in front of her, she became the first person to completely grasp the horror of what Bob Smith had seen happen.

Ragtail was dead.

Among the three hundred or so manatees that frequented Tampa Bay, Ragtail ranked as a celebrity. The animal's name came from another boating mishap years before that had sliced chunks from its spoon-shaped fluke. For more than a decade, Fick and other researchers had been monitoring Ragtail's life, documenting its travels all around Tampa Bay. Because biologists had charted so much of Ragtail's life, the Save the Manatee Club had featured Ragtail as part of its "Adopt-A-Manatee" fund-raising program. Ragtail was one of the most popular manatees in the program. Nearly eight hundred people around the country had adopted it.

After Fick's discovery, someone at the lab phoned the Save the Manatee Club to relay the grim news. The club's staff would have to write a letter to every one of Ragtail's eight hundred supporters, explaining that a boater had killed both the celebrity manatee and its unborn calf. The Save the Manatee Club quickly produced a press release noting that there were only voluntary speed limits in Tampa Bay, and suggesting that mandatory limits might have saved Ragtail's life.

"This is just awful," Judith Vallee said.

Pitchford didn't spend a lot of time brooding about Ragtail's death or whether regulations would have made any difference. He had to clean up and get ready for the next dead manatee. Hundreds came through the doors of the path lab every year, not to mention the occasional dolphin or turtle, and the staff had to be ready.

Besides, Pitchford had seen more dead manatees than nearly anyone else in the field. He had been on the front lines of what became known as "the epizootic"—the worst two months in the history of manatee science.

•

Pitchford was the fifth of ten children, seven of them boys. His father was a decorated Marine Corps colonel. His mother might have been even tougher. While Colonel Pitchford was busy in Vietnam, she somehow handled all those kids by herself.

Pitchford spent his childhood on a series of coastal military bases: Jacksonville, Norfolk, Camp Lejeune. He caught turtles and crabs and learned to sail and surf. His family nickname was Curious George, after the storybook monkey who wanted to know about everything. But he never saw a manatee in Jacksonville, or while visiting his grandparents in St. Petersburg.

After college, Pitchford worked for a museum near Chesapeake Bay. For excitement he volunteered with a group that rescued stranded bottlenose dolphins.

Then one day a manatee swam into his life.

Because they're so sensitive to cold, manatees rarely stray north of Florida. But in October 1992, a male manatee turned up in a canal lock near the Chesapeake. Since it was a marine mammal, Pitchford's dolphin rescue group went to check it out. They noticed that the manatee had some marks on its back, marks that might be scars.

Curious about what that meant, Pitchford made some phone calls. Finally he talked to Cathy Beck in Gainesville. He made a careful sketch of the manatee's scars and faxed it to her.

To his amazement, Beck matched Pitchford's sketch to photos of a manatee that had first been spotted in the Port Everglades area in 1987. Known as PE176, it had somehow managed to swim more than seven hundred miles north and find Pitchford.

"It was interesting to me you could send off a sketch, just a sketch, that's all it was, and identify the animal," Pitchford said. "It made me think they were doing some exciting things down here."

The encounter so intrigued Curious George that, three months later, he was driving south, headed for the nastiest job in Florida.

•

Back in Woodie Hartman's day, when a dead manatee turned up by someone's dock, it just floated there, drawing flies. There was no hotline to call, no one to retrieve it.

But after Congress passed the Endangered Species Act, federal and state officials became interested in finding out why manatees died. In 1974, federal biologists began systematically collecting and dissecting every stinky carcass they could get their hands on. Blair Irvine and Duke Campbell of the U.S. Fish and Wildlife Service, who had launched the first wintertime aerial survey, started the carcass recovery program on the state's west coast.

Meanwhile, after getting a federal grant, a University of Miami professor named Dan Odell began collecting carcasses in South Florida, often with the help of an eager grad student named John Reynolds.

The biologists passed the word among the state's Florida Marine Patrol officers about what they were looking for. Soon the calls started coming in about floating bodies. Dead manatees had washed up on shore, sunk under a dock, even gotten wedged into a sewer pipe.

"We extracted one from a Biscayne Boulevard storm drain," Odell said. "It got stuck and died and made a stink under this greasy spoon restaurant."

The restaurant's customers thought the food had gone bad. Finally, though, a drainage backup led highway officials to the real problem. The manatee was stuck so tightly, "we had to cut it into pieces to remove it," Odell recalled.

Some reports of dead manatees turned out to be other dead animals—Goliath grouper, for instance, and, in one memorable instance, a drowned hog (the tusks should have been a tipoff). Odell, a sardonic New Yorker with a razor wit, said they learned to ask a lot of questions before driving to collect a body that might just be someone's discarded rug.

As they pulled their smelly load back home, they were sometimes followed by suspicious police officers. The cops even stopped Odell a time or two to check out reports that he was "stealing" manatees. Mostly Odell laughed it off, until the day he got wind of an actual death threat. At that point, he said, "I went to a sign painter and got the words MANATEE RESEARCH painted on the side of the truck in big letters." The police problems dwindled after that.

Because there was no path lab then, Odell and his helpers would perform their necropsies outdoors, then bury the remains.

"We would haul the carcasses out to the zoo on Key Biscayne and do necropsies—we were literally doing it in the dirt," he said.

Meanwhile, Irvine was ready to outsource the carcass recovery on the west coast. He hired a young couple who had been working with whale skeletons at the Los Angeles County museum. Their names: Cathy Beck and Bob Bonde.

Beck and Bonde had never seen a manatee outside a zoo, or even traveled east of the Rocky Mountains. As they drove around the state hauling in dead manatees on an old trailer, Florida provided a stiff jolt of culture shock, especially when they would stop in small towns to gas up.

"We had people come out of the 7-Eleven and see this thing that's oozing blood and dripping and say, 'Mmm-mmm, mighty fine eatin' there,'" Bonde said.

No police officers ever followed them, but once a woman spotted their cargo and mistakenly assumed they had killed the manatee themselves and now were hauling it home.

"What did you do *that* for?" she yelled, clearly distraught.

Like Odell, Bonde and Beck did their necropsies in a forest outside Gainesville owned by the head of the Florida Museum of Natural History. They wrote everything down in a notebook that doubled as their expense report. One entry said, "Went to laundromat & washed three loads and still couldn't get the smell out."

At first, Bonde said, he and Beck thought of manatees as being "like cows in a pasture—they keep getting out of the pasture and up onto the highway and getting hit, so they must not be very bright."

But after the couple had been picking up dead manatees for three months, a co-worker decided to change their perspective. Buddy Powell, then working for the U.S. Fish and Wildlife Service, took Beck and Bonde to Crystal River and introduced them to the manatees he knew so well.

The first one they saw was Piety. Two decades later, Bonde vividly re-

Cathy Beck and her husband, Bob Bonde, pioneered the manatee carcass recovery program, although they sometimes got odd reactions when people saw them hauling a dead body. Photo courtesy of Sirenia Project, U.S. Geological Survey.

membered the encounter, including the fact that Piety had two young calves swimming alongside. As Powell expected, seeing live manatees in their own element showed Bonde and Beck the species in a whole new light.

"They're very fluid and mystic in the water," said Bonde, who since then has devoted two decades to following up on Hartman's studies of the Crystal River manatees.

The pioneers like Odell, Reynolds, Beck, and Bonde wrote the book on how the necropsies should be handled, including what categories should be used for "cause of death." The categories included not just collisions with watercraft but also being crushed in locks and floodgates, and natural causes such as cold stress. There was one category labeled "perinatal" for young calves that died before maturity—sometimes from poor nutrition, sometimes from disease, sometimes from cold, sometimes from being orphaned when their mother fell victim to something else.

Beck, Bonde, and a third biologist, Thomas O'Shea, wrote a procedural manual for manatee necropsies. It included a lengthy section dealing with boat collisions:

> Fresh, open propeller wounds or skeg marks provide obvious clues. Manatees can be killed by impact alone, or by crushing between the hull and the substrate, leaving no such propeller marks. . . . Broken bones, particularly recent fractures of ribs or shattered scapulae, are also frequently encountered. Massive trauma to internal organs may also be seen. . . . Broken bones may perforate lungs or blood vessels, the heart may rupture, and the kidneys may appear paler, softer, and larger than normal with loss of blood.

By studying the dead manatees, the biologists who handled the earliest necropsies were able to spot some trends. They carefully measured and documented 1,376 fatal or healed wounds on 628 dead manatees that were necropsied between 1974 and 1991. They concluded that 406 of the 628 were killed by boats.

Of the 406, being slashed by boat propellers killed 158 of them, while being clobbered by the boat's skeg killed 224, and a combination of the two accounted for the rest. In other words, more of them were killed by being hit—55 percent—than by being slashed—39 percent.

Not all boat collisions killed manatees right away. Some had been hit over and over, suffering broken ribs or maimed flippers, yet continued swimming for years—until the final, fatal wound.

"Many animals survived several boat collisions," they noted in a review published in 1995. "One manatee had 22 separate patterns of propeller cuts."

Another trend they noted in that review: Only 2 percent of the injuries were to the head. Nearly every time, the manatees were hit in the middle of their bodies, and "90 percent of the scar patterns were along the head-to-tail axis, indicating manatees were moving in response to an incoming boat when struck."

In other words, the manatees were probably trying to flee, even to dive out of the way, but the boats were moving too fast.

Federal funding for the necropsies dried up in 1985, part of the Reagan administration's cutbacks to endangered species programs. But the research provided so much valuable data that the state—that is, Pat Rose and his scientists—took over the job.

In February 1993, Pitchford landed the unenviable job of picking up every bloated, rotting manatee carcass that turned up in Collier, Lee, Charlotte, and Sarasota counties. It was dirty, nasty work. Curious George liked it.

But he was curious about something else.

Every day as he drove to work in Port Charlotte, Pitchford passed a sign for a resort called Warm Mineral Springs. The sign said the spring was eighty-seven degrees year-round. Pitchford wondered if, in cold weather, manatees might like that spot too, even though it wasn't on the list of known winter aggregation sites. So Pitchford began hunting for them.

"It became almost an obsession to go there all the time," he said. "I'd go at the crack of dawn or late at night and stand in people's backyards."

One night at dusk, his search paid off: "To see the procession of manatees coming in head to tail like RVs, twenty of them, it was just awesome to see."

Pitchford's discovery marked the first new warm-water refuge found in two decades of manatee research. Bruce Ackerman quickly added it to his list of places to check during the annual synoptic survey.

Pitchford could barely spare the time to uncover the manatees' use of Warm Mineral Springs. Nearly half the manatee population lives in southwest Florida, so he usually had his hands full with hauling dead manatees to the path lab.

"From February 1993 to December 1993 we had fifty-one dead manatees," Pitchford said. "That was a record. People were freaking out. We were the busiest in the state. I got a pin. Then the next year we had seventy-one."

Statewide, the record for dead manatees had been set in 1990, when the St. Petersburg lab handled 206 dead manatees. About 50 of them had been killed by a cold snap.

But 1995 nearly equaled the record with 201 dead manatees, even though there was no deadly cold snap to fuel the increase. That equaled roughly 10

Tom Pitchford suspected Red Tide might have killed the manatees he found in 1995. The following year, a mysterious epidemic wiped out scores of them. Photo courtesy of the *St. Petersburg Times*.

percent of the estimated population of two thousand, not a good sign for the future.

"If we have some kind of environmental disaster come along, it's really going to cause problems," said Scott Wright, the biologist then in charge of the path lab.

That year, Pitchford stumbled onto a mystery. He picked up some manatees that appeared to be completely healthy except for being dead. His bosses at the lab decided the cause was pneumonia, but Pitchford thought it might be Red Tide.

Red Tide had plagued Florida's Gulf Coast since at least the 1500s. It originates from a single-celled, plant-like organism, a microscopic alga with a pair of whip-like tails to help it move through the water. Under certain conditions, usually present during the summer, the microalgae suddenly multiply rapidly, producing what is called a bloom. During a bloom, millions of the micro-scopic algae float atop the water, turning it a rusty red color—hence the name. Scientists have long suspected that manmade pollution can fuel these massive blooms of Red Tide, but so far there is no proof that it's anything but a natural process.

Pitchford knew the waters off southwest Florida had been afflicted with a particularly persistent bloom, one that began in 1994 and would last through part of 1996. A bloom like that could be deadly.

The Red Tide microalgae produce a type of poison called brevetoxin, which affects the central nervous system of fish. During a bloom, the brevetoxin can kill thousands of fish, which then wash up on the beach, their potent stink driving away even the hardiest tourist. A bloom that occurs near the shore can send the poison wafting through the air, making beachgoers with asthma and other respiratory problems start coughing and sneezing.

In 1982, Red Tide killed thirty-nine manatees. Each victim had spent its final hours acting crazy—swimming upside down or in circles, appearing disori-ented. The necropsies found their stomachs full of sea squirts, which can con-centrate the Red Tide toxin. The poison turned the manatees' nervous system haywire before killing them.

None of the manatees that Pitchford had pulled in had exhibited odd behavior. Their stomachs were free of sea squirts. Still, Pitchford persisted. He talked to some algae bloom experts, and even found funding to pay for further tests. But his bosses said no. They were satisfied with their original findings.

Then, on the evening of March 5, 1996, the body of a dead manatee washed up on a barrier island north of Charlotte Harbor. The next day there were two more.

Pitchford picked up the carcasses and trucked them to St. Petersburg. He could tell that there was something unusual about them. Like the ones the year before, they were apparently well- fed adults with no visible signs of trauma.

Sure enough, when Scott Wright examined them, he could hardly believe they were not just sleeping.

"You open them up, and they look great," Wright said. "Except they're dead."

Four days later, two more bodies washed up, followed by two more the next day, and another one the day after that. Then, on March 12, eight dead mana-tees turned up, and on March 13 there were ten more, and another five on

March 14. All of them came from the same eighty-mile stretch of shoreline between Englewood, a small blue-collar town that straddles the border between Sarasota and Charlotte counties, and the glittering resort town of Marco Island in Collier County.

Each victim had the same symptoms: Outwardly fine, no reason to be dead. Inside, necropsies found only two unusual things: swollen brains and bright, purple-red scars on puffy lungs. Could it be a virus? The Red Tide toxin? Pesticides? Some other toxic pollution? Wright could not tell.

By mid-month, Pitchford had hauled in so many carcasses that the path lab couldn't handle them all. They were stacking up like logs at a sawmill. Pitchford helped set up an outdoor necropsy facility in the J. W. "Ding" Darling National Wildlife Refuge on Sanibel Island—a location close to the center of the die-off, but still isolated from civilization.

"We called them the pole barns," he said. "They were out of doors, away from anybody who might object. It's not an olfactory-friendly process."

They dug a pit and filled it with ice, then lined it from end to end with manatee carcasses. Soon there were too many for the pit to hold, so they just left the remainder piled up in a rickety truck with wooden sides.

Forklifts carried the manatees two at a time to flatbed trucks where Wright and other biologists who had been recruited to help stood waiting with their knives already bloody. They started on March 14, a Thursday, determined to empty the pit. By Saturday they had finally caught up.

"It felt like a big triumph," one biologist said later.

They cleaned up and called it a night—but before they could leave, five more carcasses came in.

By the end of the month, Wright had done so many necropsies that he was suffering from tennis elbow in both arms. Usually he delighted in cracking bad jokes during his necropsies. While up to his armpits in manatee guts he might start talking about how much he was looking forward to eating that meatloaf sandwich he had brought for lunch. Or he might ask a visitor if something in the lab smelled funny, then explain he couldn't tell anymore. But the rising tide of carcasses had washed away his sense of humor.

Wright's wife insisted he spend Easter Sunday with the family. Except for that, he worked every day for a month carving up carcasses, trying to solve the mystery. When a reporter asked if he was alarmed by the number of dead manatees, Wright said he preferred the word "concerned." Then he added, "We're very tired."

As the bodies piled higher, state officials declared themselves baffled and sought help from everyone they could think of. They called in the Centers for Disease Control, the Pentagon's Institute of Pathology, even an internationally recognized virologist from the Netherlands who had once diagnosed a virus in North Sea seals.

CNN and *People* magazine ran stories on the mystery. The *Los Angeles Times* declared it to be "the worst die-off of a U.S. endangered species ever reported."

By early April, the die-off had pushed the number of dead manatees past the 1990 record. It had become the very definition of an epizootic—an outbreak of a disease that affects many animals of one kind, all at the same time.

Governor Chiles personally attended a necropsy at the path lab to show his concern—and of course pose for a photo along with Pat Rose's ex-boss, Ginger Wetherell, who headed up the agency now known as the Department of Environmental Protection.

In talking with reporters afterward, Chiles mentioned one unsettling possibility, something nobody else had dared to say.

"The trouble is," the governor said, "even if scientists manage to pin down the cause, they may not be able to do anything about it."

As the mystery continued, Pitchford fielded calls from reporters from around the world. Ken Haddad, then the manager of the marine science lab in St. Petersburg, went to Sanibel to see what was happening.

"There I saw Tom in a pair of shorts, white boots, white T-shirt, with a phone in one hand, a large knife in the other hand and this, uh, let's just say a sea of manatee carcasses that had been coming in so fast that they couldn't keep up with them," Haddad said.

Complicating matters was the fact that each necropsy involved doing more than just cutting up the dead subject. Every time the biologists performed a necropsy on a manatee, they were required to collect a set of the bones and seal them up in a white plastic bucket.

"They're called a voucher set, because they vouch that it occurred," Pitchford explained. "If anybody thought we were faking the moon landing here, you would have the proof. We saved a skull, a couple of ribs, and a flipper."

Back in the 1970s all the buckets of "voucher set" bones were stored at the Sirenia office in Gainesville. When they ran out of room, they made arrangements to shift their stack of buckets to an old missile silo in North Key Largo that had been built in the 1960s, not long after the Cuban missile crisis.

Originally, soldiers stationed there guarded nuclear-tipped Nike missiles, awaiting war with Fidel Castro while fighting off hordes of bloodthirsty mosquitoes. By the 1970s the crisis had passed and the missiles were relocated. The land gained a new name: Crocodile Lake National Wildlife Refuge.

But it didn't look much like a wildlife refuge because the Defense Department had built everything at the missile site to last. The walls were made from two feet of highly reinforced concrete. Although the soldiers were gone, the buildings that housed them remained, guarded now by turkey vultures.

The U.S. Fish and Wildlife Service turned one of the empty buildings into a cavernous storehouse for evidence seized in wildlife smuggling cases, stacking it to the ceiling with boxes of crocodile skins, corals, even giant clam shells. That's where the buckets of manatee skulls wound up too. Walking through the door of the old silo was like wandering into the government warehouse at the end of *Raiders of the Lost Ark*, Pitchford said.

Although the property now was part of a wildlife refuge, no regular staff guarded the property. In the 1980s someone took advantage of the isolation and built an elaborate cockfighting ring there, perhaps the most upscale cockfighting ring ever.

"There was a two-story metal building with a restaurant and bar," said Steve Klett, who took charge of the refuge in 1997. "One wall in the restaurant and bar was lined with glass cages so you could look at the roosters and determine which one to bet on." Somehow, at the same time, the Miami police had set up a target-shooting range on the site as well. Klett—who ended up dismantling both structures when he took over—wasn't sure how they occupied adjoining spaces without any conflict.

At the height of the 1996 manatee die-off, Pitchford and a colleague had to drive down to the missile site in a truck loaded down with buckets of voucher bones from all the recent necropsies. They expected to spend at least a day unloading the truck.

But when the two scientists arrived, they discovered the police SWAT team was at the firing range, in the middle of a live-fire exercise.

"The last thing they needed was a couple of biologists with a truck full of manatee skulls," Pitchford said. "So they lined up in their black pants and black T-shirts and guns and unloaded our truck in fifteen minutes."

Toward the end of April, the biologists caught another break. On April 22, Pitchford got a call about a live manatee floundering around in Lemon Bay, offshore from Englewood. The manatee bore the same name as the town: Englewood.

Pitchford, dressed in his street clothes, including a nice pair of loafers, parked at a waterfront restaurant and immediately spotted the flailing manatee.

"It was paralyzed," he said. "I started to wade in, and soon I was swimming. I put my hand under its head and lifted it up, and it took in this tremendous snort of breath. I tried pulling him but that didn't work, so then I got behind him and pushed him to the shore."

An elderly angler fishing off a nearby bridge closely watched Pitchford struggling with his ailing manatee, but didn't offer to help. When Pitchford got close enough, though, the man called out, "You've got *balls*!"

Englewood and two other manatees that were rescued around the same time appeared to be suffering from the same symptoms. They were taken to the Lowry Park Zoo in Tampa for treatment. The zoo functioned as one of Florida's three manatee hospitals, rehabilitating animals that had been injured by boats or stressed by the cold, even raising calves that had been orphaned. Feeding and caring for injured manatees cost the zoo five hundred thousand dollars a year—nearly half the budget for all of the zoo's sixteen hundred animals—but the rehabilitation tank consistently ranked as one of the zoo's most popular exhibits.

The ailing manatees spent hours in the tank with zoo employees propping their heads up so they wouldn't drown. When the manatees had convulsions, Lowry Park's veterinarian, a blunt, no-nonsense doctor from Oklahoma named David Murphy, injected them with muscle relaxants. Soon they recovered.

To Murphy, that meant the evidence now pointed strongly to Red Tide, not some unknown virus. The other clue: once the Red Tide subsided, the manatee deaths tapered off too.

On May 13, Ginger Wetherell and Interior Secretary Bruce Babbitt held a joint news conference to declare the die-off officially over. On July 2, Wright notified reporters that they had solved the mystery. The culprit was indeed Red Tide.

The cold weather that had aided Ackerman's record aerial count had also brought high winds. The winds had stirred up the surface of the water, Wright said. As a result, the manatees not only consumed plants full of the Red Tide toxin but also inhaled it from the air. The poison affected the manatees' nervous system so that they were unable to hold their heads up, just as Pitchford's rescued manatee demonstrated.

While the discovery offered some relief, it also stood as a warning. As Governor Chiles had predicted, the scientists had found the cause but no cure. If another such Red Tide happened, accompanied by windy weather, it was possible another large die-off would follow.

"There's really nothing on hand that we can realistically use," one scientist involved in the investigation said. "We just have to accept that it's a natural event."

The final tally for the 1996 Red Tide epizootic: 158 animals. As a result, the 1996 statewide death toll set a new record: 415. That meant more than 15 percent of the animals Ackerman's squadron of volunteers had counted back in February were now dead, a statistic that left state scientists shaken.

The Miami Seaquarium's veterinarian, Dr. Greg Bossart, predicted the epidemic's impact would be felt for years to come. Because of the species' continuing human-caused problems, "this is a population that cannot stand any natural mortality," Bossart said. "And we've just lost a big chunk of the southwest population."

Some time later, a path lab staffer looked back at the 1995 necropsy reports on the manatees Pitchford had found, the ones he had been convinced died of Red Tide.

As it turned out, they had the exact same symptoms as the ones that died during the epizootic.

•

With all the worldwide attention focused on the Red Tide die-off, another statistic slipped past the press nearly unnoticed in 1996. The path lab found that, statewide, sixty manatees had been killed by boats, a new record, and an increase of eighteen over the previous year.

"The main problem is that the speed limits and regulations are not being well enforced. We need more marine patrol officers," Judith Vallee told the *Fort Lauderdale Sun-Sentinel*, one of the few newspapers to take note of the increase. "We think the root of the problem is that there's only 283 on-water officers for the whole state."

The following year boats killed another fifty-four manatees—below the 1996 level, but still higher than every other year in which the path lab had been keeping count. In 1998, when Wright quit to take a federal job, Buddy Powell put Pitchford in charge of the path lab—and the number hit a new high of sixty-six.

Pitchford decorated his new office with the plaques he received thanking him for his work during the Red Tide epizootic. But now that he ran the St. Petersburg lab, his life changed. When he worked in Port Charlotte, he could spend his drive to work looking for manatee hiding spots. Now when he climbed in the car, he tuned in to talk radio hosts ranting about politics. He said he listened "to sharpen my debating skills—yes I agree with that, no I don't agree with that."

Debate skills became an important part of his job because, as with Ackerman's surveys, the numbers from the path lab had become politicized. Manatee advocates saw the rising number of boat-related deaths as a dire sign for the future, and a reason to impose even tighter restrictions on boaters. Boating advocates contended that more manatee deaths actually meant there were more manatees, and thus there was no reason to impose new rules.

Some even challenged the path lab's findings, arguing that more manatees were killed by barges, tugboats, and cruise ships than by pleasure craft. They said the lab had misread the evidence.

"The train of thought is: If they've got massive internal injuries then it must be caused by a large vessel and we're regulating the wrong end of the spectrum," Pitchford said. He said had begun to feel like "we're getting nitpicked on everything."

One of the most vocal critics was an electrical engineer-turned-charter captain named Tom McGill, who helped run a Brevard County boating group called Citizens for Florida Waterways. He contended that Pitchford and his colleagues were unqualified and "are cooking the books regarding watercraft-related manatee mortalities."

Boaters even hired a retired large-animal veterinarian from Tennessee named Warren Compton to review the path lab's work. Compton blasted the lab staff and its procedures. But later, when Citizens for Florida Waterways took the state to court to battle proposed boat speed zones in Brevard, Compton had to admit under oath that he had no experience whatsoever with manatees. He only knew about cows that had been hit by trains. Also, he hadn't performed a necropsy on any large mammals since 1970.

As with Ackerman's surveys, the problem lay in trying to mesh science with the law. Science has no problem embracing uncertainty, while the law requires something far more definite.

On one side, manatee advocates noted that the carcass numbers, like the synoptic surveys, merely offered a minimum number of deaths. Long stretches of the state's coastline, such as the Ten Thousand Islands, offered places where carcasses could float undiscovered. Who knew how many manatee deaths the path lab missed each year?

Yet when the state attempted to impose new regulations based on where the most manatee carcasses turned up, opponents pointed out—correctly—that the path lab did not really know where those manatees had been hit. Unless someone like Bob Smith witnessed the manatee's death, the lab could only document where the body eventually turned up. Without eyewitnesses, they also couldn't say when a manatee had been hit, only that it was an unknown number of hours or days or even weeks before the carcass had been found.

Besides, what was the point of imposing more regulations when manatees kept on dying? The key, the boaters contended, lay in enforcing the rules already on the books. But that proved to be easier said than done.

# The Man in the Krispy Kreme Hat

THE TWENTY-TWO-FOOT BOAT pounded across the waves at forty miles per hour, its Mercury outboard motor roaring, the spray flying.

One of the two uniformed officers on board, Lieutenant Tim Kiss of the Florida Fish and Wildlife Conservation Commission, flipped on the blue lights mounted in the bow. His partner, Officer Darrin Riley, turned the wheel to intercept their targets: two deeply tanned Lee County men who had been spending this sunny Sunday afternoon racing a pair of Yamaha WaveRunners around the Caloosahatchee River.

Kiss and Riley were chasing the pair because their watery racetrack took them through a slow-speed zone where boats are supposed to be completely settled in the water with a minimum wake. The zone had been set up to protect manatees from being hit by boats.

Kiss and Riley pulled the WaveRunners over, questioned the men, then gave each of them a sixty-three-dollar citation. One grumbled that the officers had ruined his day. The other, also clearly unhappy, wrinkled his brow and asked, "When does manatee season end?"

Afterward, Kiss said, "That's about the average attitude for a manatee violation."

Not every violator met the same fate as the WaveRunner riders. When Kiss and Riley started their patrol that day, the very first boater they stopped for speeding was someone they knew well, a Lee County sheriff's deputy named James Erb.

Deputy Erb often helped them patrol for speed zone violators. In fact, just a few days before, the *New York Times*, to illustrate a story on manatee protection issues, had published a photo of Deputy Erb pulling over a boater who had been speeding.

Now the deputy was off-duty, taking his family out for a spin in his Carolina Skiff like any other weekend boater. When Kiss and Riley pulled him over, he was holding a beer in one hand and steering the boat with the other. He wore a baseball cap decorated with the logo of the Krispy Kreme donut chain.

The deputy insisted he had done nothing wrong. Even though they had caught Erb red-handed, Kiss and Riley didn't bother to reach for their ticket books. After a few minutes of chatting with the deputy, while his family looked on silently, they let him go—no citation, no warning, no paper record at all. If a reporter for the *St. Petersburg Times* hadn't been along for the ride, no one would have ever known.

"We've caught several deputies," Kiss said with a shrug. He explained that the state wildlife officers never give their county counterparts a ticket because "we don't want to start a war with them."

Federal wildlife officers patrolling the Caloosahatchee couldn't boast of doing much better. On the weekend before Kiss and Riley's patrol, a handful of federal agents took to Lee County's waterways to watch for speeders. In two days they charged sixty-one boaters with violating manatee zones, "and observed many more that we were unable to take enforcement action on," said Special Agent Vance Eaddy of the U.S. Fish and Wildlife Service.

This was hardly how Congress had intended the Marine Mammal Protection Act to work: selective and often spotty enforcement of little-understood and extensively disliked regulations.

Yet enforcement of the laws protecting manatees has stumbled almost from the start. In 1978, just six years after the passage of the MMPA, Marine Mammal Commission director John Twiss was already complaining to the head of the U.S. Fish and Wildlife Service that "the service's enforcement efforts are inadequate for protecting this seriously endangered species from human activities which apparently are a major source of mortality."

As for the state's rules, the picture looked just as gloomy. A year after Governor Martinez and his cabinet called for new speed zones to protect manatees, the men and women in charge of enforcing those zones were finding reasons not to hand out tickets.

John Burton, a wildlife officer patrolling the St. Johns River, blamed boater ignorance. He told the *Orlando Sentinel* that most boaters didn't even know that "slow speed" meant five to seven miles per hour.

Immediately after he made that comment, four boats zoomed past him, violating the slow-speed zone near Hontoon Island. When Burton pulled them over, one boater asked, "What's 'slow speed?' Five mph? Eight? Fifteen?"

Burton scribbled out warnings—not tickets—for each boater, and sent them on their way.

"Some people don't even know what a channel marker is," Burton said afterward, "so how are they going to understand these signs?"

•

Every year, boater ignorance became a bigger problem, because every year more and more people in Florida bought boats.

In 1994 there were 695,722 boats registered in Florida. By 1999, just five years later, the number had climbed to 829,971. That didn't include the boats hauled in by out-of-state tourists, which state officials estimated would push the total to more than a million boats.

When the number of cars and trucks increases to the point that they clog the highways, the government builds new highways. But, as with trees, only God can make more waterways. So even though the number of boats increased, the number of places for boats to travel remained constant. Crowding more and more boats into the same rivers, lakes, bays, and channels meant one thing: lots of boating accidents.

One Connecticut couple who visited Florida in 1989 told a *New York Times* reporter that they realized they had made a mistake when they took a sailboat into Biscayne Bay. It was, the husband said, "scary. Everywhere you turned there was another boat coming at us."

"We joked to one another that it looked like Grand Central Station at rush hour," the wife said.

Shortly after they set sail, they collided with a speedboat. No one was injured, but the sailboat sank.

Although other states had even more boats, Florida consistently racked up the most boating accidents. In 1999 there were 1,292 crashes involving Florida boaters, and Florida led the country in the number of boating fatalities, with fifty-eight.

Most of the accidents involved a boater cruising across a bay or running a river—usually in an idle speed, no-wake zone or in an area with a speed limit—who then collided with another boater doing the same. In more than half the accidents, the boater had been drinking. The fatalities most often resulted from boaters falling in and drowning. Most of those killed had not bothered to put on a life jacket.

Florida boaters did more than just hit each other and run over manatees. They also damaged the sea grass beds that are vital to the state's fishing industry.

Sea grasses help keep the water clean and clear, stabilize the bottom sediment, and provide habitat and food for fish, crustaceans, and other sea creatures, including manatees. Florida has two million acres of sea grass beds, more than any other state. Yet development and pollution have wiped out large portions of them. In Tampa Bay, for instance, about half of the sea grass beds disappeared between 1950 and 1982.

What was left often wound up being chewed up by boats. Boaters who misread their charts or guessed wrong on the depth of the water they were in frequently ran aground in sea grass beds. Then their propellers would grind up the sea grass leaves and stems and rip out the roots, leaving deep trenches in the bottom. Some species of sea grass may take up to a decade to grow back. Without sea grass to provide food and shelter, the fish and shrimp disappear—as well as the manatees, of course.

Scientists at the state's marine science lab in St. Petersburg spent three years in the early 1990s surveying Florida's sea grass beds. They found that more than sixty-three thousand acres had seen moderate to severe scarring from boat propellers. The counties with the worst scarring were Monroe, Lee, Miami-Dade, Pinellas, and Charlotte.

"Nearly all the shallow seagrass beds in Florida show damage caused by boat propellers," two of the scientists wrote in 1994.

After that study came out, one of the state's lawyers, Ross Burnaman, wrote a memo to his bosses at the state wildlife agency suggesting a way to protect sea grasses. He said that anytime the Florida Marine Patrol caught someone damaging sea grass beds, the officers could hand out tickets for careless boating. Burnaman's memo was ignored.

Lawyers and scientists weren't the only ones who noticed how destructive ignorant boaters could be. Dave Barry, the *Miami Herald*'s Pulitzer-winning humor columnist, wrote once that boaters were "one of the most dangerous forces in all of nature."

"I used to do some recreational motor-boating," Barry explained, "and I can tell you for a fact that there are recreational boaters out there whose nautical alertness is such that they would not immediately notice if they drove their boats into a shopping center food court."

Drivers of cars, trucks, and motorcycles must pass a licensing test in Florida. So must airplane pilots, barbers, and cosmetologists. Not recreational boaters, though, even though most of the boaters involved in accidents had never taken a single boating education course.

"Most people on the river know two and a half things about a boat," Representative Dick Locke said during a 1989 public hearing. "They know how to buy it, they know how to crank it, and they half know how to stop it."

Locke, a former Florida Highway Patrol trooper from Citrus County, backed a bill to require boaters to pass a licensing test. The sponsor, Representative Bob Shelley, said he had heard lots of horror stories about reckless boaters.

"What a license does is assure everyone that you've had the appropriate education, that you know the rules and you're willing to abide by them," Shelley said.

Public hearings showed widespread public support for requiring licenses, yet the measure failed. Powerful lawmakers derided the idea of trying to put any limits on boating.

"This is why people go out on boats, to get away from this kind of government intrusion," said Representative Jim King, a portly Republican from Jacksonville who liked to boast that he had learned how to run a boat when he was just ten. "Why should government be sticking its nose in this?"

Every time someone tried to require licensing boaters, the proposal ran into strong opposition from the people who sell boats, the National Marine Manufacturers Association.

"Why license people if the purpose is to educate them?" lobbyist Wade Hopping asked in one newspaper interview. "The general consensus is that licensing is unnecessary. . . . It's just another way for the government to gather money."

Complicating the situation further was the rise of personal watercraft—Jet

Skis, WaveRunners, and Sea Doos. First introduced as a stand-up water bike by Kawasaki in 1974, these craft were redesigned in the early 1990s to allow the user to sit down, greatly boosting their popularity. They weighed five hundred pounds and could go up to sixty-five miles per hour.

Every tourist beach in Florida offered them for rent, and pretty much anyone with a driver's license and a credit card could take one for a ride. Because the craft were so nimble, riders could roar around spraying bathers, playing chicken, jumping the wakes of passing boats. Those moves were illegal, but that didn't seem to matter, even when law officers handed out citations.

"Tickets don't seem to be a deterrent," Sergeant Dan Clemons of the Miami Beach Marine Patrol told the *Miami Herald* in 1996. "We'll talk to people and the next day they're doing the same things."

As a result, while personal watercraft made up less than 7 percent of all watercraft in Florida in the mid-1990s, they were involved in more than a third of all boating accidents. In 1995 the number of personal watercraft crashes statewide topped five hundred. One in particular became notorious.

On the afternoon of Sunday, September 25, 1995, a concessionaire near the Delano Hotel on Miami Beach rented a Yamaha WaveRunner to a Howard University law student named Howard Clark, age twenty-nine. Clark, a hardworking student, was a standout ballplayer with the university team, even pitching a no-hitter.

Clark and another Howard student, twenty-two-year-old Tisha Greene, had traveled to Miami for a quick getaway with friends. The couple climbed aboard the WaveRunner and zoomed off into Biscayne Bay—the same body of water where Fred Morse and Kirk Munroe used to enjoy a leisurely sailboat race a century earlier.

Clark and Greene zigzagged across the water, jumping the wakes of passing boats. Around 4 p.m., about a mile offshore, the WaveRunner got too close to a twin-engine Intrepid that was traveling less than twenty miles per hour. The WaveRunner smacked into the front end of the thirty-three-foot Intrepid.

The collision knocked Clark unconscious. He slid under the boat and into the boat's propellers, which sliced him up the way they would a manatee, cutting his arms, chest, and neck. The crash tossed Greene in the opposite direction, with head injuries.

This collision would have been just one of the seventy-eight boating fatalities in Florida that year—the most in the nation—except for one thing. The boat that Clark hit just happened to belong to an international singing star named Gloria Estefan.

In the 1980s, when, as the Fort Lauderdale newspaper once put it, "Miami burst from its subtropical doldrums to become the hippest, most colorful city in America," Estefan skyrocketed to stardom as a result. "If the script came from the creators of *Miami Vice*," the paper noted, "its soundtrack was sung by Gloria Estefan."

Born in Havana, Estefan became a star as the lead singer of a group called the Miami Sound Machine. They scored a string of top-ten hits in the 1980s— "Rhythm Is Gonna Get You," "Bad Boys"—infectious dance tunes suited to the shallow, party-hearty times. One of their songs, "Conga," "became the unofficial anthem of late-night, hip-shaking, cross-cultural Miami," the *Herald* reported.

On this ill-fated day, Estefan and her husband, record producer Emilio Estefan, were taking their boat out for the first time ever. They were celebrating the release of a new album.

The crash shook them badly, but Gloria Estefan pulled out her cell phone and dialed 911 while her husband leaped in to aid Clark.

"I was worried about barracudas and sharks," Emilio Estefan later told *People* magazine. "There was blood all over the place, and I'm thinking my legs are going to be eaten in front of my wife."

With help from the injured Greene, Emilio Estefan loaded Clark onto another WaveRunner and dragged him to shore. But it was too late. The law student was dead.

The crash upset Estefan so much that she decided to do something about it. Five months later she traveled to Tallahassee to testify to the Senate Natural Resources Committee about why the state should require all boaters to take a licensing exam.

"We simply need the regulation that everyone who's going to drive a motor vehicle on the water should have the same training as someone who drives a motor vehicle on the road," she told the senators. "I'm speaking from the heart, really. It's very simple."

Not all the senators recognized the star. One, upon being told that Estefan was a singer, invited her to come sing the "Star-Spangled Banner" at his hometown's Special Olympics. Actually, Estefan replied, she had a prior engagement: singing the "Star-Spangled Banner" at the 1996 Summer Olympics in Atlanta.

When she talked to members of the House, Representative King, not taking her seriously, asked her to sing something. Estefan coolly replied, "I will sing you a song when you pass that bill."

Perhaps the biggest hurdle Estefan faced sat at the head of the Senate Natural Resources Committee table. Rick Dantzler, whose father had been mayor of Winter Haven, chaired the Senate Natural Resources Committee. He didn't see any need for the government to license boaters. At nineteen, Dantzler had sold water skis to tourists visiting Cypress Gardens, and he grew up to marry into the family that owned the amusement park, headed by his father-in-law, champion water-skier Dick Pope Jr. Dantzler's parents had taught him about boating safety. He believed that was all the instruction and licensing anyone needed.

"To me boating is like the last vestige of freedom," he explained years later. Requiring a license seemed like "too much government regulation."

Dantzler acknowledged that boating could be risky. His own brother had been killed in a boating accident just the year before Estefan's crash. But his brother had been killed during a nighttime boat ride because he hit a dock he couldn't see. No amount of government regulation could have prevented that, he insisted.

Dantzler had repeatedly bottled up boater licensing bills in his committee so they didn't get voted on by the full Senate. He only allowed Estefan to testify at the request of the Senate president. Otherwise he would not have even held any hearings.

However, Dantzler at last let a licensing bill escape his committee, and it passed both houses. It passed because it was so weak no one objected to it.

The new law required boaters who were sixteen or under to take a boating-safety course before operating any vessels of ten horsepower or more. After 2001, the rule would broaden to apply to anyone age twenty-one or younger. Violators would pay fifty dollars. Stories about the bill's passage noted that even this weak attempt at regulation had passed only because of Estefan's testimony.

They also noted that, when Governor Chiles signed it into law, Estefan—as she had promised during the committee meeting—stepped up to Representative King and sang a song in his ear. The song, selected with no sense of the irony for how Clark died, was a ballad she had recorded in 1989 called "Cuts Both Ways."

The one point about the new law that no one appeared to notice is that it had nothing to do with what happened to the twenty-nine-year-old Clark. Even if this new law had been in effect the year before, he would still be dead.

•

With the number of boats increasing, and the legislature resistant to requiring that boaters know anything about their craft, is it any wonder that law enforcement officers felt outnumbered and unappreciated?

The Florida Marine Patrol, commonly known as the "grouper troopers," could field just six hundred officers on its best days when it was part of the Department of Environmental Protection (DEP). Then, in 1999, the marine patrol moved over to the new Florida Fish and Wildlife Conservation Commission, joining the game wardens from Earle Frye's old agency to form a single group of officers focused on wildlife protection.

But during the merger the marine patrol lost thirty-one investigators who stayed at the DEP to do pollution investigations.

The state routinely spent twenty thousand dollars apiece training new wildlife officers, putting them through six months of training at a special academy in Quincy, just north of Tallahassee. They had to be ready not only to chase down speeding boaters but also to arrest poachers, catch litterbugs dumping junk in state wildlife areas, and ticket fishermen who kept the little ones they should have thrown back. Sometimes the officers would get sprayed by skunks or chomped on by alligators.

Many of those highly trained officers quit after a few years, leaving for a more routine but better-paying position with a city police department or county sheriff. They left because the legislature abolished annual "step" pay increases for the game wardens in 1990, eliminating any economic incentive for the officers to stay. Thanks to the legislature, an officer with five years of experience made the same as a rookie fresh out of the academy. One ten-year veteran who left for the U.S. Customs Service wrote on his exit survey, "Pay your people or they will leave."

So even as the number of boaters boomed, the number of officers enforcing the law dwindled. In 2002, for instance, the Fort Myers wildlife commission office could put just nineteen officers on patrol, three fewer than 1990. Between 1990 and 1997, Miami-Dade County and Broward County each lost six officers.

Federal officers faced more severe constraints. When they tried, they could be extremely effective. During a five-week period from July to September 1997, for instance, the U.S. Fish and Wildlife Service deployed fifty-three employees to patrol the Banana and Indian rivers. They handed out tickets to 313 boaters, 90 percent of them Florida residents. The tickets yielded more than thirty thousand dollars in fines—but the operation cost fifty thousand.

Usually, the federal wildlife agency couldn't spare anyone to enforce manatee laws at all. In 1991, for instance, a funding crisis crippled the agency's entire southern region. For six months there was no money for investigators to do anything that might require them to leave their desks.

"Agent morale is as bad as I've seen it," said one official in the regional office in Atlanta.

Back in the 1970s, when Congress passed most of the new environmental laws, the wildlife service's Division of Law Enforcement could field 220 agents. But between 1977 and 1990, while the Fish and Wildlife Service staff increased by 78 percent, the number of agents in the Division of Law Enforcement decreased by 9 percent—even as its caseload grew tenfold.

Many agents believed their declining fortunes resulted from their unfortunate habit of arresting prominent people. One agent, assigned to patrol the eastern shore of Chesapeake Bay, repeatedly nabbed hunting law violators who turned out to be congressmen.

Regardless of the reason, the result of the declining number of agents was obvious. The General Accounting Office, the investigative arm of Congress, issued a report that said "staffing and funding shortfalls have caused [Fish and Wildlife Service] regions to selectively enforce wildlife legislation."

"When I first came to Miami, I managed to stay on top of people poaching sea turtle eggs," a special agent named Terry English told a magazine reporter in 1993. "But since 1984, I haven't been able to spare a moment to even think about turtles, much less go after poachers."

At one point, English said, he got a report that a man had tied a rope to a manatee and was swimming behind it, a clear case of illegal harassment. Although English was just fifteen minutes away, he could not get official permission to work the case. Worse, he had no boat available.

English, who had thick white hair and a bushy beard, was one of just three agents assigned to cover South Florida, the Virgin Islands, and Puerto Rico in the mid-1990s. They spent most of their time working cases in Miami because Magic City was as much a hotbed for wildlife smuggling as it was for the drug trade.

Every year, twelve thousand legitimate shipments of wildlife or wildlife products came through Miami. Nobody knew the number of illegal shipments, but the Fish and Wildlife Service ranked Miami just behind New York and Los Angeles as a conduit for smuggled wildlife.

Miami's federal agents found marmosets hidden under hats, Cuban parrot chicks tucked in a woman's bra (one per cup), and forty-five red-footed tortoises stuffed in a man's parachute pants. They caught smugglers with monkey skulls used in Santeria rituals and boa constrictors stuffed with cocaine.

Lots of wildlife smugglers are amateurs. In South Florida, the lure of easy money has snared doctors, graduate students, even a missionary who tried financing his ministry in Peru by sneaking snakes into Miami. But there are plenty of professionals too—people in the legitimate wildlife trade who have slipped across the line. Take the notorious 1993 case of *U.S. v. Bernal.*

The case started a world away with the seizure of six baby orangutans from a smuggler in Thailand. That led to the arrest of a Miami animal dealer who had brokered the illegal shipment. To avoid prison, the dealer agreed to cooperate with federal agents. When someone contacted him about buying a gorilla, he helped the agents set up a sting.

The target: Victor Bernal, director of the agency in charge of zoos and parks in one of Mexico's states. The gorilla at Bernal's zoo had died, and the state governor wanted a replacement.

Bernal traveled to Miami to see what the dealer had to offer. The dealer introduced him to an underworld figure named "Señor Blanco"—actually Fish and Wildlife Service agent Jorge Picon. "Señor Blanco" took Bernal to see primates at the Miami Metrozoo, spinning a story about how they were his merchandise and that he had bribed the zoo employees to hold them for him. (Metrozoo officials were in on the sting.)

Bernal flew home and got approval from Mexican officials to spend ninety-two thousand dollars on the deal. He said he would return to Miami to collect his ape. To seal the deal, Picon needed a real gorilla, or a reasonable facsimile. He recruited Terry English for the ultimate undercover assignment, playing the gorilla.

"I don't know where Jorge got the suit," English said. "It was probably one of the cheapest gorilla suits you can imagine. . . . We were counting on the fact it was going to be dark."

The agents borrowed a DC-3 from Customs and parked it at the Opa-Locka Airport, north of Miami. They borrowed a large Metrozoo cage and put the costumed agent inside, along with some real gorilla dung so he would at least smell authentic.

When Bernal climbed into the plane to check the merchandise "he stood looking through the little front door of the cage," English said. "I felt like he was getting too close . . . so I took my forearm and I hit the door as hard as I could. . . . He jumped back and made the statement, 'Boy, that's a big one!'"

When the pilot—also a federal wildlife agent—told Bernal he was under arrest, English figured he could step out of character and shed his hot costume.

"I was about to sweat to death," English said. "I was still a heavy smoker and I was dying for a cigarette. So I opened the door of the crate."

Hearing the cage door creak, Bernal turned around and saw the "gorilla" step out. He got so scared he tried to jump out of the parked plane.

"He thought that gorilla was going to kill him," English said. The two agents grabbed Bernal and handcuffed him. Then English pulled off his mask, and "he freaked out again."

The Bernal case made headlines around the country, many of them involving bad gorilla puns. But when the case went to trial, Bernal got just seventy days in jail.

While the federal agents stayed busy busting gorilla buyers, and the state officers handed out warnings and the occasional ticket, the number of manatee deaths continued climbing.

Some deaths, like Ragtail's, had a bigger public impact than others. For instance, in March 1991 a state park ranger named Wayne Hartley found a twelve-hundred-pound carcass in the Norris Dead River in Volusia County—near Rick Rawlins's fish camp, in other words.

From the marks on the carcass, Hartley immediately recognized it. It was Sweetgums, a well-known member of the seven hundred or so manatees that frequent Blue Spring State Park, where Hartley could call most of the manatees by name. A necropsy determined that a boat propeller had severed the manatee's spine in two places.

The ten-foot-long manatee, just like Ragtail, was among the Save the Manatee Club's oldest and most popular adopted manatees. Sweetgums had been adopted by the third grade class at Conway Elementary in Orlando. When the children heard what had happened, they absorbed the news with what the *Orlando Sentinel* described as a "combination of sadness and anger."

"I would like to know who did this," said one eight-year-old girl. "I loved Sweetgums."

She would never get the answer. While the state and federal officers who were supposed to enforce manatee protection laws did a spotty job of handing out tickets, they did an even poorer job of tracking down killers. Every now and then, as with Ragtail, they had a witness to the crime. But generally they had no crime scene, no fingerprints, no DNA, no clues to point to the identity of the boater responsible.

Usually state and federal wildlife officers didn't even bother to investigate manatee deaths, figuring it was pointless. When Dan Odell and his University of Miami students were examining manatee carcasses in the mid- to late 1970s, they would frequently pass along information that they thought could lead to charges. Not once did they ever hear back from an investigator, Odell said, "not even when a couple of times we found bullets in the animal."

Even when the killer's identity seemed fairly obvious, no prosecution resulted. In May 1990, for instance, as a tugboat captain cruised toward the Explosives Handling Wharf at the Kings Bay Naval Submarine Base in southern Georgia, the tug hit something big enough to make the vessel shudder and leave a pool of blood on the water's surface.

Some two hundred miles to the south, in Gainesville, a U.S. Fish and Wildlife researcher named Jim Reid discovered that the signal from a satellite tracking tag he had put on a pregnant manatee named Mary had fallen silent. It didn't take long for biologists to connect the two events.

Soon Reid and his colleagues would discover that two other manatees had been killed by either the base's Trident submarines or by tugs working around the base. But no one was charged with killing the three manatees.

Occasionally, state or federal officers might nab someone for harassment, but the evidence had to be strong. In 2008, for instance, they nailed two men, ages nineteen and twenty, who had filmed themselves hooking a manatee on a fishing line while they giggled about it. Then the pair posted the video on a MySpace page on the Internet, effectively handing federal prosecutors an airtight case. One got thirty days in jail, the other fifteen.

But when it came to prosecuting anyone for actually killing a manatee, for slicing up Ragtail or filleting Sweetgums, the government's track record was abysmal. In the thirty years after the passage of the Endangered Species Act and the Marine Mammal Protection Act, federal officials could point to just one case.

And they would not have made that case if a boat captain had not been hungry.

•

Through the first half of the twentieth century, some of the villages that dot Florida's coastline staked their economies on whatever their fishing boats could haul in.

In the Panhandle there was Destin, which billed itself as "the world's luckiest fishing village." Along the state's western Gulf Coast, places like Cortez and Tarpon Springs eked out a living from the sea. On the Atlantic coast there was Port Salerno, near Fort Pierce.

But waterfront land proved more valuable than any amount of fish, and condos and subdivisions soon supplanted the working wharves and fish houses. Where the fishing village motif remained, it was often just a facade for the tourists, a place to buy varnished seashells, tacky T-shirts, and postcards celebrating the Gospel of the Sand Dollar.

Still, through the 1980s, Port Salerno clung to its fishing village roots. A dozen boats might head out each afternoon to spend all night setting nets in international waters three miles offshore, hauling them in just before sunrise, and then returning to port to sell their catch. From November to March they would set gill nets for Spanish mackerel or bluefish. From April to September they would set drift nets to catch king mackerel. Other fishermen were less ambitious, working along the coast to catch whatever they could sell to the local fish houses.

In 1984, the Port Salerno fishing fleet included a boat named the *Dragon*. Its captain, Jimmy Malmsten, twenty-seven, was a husky man with a deep tan and sun-bleached hair. He had grown up in Port Salerno amid abject poverty. For the Malmstens, getting an education ranked low on the list of priorities. A minister who had known the family for a decade described Malmsten as having "a low IQ," and said he might even be mildly retarded.

But Malmsten had a reputation as a hard worker. The town's biggest fish dealer called him "the hardest working fisherman I have working for me."

Malmsten married a woman named Judy who already had three children. They soon had a fourth. Through his fishing, he got the family off the state's welfare rolls and even provided them with a home.

The *Dragon*'s crew consisted of three men: Paul Michael Mispel, thirty; Michael D. Lira, nineteen; and James M. Hughes, thirty. They were rough men, especially Hughes, who had spent five years in prison for grand theft.

About 11 a.m. on May 16, 1984, two Florida Marine Patrol officers named

Greg Moore and Ken Atkins stopped the *Dragon* in the St. Lucie River near Martin Memorial Hospital. The officers wanted to check for fishing violations. Malmsten had already been caught three times violating the rules on snook fishing.

But then the officers noticed a bundle floating about ten feet off the stern. Drug smugglers fleeing the law sometimes dropped their load in the water, leading to jokes that fishermen who hauled in floating bales of marijuana had caught "square grouper." Could this bundle be a smuggler's lost booty?

Because they hadn't found any violations aboard the *Dragon*, officers Moore and Atkins let Malmsten and his crew go while they retrieved the bundle. What they found inside made them race back and stop the *Dragon* a second time.

The bundle contained meat. The officers suspected it must be either manatee or turtle. Malmsten said he didn't know anything about the bundle. He even let the officers search the boat. Moore took a quick look around, then let the *Dragon* proceed to its destination, the C&W Fish Company in Port Salerno.

When the officers showed the bundle's contents to some other fishermen, they learned that the mystery meat was indeed manatee. So the grouper troopers zoomed over to the C&W fish house and questioned Malmsten again.

This time he refused to talk to them. They searched the *Dragon* a second time, this time more thoroughly, and seized two knives as evidence.

The next day, Officer Moore went at Malmsten again, and this time the captain opened up. According to Moore, during this interview Malmsten admitted that the bundle was his. He said he had found the manatee already dead and so he and the crew had butchered it, intending to eat it. No sense wasting the free meat, right?

However, before questioning Malmsten, Moore had failed to read him the *Miranda* warning about his rights, something every investigator is supposed to do before questioning a suspect. That meant what he said would probably not be admissible as evidence.

Officers Moore and Atkins suspected the *Dragon* had actually run over the manatee and killed it, but they couldn't prove it. So on May 18, Moore and two other wildlife officers went to C&W one more time to question Malmsten. They took him to a park where they could talk to him in relative quiet. This time they not only read him his rights, they even tape-recorded the interrogation.

Malmsten admitted to butchering the manatee, but once again insisted he had nothing to do with killing it. Instead, he said the crew had found it floating in the water, in an area just east of the hospital called the "Hospital Flats."

The next day, state and federal officers—one of them the gray-bearded Terry English—seized the *Dragon*. It was evidence, they said. They took the captain to the Stuart Police Department for another tape-recorded interview.

This time, he told them the whole story.

Malmsten said he and his crew had been fishing on the Hospital Flats about 4 a.m. when they ran over a five-foot-long manatee calf. Initially the captain thought they had hit a log. But then he spotted the calf and its mother, tangled in their nets. The mother managed to work free of the tangle, but not the wounded calf.

"When I looked, I seen what it was," Malmsten said later, telling the story in court. "It was bleeding. . . . It looked to me like it was dead. I heard it was good eating. I just took a couple chunks out of it."

English asked him why he didn't try to get the wounded calf some help. Malmsten said he was too scared.

Officer Moore charged all four men under state law with killing a manatee, as well as illegal possession of its carcass. But prosecutors soon dropped the charges against the teenage Lira. Then Mispel cut a deal where he paid four hundred dollars to the Save the Manatee Committee (still a quasi-state agency at that point), and the prosecutor dismissed his charges too.

In July 1984, Malmsten and Hughes pleaded no contest to one charge, illegal possession of manatee parts, and a judge fined them five hundred dollars. Headlines about the size of the fines prompted angry phone calls to the U.S. Fish and Wildlife Service. As a result, Terry English got the green light to build a federal case.

"The outcry we heard showed the public is not going to sit back while these people are out killing an endangered species," the agent said. He called manatees "one of the easiest species on earth to kill." He said his agency received many reports of manatee deaths, "but proving the charges is another matter."

In August 1984, federal prosecutors charged Malmsten, Mispel, Lira, and Hughes with taking a manatee and possessing manatee parts. Each was a misdemeanor violation of the Endangered Species Act, carrying a maximum sentence of a year in prison and a fine of thirty thousand dollars. (For some reason, no one charged them with violating the Marine Mammal Protection Act.)

Three of the *Dragon*'s crew appeared in federal court in Fort Lauderdale for their arraignment, but not Hughes. The ex-con fled. The magistrate put out a warrant for his arrest that remains on the books, even though he later went back to state prison for a variety of violent crimes.

If Hughes had not fled, he might have gotten off even more lightly than he did before. Just as in state court, prosecutors dropped the charges against Mispel and Lira. Only Malmsten, the captain, wound up on the hot seat. After all, he was the one in charge. He was the one on tape. He was the one who admitted killing the manatee and cutting it up.

Even then, Malmsten's public defender worked out a deal that would spare him from jail time. In exchange for a guilty plea to the charge of possessing manatee meat, he would be fined $750 and put on probation for a year. After all, his public defender argued, the manatee's death was an "isolated" incident.

When it came time for a judge to sentence Malmsten on July 31, 1985, though, the deal fell apart.

U.S. Magistrate Ann Vitunac took note of Malmsten's three prior snook violations. She questioned the captain at length about them. It seemed to her that, rather than an isolated violation, Malmsten's manatee crime fit a pattern of ignoring the laws protecting marine species. Vitunac rejected the plea bargain and instead sentenced Malmsten to pay the $750 fine he expected, but also to serve a year in a federal jail, followed by a year of probation. She suspended half the jail sentence—but that meant he would still spend six months behind bars. Upon the conclusion of the sentencing hearing, Malmsten was immediately taken into custody and shipped off to a federal jail in Miami.

As often happens with a criminal case, the sentence took a toll on the perpetrator's family. Malmsten's wife, then twenty-eight, had never worked before, spending all her time taking care of their four children, ages six to thirteen. She found a job in a flower nursery for $3.35 an hour, but that was hardly enough to feed the family.

"My husband being in prison causes a lot of hardship for me and my children," Judy Malmsten later wrote to the judge. She said she couldn't even take the kids to visit their father because she couldn't afford gas for her car.

"Other kids make fun of my kids because their dad is in prison," she wrote. "So my kids and I are the ones who are really being punished."

Malmsten's attorney tried to get Judge Vitunac to reduce the sentence, but she refused. So the captain served his six months, and when he got out he paid off his fine by sending in sixty-five dollars a month from what he earned fishing.

The *Miami Herald*'s editorial page praised Vitunac for taking such a hard line against Malmsten.

"There is no point to any law unless it is taken seriously," the *Herald*'s editorial board wrote. "Scientists believe that there are only 1,000 manatees left in Florida. . . . No excuse can be a good excuse for killing off the last few remnants of Florida's wildlife heritage. By demanding a jail sentence for Jimmy Malmsten, Judge Vitunac rightly sent that clear message."

However, bringing that message home would require jailing more than one poor fisherman who had foolishly kept the meat from an endangered species he had accidentally killed. It would require the jailing of dozens of boaters for zooming through manatee zones and slaughtering sea cows—and that just wasn't going to happen.

In fact, scores of them were about to get state permission to ignore the law whenever they chose.

•

Four years after Jimmy Malmsten went to jail, Governor Bob Martinez and his cabinet ordered the thirteen coastal counties to impose slow-speed zones to protect manatees. But a group called Organized Fishermen of Florida objected that the new zones would ruin commercial fishermen who were putting out nets to catch mullet.

"They argued that the nets had to be set at speed," said J. Kipp Frohlich, who took charge of the state's Bureau of Protected Species Management when Pat Rose left in 1996. "To set several hundred yards of net around a school of mullet, they needed to do it quickly."

State officials agreed to let the mullet fishermen be exempt from the new rules—in other words, to allow them to go fast in areas where other boaters had to slow down.

Then the state's fishing guides contended that they deserved to be exempt too, Frohlich said. State officials approved adding them to the list of people who could ignore the speed zone rules.

When Florida's voters approved a ban on gill nets in 1996, that killed the mullet fishing industry far more effectively than any manatee speed zones would have. That meant most of the people getting exemptions were fishing guides.

To get their exemption, the guides had to attest that obeying the speed zone rules would cost them 25 percent of their income, but state officials didn't ask for proof. Between July 1998 and June 2000, the state issued 157 exemptions. It didn't turn down a single request.

Although the exempt guides were supposed to keep their speed below twenty miles per hour, a veteran Cocoa flats guide named Tony Perez told a reporter that nobody bothered with slowing down.

"If you sit in a boat at Banana Creek," he said, "I guarantee all those guys will be going full speed through there."

Not until 1999, when the Save the Manatee Club protested an exemption given to a Collier County airboat operator, did state officials reconsider the whole exemption program.

A poorly enforced law is obeyed only when it's convenient to do so—and then only by those who agree with it. After Martinez and the cabinet ordered the new speed zone rules, plenty of boaters who were angry about being told to slow down simply ignored the rules, counting on lax enforcement.

After all, the boaters greatly outnumbered the men and women enforcing the law. In 1996, for instance, thirty-six officers patrolled the Dade and Broward waterways that Fred Morse and Joe Moore once cruised around, and they had to keep tabs on more than ninety-two thousand boats.

"What I do is cheat," a bass fisherman plying his trade on the St. Johns River told a reporter. "I'm being honest. . . . Any fisherman who tells you he's going [the speed limit] from one hole to the next, he's lying. The only thing you can do to get to your spot is to go like hell."

Others actually tried to get caught. They wanted a ticket so they could challenge the speed zones in court.

Leading the charge, as usual, was Rick Rawlins, the Volusia fish-camp owner. In 1992 he managed to get not one but two speeding tickets. At trial, he persuaded a county judge to toss them both out on the grounds that the speed zone rules were too vague.

Two months later, in January 1993, another Volusia County judge tossed out a ticket given to another boater, Michael Paul Lindstrom. The judge ruled that the speed zones violated the provision in the Manatee Sanctuary Act that said the state should not "unduly interfere with the rights of fishermen, boaters, and water skiers."

State officials persuaded an appeals court to overturn those decisions. So in 1995, Rawlins tried again, once again persuading a Volusia County judge to toss out his ticket. This time the judge ruled that the state had failed to provide sufficient scientific data to justify ordering boaters to slow down. He also raised questions about how to define "slow" boat speeds, and whether there should be fast lanes for some boats through the slow-speed zones. Once again, the appeals court overturned the ruling.

Rawlins tried one more time, in 1996, racking up yet another speeding ticket, this time in Lake County. But after a trial, Lake County Judge Donna Miller found him guilty. She said Rawlins's own testimony convicted him.

"He admitted there was a sign that said, 'Slow,' and he admitted he wasn't going slowly, and therefore he was in violation," Judge Miller said.

Rawlins contended that losing in court proved his point just as well as a win would have: "I believe this illustrates exactly how confusing, contradictory, and controversial these manatee speed rules are."

While Rawlins battled on largely alone, boaters in Lee County got help from a major developer called Bonita Bay Properties. The developer had built a marina with 126 wet slips and 350 dry slips on the Imperial River, which flows into Estero Bay. The marina was such a boon to the waterfront development that the developer was willing to operate it at a loss for ten years.

But then the DEP proposed new regulations to slow down boats in that area. A pair of boaters joined Bonita Bay in challenging the new rules in 1995. The marina's manager, Jim Hohnstein, timed his run from the marina through the Imperial River and southern Estero Bay to the Gulf of Mexico. Without the new rules, the trip took eighteen minutes, he testified. If he followed the new regulations, he said, the trip would take forty minutes.

By adding twenty-two minutes to the trip, Bonita Bay's attorneys argued, the new rules would cripple the demand for the developer's boat slips. That would upset the company's calculations about the marina's financial future, and put it at a disadvantage when competing against other marinas, they said. Bonita Bay's lawyers calculated the loss from that additional twenty-two minutes would amount to seventy thousand dollars a year.

The judge who heard the case for the Florida Division of Administrative Hearings, Linda Rigot, agreed with Bonita Bay, noting that the DEP had failed to properly calculate the economic impact of the rules. She also criticized the fluctuating definitions and standards the DEP had used in drawing up the rules. For instance, the judge noted, the top speed in the Lee County rules was twenty-five miles per hour, while in other counties the top speeds went up to thirty-five.

"The department has no scientific basis or formula for establishing the top speeds allowed," Rigot wrote. Then the judge nailed the whole problem in a single sentence: "The disparity in speeds among counties is the result of political compromise."

Rather than appeal, the DEP rewrote the rules. Once again Bonita Bay joined with boaters, in this case the Southwest Florida Marine Trades Association, to challenge them.

By then, Lee County had tied with Brevard County over on the east coast for the most boat-related manatee deaths in the state in 1998—nine for each of the counties, out of sixty-six statewide. But Marine Trades Association president Ken Stead contended that wasn't a good reason to impose the new regulations. Instead, he called for "increased enforcement."

Finally, though, the developers and boaters worked out a settlement with the DEP to impose some new regulations.

The Bonita Bay case pointed to the strong interest that the state's developers had taken in the push for boat-speed regulation. But while the state's regulators battled county by county to slow down boats, nothing slowed down the conversion of manatee habitat into canal-lined subdivisions, marinas, and waterfront condominiums.

Under a law called the Rivers and Harbors Act, passed in 1899, the U.S. Army Corps of Engineers issues permits for all dredge-and-fill work that affects the nation's waterways. For decades the only question the Corps cared about was whether the project would harm navigation.

Then, in 1967, the colonel in charge of all the Corps permitting in Florida, a World War II veteran named Robert Tabb, upended the Corps' permitting tradition. He denied a pair of developers a permit for filling in eleven acres of Boca Ciega Bay to expand their St. Petersburg–area mobile home park. Colonel Tabb turned the permit down because the project would have harmed the bay's ecology, and thus would not be in the public interest.

The developers battled that case all the way to the U.S. Supreme Court and lost, establishing Tabb's "public interest" test as a standard for all subsequent permits issued by the Corps.

In 1972, Congress added to the Corps' authority by passing what became known as the Clean Water Act. Under the new law, no one was supposed to dump fill in a wetland without a Corps permit.

Three years later, the colonel then in charge of Florida, a Vietnam veteran named Don Wisdom, persuaded his superiors to reject a Clean Water Act permit for a politically influential developer on Marco Island. The reason: the housing the developers proposed did not have to be built amid filled-in coastal mangroves, and anything that did not need to be built in a wetland should probably be built elsewhere.

Once again the developer fought the permit denial all the way to the Supreme Court and lost. The Marco Island case established a precedent that housing was not water-dependent, and developers of subdivision projects should look to dry land first before asking the Corps for a permit to build in wetlands.

From 1975 to 1981, the Florida division of the Corps led the nation in rejecting permits to build in wetlands, usually because the permits flunked the tests established by Colonel Wisdom and Colonel Tabb. But when Ronald Reagan moved into the White House, the civilians he picked to lead the Corps pushed the agency to treat its permits like a product and its applicants like customers. Reagan's top civilian Corps overseer even made a trip to Florida to tell Corps regulators to stop saying no to so many permits.

As a result, permit denials virtually dried up. Between 1992 and 2001 the Corps denied only nine dock-building permits in Florida, approving thousands more. Now the entire permitting process concerned finding a way to say yes. When it came to manatees, that usually meant the permits came with conditions requiring the developers to post speed limit signs.

However, in 1990, the U.S. Fish and Wildlife Service discovered that of twenty-seven recently built Florida marinas, only nine complied with their Corps permit requirements. In a letter, the service's David Ferrell told the Corps that "our study indicates a high level of non-compliance. . . . We recommend that you take appropriate enforcement action."

In response, Corps officials said they simply didn't have the manpower to go back and check on whether developers had been too lazy to post the required signs. They were too busy issuing new permits to enforce the old ones.

Over the next decade, the Corps approved more than two hundred permits for waterfront development that wiped out manatee habitat around Florida's coast. Every time a development destroyed several acres of sea grass beds, that meant the manatees living in that waterway would have to find a new place to feed—or if they stayed, they would have to dodge more boat traffic.

From 1992 on, the Save the Manatee Club, now independent of the state, repeatedly went to court to stop or at least alter the worst of the developments.

"We were taking on these development projects piecemeal and we were succeeding, but it was getting very tiring," the club's biologist, Patti Thompson, said.

Meanwhile, though, the number of manatees dying continued to rise.

"We had all these boat speed zones in place and mortality escalated," Thompson said. "It was a big frustration for us. . . . Compliance was abysmal, and there was nobody out there to enforce compliance."

By the end of the 1990s, a vast machine had been put into place designed to protect the manatees, with "some 80 professionals working on research, management, education, legal protection, and advocacy," Woodie Hartman wrote in his unpublished study for Buddy Powell. "Annual expenditures for manatee recovery are now approaching $10-million."

Yet, despite all that, Hartman wrote, "a growing sense of resignation is pervading the manatee conservation community as it becomes harder to deny that the status of sirenians in the United States today is hardly less precarious than when regulatory maneuvering on their behalf began almost 30 years ago." Its habitat continued to dwindle, and its mortality rate continued to rise, Hartman noted.

Despite attaining its hard-won independence, despite the evidence that the big manatee protection machine simply wasn't working, the Save the Manatee Club board for the most part continued backing the state on all its regulations.

"We were running on automatic pilot for quite some time," Thompson said.

She could see it was time for a change—starting with the Save the Manatee Club's own board.

# Pegasus Rising

AS PATTI THOMPSON TRAVELED the state visiting counties where new speed zones were being considered, she chatted up the local officials. Sometimes she encountered hostility, but not always.

At Collier County's environmental services department, she ran across a feisty little man with muttonchop whiskers. His high-pitched voice still carried the backwoods twang of his native Carrabelle, a small fishing village in the Panhandle.

E. F. "Fran" Stallings sounded like a redneck and swore like a sailor. But he had earned a Ph.D. in education and once taught at Florida State University. Over the years he had come to think of himself as an independent environmental activist, beholden to no one single organization, carving out his own path financed by various foundation grants. He joked that he was like the freelance assassin Paladin from the old TV show, whose motto was, "Have gun, will travel."

Stallings's own motto was: "Leave no stone unturned, no ass unkicked, and God help Satan if he gets in the way."

With his independent streak, Stallings frequently ruffled the feathers of other environmental activists by refusing to compromise. Cutting a good deal could boost an environmental group's power and visibility. It could even look like success.

But Stallings had no allegiance to an organization, so he seldom saw any reason to make a deal, even if that angered his own allies. To him, taking a hard line was the only way to be sure he was taken seriously.

"I'm the kind of guy who believes in going balls to the wall if it's worth doing," he explained. "Nobody pays any attention to you unless you take them to court and show up with your attorney."

To Thompson, tired of the compromises she saw taking place on every front, Stallings's attitude seemed refreshing—and right.

"I immediately thought, 'This is a man who thinks like me,'" Thompson said. "I was impressed with his 'let's get 'em' approach."

Thompson and Stallings worked together drawing up a manatee protection plan for Collier County, but their labor came to naught. The county commissioners, a strongly pro-development group who disdained environmental protection as a plot by the United Nations, pulled the plug.

Stallings quit his county position. True to form, he subsequently filed an ethics complaint against one of his former bosses on the county commission, who ended up pleading no contest to charges he took a payoff from a developer. Stallings then opened the Florida Wildlife Federation's first branch office in southwest Florida.

Meanwhile, Thompson began lobbying Judith Vallee to put Stallings on the Save the Manatee Club board. Now that the governor no longer made the appointments, the club's own officials picked who their overseers would be. In 1995, when Stallings joined the board, Thompson rejoiced at his arrival, figuring she would see things start to change.

"It was helpful to start having people on the board who were *not* appointed by the governor, people who thought for themselves, and thought not enough was being done," Thompson said.

Stallings didn't think much of his fellow board members—or of the club's employees, either.

"It to me was a little bit too quiet," Stallings said. "They were activists, but I wouldn't characterize them as playing hardball."

Vallee kept the door to the club's office locked because the staff had once gotten a few death threats (the caller turned out to be a deluded Midwestern teenager). To Stallings, that became a symptom of what he called "a siege mentality" among the club's employees. Most were women, and he joked that hiding behind a locked door made them seem "like a bunch of cloistered nuns."

Stallings thought it made no sense to wait behind a locked door for an attack. He would rather take the fight to the enemy—and take no prisoners.

In April 1996, the assertive Stallings became co-chairman of the board with Jimmy Buffett. Buffett had become far too busy to actually attend board meetings, though. Not only was the Chief Parrothead selling records, he was also writing books and marketing a line of tropical wear and running a restaurant in Key West called Margaritaville and helping Democratic politicians like Bob Graham and Lawton Chiles get reelected.

That left Stallings in charge. He set to work revamping the board's membership and its strategy. He wanted "people who were interested in seeing a change," people who like him would not be afraid to go on the warpath.

They arrived on a winged horse.

•

Although Cynthia Frisch hailed from Marblehead, Massachusetts, a coastal town just north of Boston, her voice betrayed no trace of the famous Baaahstahn accent. That was probably for the best. A longtime devotee of meditation and yoga, she was prone to coining pseudo-koans like "We have a way of moving through nature that is contrary to nature." An accent would have made that sound silly.

Frisch lived for causes that might better the world. In early 1997 she was working on a project to help Amazonian Indians learn to make products that would not harm the rain forest. To become accustomed to a warmer climate, she moved from New York to Fort Lauderdale.

On a trip to see a potential supporter in Maryland, she stumbled across a conference of the Humane Society of the United States. There she met a man named Peter Bender. A New Hampshire resident, Bender sat on the Humane Society board. But more importantly, he was the executive director of a new organization called the Pegasus Foundation.

Pegasus billed itself as "A Strong Voice for All Creatures." Its symbol was the winged horse of Greek mythology which, as the foundation's Web site put it, "created a spring where its hoof touched the earth." Similarly, "the Pegasus Foundation taps the spring of hidden capacity in communities and organizations."

Actually, Pegasus did less tapping of springs and more priming the pump. The foundation picked a select few animal-welfare causes and sent them money—a total of $123,000 in 1997, another $230,000 in 1998, and $313,000 in 1999. The foundation's causes included a Navajo-run animal clinic in New Mexico, an orphan elephant project in Sri Lanka, and rain forest research in Paraguay.

Not long after Frisch's encounter with Bender, he called to offer her a job as the official Florida representative of Pegasus. Her first assignment: find out everything she could about manatees.

Frisch covered the phone with her hand, turned to a friend and said, "Manatees—big marine mammal, right?"

When she took her hand off the phone, Frisch accepted the job. At that point, she had never even seen a manatee. She also had never organized an environmental campaign.

That night, she spent hours on her computer, searching the Internet for everything she could find about manatees. What she learned appalled her: the scars, the rising death toll from boats.

Next she began making phone calls and quizzing various officials. When she asked a marine patrol captain why boaters couldn't just slow down, he told her that "the water is like the last frontier, people feel like it's their God-given right to be able to do as they please—the last place they feel unrestricted freedom—regardless of the consequences."

To Frisch it all seemed horribly cruel. "What right do we have to abuse this animal?" she said in an interview several years later. "And for recreational purposes, not for our survival?"

The manatee's future seemed particularly bleak at that moment. Bender had called Frisch just a few months after the end of the Red Tide epizootic. Questions about whether the manatee might go extinct had popped up in newspapers and magazines around the globe, many of them noting that "only" two thousand or so manatees remained. With a total of 415 dead by year's end, anyone with a calculator could see that nearly 20 percent of what was then believed to be the entire manatee population was now fertilizing the banana plants at the path lab.

Those dire Red Tide stories were the reason Bender had called Frisch. The Red Tide epizootic had caught the attention of Pegasus's founder, an animal lover named Barbara Birdsey, who, like Frisch, had recently moved to Florida.

Birdsey was a soft-spoken blond-haired woman from New England. Since she was three years old, Birdsey had lived in a classic Cape Cod beachfront home with a cedar-shingled facade and windows with blue shutters. Her parents had fished in Horseshoe Shoals and sailed with the Kennedys of nearby Hyannis Port.

Her father, a Navy veteran, started a car dealership after World War II.

But what he really enjoyed was tinkering with his various inventions, which turned out to be a lucrative hobby. He had "once flown biplanes, which somehow led him to invent some kind of widget that is now widely used in the manufacture of airplane engines," Birdsey wrote in a memoir. "I'm not sure what Dad's widget does, but I do know that it made him a lot of money." As a result, she wrote, she and her husband enjoyed "the financial independence to live our lives without worrying about where our next meal is coming from."

Birdsey's husband had known her since childhood, and they married as soon as he finished a stint in the Coast Guard. He ran a boat-building shop on Main Street in West Barnstable, Massachusetts. They were the kind of couple who would attend a glamorous benefit wearing what the *Boston Globe* described as "white period summer clothes" and driving "his pristine, lemon-yellow 1930 Willys Whippet, its mocha-colored cloth top down and its rumble seat open to the summer sky."

With that kind of money, Birdsey could have spent all her time partying with the jet-set crowd or collecting Tiffany lamps or pursuing some other frivolous pastime. Instead, she chose to use her money and influence to promote various causes.

Birdsey put in some time as a Massachusetts social worker. Then for ten years she ran an adoption service that found homes for Third World orphans. However, a couple of con artists fleeced her and several clients out of thousands of dollars by promising to arrange adoptions from the Philippines that never happened. When the grifters were caught, they got off with what Birdsey regarded as a mere slap on the wrist.

Embittered, she got out of the adoption business. Instead she focused her energy—and her money—on a new cause: the environment. First, Birdsey launched a land trust to preserve wildlife habitat in New England. She also became active in opposing the construction of massive wind turbines in Nantucket Sound that would produce clean power but, opponents warned, at the cost of ruining the sound.

Soon Birdsey's perspective expanded beyond New England. In 1996 she and her husband bought a winter home among the wealthy families of Jupiter Island, a place with lush tropical landscaping and an ocean view. Her attention became drawn to Florida's environmental causes as well, and in particular to the manatees dying in droves along the southwest Florida coast.

Birdsey wanted someone to find out what her foundation could do to help save this poor, strange creature, which led to Bender calling Frisch out of the blue.

"My mandate," Frisch said, "was to find out what was going on with the manatee and what we could do to help."

Soon Pegasus's newest employee was on the phone to the Save the Manatee Club's newest employee: Pat Rose.

•

Rose had stuck to his guns at the DEP for as long as he could, aided by McVety's protection. But after McVety got the boot, "the hell just continued," he said. "They started taking me out of the negotiations with the development community."

The DEP under Ginger Wetherell had a reputation for being overly friendly to the industries it was supposed to regulate. So instead of Rose commenting on what might be wrong with a development, he would be handed the department's decision, made without his input. Invariably, he said, it would be whatever the developer wanted.

Nevertheless, when the top job overseeing all of Florida's endangered species came open, Rose applied for it. He drew support from many environmental activists who had worked with him on manatee protection. But he was passed over in favor of a biologist who had specialized in turtles.

"It was like a dart in the heart of the manatee community," Vallee said.

The final straw came when Rose's bosses began threatening to break up the entire manatee program, sending the various biologists to different sections rather than keeping them together, Rose said.

He offered to resign if it would spare the manatee program. The sacrifice worked. In 1996, the worst year ever for manatees, their most vocal advocate in state government left his job.

In his usual meticulous way, Rose had prepared for this day by compiling extensive files and memos, just as he did with the documents that ended up winning the lawsuit with the Florida Audubon Society. In this case, though, Rose was laying the groundwork for a lawsuit against his former employers. He hoped the suit would expose all the political wheeling and dealing that had gone on behind the scenes, at the manatee's expense.

But when the time came for Rose to go to court, he couldn't do it because of his new job. Instead of finding work with some other government agency or university as a biologist, Rose had been hired as the government affairs director—in other words, the lobbyist—for the Save the Manatee Club. He knew that suing the DEP would hurt his efforts to lobby state officials for the club. He would be seen as someone who was asking the state for help with one hand while using the other to beat the government over the head.

"Although I had prepared for a lawsuit, as director of government relations there was no way I could go forward with that," Rose said.

Even though he had a new job, Rose's stress level did not drop a single notch. Lobbying requires charm and gentle persuasion, a different set of skills than those required for being a hard-nosed state regulator enforcing the law. Rose frequently found himself seeking help from the same people he had clashed with in his old job.

Meanwhile, he continued to be a lightning rod for those who disliked government efforts to slow down boats. They frequently accused him of hiding an ulterior motive, over and over bringing up his 1990 comment to the *Orlando Sentinel* about using manatee protection as a way to "put a lid on growth."

Now, to add to his load of woe, here was some well-meaning woman on the phone offering to bring in some group he'd never heard of to help save the manatee.

Rose could tell Frisch had no idea what she was talking about. The people at Pegasus "thought the manatee was on the brink of extinction," Rose said. "They had no understanding of everything that was going on with manatees. They felt like there was nothing happening. They felt like they needed to come in on a charging white stallion to save us."

Rose bluntly told Frisch that she was on the wrong track. If she and Pegasus really wanted to help the environment, he said, they would focus on something even more endangered than the manatee. They should focus on saving Florida from poorly planned sprawl.

"I told them the most critical issue they could get involved in is growth management," Rose said. "The future of manatees and all these other aquatic ecosystem issues depends on what Florida is going to do about growth management. They didn't want to hear that."

Finally, reluctantly, Rose agreed to join Frisch and several other environmental and animal-welfare activists at the Clarion Hotel in Hollywood for what Frisch called "a brainstorming session" on manatee protection.

When Rose showed up the night before the meeting, he bumped into Frisch. After he introduced himself, "the first thing she did was ask me to carry her bags to the hotel," he recalled, chuckling.

Although at the time it seemed rude, Rose said the request taught him something important about Frisch: "She was not shy to ask people to do things for her." To him, that was the sign of someone who can get things done.

In addition to Rose and Frisch, the other attendees at that spring 1997 meeting near Fort Lauderdale were Bender; a biologist from the Humane Society; an activist from a group called the International Wildlife Coalition; and a Florida Wildlife Federation lobbyist.

They did not, to Rose's disappointment, talk about growth management. Instead, they talked about manatees, and how to get state and federal regulators to follow the law instead of caving in to political pressure.

To Frisch, and to Pegasus, this effort to help the manatee marked the first step in an effort to help other, less popular animals.

"We saw the potential of a precedent-setting campaign," Frisch said. "If we can't save an animal like the manatee, then what are the chances of us saving an endangered fly or a flower? So this is the leading edge of the animal-welfare movement."

At one point during the meeting, though, the activist from the International Wildlife Coalition made a prediction that lobbying, letter-writing, media campaigns, and every other tactic would probably fail.

"He said, 'I guarantee you're going to end up doing a lawsuit,'" Frisch recalled. But everyone agreed that would be the last resort.

That was before Fran Stallings got involved.

•

In his crusade to toughen up the Save the Manatee Club board, one of the places Stallings went looking for help was the annual meeting of the Everglades Coalition.

The coalition was a consortium of about thirty-five environmental groups pushing for the restoration of the River of Grass. It had been originally formed in the 1960s to battle a proposed jetport that Miami officials wanted to build in the Big Cypress Swamp. The project was ultimately canceled by President Nixon (with a big push from Nat Reed). Afterward the coalition evaporated, but Governor Graham revived it in the 1980s as part of his drive to restore both the Everglades and his own reputation.

Over the years the coalition meetings had grown into a place for Florida's many environmental activists to network with potential allies while knocking back a cocktail. The meetings had also become a prime photo-op spot for politicians sprucing up their green credentials.

The January 1998 Everglades Coalition meeting was held that year at the Westin Beach Resort in Key Largo. While there, Stallings fell into conversation with Frisch, who was still trying to learn everything she could about manatees. Stallings, ever on the hunt for foundation money, turned on the charm. Soon Pegasus was offering financial aid in addition to its moral support.

Nothing gets an environmental organization's attention faster than an open checkbook. That was especially true with Stallings. He began talking frequently with Birdsey, Frisch, and Bender.

In one of those conversations, Stallings said, Bender pointed out that a big federal lawsuit had recently been filed in his own backyard. The Sierra Club and the National Wildlife Federation had joined forces to sue the Corps of Engineers and the U.S. Fish and Wildlife Service over the rampant development of wetlands in southwest Florida in violation of the Clean Water Act.

"Why aren't you doing something like that with manatees?" Bender asked him.

"Hell if I know," Stallings replied.

According to Stallings, Bender then offered to "put together a group to sue. . . . We discussed the possibility of filing suits to try to ramp up the level of protection, get those agencies to ramp up the enforcement of the laws for protecting manatees."

To Stallings, that sounded like exactly what the Save the Manatee Club needed to do.

"If you're going to take people's money to protect these animals," he explained, "then you should be doing everything you can do."

But to join forces with other groups and file a big lawsuit, Stallings needed the approval of the rest of his board. At that point he didn't think he would get it. The Save the Manatee Club had been an independent entity for just five years, and many board members still regarded the government as an ally. Suing would seem rude, and it might be counterproductive.

"The staff was hesitant to piss off the agencies" they had worked with for so long, Frisch said.

So instead of asking for permission to sue, Stallings asked for something that appeared to require less of a commitment.

"I had watched how developers work with politicians and I figured it might work for me, too," Stallings said. "So I asked for *conceptual* approval first."

Stallings had seen over and over again how developers would ask county officials for "conceptual approval" of their plans, just to get their foot in the door. Although the term sounded tentative, it actually guaranteed that the developer would get every permit he needed, Stallings said. Once the ball was rolling, hardly anything could stop it.

So Stallings told his board that he just wanted permission to explore the concept—to look at the possibilities of such an alliance, and whether there might be grounds for any lawsuit.

"I said, if it works, then we'll go forward," he said. "Then of course you come back and say, 'Hey, y'all already approved it.'"

No one noted the irony. The club that had fought so hard to be free of a larger environmental group now wanted to partner with other big environmental groups to pursue its mission. Stallings got what he asked for, setting in motion everything that would follow.

•

With the Save the Manatee Club board's conceptual approval in hand, Frisch began pulling together organizations that might work well together in filing suit. If Stallings was Paladin, the gunslinger-for-hire, then Frisch was more like Yul Brynner in *The Magnificent Seven*, assembling a handpicked team to take on a risky mission.

"She was amazing at getting people to sit down at the table together," Patti Thompson said.

Frisch said she viewed it as essential "to bring the issue to national and international attention and to create a coalition in the broader environmental and animal welfare community. I knew that although [the Save the Manatee Club] was doing good work, it would take greater numbers and a broader perspective of talents and experience . . . to make a more powerful impact."

It helped that Bender sat on the Humane Society's board. That guaranteed the Humane Society would take an interest joining Frisch's manatee campaign. Once the media-savvy Humane Society was on board, others began to join as well, because they knew what an impact the Humane Society could have.

To most of the public, the Humane Society enjoyed a fairly benign image as the operator of small animal shelters, not a rabble-rousing group like People for the Ethical Treatment of Animals (PETA). In truth, though, the Humane Society had no direct connection to any animal shelters. It was actually a direct-mail and lobbying operation that had become the nation's largest and most influential animal-welfare organization.

Founded in 1954, the Humane Society grew from about 15,000 members in 1976 to about 725,000 as of the mid-1990s. A 1995 scandal showed just how big it had become. Two female employees accused one of the Humane Society's top executives of sexual harassment, and he was arrested on charges he embezzled sixty-eight thousand dollars from the organization. The executive then accused his bosses of sacrificing him to protect their own jobs, which paid each a salary of more than two hundred thousand dollars a year.

Some former board members and employees said they had been warning the Humane Society's leadership for years about how fat salaries and big expense accounts were draining the organization's twenty-four-million-dollar budget.

"The Humane Society should be worried about protecting animals from cruelty," Robert Baker, the Humane Society's former chief investigator, told a magazine. "It's not doing that. The place is all about power and money."

Rather than really nail down the facts before going public with cruelty charges, Baker told a reporter, the society had begun relying on legally shaky but high-profile cases to drive its fund-raising: "Make the splash and get the publicity and get the money and don't worry." That's how the accused executive got away with listing payments to nonexistent informants in his expense reports. He wound up sentenced to six months behind bars.

Like PETA, the Humane Society opposed hunting, the wearing of animal pelts, and the use of animals in product testing. But unlike PETA's outrageous publicity stunts—throwing paint on women wearing furs, or wrecking testing labs—the Humane Society took a fine-tuned approach to using the media to achieve its aims. The organization cranked out dozens of targeted press releases and bought ads in major newspapers to help its lobbyists pressure Congress on various bills.

For instance, the Humane Society garnered reams of free publicity by raising money to find a better home for the whale featured in the movie *Free Willy*. But the best example of its approach was its First Strike campaign: a coordinated, state-by-state drive employing all of its public-relations and marketing techniques to use research tying animal abuse and domestic violence as a tool to persuade lawmakers to toughen the penalties for crimes related to animal cruelty.

With the Humane Society on board with Frisch's budding manatee coalition, things moved quickly. In February 1998, just a month after her encounter with Stallings in Key Largo, Frisch set up something she called "a manatee action workshop and congressional briefing."

The session, held in the Russell Senate Office Building in Washington, D.C., drew attendees from twenty-five environmental and animal-welfare organizations, plus officials from the U.S. Marine Mammal Commission and several congressional staffers.

The invitation Frisch sent out played up the rising number of manatee deaths of all kinds without focusing on either boats or Red Tide: "In 1996 there were 415 Florida manatee fatalities, close to a fifth of the entire population of this very endangered species and the highest annual mortality count on record. The death toll in 1997 was 242, the second highest on record."

The opening speaker was former governor Bob Graham, now the state's senior U.S. senator. Frisch worried Graham might cancel because the deadliest tornadoes in Florida history had just laid waste to Central Florida. Generally a politician's first instinct in the face of a natural disaster is to proceed directly to the center of the carnage to show the TV cameras how much he or she cares about the victims. Without Graham, the meeting Frisch had set up would lose credibility with the government officials who were attending. Frisch said she "called every friend I had that knew how to pray" to ensure Graham would show up.

Sure enough, Graham arrived at the Washington meeting promptly at 8:30 a.m., dressed as usual in a suit, a button-down shirt, and a tie decorated with silhouettes of his state. He made his speech, then flew to Orlando with President Clinton, Governor Chiles, and other dignitaries to visit the tornado victims.

In his speech, Graham told about attending the Buffett concert and going backstage to chat about manatees, and "he said he had this epiphany that Jimmy Buffett was the man," Frisch recalled. Although Graham had had little involvement with the Save the Manatee Club since he and Buffett set it up, the senator proved to be the ideal man to kick off the gathering, filling everyone in on some crucial history about the club. Until Graham spoke, some of the other activists had no idea what the Save the Manatee Club was. That was partly Frisch's fault, Thompson said.

"What was infuriating to me, what got me bent out of shape and other staffers too, was the impression that Cynthia gave that *nothing* was being done for the manatees," Thompson said. "We were suing already over various projects, doing things more on a piecemeal basis. . . . We would either win or get a favorable settlement. Then Pegasus came in and said, 'Oh these poor manatees, nobody is doing anything for them.'"

After Graham—who walked off with an award that Frisch had invented for the occasion—came the next speaker, Pat Rose. Rose talked for more than an hour about the threats facing manatees, the stalled manatee protection plans, and the development wiping out manatee habitat.

After lunch, the group got a lecture on endangered species law from an attorney from the Earthjustice Legal Defense Fund. Then the various organizations talked about what they had just heard and what they could do about it.

"We agreed we should begin building a coalition and building grassroots support," Frisch said. "It became very clear that what was preventing manatees from being protected was politics and associated business interests."

Many of the groups attending Frisch's Washington summit belonged to something called the Endangered Species Coalition, which had a membership roll that ran from the Alabama Environmental Council to the Zoological Society of Philadelphia. From them Frisch obtained a list of other possible allies for the Save the Manatee Club.

"One name jumped off the page," she said. It was a Washington law firm: Meyer and Glitzenstein.

•

That that particular firm's name would leap off the page should not be too surprising. Married partners Katherine Meyer, then forty-five, and Eric Glitzenstein, then thirty-nine, had been involved in nearly every major endangered species case in the past decade.

Over the years they had handled cases involving wolves, bears, owls, salmon, lynx, and buffalo. *Washingtonian* magazine listed them among the most influential and effective lawyers in the District of Columbia.

Their expertise extended beyond endangered species. Both Meyer and Glitzenstein had worked for Ralph Nader's Public Citizen consumer action law firm, learning how to take on government agencies that were failing to follow the law. Then they hung out their own shingle in Washington.

Glitzenstein, who looked like a tweedy professor but talked like a Brooklyn prosecutor, had handled several cases involving the licensing of nuclear power plants. In one case he won the lawsuit, only to lose everything because a congressman friendly to the nuclear industry stuck an obscure rider on a barely related bill that overturned the ruling. As a result, the firm had branched out from simply suing the government to start a lobbying arm, called the Wildlife Advocacy Project, which would push for laws that would better protect animals.

His wife, meanwhile, had become known as an expert in using the Freedom of Information Act. She was hired by *The Nation* magazine to force the government to release documents revealing Texas billionaire Ross Perot's involvement in foreign affairs. Meyer garnered even greater fame with her work for Oregonians for Ethical Representation, finding the evidence that ultimately forced Senator Robert Packwood to resign for lying about his sexual harassment of female employees.

The couple, who had two children, had some prior experience defending Florida wildlife in court. When the U.S. Fish and Wildlife Service decided to capture endangered Florida panthers for a captive breeding program, the Fund for Animals hired Glitzenstein to go to court to stop it. The federal agency settled, agreeing to draw up a plan for where the panthers would go once they were grown—something no one had considered. Ultimately, the breeding program never got off the ground.

Although the couple kept a full calendar of cases, Frisch had no trouble getting them to join the team. She simply called Glitzenstein "pretty much out of the blue one day," the lawyer recalled. "She said, 'We're putting together a coalition of groups to look at the situation with the manatee, which is bad.' She said they would be looking at a variety of things, including a 'creative legal strategy.' When anyone says 'creative legal strategy,' I get intrigued."

One problem, though: Glitzenstein, as well as several members of the newly minted Manatee Coalition, had never actually seen a manatee.

Frisch arranged for the group—accompanied by her and Fran Stallings—to tour the SeaWorld theme park together. She snapped photos of them all peering down at an orphaned manatee swimming around in one tank as proof that they did, in fact, know what they were doing. Sort of.

•

Stallings, not an easy man to impress, called Glitzenstein "one of the brightest and best attorneys I've ever seen. He's got an IQ that's just off the scale." But the kind of expertise that Meyer and Glitzenstein offered did not come cheap, either.

When Stallings talked to his board about hiring the couple, "one of the questions was, 'Do we pay the bills? Or do we depend on other groups?' And I said, 'He who pays the bills drives the vehicle.'" The board agreed to take on the lion's share of the attorneys' fees—although it still had not formally made the decision to sue.

Similar concerns cropped up at Pegasus, Frisch said. "Peter and Barbara and I were all at Barbara's house in Jupiter . . . and we were under the full recognition that we were headed to a suit," Frisch said. "Peter was usually very bold all the time, but this time he stopped and said, 'And where the hell are we going to get the money for all this?'"

Frisch said she told him, "Don't worry, Peter. If this is the right thing, then the money will come."

In June 1998, Frisch and Pegasus convened another meeting in Washington, this time at the Humane Society's offices. "We gathered the best legal minds from the Endangered Species Coalition, to explore whether we even had a case," she said.

The lawyers—not just Glitzenstein, but also attorneys representing the National Wildlife Federation and several other environmental groups—went over what a potential case could aim for and what might happen. What Frisch was talking about doing departed from the usual environmental lawsuit. Most such suits involve trying to stop or alter one particular project.

"But this wasn't a case where we were saying, 'Let's stop Project X,'" Glitzenstein said. "It was, 'We have a problem with increasing mortality from boats. We've got a huge number of boats hitting manatees and manatees dying in record numbers.' We didn't know what the case *was*."

Glitzenstein set to work trying to decide how to tackle the situation, aided by "my ignorance or my fresh perspective, depending on what you want to call it."

At Frisch's urging, the various groups fired off a letter to Interior Secretary Bruce Babbitt urging him to step up enforcement of the speed zones. They also told him to take a look at what might happen if power plants stopped putting hot water into various rivers and bays, and to set up a new group of science experts to write an updated recovery plan for the species.

Meanwhile, Frisch and the leaders of the other groups began figuring out who should play which roles in this new Manatee Coalition. They set up a legal team to deal directly with the lawsuit. There was a media team to handle publicity. They set up a fund-raising team to handle paying the bills. And they named a legislative team to focus on Congress, trying to get more money for enforcing the law.

Frisch's job: make sure the teams continued working together and, when necessary, smooth any ruffled feathers.

"I was an 'ego manager,'" she said. "It made me glad I had meditated for twenty years. As a result, I had some insights into the human psyche."

Before any suit could be filed, the first step, Stallings said, was "an investigation to get the lay of the land. . . . We were looking at different cases and actions that the agencies had taken." He figures the Save the Manatee Club spent more than one hundred thousand dollars on the investigation to collect the evidence they needed, even before any legal paperwork was filed.

They sent the government agencies massive Freedom of Information Act requests for documents relating to their permitting decisions. That included biological opinions from the Fish and Wildlife Service, issued under Section 7 of the Endangered Species Act. The opinions said that all these new marinas would not put manatees in any kind of jeopardy, thus allowing the Corps to rubber-stamp the permit. When the documents began flowing in, Glitzenstein spent hours going over them all.

"I read every biological opinion and every other consultation document for the last ten or fifteen years, and every single Corps permit in manatee habitat," the lawyer said. He soon spotted a pattern of what he called "egregious illegal activity."

Each time the Corps and Fish and Wildlife Service would review a development permit in manatee habitat, they would not bother doing an analysis of how this particular project fit in with all the other projects that had been approved. They didn't look at what the cumulative impact might be of all those projects on manatee habitat. Instead, all Glitzenstein would find in each permitting file would be some boilerplate language that said, "There should be no cumulative impact."

He remembers thinking, "Okay, is that a wish or a reality?"

Even worse, he said, was the feeble attempt to comply with the Marine Mammal Protection Act. The act prohibits any incidental take—defined as death, injury, or even harassment—of species like the manatee unless there are rules in place to allow it in certain circumstances. The Fish and Wildlife Service's rules for incidental take were supposed to guarantee that the population would not be generally harmed.

But the service had never come up with any rules for take of the manatee.

If there were no rules, the law said there could not be any "take" of the species whatsoever—no deaths, no scarring by boats, no Crystal River tourists harassing calves, nothing.

The Corps and the Fish and Wildlife Service handled this problem very simply: they ignored it. They produced permits that said, in effect, "Since we don't have any regulations authorizing incidental take, we can't authorize incidental take, and therefore we approve this permit," Glitzenstein said. "There was a huge legal flaw in the syllogism."

But finding the legal grounds for a wide-ranging lawsuit left a far larger issue yet to be resolved.

"The difficult question was, what are you trying to get out of this process?" Glitzenstein said. "You're trying to get at an entrenched statewide problem and you're trying to change an entrenched way of doing business. How do you do that with a lawsuit?"

While Glitzenstein and his clients struggled with that question, the staff and leaders of the Save the Manatee Club edged closer to leaping into a major lawsuit. In the meantime, though, the club continued to pursue smaller ones. One of them led to a break between Stallings and his biggest supporter, Patti Thompson.

"Fran and I started to be at odds," Thompson said. "Fran was willing to jump in and sue anyone and everyone."

One Stallings lawsuit concerned how the Corps and the South Florida Water Management District handled the water level in Lake Okeechobee. The lake had once fed the flow of water into the Everglades. But a hurricane in 1928 sent so much water washing out of the lake that it killed three thousand people. The Corps built a dike around it, as well as a network of canals, pumps, and levees after a 1947 hurricane.

Now it operated like a combination of reservoir and toilet. Small cities around the lake tapped it for their drinking water, but when there was too much rain, sugar and vegetable growers back-pumped their fertilizer-laden irrigation into the lake to dry out their fields.

Meanwhile, because the Corps had straightened all the bends out of the Kissimmee River, which carried water into the lake, nothing impeded the flow of pollution into what was once known as "the liquid heart of Florida." As a result, the lake had become extremely polluted with nitrogen and phosphorus.

If heavy rains left the lake's water level too high right before hurricane season began, the Corps and the water district would become concerned about the lake overtopping the dike. To blunt the threat, they would release a lot of lake water into canals leading to the Caloosahatchee River and the Indian River.

Opening the tap like that would send the polluted water sluicing down into the sensitive estuary around Fort Myers on the Gulf Coast and a similarly sensitive estuary at Fort Pierce on the Atlantic coast. Sea grass would die, fish would get sick, and then a nasty bloom of toxic algae would drive tourists away.

Stallings wanted to sue the Corps and the water district over the Caloosahatchee releases, contending that the toxic water that wiped out the sea grass would actually kill manatees because they would starve.

"I stated that I didn't think that was true," Thompson said. "Manatees move. They will find food. . . . Fran didn't like that. I was somewhat appalled at what they were claiming was going to happen. Fran was furious with me. At that point, I was out of the game."

So Stallings shut out the club's biologist from participating in the planning of the biggest lawsuit in the club's history. Of course, the club had another manatee biologist on the staff, Pat Rose—but events would soon force Rose to the sidelines as well.

•

By early 1999 the big lawsuit was ready, only now it split to become two suits. One would be filed in federal court in Washington, D.C., against the Corps and the U.S. Fish and Wildlife Service. The other would be filed in federal court in Florida against the state Department of Environmental Protection. Both the federal and state agencies would be accused of failing to follow the Endangered Species Act and the Marine Mammal Protection Act.

"We called them the D.C. case and the Florida case," Frisch said. As the cases divided, so did the legal representation. Meyer and Glitzenstein would handle the D.C. case, and the Earthjustice Legal Defense Fund would handle the Florida case.

Earthjustice used to be the Sierra Club's in-house law firm, but now it functioned as a public interest firm dedicated to protecting the environment. Its top litigator in Florida was a University of Chicago Law School grad named David Guest.

Guest had the beard of a rustic mountain man coupled with a nightclub comic's penchant for withering sarcasm. His sense of humor skewed to the darker end of the spectrum. For years, Guest relished pointing out to people how much he resembled police sketches of a domestic terrorist called the Unabomber.

Guest had spent two decades battling phosphate mines, pulp mills, and sugar companies. His biggest case required him to take on one of the state's most powerful corporations, Lykes Brothers, which had fenced off public access to Fisheating Creek in Glades County, claiming it was private property. He spent hours pouring over ancient maps, military records, and century-old diaries, trying to prove that the creek was a navigable waterway and thus belonged to the people of Florida. One interview with a potential witness had to be delayed while the man chased a snake out of his living room.

As happens with many environmental lawyers, Guest felt a personal commitment to saving Florida's wilder areas. He even built his own pontoon boat for wildlife watching. Pursuing his cases, he once wrote, meant "scores of hot days wading waist-deep in alligator-infested rivers, marshes, and swamps, finding relief only with the driving rain of the late afternoon."

Unlike Glitzenstein, Guest's expertise lay in water law, not endangered species. Although he knew the state permitting process better than most other attorneys in Florida, this suit would mark a departure from his previous work.

Stallings really wanted Guest on the state case, but he knew that Guest's services were difficult to get. So Stallings mentioned what he wanted to Bender and the head of another foundation that donated to both the Save the Manatee Club and Earthjustice, counting on the power of the almighty dollar to do the rest. Before the day was over, Guest had called to ask what he could do to help. Earthjustice, unlike Meyer and Glitzenstein, handled the case pro bono, asking only to be reimbursed for expenses.

Still, Guest wasn't all that thrilled about working with a bunch of animal-welfare activists. They had similar reservations about Guest.

"I told them I'd touched a manatee once at Crystal River, and the way they looked at me, I felt like I'd rolled over and screwed the thing," he joked.

At one point, during a strategy session at the Humane Society's headquarters in Washington, the group broke for lunch, Guest said, "and I committed a crime against all eternity by ordering a *ham* sandwich. I was told very quickly I should *never* do that again."

Even the Save the Manatee Club folks struck the free-spirited Guest as a bit uptight.

"They did not see the manatee as a species in need of protecting," he said. "They saw them as a collection of individual manatees with human attributes, human emotions, being slaughtered. They were feeling in their hearts like they were at a Roman coliseum watching the Christians being fed to the lions."

Although he hadn't handled an endangered species case before, Guest grasped the basic issue immediately. It was all about convenience.

"The proposition that we should allow fishermen in twenty-thousand-dollar boats to shave ten minutes off a trip by rocketing through their habitat, it's disgusting," he said. "It's like encouraging the Hell's Angels to ride through your tulip patch."

Legally, though the state case required a little finagling. Guest would have to argue that the state of Florida, by allowing people to go too fast in their boats, had violated federal laws protecting endangered species, "just as if I handed you a gun and said, 'Go blow the head off that panther.' They knew full well that people in these huge motorboats were rocketing around killing manatees."

Fortunately, another Florida case had set a precedent for Guest to make such an argument. People had been driving on Daytona Beach since the days of Henry Ford. The tradition had become ingrained, even though the cars frequently destroyed the nests of sea turtles as well as mowing down the occasional tourist. Two women who cared about the turtles, if not the tourists, decided to take on the practice.

Their lawsuit, *Loggerhead Turtle v. Volusia County*, went all the way to the U.S. Supreme Court, and ultimately they won. Volusia County officials had to ban cars from portions of the beach—no doubt to the relief of tourists who wanted a tan, not a set of tire tracks.

Before filing any lawsuit, federal court rules required the Manatee Coalition plaintiffs to send the government agencies a notice giving them sixty days to fix whatever was wrong. Filing the sixty-day notice meant putting a signature on it, and "here was where the men were separated from the boys," Frisch said. Some of the groups that had been part of the meeting with Bob Graham began to get cold feet.

"Some groups simply were not able to participate in suits," she said. "Some were concerned about the costs. Some don't like litigation."

One of the people hesitant to sue had the power to stop the whole thing. Jimmy Buffett still co-chaired the Save the Manatee Club, and his contributions—and the contributions of his Parrotheads—helped pay the bills.

Buffett "had been involved in lawsuits over copyright issues, and it made him cautious about getting involved in another one," Fran Stallings said. "So I pushed him on it, which I felt a little bad about."

Stallings met with Buffett and told him, flat out, that this was the only way the club could do what it had been set up to do. Nothing else had worked.

"We're out there to protect these animals, then by God we ought to do it," Stallings told the singer.

Finally Buffett agreed—but with a condition. He insisted that, as a courtesy, he had to meet with one person to warn him what was coming. He wanted to talk to Florida's newly elected governor, Jeb Bush.

## The Time Has Come

JOHN ELLIS "JEB" BUSH, the son of a president, the grandson of a U.S. senator, had spent years trying to find his way in life.

He had sold water pumps in Nigeria and mobile phones in Miami. He tried banking in South America. He became part-owner of the Jacksonville Jaguars football team. He even spent a brief term as Florida's secretary of commerce under Governor Martinez.

At last Bush was taken in hand by a Miami developer named Armando Codina, who also happened to be a major GOP contributor. Codina's assistance made Bush a millionaire. Then he could focus on politics, where his family had succeeded so well.

Jeb Bush had long been regarded by Republicans as their best shot at continuing the family dynasty. In 1994 he launched his first political race. He ran for governor despite having virtually no experience in government, and no experience even running a large organization of any type.

Yet Bush didn't pander to the voters. He made it plain he was not a Republican moderate like Bob Martinez. He was an arch-conservative, someone who despised government bureaucrats and valued private enterprise. The list of government programs he wanted to toss out included a wildly popular program that bought environmentally sensitive land for preservation. And when asked what he would do to help black Floridians, Bush responded, "Probably nothing."

Still, the young and energetic Bush ran well against the rumpled Democratic incumbent, Lawton Chiles. Bush frequently succeeded in painting Chiles as the prisoner of old ways and old ideas while portraying himself as the harbinger of a new day. But with the polls showing them neck and neck, in their final TV debate Chiles warned the television audience not to count him out, explaining, "The old he-coon walks just before the light of day."

Like the wily he-coon, Chiles then pulled a fast one on his young challenger. On the weekend before the election, Chiles deployed an army of campaign workers to call older voters warning that Bush would slash their Medicare benefits. That Chiles's claim was false did not make it any less effective.

In the closest gubernatorial vote in Florida history, Chiles won, even as Republicans took control of Congress and the Florida Legislature. (Meanwhile, Bush's brother George won election as governor of Texas, beginning a climb to the White House along what many Republicans had thought would be Jeb's path.)

Bush went into an exile of sorts. He went back to Miami. He established a foundation that collected corporate contributions and produced conservative, pro-property-rights position papers—and helped him build an organization for the next gubernatorial race. And he co-founded a school in poverty-stricken Liberty City.

When Bush ran again in 1998, he faced Chiles's lieutenant governor, Buddy McKay, who was just as folksy as Chiles but far less adept at playing the wily he-coon. Bush, on the other hand, had learned a thing or two about politics since 1994. While his views had not really changed, his tactics had. He now positioned himself as less of an ideologue and more of a caring conservative. He reached out to black and Jewish voters who traditionally voted Democratic. He even showed a newfound concern for the environment. He said he wanted to restore the Everglades, just like Bob Graham, and he called for renewing the state's land-buying program, not ending it.

At one campaign stop, Bush helped SeaWorld release a pair of rehabilitated manatees at Blue Spring State Park. One was named Ajax, and the other, Little Jeb. Television cameras caught the whole scene of Bush helping release Little Jeb, of course.

There were signs, though, that Bush's concern about manatees might go deeper than a photo-op smile. The candidate carried a stuffed manatee named Marty along on his campaign travels. He even used a photo of Little Jeb as the screen saver on his computer.

On Election Day, Bush crushed McKay and swept into office vowing to change state government.

Although Jimmy Buffett had campaigned for McKay, he and Pat Rose agreed that Bush might be just the savior the manatees needed. After all, everything that had gone wrong—the poor enforcement of the speed zones, the political interference at the DEP, the failure to force all thirteen counties to draw up protection plans—had happened before Bush took office, under a governor who didn't care about manatees the way Bush apparently did.

By the time Bush took office, the twin duties of manatee research and manatee protection had been taken away from the politically hamstrung DEP and handed over to a newly created agency. The voters had approved a merger of Earle Frye's old Game and Fresh Water Fish Commission with a small, obscure body called the Marine Fisheries Commission, which oversaw saltwater species. The merger created an entity called the Florida Fish and Wildlife Conservation Commission. As its name implied, the new agency was supposed to focus less on hunting and more on conserving species.

In yet another promising sign, state officials—in response to criticism from the group of manatee experts that Rose had set up in 1981 called the Manatee Technical Advisory Committee—had recently hired a new biologist to oversee all manatee-related research. His name was Buddy Powell.

Powell, the Boy Wonder Biologist who grew up swimming with Crystal River's manatees, had left Florida behind after he quit the U.S. Fish and Wildlife Service. He studied dugongs in Africa and South America. He contracted such a nasty tropical disease that Nat Reed had to find him a doctor in New York who could deal with it. There weren't any in Florida.

But now Powell was married to an anthropologist and they had a daughter, so he wanted to return to his home state. He seemed like the ideal scientist for what the wildlife commission had in mind. Powell started his new state job in 1998, ready to pull together all the diverse strands of manatee research and manatee protection, ready to carry on Woodie Hartman's legacy.

With a new governor in charge, a new agency handling both manatee research and enforcement of the speed zones, and a veteran scientist in charge, conditions seemed promising for a fresh start.

Rose set up an appointment with Bush on May 19, 1999. Before the visit, Rose filled in a Bush aide about what he and Buffett wanted to discuss, so that Bush would be prepared.

"The governor was supposed to be completely briefed on the suit before we met with him," Rose said. "Jimmy and I were going to see him and tell him that the suit against the state was against what the DEP had done, not against the new Fish and Wildlife Commission. . . . So we go into the meeting thinking, 'This is going to be great. It's going to be cordial.'"

The first few minutes went well, Rose said. "The governor was talking about his love for manatees. And finally we said, 'So, let's talk about the lawsuit.' He goes, 'LAWSUIT?!' And he stood up, and I could see everything just drain out of him. He had *not* been briefed."

Years later, Rose could only shake his head over the foul-up: "If only I had double-checked things, had gone back to make sure things had been done that I was told were done, the outcome may have been very different."

Bush already had a reputation for being thin-skinned. After his outburst, he sat back down and listened to Buffett and Rose talk about the lawsuit, but offered little in response.

"He was reserved, but you could tell he was mad," Rose said. "I can't blame him. He looked like he'd been cold-cocked."

Somehow the pair stumbled through the rest of the meeting, then stepped out of Bush's office to face a gaggle of reporters curious about what the singer and the governor had discussed.

Neither Buffett nor Rose mentioned Bush's anger at being blindsided. Instead, Buffett called the new governor "charming" and said that Bush displayed an "obvious, personal affection" for manatees. Overall, Buffett said, he was encouraged.

"The atmosphere is one where I think there's a great opportunity for cooperation," Buffett told the reporters. The main problem, he said, was that "there's not a lot of enforcement of the laws designed to protect manatees" and "the mortality rate is way beyond what it should be."

Then the rattled Buffett seemed to argue the other side of the debate as well, as if he were suddenly possessed by the spirit of Wade Hopping: "How are we going to deal with this? How are we going to take time out of our development life and our personal life and slow our boats down? How much are we willing to sacrifice for these creatures?" He didn't answer his own questions.

Rose, still trying to salvage relations with Bush, made sure to tell the press, "This is not an attack on his administration. These problems started a long time before. He could be the one who really helps turn this around."

Bush, conspicuously, had nothing to say to the reporters. Instead he dis-

When Jimmy Buffett tried to warn Governor Jeb Bush about the impending lawsuit, the meeting did not go well. Afterward, Buffett tried to put the best face on the situation for the press. Photo courtesy of the *St. Petersburg Times*.

patched a spokesman to announce only that the governor "cares about issues surrounding manatees."

Still, Bush gave the manatee advocates more attention than the Democrats in the Clinton administration in Washington had. One of the club's donors had urged Stallings to put in a courtesy phone call to Interior Secretary Bruce Babbitt.

Ever eager to please a donor, Stallings made the call, only to wind up on the phone with a low-level functionary who took a message, nothing more.

"They didn't even ask for my number," Stallings said. "They didn't give a shit what we did or didn't do.

•

The day after Buffett's botched meeting with Governor Bush, Meyer and Glitzenstein faxed out the two sixty-day notice letters, each signed by a coalition of twenty-two organizations. The letters warned state and federal officials that they were going to be sued in federal court if some settlement could not be reached within two months.

The signers included the Save the Manatee Club, the Humane Society, and the Pegasus Foundation, of course, but also Defenders of Wildlife, the Center for Marine Conservation, Earthjustice, and, despite their past differences, the Florida Audubon Society. Getting the Audubon Society to join in wasn't hard, Rose said, since Yokel was no longer in charge.

The letters were sent to the heads of the DEP, the Corps, the Fish and Wildlife Service, the Department of the Army, and the Interior Department. They noted that the 1998 death toll from boats had set a new record and that the first three months of 1999 had registered the highest number of boat-related deaths—twenty-two—of any first quarter since the state began keeping track. The rising death rates "paint a bleak picture of the manatee struggling to survive."

Because of the agencies' failure to prevent those deaths, the letters said, the government was responsible for violating the Endangered Species Act and the Marine Mammal Protection Act, not to mention the National Environmental Protection Act.

The Fish and Wildlife Service and the Corps were both guilty of cranking out hundreds of permits a year that allowed harmful coastal development, the letters warned. The cumulative effect of all that development constituted a "taking" of manatees without the necessary permits, the attorneys argued.

Worse, the Fish and Wildlife Service's recovery plan for how to help the manatee get off the endangered list—the latest version had been approved in 1996—fell short of what the law required, according to the notice letter to the federal agencies.

The recovery plan "does not establish objective, measurable recovery criteria" that would show how well or how poorly manatees were doing, the letter complained.

As for the state, it had failed to comply with not only the Endangered Species Act but also the state's own Manatee Sanctuary Act, the attorneys argued. The best example of its failure: the fact that of the thirteen counties that were supposed to draw up manatee protection plans in 1989, only Citrus, Dade,

Duval, and Collier had followed through—and the plan that Collier had come up with after Fran Stallings left was, the letter said, "woefully inadequate."

The letter to the DEP effectively spelled out all the things that Pat Rose had tried to implement while he worked there, only to be thwarted by political interference and bureaucratic infighting. Although Rose had never had a chance to file his personal lawsuit against his bosses, here at last was a day of reckoning for all the things he believed they had done wrong.

Yet hardly anyone at the state saw it that way. Just the idea that the Save the Manatee Club, once a part of state government, might sue the state for poor job performance caught many state officials off guard.

"They really thought they were doing their jobs," Patti Thompson said. "They were so deluded. So there was puzzlement and surprise."

One person in particular had been caught flat-footed: the newly hired Buddy Powell. He thought he had built up a good rapport with the environmental groups interested in manatee protection. Yet he had no idea any lawsuit had been brewing. Like Bush, he felt blindsided.

Powell passed along a copy of the letter to a lawyer friend and asked his opinion. His friend said, "They've got a case. It's going to be very important— and very clever."

That's not the way Powell's boss saw things, though. The turtle biologist who had been promoted over Rose called it "frustrating" to be told that "our efforts all these years have been meaningless."

But then he himself admitted that politics had hampered their work.

"It's a very politically contentious business to regulate boats and boat speeds," said the DEP's top imperiled species official. "Can we make the entire state of Florida a slow speed zone? Realistically no, so we are trying to regulate where appropriate."

The sense of outrage over the sixty-day notice went all the way to Governor Bush's staff, despite Rose's efforts to point all blame at the Chiles administration. At a conference in Tampa, Stallings bumped into one of Bush's advisers, a diminutive former judge who had once been on the board of the Audubon Society. Stallings said the Bush aide "took me aside and chewed my ass out. 'How dare you do something like this? This is an embarrassment to the governor! This is the governor's favorite animal!'"

Stallings, of course, took the confrontation in stride, more amused than abashed.

However, Rose emphasized over and over in interviews that the Save the

Manatee Club did not really want to sue anyone. This was a chance to work things out before any suit was filed, he said.

A sixty-day notice serves as an opening bid, laying out the upper range of what the plaintiffs would take to settle the case out of court. In this case, the letters spelled out a long list of what it would take to avoid a suit, including sending a "strategic enforcement task force" out to stop boaters from speeding; hiring more law officers to patrol the waterways; creating a series of sanctuaries and refuges like the ones in Crystal River where manatees could get away from all motorboats; ensuring that manatee protection plans were adopted by the other ten counties; setting minimum flow levels to the springs and other water bodies frequented by manatees; and restoring water bodies that had become too polluted for manatees to use them anymore.

They put the most radical demand of all last on the list: "suspend permitting on all new coastal construction activities . . . with the exception of single family docks."

During the suspension, the letter said, the DEP, the wildlife service, and the Corps must analyze the cumulative impact of all the destruction they had already permitted to occur and then adopt "effective, peer-reviewed strategies for addressing the cumulative adverse impacts to manatees" in future coastal construction.

The letter to the Corps and the wildlife service got their attention. Glitzenstein said he had two meetings in Jacksonville with the top Florida officials from both agencies to talk about a possible settlement.

The boss of the Fish and Wildlife Service office was Dave Hankla, who had an odd connection with both Pat Rose and with Fran Stallings—and as a result they had opposing opinions about him.

Hankla's father, Don, had worked for the U.S. Fish and Wildlife Service. Back in 1978, Don Hankla was the federal bureaucrat that the Marine Mammal Commission's John Twiss had accused of not taking the killing of manatees seriously. Not until the Marine Mammal Commission came up with the money did Hankla's father agree to hire a biologist Twiss had recommended to oversee manatee recovery—Pat Rose.

So Rose knew both Hankla and his father well, and he could see a strong resemblance in their attitudes.

"I am afraid that in some ways the apple did not fall far from the tree," Rose commented years later.

Stallings had a higher opinion of Hankla—but his reasoning would not have convinced Rose. Stallings knew Dave Hankla from early in his career with the Fish and Wildlife Service, back when Hankla ran a small government office in Louisiana that dealt with permitting for the oil and gas industry. Stallings had been a consultant for the oil industry, and he and Hankla got along just fine, he said.

Of course, that was now the Save the Manatee Club's complaint about Hankla, namely, that he and his wildlife agency got along a little too well with the development and marine industries, rather than acting as tough regulators.

However, Hankla contended that his agency took a tougher stand on manatee issues than it was given credit for. He insisted his agency wrote more jeopardy opinions on projects affecting manatees than it wrote for projects affecting any other species.

That standard was lower than it sounded. Since 1993, the Fish and Wildlife Service had not written a single jeopardy opinion blocking development in the habitat of the Florida panther, at a time when there were fewer than one hundred panthers left.

The keen-eyed Woodie Hartman, in his 1999 study on the status of the manatee, wrote that the Fish and Wildlife Service office that Hankla ran had all but given up the struggle against poorly sited waterfront development.

"Federal agents in Jacksonville, instructed by their superiors to soft-pedal the issue of critical habitat, contend that boat slips need not be regulated nor the number of powerboats restricted, on the grounds that enforced compliance with boat speeds in manatee protection zones is sufficient to lower watercraft-related mortality," he wrote. However, he noted, the argument was undercut by the fact that the number of officers on the water "has declined in recent years."

Hankla, years later, contended that Hartman got his facts wrong. His biologists weren't soft-pedaling anything, he said. But it was true they had pretty much stopped writing jeopardy opinions on projects affecting manatees, he said, because of the same problem Glitzenstein had discovered with the lack of rules for incidental take.

Also, Hankla had abolished the job of manatee coordinator, the job Rose had once held, and spread those duties out among several employees. That, Hankla contended, angered the Save the Manatee Club more than anything else.

Representing the Corps in the negotiations was John Hall, a crusty paraplegic with a neatly trimmed mustache. Hall, a Virginia native, had run the regulatory office in Jacksonville for more than a decade. An avid sailor with a Ph.D. in biology, he traveled the country teaching other Corps biologists how to do their jobs. Although Hall was a staunch advocate for the Corps, when pressed he admitted that its permitting program did little to stop development from paving over most of Florida's environmentally sensitive land. His only argument was that the least valuable wetlands and wildlife habitat had been wiped out first—a dubious contention at best, and one he admitted he could not prove.

In negotiating with Glitzenstein, Hall and Hankla did not even try to defend their agencies' actions. Instead, Glitzenstein said, they talked of trying to find a way to take a new approach to permitting that would look at the impact on the whole ecosystem. However, they had no timetable for making such a change—and while they were trying to produce this new system, more and more permits would be approved the old-fashioned, flawed way. What they were offering, Glitzenstein said, simply wasn't enough.

Meanwhile, despite the big splash that the notice letters made in the press, despite the strong demands they contained, the DEP's top brass brushed the whole thing aside. They didn't even bother to meet with Guest or his clients to negotiate for a settlement.

Wade Hopping, doing some investigating for his boating-industry clients, asked people he knew at DEP how they planned to defend themselves. DEP officials told him they would just dump the problem in the lap of the new wildlife commission, period.

Hopping then asked the wildlife commission's leaders what they would do. They, too, didn't even mention negotiating. They said they planned to "vigorously defend" the state against a lawsuit that seemed to them inevitable.

The suit seemed inevitable to Hopping, too. The sixty-day notice created a flurry of activity among his clients. They could see that even if the Manatee Coalition plaintiffs didn't get everything they wanted, there would still be new limits on the number of docks and marinas as well as on how fast boats would be allowed to go.

So at the end of August 1999—after the sixty days had expired, but before any suits had been filed—the boat dealers and manufacturers convened a meeting of what they called the Boating Coalition in Orlando to talk about launching a counterattack.

"They believe they have been on the defense far too long," Hopping wrote

Lobbyist Wade Hopping suggested to his clients that it might be time to try to take manatees off the endangered list. Photo courtesy of the *St. Petersburg Times*.

in a memo afterward, "and therefore they are planning to create a proactive program on manatee issues."

Hopping's memo made it clear that the sixty-day letter had sent his clients into a panic.

"Their fear is that the thrust of all the manatee protection activities are designed to limit the number of docks and marinas, and to limit the number of boats that are on the water," he wrote. "Obviously, they have a tremendous interest in this issue."

To strengthen their position, the lobbyist wrote, the industry officials planned to meet with the state's two leading pro-development groups, the Florida Home Builders Association and the Association of Florida Community Developers, as well as the Florida Association of Counties.

Their goal, he wrote, was "to seek a united front."

Their first target, Hopping wrote, would be to get the legislature to eliminate the strict state scrutiny of new waterfront developments that included marinas. They would do that by striking the requirement that new marinas would automatically be classified as a "Development of Regional Impact," since such large developments faced greater regulatory scrutiny. Getting rid of that requirement would make life much easier for waterfront developers.

The second target was the one that would prove the most controversial: "Begin the process of down-listing or de-listing the manatee."

In his September 3, 1999, memo, Hopping explained that the time seemed right to take such a bold step—and the boaters had an inside source urging them on.

To oversee progress on the manatee recovery plan, the U.S. Fish and Wildlife Service had picked several people to serve on what it called the Manatee Recovery Team. One of the team members was a Lee County marina owner named Pat Riley. Riley attended the August meeting of the Boating Coalition to report on everything he had heard, Hopping wrote, and what he had heard was that manatees were doing fine.

"All of the evidence currently available indicates that the manatee population is stable and growing at somewhere between 3 and 10 percent a year," Hopping wrote, twisting the findings of the synoptic aerial surveys to suit his argument. "The current population is estimated to be somewhere in excess of 2,500 manatees. This is a great improvement over ten years ago when they [*sic*] were only reputedly 1,100 manatees in Florida. Perhaps the time has come to delist the manatee, much as the alligator and the eagle have been delisted." (Hopping again had mangled the facts—eagles would not be taken off the endangered list for another nine years.)

In addition, Hopping said, the boating industry wanted to see if the millions of dollars pouring in from selling Save the Manatee license plates could be steered away from research—in other words, away from paying for those expensive synoptic surveys, not to mention the carcass recovery program. Instead, his clients wanted that money to be spent on "putting more marine enforcement officers on the water to enforce the current speeding and other laws."

Hopping's memo found a welcome audience in some areas. The president of Brevard County's Citizens for Florida's Waterways, George Reynolds, wrote to say his pro-boating organization would be happy to help.

"We believe that the over-zealous environmental groups are not addressing the manatee mortality rate with scientific data, but with emotion and profit motives," he wrote, not mentioning that the boating industry had profit motives too.

Unfortunately for Hopping, someone leaked a copy of his memo to a reporter for the *St. Petersburg Times* named Julie Hauserman. Her September 30, 1999, story about the memo was headlined "Trade group will fight manatee protections: State marine interests want the mammals off the endangered list." In the story, she quoted Hopping's memo at length, and then showed how off-the-mark the lobbyist was.

"Scientists working to protect manatees say the idea of stripping away protections is ridiculous," Hauserman wrote. "Manatee populations may be stable or even growing a little in some locations, they say, but the number of boats is growing too. This year, they predict, Florida will set a record for the number of manatees killed by boats."

Hauserman's scoop, picked up by papers across the state, put Hopping on the defensive. The Tallahassee spinmeister complained to the *Palm Beach Post* that angry manatee lovers were unfairly portraying him as a male version of Cruella de Vil.

"They've been siccing school children on me and publishing my address," he grumbled.

Really, Hopping said, he wasn't so evil. "We don't see the death of manatees as beneficial to us," he said. "We're opposed to regulation, but we need more on-water law enforcement. That would be good for the manatees and for people."

Despite the bad publicity, the campaign that Hopping outlined in his memo soon began. Boaters and home builders joined forces against a common enemy, using their combined clout to push their agenda.

Just as the Save the Manatee Club savored its greatest triumph, just as its bold move to enforce the law began to yield results, Hopping's long-ago prediction came true, and the pendulum began to swing back the other way.

# Oh No, Mr. Bill!

PURSUING A PAIR OF MAJOR federal lawsuits costs money—far more money than the Save the Manatee Club, with its $1.7 million budget, had on hand.

After all, the organization's major fund-raiser each year was a dinner dance and auction called the Manatee Ball. It was a step up from Pearl Dick selling T-shirts in front of the Crystal River Winn-Dixie, but not a big step.

The Manatee Ball was sponsored by the Tampa Bay Parrotheads in Paradise Club. The auction offered goods ranging from autographed sports memorabilia to an all-expenses-paid visit to a nudist resort. It usually brought in between fifteen and twenty thousand dollars.

With nearly two thousand members, the Tampa Bay chapter was the largest among the 175 Parrothead fan club chapters worldwide. The members included every brand of Buffett fan: surgeons, lawyers, construction workers, police officers, and janitors. They showed up at the ball dressed in a variety of tropical costumes that usually involved some combination of flower prints and sandals, with the occasional fake parrot thrown in for comic effect.

This particular Parrothead chapter had been founded in 1994 by Harry Fink, who liked to be called "Captain Harry," and his girlfriend at the time, who went by the name Sarah Sunshine. She owned a travel agency. Fink, a skinny man with a gunfighter's downturned mustache, worked in what he called "the debt management business." But what Captain Harry really lived for was heading out into the Gulf of Mexico in his forty-six-foot powerboat.

He said his appreciation of life on the water dated back to his childhood up in north Florida.

"I probably hit over a hundred manatees growing up, because I grew up skiing on the St. Johns River," he said. "I water-skied to high school. I was a river rat. I loved it."

The Parrotheads in Paradise wanted to party, not talk about politics or lawsuits. Many of them were boaters as well as Buffett fans. But if pressed, Fink would wave his drink around grandly and declare the manatee was "the most gentle creature in the world." Now, when he took his boat out, he said, "I can slow down."

Paying the bills being racked up by the dual lawsuits would take about ten or twelve Manatee Balls all at once. So in October 1999, Fran Stallings decided to further cement the financial relationship with Pegasus. He talked Barbara Birdsey into joining the Save the Manatee board.

"One of the things you've got to do is get the people forking out the green stamps involved in the process," Stallings explained.

Still, even Pegasus couldn't come up with enough money on its own. Then one day Stallings got a call to have lunch in Bonita Springs with a couple of visitors from the Pacific Northwest.

"They were members of the club and just flew in out of the blue, literally, to assist in the suit," Stallings said.

They were Gordon and Rose Letwin from Redmond, Washington. Although those names were virtually unknown to the public, the Letwins were extremely wealthy people.

Gordon Letwin had been one of the original eleven employees of Microsoft, the ones who got company stock early on before the company's software wound up on so many computers that it seemed ubiquitous. Bill Gates said Letwin was the only programmer who had skills equal to his own. Gordon Letwin stayed with Microsoft until 1993, then retired a very rich man. *Time* magazine estimated his fortune at twenty million dollars.

Letwin met his wife, a mechanical engineering student, when they were both attending Purdue. They never had children. Instead, after Letwin retired, the couple spent their time tinkering with electronics and traveling to exotic locales like Mount Kilimanjaro. They also set up a foundation that donated to environmental groups throughout the western United States and Canada.

Now they were ready to help a cause in Florida too.

"They had come to town a week earlier and hired someone to give them a private tour of various nature sites and the like in South Florida," Stallings said.

At some point, they heard about what was happening with the manatee lawsuit and asked for a briefing from the top man at the Save the Manatee Club. At lunch, Stallings filled the couple in on what was going on and invited them to the next meeting of the coalition of environmental groups.

Rose Letwin flew to the meeting in Washington, D.C., "accompanied by a private security detail who remained within a short distance at all times," Stallings said. "She also asked that she be introduced as a club member without reference to her foundation."

Just her presence at the meeting "gave the whole process a big boost," he said.

But then she boosted the lawsuits in a far more substantial way. First she donated $50,000 to the cause. Then she offered to donate another $100,000—but only if the Save the Manatee Club could match it. Half the match had to come from the club's allies in the lawsuit, she said, and half had to come from the club's other members.

"The Humane Society gave us $20,000," Judith Vallee said. "The International Fund for Animal Welfare gave us $20,000. Defenders of Wildlife gave us $1,000. The International Wildlife Coalition gave us $2,000. The Pegasus Foundation gave us $10,000."

Vallee sent out a quick fund-raising alert to the club's forty-five thousand members. Within ninety days the rest of the matching funds were in hand, Stallings said. The replies came from as far away as the Middle East. All told, Rose Letwin had helped the club raise about $250,000 in a very short time.

Now the two suits could proceed. On January 13, 2000, Eric Glitzenstein filed one suit in federal court in Washington, D.C., while David Guest filed the other one in federal court in Tallahassee.

Even those Save the Manatee Club officers who had been reluctant to go to court had to admit, after the poor outcome of their notice letters, that all other options had been foreclosed.

"We figured there was no choice. It was a last alternative," Vallee said.

The lawsuits focused on the actual harm being done to the species—how they manatees repeatedly hit and cut and killed by boats, how they were losing habitat, how all of this violated the laws designed to protect them.

The complaints cited the numbers produced by Tom Pitchford's crew at the path lab: a record 82 manatees killed by boats in 1999, and 268 dead from all causes. That was the second-highest number ever, which was especially alarming since the record year of 1996 included the Red Tide epizootic. There had been no Red Tide to boost the mortality figures in 1999.

The Save the Manatee Club faxed out a press release headlined "Environmental and Animal Protection Groups Announce Federal Lawsuits to Save Manatees" that started dramatically: "As boat collisions and habitat destruction cause the Florida manatee to sink further toward extinction . . ."

Patti Thompson saw that line and sighed. She knew it was wrong. Not one marine mammal biologist believed manatees were anywhere near extinction. The species was not in good shape, but it was not about to disappear either.

She also noticed a line that said, "Only an estimated 2,400 survive in the wild in Florida coastal waters."

That was wrong too. It misrepresented the results of the synoptic surveys, which Ackerman always said were a minimum number for the manatee population, not the maximum. Once again, the word "only" had created a misleading connection between the manatee's endangered status and the number of manatees.

But Thompson's opinion about all this did not count. Since Stallings had frozen her out, nobody had bothered to consult the staff biologist about the language in the press release, she said later. In fact, the only person quoted in the press release was Fran Stallings. In some of his statements, Stallings correctly analyzed the situation: "The root of the problem is continued and unabated coastal development and the resulting increase in dangerous boat traffic."

However, other quotes carried an apocalyptic flavor that suggested the last manatee in Florida would soon join the Steller's sea cow in the Hall of Extinct Marine Mammals.

"We must decide now as a nation whether to honor our legal and moral commitment to the manatee or fail as environmental stewards and allow their extinction," said one Stallings quote.

Another said: "Maybe the Clinton Administration can wait until the manatee has disappeared, but we're not going to sit by without taking action."

Glitzenstein took a more measured tone, while still talking about the urgency of taking action because of the rising number of manatees being killed by boats. "There is widespread acknowledgement that the system has broken down," he told the *St. Petersburg Times*. "Based on the most recent mortality figures, we felt the situation had reached a crisis level."

Meanwhile, officials from the boating and building industries suddenly discovered how much they liked the network of boat speed restrictions that were already in place.

"I think the restrictions have done a good job," said Ed Day, who had been one of Marco Island's first city council members and now served as the executive director of the Florida Marine Contractors Association. "I think it's fairly clear that the manatee herd is growing."

Over at the U.S. Fish and Wildlife Service office in Jacksonville, Dave Hankla said he was "disappointed" that the environmental groups had sued. He also contended that, by focusing on all the waterfront development that his staff had allowed over the years, the lawsuits had taken a simplistic approach to the loss of manatee habitat and proliferation of boats.

"It's a more complex scenario than that," Hankla insisted.

Two months after the suits were filed, a new party joined in. The Association of Florida Community Developers—an organization that represented every major developer in the state—won permission from the court to intervene in the lawsuit against the Corps and the Fish and Wildlife Service.

The move made tactical sense. Joining the suit gave the association a seat at the table during any settlement negotiations. Soon the National Marine Manufacturers Association, the Marina Operators Association of America, and the Marine Industries Association of Florida jumped in too.

The same groups also tried to intervene in the lawsuit against the state, but David Guest fought them off, privately joking that they represented "Boaters for Hitler." Guest had already beaten back an attempt by the state wildlife commission's attorneys to get a judge to dismiss the case. Now they had begun negotiating a settlement, and to Guest those negotiations were already tough enough without letting the boaters and developers get involved.

The animal-welfare groups in the coalition did not like negotiating with a state agency that supported the killing of animals by hunters and anglers, Guest said. That made it tough to find any common ground. To add in people who would be opposed to any new government regulations "was just going to put a monkey wrench in it and make it harder to settle," he said.

Then, in mid-April, the legal fight suddenly took on a new urgency. Despite the pending lawsuit, the Corps approved a permit for the Naples Bay marina, putting 180 new boat slips in an area of Collier County that had been classified as critical habitat for manatees. As a way to make up for destroying manatee habitat and putting more boats on the water, the Corps allowed the developer to pay a $450 fee per boat slip into a fund to boost federal enforcement of the speed zones—a move that Glitzenstein called "unprecedented" and "flagrantly illegal."

Stallings blew his stack. Already one hundred manatees had died that year, more than thirty of them killed by boats. Now the Corps had seemingly thumbed its nose at the lawsuit.

"The Corps is issuing manatee hunting licenses that never expire," Stallings said. "You've paid your money, now go ahead, build your marina in critical habitat . . ."

Glitzenstein went to court seeking a temporary injunction against the Corps and the Fish and Wildlife Service to prevent them from issuing any more permits like that one. Initially, wildlife service officials talked tough about the battle. "There's a lot at stake here for people who want to do things on the waterfront," one official said. The injunction "is aimed at bringing things to a screeching halt."

Ultimately, though, Glitzenstein didn't even have to make an argument. The lawsuit was making the Clinton administration look bad at a time when his vice-president, Al Gore, was running for president and boasting about his environmental credentials. Gore's campaign staff knew that Florida held a lot of electoral votes as well as a lot of manatees.

"They basically capitulated," Glitzenstein said. "We were able to work out a stipulation with the government that they were not going to permit any project during the case without giving us thirty to sixty days' notice. That effectively shut down permitting in most of the places we were concerned about."

The Corps did not out-and-out reject any dock permits. They just did not approve any in counties that the Fish and Wildlife Service had classified as high-risk areas for manatees.

With hundreds of dock permits in limbo, developers who wanted to build marinas or boat ramps got caught in the freeze, fouling up their work schedule and their ability to pay back bank loans. Ed Day's dock builders found themselves with no work to do, since hardly anyone could get a permit.

Suddenly the tension over the manatee case ratcheted higher than ever. In a state where the entire economy is geared toward one major profit-producer—development—a legal proceeding in faraway Washington, D.C., had suddenly jammed the machinery. And for what? For the benefit of some ugly animal?

If any developers still believed they had nothing in common with the boating industry, the freeze on permits stripped away that illusion. They were all part of the growth machine, and it wasn't made to slow down for anything.

The battle over manatee protection had spread beyond a simple activists-versus-government dispute. It had become a struggle for the future of Florida, a war over the continued development of the state's coastline.

Now the governor jumped in too.

•

The agenda for the July 25, 2000, meeting of the governor and cabinet seemed fairly routine.

As usual, the list of items included a marina seeking state permission to add new boat slips. This time, it was the Sarasota Yacht Club, requesting to enlarge its marina from 84 slips to 108. Since all submerged lands belong to the state, adding slips requires the cabinet's permission. Normally such requests would be granted with little discussion.

Not this time.

"There's an endangered species that's close to being extinct in Florida waters, and I don't want to be part of that," Governor Bush announced. "It's my favorite mammal."

Bush and the cabinet voted to hold off approving the request because Sarasota County had never adopted a manatee protection plan. Bush noted that, of the original thirteen counties that had been told in 1989 to adopt manatee plans, Sarasota was one of nine that had so far failed to do so.

"I don't think it is appropriate for the [state] to allow for expansion of these facilities unless there's some indication that the counties are sincere about working to develop their plan," Bush said.

Bush noted that 175 manatees had died from all causes so far that year, an average of about one a day.

"We have to come to grips with this," the governor announced.

The news of what Bush had done shocked Ed Day, the head of the dock builders' group.

"I think the governor is grossly misinformed and he's overreacting on the side of the radical environmentalists," Day said. "I'm sorry the manatee is his favorite mammal. Humans are my favorite mammal."

Then Day made a comment that echoed a sentiment once put forward by Big John, the Volusia County councilman, during the debate on speed limits near Rick Rawlins's fish camp: "Marinas and boat slips don't kill manatees. Irresponsible boaters do."

Bush's "favorite mammal" comment sent ripples of giddiness through the

Save the Manatee Club. Could this be a sign that one of the most powerful political leaders in the state might take their side? Could this be the second coming of Bob Martinez?

Further fueling their excitement, some news organizations mistakenly reported that Bush and the cabinet had "rejected" the Sarasota Yacht Club application. That made it sound like a final decision. Actually, they had only voted to defer it.

Jeb Bush was no Fran Stallings. When it came to the environment, Bush preferred making deals to taking a hard line. Four months after loudly chastising Sarasota County, Bush and the cabinet reversed course and approved the yacht club's new slips.

Bush's DEP secretary, David Struhs, contended the change was justified because Sarasota County had made "significant progress" on its manatee protection plan. In this case, though, "significant progress" did not mean the county now had a finished protection plan, or even that it had a draft. It meant only that Sarasota County officials had agreed to apply for a fifty-thousand-dollar grant from the state to pay for *starting* on the plan sometime soon.

"It didn't matter how much you've done on the plan itself," a Sarasota County official told the *St. Petersburg Times.*

Something similar happened with Bush's next big initiative. In August 2000—when there had already been sixty-one boat-related manatee deaths—he unveiled a series of steps to combat the increase in manatee deaths. One step in his plan called for Bush himself to record public-service announcements urging boaters to slow down. Another would involve asking the legislature to increase the fine for boaters caught speeding.

The centerpiece of Bush's plan called for a "manatee summit" in Tallahassee. Boaters and manatee advocates would sit down together in one room to hash out their differences. To build public interest in the summit, it would be preceded by an online survey allowing anyone anywhere to voice an opinion about what the issues should be.

"No other animal is as endearing a symbol of our state as the gentle manatee," Bush said in announcing his plan. "Anyone who has seen or come in contact with these gentle, aquatic mammals are hard pressed not to be able to feel an attraction."

Boating-industry officials did not feel such an attraction.

"We must first strive for a balance between the protection of the manatee and Florida citizens' rights to have access to the state's beautiful waterways," said David Ray, executive director of the Marine Industries Association of Florida.

Following the Wade Hopping playbook, Ray brought up the question of whether manatees were really in danger of extinction, as Bush had claimed. Like Hopping, Ray focused on how many manatees existed, not on the escalating threats they might face.

"We've heard numbers over 4,000," Ray told reporters, citing no sources for that estimate. "We believe there may be as many as 10,000."

On October 19, Bush convened his summit in a large hotel ballroom in Tallahassee. The online survey had drawn eight hundred responses, which were collated and summarized for use by the thirty participants in the summit. Some offered serious advice, but plenty more ran the gamut of absurdity.

"Arm the manatees or in the alternative use decoys similar to deer decoys," one person suggested. Another recommended that the state "implement a pilot program to take about 100 manatees and put them in a lake where they can be provided food and medical treatment. Save the Manatee Club could conduct manatee safaris."

Bush's staff had handpicked all the summit panelists. On one side sat representatives from the Save the Manatee Club and Florida Audubon, as well as the Center for Marine Conservation, the Florida Wildlife Federation, and the Sierra Club. On the other sat representatives from the Association of Florida Community Developers, the Marine Industries Association of Florida, and the National Marine Manufacturers Association. Bush's staff had also brought in an assortment of elected and appointed officials, as well as a few scientists.

About 150 spectators showed up to watch, plus the usual gaggle of television, radio, and newspaper reporters and camerapeople who normally covered state government. As Bush walked in, one of the spectators handed him a paper manatee made using the ancient Japanese art of origami. He stuck it in his pocket.

The first speaker of the day turned out to be the most dramatic: Buddy Powell. He came armed with a grisly slide show reminiscent of the one Woodie Hartman had shown to Congress. His images were shots of dead manatees, their hides slashed open by propellers "like a hard-boiled egg put through a slicer," Julie Hauserman reported in the next day's *St. Petersburg Times*.

Powell talked about all the ways a manatee can die: hit repeatedly by boats, stunned by the cold, poisoned by Red Tide, even crushed by the locks in one of the state's old dams. The graphic pictures made the panelists wince.

Powell also talked about Bruce Ackerman's synoptic surveys. He made sure that he "presented that with a lot of caveats," Powell said years later.

Although Powell had helped Woodie Hartman with the first aerial survey back in the 1970s, he had a low opinion of Ackerman's head counts and the way they were manipulated by activists on both sides. There were always too many variables affecting the results. The data the surveys produced might seem interesting on the surface, he said, but "it was difficult to use it from a scientific standpoint."

Powell's appearance at the manatee summit marked his final bow as a state employee. He had been hired to oversee certain research projects, but the lawsuit had changed the state's focus.

"Everything we did from that point forward was based on the litigation," he explained.

Because every ounce of the state's resources had been committed to fighting the suit, none of the experiments Powell wanted to do could be carried out. He could no longer talk to either the boating-industry people or the Save the Manatee Club because they were in litigation. Fine, he said, fight it out among yourselves. Four months after the summit, he quit.

After Powell's horrific slide show came a pair of state biologists who took the panelists through a seminar on the state's effort to regulate development and boat speeds. One point the two biologists made was that no state law required the counties to pass the manatee protection plans. Unless something like the Sarasota Yacht Club expansion came up again, there was little the state could do to force the counties to enact those plans.

The next act offered dueling talks by Pat Rose and the president of Florida's boating-industry trade group, a man named John Sprague, each offering his take on regulating waterways.

Sprague, then in his early fifties, had hair that shone like a schoolgirl's Mary Janes, a deeply lined face, and a perpetual slump to his shoulders. He had an easygoing manner that enabled him to make the most outrageous statements sound perfectly reasonable—for instance, claiming that making boats slow down actually led to more boating accidents, not fewer crashes.

Although he lacked Rose's scientific background, Sprague knew the boating business backward and forward. His father had owned a marina in Riviera Beach, and Sprague learned the ropes working there while he was growing up. After Sprague inherited the business he sold it to a yacht company. Now he co-owned a marina and campground on the shores of Lake Okeechobee. Because of his vast expertise and backslapping manner, Sprague frequently served as his organization's lobbyist in Tallahassee.

When Rose and Sprague finished, about an hour into the program, Bush himself stood up. The governor gave a short speech, noting that state government had been promising for years to protect manatees, and failing.

"We have an obligation that hasn't been fulfilled," Bush said solemnly. "I love the manatee. I think this docile, beautiful animal should be protected."

Then, although the summit was scheduled to last most of the day, Bush ducked out to attend to other state business. The reporters tagged along, clamoring for a comment. Suddenly the governor stopped and turned his back to the television people.

"I don't want the cameras to see this," he told Hauserman.

Smirking, Bush reached into his pocket and pulled out the origami manatee. He pinched its flippers and made it appear to swim. Then, imitating the squeaky voice made famous on *Saturday Night Live* by a repeatedly clobbered Claymation figure known as Mr. Bill, the governor said, "Oh noooooooo! I'm stuck in the Rodman Dam! Ooooh nooooo!"

Because Bush left early, he missed most of the discussion and debate that followed. His summit could have degenerated into name-calling and chair-throwing, but it did not.

The participants actually found some things they all agreed on. They agreed the state needed to step up enforcement of its speed zones. They agreed the state should find a way to pay for more officers to patrol waterways. They agreed that one way to do that would be to charge a ten-dollar fee on every new boat registration.

Remarkably, idea for the ten-dollar fee came from none other than John Sprague of the Marine Industries Association. He said this small increase would raise eight million dollars a year, enough to add one hundred new wildlife officers to patrol the speed zones in the thirteen counties. Even better, Sprague said, the money would become a reliable, continuous source of funding, something not affected by the vagaries of the state's own budget. Anyway, ten dollars per boat did not seem like a steep price to pay to avoid both a nasty lawsuit and tighter regulation of the state's waterways.

Sprague's willingness to compromise won him at least one fan: Dave Hankla.

The Fish and Wildlife Service official had shown up at the summit just to observe what happened. But when it ended, Hankla felt compelled to track Sprague down in the parking lot and tell the marina owner how much he admired him for putting forward such a bold proposal. From then on, whenever Sprague talked, Hankla paid close attention to what he had to say.

But the summit's brief moment of compromise and consensus didn't last long. Despite Governor Bush's avowed love for manatees, the second he was asked about the fee idea, he all but killed it.

"It smells like a tax," he grumbled.

In Jeb Bush's world, new taxes were *verboten*, even when they were actually a user fee to benefit his favorite mammal, even when they were proposed by the industry that would be "taxed."

As a result, the whole manatee summit—the planning, the discussions, the final report from the conflict resolution experts hired by the state to review the process—went for naught. A second summit had been scheduled for the following year, but it never materialized.

Not only did Bush's summit fail to yield any substantive results, it actually tossed gasoline on some activists' smoldering anger. The Brevard County boating group known as Citizens for Florida's Waterways complained that the summit was "a game with a stacked deck" because none of its members had been invited.

Meanwhile, Ed Day complained loudly about how his Marine Contractors Association had not been among the thirty panelists given a seat at the table, even though his industry was suffering more than any other. Day issued a statement to the press calling the ongoing suspension of dock-building permits "a 9-month-old manatee war"—the first time that martial image would be invoked by one of the participants, but far from the last.

However, there was one marine contractor who did get to participate in the summit. He had somehow wangled an invitation from Bush's staff even though the organization he represented had begun signing up members two months before. The one lasting legacy of Bush's big manatee summit, in fact, was that it inflated the influence of Jim Kalvin and his brand-new pro-boating coalition, Standing Watch.

•

With his shaggy blond hair and thick blond beard, Kalvin looked noticeably out of place among the scientists and bureaucrats and well-heeled lawyers gathered to talk about manatee regulations.

When he showed up for events like the manatee summit, Kalvin usually wore a blue blazer stretched tight across his muscular shoulders, along with a

Jim Kalvin became the face of the boating rights movement after he founded Standing Watch. Photo courtesy of the *St. Petersburg Times*.

loud plaid shirt with no tie, a pair of perpetually wrinkled khakis, and some battered Topsiders. He was no blow-dried, camera-ready politico. Still, he knew his way around politics, and not just from being class president in his sophomore year at Naples High School. He had picked up lessons on political savvy from his mother, who for six years served as chairwoman of the Collier County School Board. Her term occurred during a bitter struggle over integration of the schools.

Kalvin spoke with the drawl of a native Cracker, and his thick-fingered hands clearly belonged to a man familiar with manual labor. The combination often misled people into thinking he was an uneducated redneck. But Kalvin's father had been a successful ophthalmologist, providing him with all the trappings of a comfortable upper-middle-class childhood.

However, for a boy growing up in Naples in the 1960s, "you either went fishing or went into the woods—or you got in trouble," Kalvin explained. He chose to skip the troublemaking and head for the outdoors. In those days, it wasn't that far away.

"I could walk from our house four blocks to the beach or to the woods," he said. Being a kid back then was "absolutely awesome. We had two seasons. In the summer the swamps were all full of water and mosquitoes but the Gulf was clear and calm and pristine, so we went fishing. In the winter it was extremely rough in Florida Bay, but the woods were dry and the mosquitoes were gone so we could go into the woods."

Thanks to the rapid development of southwest Florida, though, those days were long gone. The woods Kalvin had enjoyed so much were cut down for a mall, he said. Now when he wanted to get out in the woods, he and his wife would load their all-terrain vehicles on a trailer and drive for an hour to the Big Cypress National Preserve, where they would splash around in the mud and shoot photos of wildlife.

Kalvin's childhood enjoyment of the woods and the water guided his career choices. He worked a variety of jobs related to boating, including spending five years running a Naples marina. It ended badly.

"I had a crew of fourteen people, taking care of some sixty-plus boats," he said. "I was leasing the property. It was sold to another property and I got a two-week notice to vacate with fourteen yachts in the yard."

What happened to his marina happened to a lot of his competitors as well. "All the marinas in Naples are gone," he said. "They've been redeveloped into office condos with waterfront retail. There's a tremendous dock shortage now. Most active boaters live on the water or store their boats at a landlocked facility."

During a divorce from his first wife, Kalvin lived aboard a thirty-foot running sloop named the *Knucklehead*. The name came from a 1946 Harley-Davidson Knucklehead that he spent years restoring.

Motorcycles led to his first grown-up taste of grassroots political activism. For years, bikers had lobbied the legislature to revoke a state law requiring them to wear helmets, arguing it was an unjustified limit on their freedom and ruined the experience of riding. They formed a group called A Brotherhood Against Totalitarian Enactment, abbreviated as ABATE. Every year during the legislative session, ABATE would ride through downtown Tallahassee waving banners that said "Let Those Who Ride Decide." Kalvin became an officer in ABATE's Gator Alley chapter.

That's also where he met his second wife, Ruth, an avid outdoorswoman who, he said, "taught me things about camping and being outdoors." She also had a high tolerance for pets. The Kalvins owned two dogs, a cat, a macaw, a ferret, and a bald python named Snake. The sloop was gone, but Kalvin kept a flats boat parked in the driveway for whenever he got to go fishing.

Kalvin never saddled up with the ABATE members who roared through Tallahassee. Instead, the road that led him to Bush's manatee summit took him through six years of building docks at Port of the Islands, a development south of Naples.

For two years he worked for someone else, and then he spent four years running his own business, generally working from a barge anchored in the canal where his customer was building a million-dollar waterfront home. Kalvin's dock-building business depended on the continuing success of the home-building business.

"It was a nice steady progression of people building homes, a nice pipeline of steady work," he said. Yet the job left him plenty of time for coaching his kids' soccer team: "In the summer we generally got rained out by 2 p.m. In the season we did a max of five days of work a week."

Port of the Islands existed far from the leading edge of civilization, so he faced no competition. "It was a niche market—none of the other contractors wanted to go down there," he said.

Because it was such a long haul back to Naples, a dock contractor could not easily make a run for supplies. The barge carried every piece of hardware that might be needed. Kalvin also kept a short PVC pipe nailed to the barge to hold what he called "the fishing pole of the day." By dangling a line in the water while he worked, he caught plenty of snook. He also kept a cast net nearby because, he said, the mullet were "just phenomenal."

The twelve- by thirty-foot barge floated atop four fiberglass pontoons with a hole in the center. Frequently, Kalvin said, he would spot manatees floating in the shade under the barge, taking life easy.

"The manatees would lay up in there and be out of the sun, and be able to breathe," he said.

Then came an edict from the Fish and Wildlife Service, an edict designed to protect manatees that, he said, drove him out of business.

"All these little docks here, we built these," he told a reporter while conducting a boat tour of his old stomping grounds one sunny August afternoon. As he cruised along past the docks, where boats called *Chillin' the Most* and *Spare Parts* bobbed at anchor, a few people lingered outside despite the heat. Kalvin mentioned that his customers had been so friendly that they brought his crew beer and sometimes even grilled steaks.

As the boat zoomed along, Kalvin smiled and waved at an elderly woman eyeing him from a balcony. Instead of waving back, she shouted at him, "No wake!" and motioned for him to slow down.

Reddening with embarrassment, Kalvin grumbled that a few old Parrot-heads were hiding among the retirees. He gave the reporter a rueful look and said, "I suppose that'll be in your story."

Kalvin knew a bit about journalism. In the 1980s he wrote a troubleshooting column for a marine-industry publication. He called the column "Standing Watch," because he likened himself to a sailor standing watch on the deck, looking for hazards. Later, when he became the boating columnist for the *Naples Daily News*, he used the same column name.

What landed him in the statewide spotlight, though, was not a column but a letter to the editor that was published in the *Daily News* in mid-2000. In his letter, Kalvin sharply criticized the Save the Manatee Club.

"I asked them to disclose the salaries they pay themselves and stick to science," Kalvin said. "It was circulated around the state via e-mail. I put my home number in that . . . and that was a big mistake."

The letter generated so many phone calls from people who agreed with him, Kalvin said, that he rented a hall in Naples to convene a meeting of like-minded boaters. They decided to form an organization named for his old column, Standing Watch.

In September 2000, Kalvin helped organize a meeting of about thirty boating activists in Orlando, where they agreed to make Standing Watch a statewide group, with Kalvin as its leader.

"He had the fire in the belly," said Ron Pritchard, one of the leaders of Brevard County's small but vocal Citizens for Florida's Waterways. Pritchard wound up as Standing Watch's first vice-president, and Volusia County's pioneering boating-rights activist Rick Rawlins became one of the board members.

Pritchard's group and Rick Rawlins's Citizens for Responsible Boating had both tried in the preceding decade to form a statewide group that spoke for boaters. But their efforts failed to catch on the way Standing Watch did. They couldn't tap into any widespread outrage similar to what the dock-building freeze had generated. Standing Watch came along at just the right time, with the right leader. Kalvin credited his selection as president to the fact that he had communication skills those other activists lacked.

"I wanted to be able to stick to a proactive message," he said. "There were people in the room who do not, people who like to belittle and verbally abuse those present."

The hard part, Kalvin said, was getting different types of boaters to work together: the yacht owners, flats fishermen, personal watercraft users, power-boaters, and live-aboard sailors. The fishermen didn't like having their angling disrupted by the personal watercraft hotshots. The live-aboards looked down on the anglers and powerboaters. The yacht owners looked down on everyone.

But Kalvin had been a live-aboard, a powerboater, and a fisherman, and he had worked with yacht owners at his marina. His broad background enabled him to talk to all of the factions in language they understood. He told them they didn't have time to deal with petty differences. As long as the manatee lawsuits were threatening to shut down their favorite boating areas, they had to stick together.

"I tell people in our meetings, 'Hey, we can fight later,'" Kalvin said.

The others listened to Kalvin because he had a compelling personal story to tell, the one about how manatee regulations had forced him to close his business. However, any reporter who checked out his story learned that it wasn't quite as clear-cut. The U.S. Fish and Wildlife Service had not exactly shut him down. Hankla's agency had limited Kalvin's use of the barge to seven months of the year so manatees could flock to Port of the Islands in the winter months without worrying about being hit by boats.

Kalvin could have kept building docks, albeit with a higher overhead because he couldn't use the barge year-round, state and federal officials said. Kalvin himself chose to shutter the business and let his crew go. But Kalvin continued working part-time, doing dock repairs. He still had the barge, too.

As he traveled the state in his Ford F-150 making speeches, Kalvin frequently repeated the theme of his letter to the editor: the Save the Manatee Club was nothing but a money machine.

"The groups we're up against are well funded by donations from large corporations and grants from national foundations with very deep pockets," he would say. "They have the money for high-powered lawyers who can manipulate the system, particularly the endangered species laws, to impose their concept of how our environment should be managed."

Kalvin seldom mentioned how Standing Watch got its money. One of its largest contributions, ten thousand dollars, came from the Florida Association of Realtors—part of the same growth apparatus that Kalvin blamed for ruining the wilderness of his childhood. Another ten thousand came from a member of Safari Club International, which draws its members from the ranks of exotic game hunters who tend to oppose endangered species laws that limit what they can shoot.

Thanks to Kalvin, Standing Watch had become the living embodiment of Hopping's idea of a united front. In fact, Kalvin said, Hopping "was a very big help to us." The lobbyist routinely supplied him with the boating and development industries' analysis of the latest synoptic surveys and mortality data, he said. That way, they were all singing from the same hymnbook.

The other players on the boating side helped boost Kalvin's profile too. John Sprague hailed Standing Watch as a "welcome ally" to the boat-building industry. Sprague explained that it was perceived as more of a champion of individual boaters, not a bunch of businessmen like the Marine Industries Association.

By attending Bush's manatee summit, Kalvin said, "I was able to meet the key people from the agencies. They got to see that we were not the type of rabble-rousing, picket-carrying person they're used to dealing with."

Sure, they included many of the same members, people like Rick Rawlins who were just as rabble-rousing as ever. It's just that now they had a more acceptable front man.

•

While Kalvin's star rose, Pat Rose virtually vanished.

First, Rose lost a race for a seat on the Leon County Commission, despite an endorsement from Buffett. Then he was diagnosed with a serious heart ailment. He had to undergo surgery to have a stent implanted. When the stent failed, he had to have more surgery, and then finally an emergency bypass. While Rose was recovering from the bypass, his doctors discovered he had prostate cancer, too, so he began treatment for that. Recuperating from those multiple medical ailments kept him mostly on the sidelines for the next two years.

With Rose unavailable, Eric Glitzenstein needed someone else from the Save the Manatee Club to advise him while he jousted with the Corps, the Fish and Wildlife Service, the state's developers, and the boating industry. The job fell to Patti Thompson.

"We had a fabulous rapport," the attorney said. "I would try to do something from a legal standpoint, and I would show it to her and say, 'Does this make any sense?'"

He particularly needed her help when the Fish and Wildlife Service agreed to consider creating some places where all boating would be banned so manatees could find refuge from being hit so often. At Glitzenstein's request, Thompson put together what she called a "pie-in-the-sky" list. It covered 150 possible locations for new refuges and sanctuaries. She intended it as a menu for the feds to choose from, not a list of demands to be met. That crucial distinction would soon be lost in the heat of the struggle.

As Thompson regained her influence, Fran Stallings's fortunes went into decline. The feisty co-chairman of the Save the Manatee Club had pushed the rest of the board into pursuing the big lawsuits, but now some of them began to feel that he had become too pushy, too inclined to pick a fight.

"Somehow I have a gift, definitely not God-given, for either falling into controversy through no fault of my own or creating it myself, or more likely some combination of the above," Stallings explained. "Basically I am a button-pusher. If you punch enough buttons, sooner or later you will hit the panic button where all hell breaks loose."

Stallings's term as co-chairman expired in November 2000. Normally the Save the Manatee Club board offers to renew its officers' terms as often as they would like to serve. Some board members have been in office for more than a decade. Stallings got no such invitation.

"Fran got the boot because he was difficult to work with, he was making important decisions on his own without board input. . . . In other words, he got the Big Head," Thompson said.

By the following spring, Stallings had left the board. Soon afterward he moved out of Florida. Like Moses, another leader with a volatile temper, he would only catch a glimpse of the Promised Land, while others would reap the reward.

•

During settlement negotiations, the judge presiding over the Washington case sent all the parties over to see U.S. Magistrate John Facciola. The magistrate was a former federal prosecutor with graying hair and glasses. He had a sideline as a law professor at Catholic University. He also had a hobby that gave him an interesting perspective on the case.

When the attorneys went to meet Facciola the first time, they noticed that his waiting area was decorated with photos of sailboats. The lawyers all exchanged looks. When they got back to the magistrate's chambers and asked him about the pictures, he confirmed what they suspected.

"He was actually an ardent sailor in Chesapeake Bay," Glitzenstein said. And, as if he had descended from the founders of the Biscayne Bay Yacht Club, Facciola was none too happy about the motorboats he encountered there, telling the attorneys, "Yeah, it can really be annoying when you're out there trying to sail." The attorneys for the boating industry "did not look pleased," Glitzenstein recalled, chuckling.

Although the Clinton administration wanted to settle the case, the intervening parties—the boating and development industries—fought with Glitzenstein over every phrase and every clause, he said. For months all the sides argued with each other, repeatedly going to Facciola to settle disputes. Hashing out their differences often required a daylong work session with him.

The magistrate knew how to hold everyone's feet to the fire, Glitzenstein said. Facciola would ask Glitzenstein if he really wanted to take his chances on a trial, knowing that even if he got a favorable outcome the case would be appealed. Then he would ask the boating and development attorneys if they really wanted to risk having all permitting shut down for several years while the case ran its course through the court system. Neither side liked the idea of a trial, so they pushed ahead with the negotiations.

Glitzenstein had another strong motivation to get a deal nailed down as quickly as possible. "We were trying to reach a settlement before the Clinton administration left office," he said.

The reasons weren't political, he said. By then he and his clients knew the current crop of federal officials on the other side of the suit. They had no appetite for starting over with a brand-new bunch. No matter which party wound up in the White House, changes in the wildlife service seemed likely.

The final phases of the negotiations played out over the final days of the election, as Al Gore battled Jeb Bush's brother for the White House. Florida did indeed become crucial to the outcome, in a way no one had expected. The U.S. Supreme Court shut down the statewide recount of Florida's votes on December 12, and a day later Gore conceded.

Now the rush was on to end the manatee case.

On Wednesday, January 5, 2001—the same day Congress met to tally the Electoral College results—the D.C. case was over. The Corps, the Fish and Wildlife Service, the environmental and animal-welfare groups, the developers, and the boating industry had at last reached a deal they could all live with.

The federal agencies did not admit to anything illegal, but they committed to quickly make changes in how they handled manatee protection:

- The Fish and Wildlife Service agreed to set up a lot of new manatee refuges and sanctuaries like the ones in Crystal River, to give manatees a place where they could get away from all speeding boats. In the refuges, water-related activities by humans would be restricted between November 15 and March 31, cold months when manatees would congregate for warmth. In the sanctuaries, all human activities—not just boating but swimming, diving, snorkeling, and fishing—would be banned. The agency agreed to produce a list of proposed sites by April 2, 2001, and then after hearing public comment it would adopt the final list of sites by September 28, 2001.

- The Fish and Wildlife Service and the Corps agreed to produce an analysis of "the direct, indirect, and cumulative impacts on manatees and their habitats" of all Corps-permitted projects along the Florida coast.

- By 2003, the Fish and Wildlife Service and the Corps would produce regulations for ensuring that all new permits for docks, piers, boat slips, and other aquatic structures to be built in manatee habitat would have no more than a negligible effect on the species.

- In the two-year interim, the Fish and Wildlife Service and the Corps would come up with new, stringent criteria for permits for any projects that might increase boat traffic in manatee habitat. Of particular concern were counties where the service had determined manatees faced a higher than usual risk for being killed. In those areas, no permits would be issued unless adequate boat speed zones had been established and were being enforced.

- The Corps agreed to allow greater public scrutiny of its permitting so that the Save the Manatee Club and other environmental groups could monitor how it was making its decisions.

- The Fish and Wildlife Service promised to explain how it planned to beef up its enforcement of the existing speed zones in the coming year.

- Finally, the Fish and Wildlife Service promised to write a new, updated version of its plan for helping manatees recover from being endangered by February 28—a little more than a month away.

In announcing the settlement, Glitzenstein told reporters he was particularly happy with the promise of a cumulative impact study.

"For too long," he said, "the manatee has been balancing on the knife edge of extinction. Taken as a whole, we believe this settlement is a tremendous step forward in regard to federal agencies acknowledging their responsibilities."

Even the Washington attorney representing both the boating industry and the developers, Virginia Albrecht, praised the settlement. After all, it was better than the full-bore dock-building moratorium the environmental groups had sought.

"Our view all along is that you can have manatee protection and reasonable development, and we think this does that," she said. "We're copacetic with it."

That Albrecht's clients had agreed to such a far-reaching settlement seemed to Glitzenstein "miraculous on some level."

The Save the Manatee Club and its allies made sure to mention that the case against Florida's state agencies had also been settled "in principle," with just a few details to clear up. They made it sound like that settlement would be done in a week or so, which turned out to be more wishful thinking than actual fact.

Still, the big lawsuit that had begun with such tremendous trepidation had yielded a grand-slam homer, bringing the Save the Manatee Club nearly everything it had sought.

"Today is a good day for the manatee," proclaimed the club's new co-chairwoman, Helen Spivey of Crystal River. The ex-councilwoman and ex-legislator was no Stallings. She was a grandmotherly woman, soft-spoken, not as inclined to pick a fight.

Not everyone was quite so thrilled with the settlement, though. As Dave Hankla read it over, he realized that it put the burden of compliance on his agency, and none on the agency actually issuing the permits, the Corps of Engineers. He sensed trouble ahead, although he had no idea how bad it would get.

As it happened, the day the settlement was signed in Washington turned out to be a cold one in Florida—cold enough for Bruce Ackerman to dispatch his squadrons of scientists to count manatees around the state. Over the next forty-eight hours, biologists circled and circled, counting noses in murky water.

For once, all the variables clicked the right way. "This was probably our top score for good: cold winter, cold week, but it warmed up around here," Ackerman said years later.

When he saw the numbers that the biologists turned in, though, "I was shocked," Ackerman said. "We kind of had to huddle and decide if we really believed our own numbers, and how to present it."

The outcome that Ackerman announced on January 10, 2001, caught everyone off guard. His flying scientist squadron had counted 1,756 manatees along the Gulf Coast and another 1,520 along the Atlantic. The statewide total: 3,276 manatees, the most ever.

Records fell across the state. In Citrus County, biologists with the federal wildlife refuge counted 377 manatees, far more than Woodie Hartman ever saw. In the Tampa Bay area, researchers found a record 356 manatees, a number so high that Ackerman said it "blew us out of the water."

As he had in 1996, before the Red Tide epizootic, Ackerman would not credit the higher synoptic survey results entirely to the weather. Instead, buoyed by success, he told reporters that this high count could mean the manatee population was rebounding.

"It probably is growing a little," he said.

This was the day of reckoning that Patti Thompson had long feared would come, the day when all the "onlies" the club had attached to previous numbers became exposed as a manipulation.

Still, when she heard how many manatees Ackerman's crew had counted, the implications didn't sink in right away: "I was like, 'Wow! Cool! . . . Uhhh-ohhhh!'"

She knew the Save the Manatee Club was about to be clobbered like Mr. Bill.

## Eat Umm

ON THE DAY BRUCE ACKERMAN dispatched his scientists to record what would turn out to be a new record for the synoptic survey, one of the fliers took along a fairly important passenger. Tom Pitchford, the head of the state's marine mammal pathology lab, flew the designated routes around Collier County accompanied by none other than Jim Kalvin, founder of Standing Watch.

It's hard to picture a more mismatched pair than mild-mannered Curious George and Kalvin the modern Viking, partnered in the same small aircraft buzzing around Marco Island and Naples and even Kalvin's own Port of the Islands, skimming over the waves to search for sea cows.

They both gained something from the trip. Kalvin pointed out a few spring holes where Pitchford had not known to look for manatees. And Pitchford showed Kalvin just how difficult it is to pick out surfacing manatees from a circling plane.

"The animals are coming up and going down," Kalvin said. "Just as you think you get them all counted, more would come up and others would go down, and then the sun would glare in your eyes."

So when Ackerman announced the stunning results the following week, Kalvin was better prepared for it than anyone else on the boating side of the battle. He pointed out, accurately, that the 3,276 manatees spotted by the scientists was merely the minimum number, meaning the real number was probably higher—and thus, far beyond what the Save the Manatee Club had ever admitted might exist.

"This tells me that the population is doing quite nicely," he told a *Fort Myers News-Press* reporter. "The animal is flourishing in spite of the boats."

Other boating advocates took an even tougher stance. Ron Pritchard, the retired firefighter who was Standing Watch's vice-president and the head of the Brevard County group Citizens for Florida's Waterways, contended that because of the new survey results "some adjustments should be made" in the lawsuit settlement. Since there were more manatees than ever, he contended, everyone should agree to ratchet down any of the new restrictions on boating that had been envisioned.

To boaters, dock builders, and developers across the state, Pritchard's argument made perfect sense. The lawsuit was based on the Endangered Species Act. So was the settlement. Yet the manatee's numbers had grown. Therefore manatees couldn't be endangered anymore, could they? If they weren't endangered, then the Endangered Species Act no longer applied here. Therefore, all those new speed zones and sanctuaries and refuges should be tossed out as unnecessary.

The entire argument was based on a faulty understanding of what made a species endangered. Endangered didn't necessarily mean "few." Instead, it usually meant "facing major threats." This misunderstanding had been pushed for years by the Save the Manatee Club, with all those press releases about "only twelve hundred left" that had made Patti Thompson wince.

Then, to make things worse, the Fish and Wildlife Service had published Thompson's "pie-in-the-sky" list of 150 possible refuges and sanctuaries for the public to comment on which ones should be chosen. Some people thought that public notice meant every last one of the sites on her list would be declared off-limits. The idea of closing down so many of the state's waterways seemed particularly outrageous if the species was thriving.

Columnists at several newspapers quickly echoed Pritchard's argument. Frank Sargeant, the outdoors columnist for the *Tampa Tribune*, branded Glitzenstein's "knife edge of extinction" quote from only a few days before as "clearly false." He wrote that Ackerman's new number should put to rest "the fable that the manatee is disappearing—that we are 'down to the last few' as is so often repeated by television news anchors after prompting from those who depend on an 'endangered' manatee to justify their agenda. . . . And regulations should be made based on biological realities instead of trumped-up, emotional half-truths."

Sam Cook, a columnist for the *Fort Myers News-Press*, sneered that manatees floating in one waterway looked to him like "cigars in a toilet bowl that won't flush." He recommended that federal officials "flush the new manatee laws and give the waterways back to the boaters and anglers. They deserve as much. People are warm and fuzzy too."

Cook's column resonated well with his readers. In the post- settlement era of the manatee war, southwest Florida, particularly Lee County, became the major battleground. Cars and trucks featured window decals showing the mischievous cartoon character Calvin flashing an evil grin while urinating on a manatee. Bait shops advertised "manatee burgers" on their menus, although the main ingredient was actually something easier to obtain.

A Fort Myers boat captain made statewide headlines when a reporter discovered he had bought a "Save the Manatee" license plate for his pickup truck that said "EAT UMM." Humorless bureaucrats demanded he return it because it was in poor taste—the plate, that is, not the manatee.

Boating ranked as a pleasant pastime in most of Florida. In Lee County it had become a passion. That's because Lee County has more than a thousand miles of natural shoreline and 232 square miles of inshore waters, the handiwork of a pair of brilliant salesmen from Baltimore who over twenty years conjured a city out of a mangrove swamp.

Leonard and Julius Rosen had already made a fortune hawking hair-care products on television. Then they figured out they could make more money selling land than lanolin.

The Rosens moved to Florida and invested more than six hundred thousand dollars buying 1,724 acres on the northern bank of the Caloosahatchee River. The locals called it Redfish Point. They laughed at anyone who would be dumb enough to build on such a swampy spot. Heck, it was the site of an Indian massacre during one of the Seminole Wars. Who'd live there?

The Rosens rechristened it as Cape Coral, Florida's Water Wonderland. In ten years, the brothers were multimillionaires. Nobody was laughing at them anymore. The key to their success, of course, was selling home lots the same way they sold shampoo: advertising.

Even before they put up the first model home in Cape Coral, the Rosens unleashed a nationwide ad blitz, with commercials airing on TV as well as in newspapers across the country. They did more than just advertise, though.

They used their marketing savvy to burn their brand name into the brain of every northerner who ever got tired of shoveling snow.

They gave away unbuilt Cape Coral homes as prizes on popular TV shows like *Queen for a Day* and *The Price Is Right*. They bought a fleet of planes for a "fly and buy" program to bring in customers. They treated visitors to free dinners. They hired an army of salesmen trained in high-pressure tactics. If anyone forgot to bring along a checkbook for closing the deal—hey, no problem! The Rosens' salesmen kept a collection of blank checks from every bank in the nation. When all else failed, the salesmen would bug rooms to spy on customers and find out how to manipulate them into signing the contract.

Buyers were actively discouraged from inspecting their lots—after all, there often was no actual dry land yet. Still, a few would insist. In those cases the Rosens employed a pilot to fly these customers over the swampy land, zooming in low enough to toss out a bag of flour to mark their future home lot. The Rosens deemed accuracy less important than a convincing performance.

While the boiler-room sales tactics pushed the product, dredges set to work digging out canals and dumping the fill into the wetlands, converting soggy, muck-filled Redfish Point into Cape Coral homesites that all offered a water view. To create their new city the Rosens dug out some four hundred miles of finger canals, creating a maze of waterways sure to baffle any Minotaur.

Cape Coral became the second-largest city in Florida by area, though filling in the population would take longer than filling in the swamp. By 1967 the Rosens had sold ninety-two thousand homesites—but only thirty-one hundred families had actually moved in. Many of them got a shock. Only 5 percent of the lots had roads, drainage systems, central water lines, or a central sewer system. The land itself, according to a mid-1970s analysis, was "a virtual desert, dehydrated and devegetated except for . . . growths of noxious aquatic weeds in the so-called freshwater canals."

Then the *Wall Street Journal* ran a story exposing all the salesmen's dirty tricks. Governor Claude Kirk denounced the Rosens as "scoundrels" and told his staff to find a way to shut them down. The Florida Land Sales Board ordered them to suspend sales for a month.

The Rosens realized it was time to dump the mess in someone else's lap, so the brothers sold their development company to a Pittsburgh corporation for $250 million. Like Julia Tuttle and William Brickell in Miami, the Rosens didn't enjoy their newfound wealth for long. Julius, better known as Jack, died of a heart attack that same year. Leonard took off for Vegas, but soon wound up pleading no contest to charges of tax evasion.

The new owners took charge of Cape Coral's future just as all the regulators began to crack down, targeting not only the unscrupulous sales tactics but also the fact that the Rosens had never bothered to apply for a dredging permit. The Corps of Engineers notified the company that all excavation must immediately stop—bad news for any homebuyer whose lot was still under water, and worse news for the company's cash flow. By 1975 the company responsible for turning the Rosens' lies into reality had slid into bankruptcy.

Still, slowly, people came to Cape Coral. Waterfront property is waterfront property. By the late 1990s more than one hundred thousand people called Cape Coral home—double the population of the county seat of Fort Myers, right across the river. Another sixteen thousand would pour into the city between 2000 and 2003.

Cape Coral became the largest city in southwest Florida, with a parade of new homebuyers "turning musty flatlands into a grid of ranch homes painted in vibrant Sun Belt hues: lime green, apricot and canary yellow," the *New York Times* later reported. Fueling the boom: creative financing by mortgage brokers who were eager for buyers, no matter what the risk. The brokers made it ridiculously easy for buyers from as far away as Europe to snap up homesites while taking on more debt than they could handle.

Cape Coral benefited from another factor, something the Rosen brothers would have loved if it had been around in their day. "The Internet made it possible for people ensconced in snowy Minnesota to type 'cheap waterfront property' into search engines and scroll through hundreds of ads for properties here," the *New York Times* wrote after the real estate bubble burst. "Cape Coral beckoned speculators, retirees and snowbirds with thousands of lots, all beyond winter's reach."

As Cape Coral boomed, everybody who moved in wanted a dock behind his or her new house. By mid-2001, about 6,500 docks had already been built on the Lee County shoreline, and there was room for another 13,500.

During the manatee lawsuit, the Corps issued permits, but only after the plaintiffs looked them over, which slowed down the approval process. After the settlement, getting a permit got a lot harder. The Corps issued a notice that new dock permits would now cost an extra $542 per boat slip, with the money going into a fund to boost enforcement of manatee speed zones. Corps and wildlife service officials said that fee would be the equivalent of 1.65 hours of waterway enforcement over ten years.

The review process for dock permits now took months. One Cape Coral resident applied for a two-slip permit in February 2001, paying more than a thousand dollars, and got her permit in June. She griped to the *Fort Myers News-Press* that the fees were "extortion."

Yet the permits did get approved. Through the end of 2001, the Corps okayed nearly six hundred dock permits in Lee County, more than any other coastal county.

Miffed at the slowdown, Cape Coral city officials tried to issue their own dock construction permits. But if there's one thing Corps officials won't stand for, it's someone challenging their power to issue permits, no matter how slowly. The Corps told the city to knock it off or face criminal charges. City officials ignored the threat for a few months, but finally surrendered.

Although Cape Coral residents could dock their boats behind their houses, not everyone was so lucky. Boaters who couldn't afford waterfront property relied on commercial marinas and ramps to launch their boats. But through the 1990s, as Jim Kalvin discovered, those marinas began to vanish as developers took them over. They would become part of a waterfront condominium where only the owners could use the water. Although there were still a few public ramps, every year the line of boaters waiting to use them on the weekends got longer and longer.

Yet the loss of access did nothing to halt the boom in boating there. By 2000 Lee County was home to more than forty thousand boats, nearly all of them pleasure boats. The next county to the south, Collier, had only half that many. The annual boat show in Fort Myers drew more than ten thousand people to look at the latest seventeen-footers from Sea Fox or the new ninety-horsepower Mercury engines.

The downside to cramming so many boats into the local waterways: the danger, not only to manatees, but also to people. One four-year study by Mote Marine Laboratory in Sarasota found that there were so many boats crowded into the Caloosahatchee and other Lee County waterways that "it's like a boat parade" on weekends, said Mote researcher Jay Gorzelany. "It averages out to one boat going through every eight seconds."

In 2000, Lee tied Brevard County for having the most manatees killed by boats—thirteen—and led the state in the number of people killed by boats, with seven. Boating had become so dangerous that even people like Bonita Springs dock builder Ben Nelson and his wife gave it up.

"It's just not worth it," Lori Nelson said. "There's no licensing, no mandatory boater education, and it can be quite frightening. . . . We've reached our carrying capacity. We're way beyond it."

Still, for many Lee County residents, the sound of a rumbling Evinrude symbolized "everything dear to those who love the Southwest Florida lifestyle—boating with the wind in one's hair, the horizon as the only boundary, and a pocket full of keys to the tallest waterfront house with the biggest dock out back. Stuff that is probably protected in the Bill of Rights," wrote a *News-Press* columnist.

Now here came a federal court settlement that threatened to limit the boaters' already diminishing access to the water. People in Lee County were already inclined to view with suspicion anything involving federal authorities. After all, this was the county named for the most famous rebel of all, General Robert E. Lee.

The personification of the disdain that Lee County and its leaders had for manatee rules was a man named William "Doug" Wilkinson. In February 2000, Wilkinson took his nineteen-foot Hewes flats boat into the Caloosahatchee and deliberately violated a manatee speed zone to get a ticket.

Then, just like Rick Rawlins, Wilkinson used his ticket to challenge the legality of the manatee regulations. He argued that the rules were not based on science. Worse, he said, the state had usurped his "constitutional right to travel." Also, he testified later, he thought the rules as written were incomprehensible.

"I don't understand any of the rules," he said. "I don't know where you can and can't go. I don't think there is anybody that can interpret any of this."

Wilkinson then filed suit against both the state and Lee County for trying to enforce the zones. He said he wanted to ensure that "everybody who is a fisher and a boater and a water skier's voice can be heard" because "these rules have been adopted and no one is taking into any consideration any of the rights of any of these folks."

This was no camouflage-clad kook screaming about black helicopters swooping down on freedom-loving Americans. Doug Wilkinson was Lee County's circuit court administrator. He ran the court system.

Although he had sued his own employer, Wilkinson probably felt sure of keeping his job no matter what. During a pretrial deposition, an attorney for the Florida Fish and Wildlife Conservation Commission asked him about something called the "Old-Timers" list, people with whom Wilkinson regularly went fishing.

"I notice several people whose address is listed as the Lee County Justice Center on the Old-Timers' list," the attorney, Ross Burnaman, said to Wilkinson. "Could you tell me who these people are and what they do?"

So Wilkinson ran down the list. One was a county judge, one a circuit judge, then another circuit judge, then another. . . . All told, there were seven sitting judges on the list of Wilkinson's fishing buddies. And one of the attorneys representing Wilkinson happened to be the guy who oversaw the operations of the state attorney's office.

Because of Wilkinson's extensive connections, none of Lee County's judges could hear the case. A retired judge came in to try the ticket charge. He listened to detailed testimony from Bruce Ackerman about the science behind the speed zones. He also listened to testimony from an expert that Wilkinson called who repeatedly admitted he didn't know what data the state had used.

Then the judge declared the speed zones appeared "arbitrary and capricious." He tossed out the charges against Wilkinson and eight co-defendants who, like him, had incurred speed zone violations to challenge the rules.

However, Wilkinson and his co-defendants lost their civil suit, with one appellate decision observing that speed zones for boats did not interfere with any "right to travel" because they were "no more burdensome than speed limits or road closures commonly enforced on Florida roads."

Amid such widespread pro-boater sentiment in southwest Florida, the settlement between the federal agencies and the Save the Manatee Club's coalition sparked vehement opposition. There were complaints about new rules being formulated during closed-door negotiations, rather than in an open public hearing.

It didn't help that rumors ran rampant about an impending clampdown by federal officials. One Lee County real estate agent sent out a letter to waterfront property owners warning them to sell their properties fast before the feds shut down every last waterway to boat traffic.

People upset about what was happening inundated their region's legislators with phone calls urging them to do something about it. Cape Coral's state representative, a Republican lawyer named Jeff Kottkamp whose house sat on a canal, wanted to appeal to a higher authority. He proposed a bill calling on

Congress "to assure all Floridians than their boating rights will not be abridged by federal designation of manatee protection refuges and sanctuaries." (The bill failed.)

Many in southwest Florida wanted their legislators to step in and block the wildlife commission from settling its lawsuit behind closed doors, the way the feds did. The representative for the Fort Myers area, a real estate agent named Lindsay Harrington, shared their concerns.

"We're tired of the federal government telling us how to live; we're tired of court's rulings telling us how to live," Harrington told one gathering.

Harrington didn't think much of environmental activists like the ones from the Save the Manatee Club, comparing them to watermelons: "Green on the outside, red on the inside."

When a *St. Petersburg Times* reporter asked Harrington what he had against the Save the Manatee Club, his face turned bright red and his voice rose to a near-shout.

"Just follow the money!" he yelled. "The machine—the Save the Manatee Club—has gone too far. They are fighting this issue because once you start recovering this critter, it's not an issue anymore! They won't have anything to do!"

Since Harrington at that point chaired the House Natural Resources Committee, controlling all the legislation involving the state's wildlife agency, he was in the perfect position to do something. On March 1, 2001, just two months after the federal settlement had been announced, Harrington called his own version of Jeb Bush's manatee summit. He scheduled it for Charlotte County Memorial Auditorium in Punta Gorda, where he had once been mayor. The speakers included representatives from Governor Bush's office, from the state Fish and Wildlife Conservation Commission, and from the U.S. Fish and Wildlife Service, Dave Hankla.

Hankla said later that if someone had stuck all of that night's speakers in a dunk tank and charged five dollars a throw, "they would've made a phenomenal amount of money. If they had offered to let them use live ammo, they probably would've made even more."

The panel of speakers had to contend with frequent interruptions from the rowdy crowd of about a thousand people who showed up, Hankla said. At one point during the forum, while Bush aide Colleen Castille was trying to explain the governor's position, one man in the crowd shouted out, "Why don't we all just get up and walk out? You've already got this settled."

But later Castille won applause by reminding everyone that Bush opposed any increase in boater registration fees to pay for increased law enforcement and boater education—even though that might reduce the need for new speed zones.

The forum grew worse around midnight, Hankla said, because "the moderator turned on us. We answered questions until 3 a.m., and then we went to a bar and just *drank*."

Many of the people who attended Harrington's forum were members of the Coastal Conservation Association of Florida (CCA), an organization with about ten thousand members interested in recreational fishing. CCA drew some of its financial support from the boating industry, particularly Mercury Marine. But the organization had not previously gotten involved in any skirmishes over manatee protection, and it did not participate in the settlement negotiations.

Now the executive director, Ted Forsgren, came down from Tallahassee to speak at Harrington's forum and join the fray. Forsgren said he had been incensed at seeing Patti Thompson's "pie-in-the-sky" list of 150 potential refuge or sanctuary sites.

"They're taking some entire stretches of prime saltwater fishing waters and closing them," complained Forsgren, a bearded Tampa native who usually wore a vented fishing shirt with the CCA logo to such events, as if he intended to leave shortly to go looking for snook. "We've been willing to accept speed zones and restrictions, but when you talk about closing entire waterways, then we're going to fight it."

Quite a few of the other attendees wore T-shirts decorated with a fake license plate that asserted Florida boaters, not manatees, were the true endangered species. They trailered in their high-powered skiffs and left them parked outside to make it plain which side they were on.

There was no mistaking what side Harrington was on. "If those boating rules are created, we're talking about restricting areas that mankind . . . has always walked and waded," the state representative said. "I think that is very, very drastic, and what I consider an imbalance."

The crowd at the forum got what they wanted. A spokesman from the Fish and Wildlife Conservation Commission said the state's settlement would not be signed until the agency gauged public sentiment. Meanwhile, Hankla promised that what his agency had in mind for refuges and sanctuaries would not be as restrictive as what the audience feared.

In fact, as 2001 turned into an all-out assault on the whole concept of manatee protection, the Save the Manatee Club had reason to worry that the feds might renege on the whole agreement.

•

The first signs of trouble came from Fred Morse's town, around the same time as Harrington's forum. The Corps of Engineers surprised Glitzenstein and his clients by approving a seventy-slip marina on Miami's Brickell Key, just south of the mouth of the Miami River in the Biscayne Bay Aquatic Preserve. The Corps said yes because the Fish and Wildlife Service had signed off on it.

The builder, Swire Properties—one of the largest property investment firms in Hong Kong—had already developed condominiums for three thousand residents, a restaurant, and the grand Mandarin Hotel on its land. The site: a forty-four-acre artificial island made from piled-up dredging spoil in the middle of Biscayne Bay.

To blunt objections to their plan to put more boats into the middle of an aquatic preserve, Swire officials promised to set aside a few boat slips for wild-life officers and to set up an observation post so they could watch for speeding boaters.

"This waterway will absolutely benefit from this marina," said Swire's lob-byist, Frank Matthews, who worked for Wade Hopping's law firm. Matthews pointed out that the Fish and Wildlife Service had determined that the marina would actually *benefit* manatees, thanks to the increase in law enforcement it would provide.

But both the state wildlife commission and the Miami-Dade County De-partment of Environmental Resource Management objected to the Brickell Key project. Not only was it in an aquatic preserve, but it appeared to violate the county's manatee protection plan.

Glitzenstein was furious. After working out the lawsuit settlement, the Save the Manatee Club had reviewed two dozen dock-permit applications sent over by the Corps. The Brickell Key marina project was the only one they had ob-jected to. Yet the Fish and Wildlife Service and the Corps had given it a green light anyway, and without any warning to the club.

One call from Glitzenstein had federal officials backpedaling. Corps officials suspended Swire's permit.

Then the Brickell Key project came up for a vote in front of Governor Bush and the cabinet, which had final say over the use of state-owned submerged land. Miami mayor Joe Carrollo showed up to endorse the marina as "a gateway to downtown Miami," not to mention "a critical linchpin in crime prevention, boating safety, and manatee protection."

However, Carrollo—in Miami his nickname was "Crazy Joe"—had himself just been arrested, accused of domestic violence amid reports he had beaned his wife with a terra-cotta tea container. Months later those charges were dropped, but at the time the mayor was probably not the most effective advocate for the crime-busting aspect of Swire's boat slips.

Another Swire supporter, a Miami police officer, might have done better, except he went too far. He contended that putting a marina in that spot could halt the flow of drugs into Miami.

"Are you saying that parking a couple of boats and having a little observation tower is going to stop drugs coming into Miami?" asked Attorney General Bob Butterworth, skepticism dripping from his voice. Butterworth had previously been the sheriff of Broward County. He knew the South Florida crime picture better than that. He joked that it might be more effective to post a couple of undercover agents on the riverbank, armed with cane poles.

In the end, the vote went five to two against the marina. Bush voted no, as did Butterworth and even Secretary of State Katherine Harris, who described herself as "pro-boating and pro-marina." One of the votes for Swire came from the state's education commissioner, widely regarded as an overly ambitious lightweight. His name was Charlie Crist.

Swire's president, an avid boater, complained loudly about seeing his multi-million-dollar plans thwarted by a lumbering marine mammal and its fans.

"The passion and the fanaticism of the manatee cause is such that any marina is a bad marina," he griped to reporters.

After the cabinet blocked the Brickell Key marina, the controversy settled down briefly. But as the April 2 deadline approached for the Fish and Wildlife Service to produce its list of proposed sanctuaries and refuges, Hankla's staff told reporters that they needed more time.

When one newspaper reported that the wildlife service was going to miss its deadline, an agency spokesman insisted that that was an inaccurate characterization.

"A press account used the term 'miss' the deadline, and it should have used 'postpone,'" the spokesman said. "We're synchronizing our timeline with the state's timeline, which could in fact change our deadlines."

Glitzenstein could see that this was more than just a technical glitch. It was an omen.

## 14

Bad Boys

THE PROBLEM WITH THE NEW ADMINISTRATION lay with whom the new president had chosen to run things, and how.

During the presidential campaign, Texas governor George W. Bush had promised voters he would "change the tone in Washington" and work to be "a uniter, not a divider." But after he beat Clinton's vice-president in the disputed 2000 election, all that anti-partisan rhetoric went out the White House window. Instead, as former Bush press secretary Scott McClellan wrote in his memoir, "the mantra of the new administration was 'anything but Clinton' when it came to policies."

Rather than govern as a moderate the way his father had, the new President Bush modeled himself on a more conservative GOP father figure, Ronald Reagan. In selecting who would lead his federal agencies, Bush frequently put ideology ahead of all other considerations, including experience and even competence.

A prime example was his selection for the Interior Department, which oversees the U.S. Fish and Wildlife Service. He picked a silver-haired attorney from Colorado named Gale Norton, who was no fan of the Endangered Species Act. While Norton was Colorado's attorney general, she had urged the U.S. Supreme Court to declare the Endangered Species Act unconstitutional. She backed drilling in the Arctic National Wildlife Refuge as far back as the 1980s, when she was working in Reagan's Interior Department. She was so enamored of putting the states' rights ahead of federal regulation that she once lamented the fact that Robert E. Lee's side lost the Civil War.

"We certainly had bad facts in that case where we were defending state sovereignty by defending slavery," Norton said in a 1996 speech that came back up during her confirmation hearings. "But we lost too much. We lost the idea that the states were to stand against the federal government gaining too much power over our lives."

So when the president's brother, Jeb Bush, said his state wanted to take the lead on manatee protection regulations, Norton was inclined to do what he wanted—no matter what it said in that federal court settlement that those despised Clintonites had signed.

On March 26, 2001, the U.S. Fish and Wildlife Service announced that the deadline for producing its list of refuges and sanctuaries would be pushed back a month, to May 2. An agency spokesman first said the idea came from the service's Jacksonville office. Then Governor Bush issued a statement explaining that the delay actually resulted from his pulling strings in Washington.

"Recognizing the frustration and heavy burden on Florida boaters," the governor said, "earlier this month I appealed to Gale Norton . . . to delay any announcement and possibly forgo implementation of federally designated refuges and sanctuaries." Delaying the federal action "would enable the state to consider implementation of its own protective measures," he said.

Glitzenstein's clients agreed to this postponement, reluctantly. After all, the governor was promising state action that would be better than the fed's promises—even though his state wildlife commission had yet to approve its own settlement.

Getting to the point of having a settlement with the state had taken months longer than the January announcement promised. The two sides slugged it out over every syllable.

"We were doing twenty-foot segments of the Indian River, when the negotiations were supposed to be covering the whole state," David Guest said. "It was absolutely inch by inch."

As with the lawsuit against the federal agencies, the developers and the marine industry filed motions to intervene. Patti Thompson said the Save the Manatee Club had no objection, but Guest opposed it. He successfully kept them out, at first. By the time an appeals court ruled that those groups did in fact have a right to be a part of the case, Guest and the wildlife commission had at last hammered out a settlement.

Once the basics of the agreement had been nailed down, the exhausted Guest—a frequent sufferer from extreme wanderlust—left a young associate to work out any final details while he went hitchhiking through Canada.

The deal called for a template set of regulations to be imposed on Brevard County. Once those were in place, the template would be applied to other hot spots throughout the state. Such a loose approach seemed logical as a way to resolve such difficult negotiations. In retrospect, Guest said, that approach "was a mistake." It left far too much wiggle room for the defendants.

Guest's clients felt singularly unenthusiastic about the final version, too, but said they would accept it.

"This is the bare minimum that is needed to protect manatees in Florida, and without a lawsuit, we would not have even gotten this far," Patti Thompson said.

State wildlife officials made it plain they didn't like it either. By this time the head of Pat Rose's old Bureau of Protected Species was one of his first hires, Kipp Frohlich. Slender and acerbic, Frohlich usually showed up at public hearings looking like a refugee from a Rotary luncheon, dressed in neatly pressed khakis and a blazer. Frohlich had actually gotten his start looking far less natty. He had been the biologist picking up smelly, dead manatees in southwest Florida in the early 1980s, the job Tom Pitchford later took over. Frohlich had grown up in a finger-canal community in St. Petersburg called the Isle of Capri, and he had seen how the state had changed.

"We're like a bunch of crack addicts for development," he once quipped. "We just can't get off the habit."

Now, though, Frohlich took the part of dutiful bureaucrat, explaining to reporters that "the Save the Manatee Club had a huge menu of areas, which we didn't feel we could support. But we didn't want to go to court. . . . Management options handed down by a judge might not balance the public interest. We'd much rather do this ourselves."

For the pro-boating groups that had been kept out of the negotiations, the idea of approving a settlement without hearing from the people affected by it seemed downright criminal. Tom McGill, a retired electrical engineer who helped found Citizens for Florida Waterways, compared the negotiations between the state and the manatee advocates to "two crooks who decide to rob somebody and have a meeting, and the person they're going to rob isn't at the meeting."

But Judith Vallee contended that it was the boaters who were taking advantage of everyone else, for their own convenience.

"They see boating as a right, but they forget that sovereign submerged lands are public land," she said. "They belong to everybody, not just boaters. I'm not a boater, but I have as much right to say what happens to submerged lands as boaters and riparian owners do. It's shortsighted for them to say, 'This inconveniences me, so I don't want it.'"

The final say on the settlement belonged to the wildlife commissioners. They drew no salary but could claim reimbursement for their expenses, so they routinely held their meetings at resorts around the state. That allowed them to get in some golf or fishing between sessions revising the rules on turtle harvests or exotic wildlife possession. Once or twice a year they met in Tallahassee, and now it was time for one of those meetings.

They were supposed to take up the settlement during their Tallahassee meeting on March 30, 2001. Instead, because of the outcry against the federal settlement for taking place behind closed doors, they decided to postpone their vote. They said they would wait two weeks until they could hear from everyone who wanted to express an opinion.

During that Tallahassee meeting, a young representative of the Save the Manatee Club presented the commissioners with the results of an opinion poll showing widespread support for manatee protection. In response, one of the commissioners took the club to task for its long years of claiming manatees were endangered.

"The commission and the public is being misled on this issue," said Quinton Hedgepeth, a Miami dentist who had been appointed by Governor Chiles as the commission's first black member. "We may need to do something as far as a study to determine the status of the manatee."

As it happened, someone at the meeting had such a study in hand.

Ted Forsgren of the Coastal Conservation Association proudly presented the commissioners with a manatee study that had cost his fishing group ten thousand dollars. The study had not been done by a manatee biologist. The author, Thomas Fraser, had a Ph.D. in marine biology, but he specialized in the study of various kinds of fish. He had once been chairman of the state Marine Fisheries Commission, an agency that had never dealt with manatees. It specialized in stock assessments of sport fish.

Fraser now worked as the partner in a big environmental consulting firm in Fort Myers, where many of the clients happened to be developers who needed dock permits. The note about him at the end of his report said, "He has had, and is working with, a number of marina projects that must address manatee protection issues."

In other words, he wasn't an independent scientist reviewing data in an impartial way. He had a rooting interest in the outcome of his own report. Cynthia Frisch sniffed that he was nothing but a "biostitute."

Fraser's report was really just a comparison of those same synoptic survey results that the marine-industry groups had previously questioned. Acker-man's count of three thousand plus had turned those surveys into a gold mine for pro-boating forces.

In the report, Fraser contended that the surveys showed the manatee popu-lation appeared to be "growing at a healthy rate" of 6 to 7 percent a year, so there was "virtually no real probability of the manatee becoming extinct in the next 100 years due to boat interactions."

In fact, Fraser wrote, "Manatees showed a spectacular recovery in Lee County from all causes of mortality, especially the . . . Red Tide related deaths in 1996, based on comparative synoptic survey counts in 1996 and 2001."

And what of all those dead manatees, the ones killed by boats as well as all the rest? "Increases in the manatee population should be expected to coincide with increasing numbers of dead manatees from all causes including boats over time," Fraser wrote.

So the increasing number of dead manatees—creeping from 150 to 200 and then 250 and now, in 2001, climbing to a record high of 325, with 81 of them killed by boats—was not really a problem, Fraser wrote.

"This is not a sign of failure to adequately protect manatees," he wrote, "but a positive indication of successful population growth."

The Save the Manatee Club and the Humane Society quickly deployed staff biologists to poke holes in Fraser's report for reporters. The experts on the Manatee Technical Advisory Council took things more carefully.

In July 2001 the MTAC met with Fraser and, after hearing him out, easily uncovered his report's weak spot: "Dr. Fraser's calculations show differences between death and count indices. If his theory that population growth explains increase in deaths, then both rates should be similar. . . . Boat mortality seems to be increasing faster than natural mortality. This might mean that there is a problem with boat mortality."

But Forsgren argued that the report he had paid for showed "there's been a fairly substantial increase in manatees." He got right to the point about why he hired Fraser, asking a reporter: "At what point do you declare success so you don't have to crack down on boaters?"

Actually, a panel of manatee biologists that included Buddy Powell had been working on that question. As required by the settlement, they had been trying to craft a new recovery plan for the species. The plan would set out scientifically sound criteria for when manatees could be reclassified as threatened instead of endangered, as well as criteria for taking them off the list entirely. The criteria wouldn't be based on just the number of manatees. Instead, the plan would focus on more important questions, such as the survivability rate of adults—in other words, how many survived from year to year. The panel concluded that a 94 percent survivability rate would show sufficient growth in the population to merit reducing the level of protection to threatened, instead of endangered. It would mean the population would grow 4 percent a year, a healthy rate.

Yet before the year was out, the scientific study that would have the greatest political impact would be the overly simplistic Fraser report, not the work of the nineteen manatee experts.

•

A week after the Fraser report became public, one of Harrington's Republican colleagues, Representative Bob Allen of Merritt Island, decided to copy him and hold what he called a "Brevard County Boating Summit."

The April 7 gathering drew 250 people, all of them opposed to new manatee regulations. One of the speakers was Harrington, now taking a more strident tone in his attacks on the closed-door negotiations that produced the federal settlement—even though the marine industry had been involved in those negotiations.

"What we are seeing is a lack of democracy, and now we are going to extremes," Harrington told the crowd.

Then came the Fish and Wildlife Conservation Commission's hastily arranged public hearing on April 19. Held in an opulent Orlando hotel ballroom, the hearing lasted five hours but seemed far longer. About two hundred people showed up, some wearing white buttons urging approval of the settlement but far more wearing dark pink buttons vowing loyalty to the boaters.

The speakers included Ron Pritchard from Citizens for Florida Waterways, who complained that the commissioners had been "bamboozled by eco-radical groups." He gave the commissioners a two orange life vests decorated with the slogan "Save Boating."

Jim Kalvin from Standing Watch took his turn at the microphone, contending that the synoptic survey results proved there were now more manatees than ever. He urged the commissioners to set a numerical limit past which manatees would no longer be endangered.

"We want to know when enough is enough," he said.

One of the strongest voices belonged to someone who wasn't there: Governor Bush.

Bush had dispatched his top cabinet aide, Colleen Castille, to smooth over any objections to the state's settling the lawsuit. She told the commissioners that Bush wanted state officials, and not a federal judge, making decisions about which Florida waterways would be restricted. She also promised that if the state settled the case, it would help persuade the Fish and Wildlife Service and the Corps to drop consideration of some of their more onerous measures.

After making her public statement, Castille spent the remainder of the meeting scurrying back and forth among groups of angry boaters and suspicious manatee advocates, trying to work out any obstacles to the settlement. Castille, an avid hiker and canoeist, was an imposing blond woman with a steel-trap mind. A veteran of many a political campaign, she knew how to sprinkle calming words on a roaring argument, as well as how to spit out a sentence packed with sharpened steel.

In the end, the wildlife commission voted five to one to approve the settlement with the Save the Manatee Club and its fellow plaintiffs. The no vote came from the Miami dentist, Dr. Hedgepeth, who thought it should go to trial.

"I don't feel the state of Florida is guilty," Hedgepeth explained. "I don't think that settling this lawsuit is the way to make rules."

This settlement did not contain as many far-reaching promises as the one with the federal agencies. Under this settlement, the wildlife commission pledged only to *consider* imposing new speed zone rules around the state, beginning in Brevard County. Meanwhile, the state, like the feds, would draw up a list of potential "safe havens" for manatees, where all boat traffic could be limited to certain times of the year or forbidden entirely—but they didn't have to adopt them.

Castille had worked out a few amendments to the original agreement, just to make the boaters happy, that said the wildlife commission wouldn't even think about putting a few areas off-limits. The changes didn't make a big difference, Guest said. When he returned from his walkabout across Canada, he found the version he had seen before he left "largely intact" in the final settlement.

But to some of the people at the Orlando meeting, just the idea of a whole new layer of rules seemed wrong, especially given the numbers from the latest synoptic survey count.

"We're setting up this mosaic of regulation on the waters of Florida, and eventually this mosaic is going to cover all of Florida," griped John Sprague, not mentioning that the Marine Industries Association had agreed to the federal settlement. "That mosaic has got to stop, or else boating as we know it in Florida is going to end."

That prospect greatly concerned one of the most powerful media moguls in the state: Karl Wickstrom, publisher of *Florida Sportsman* magazine.

As an energetic young *Miami Herald* reporter, Wickstrom had focused on rooting out Mob-connected public officials. Now he was much older, with thinning blond hair and thick glasses, but he still had a reputation for ruthlessness.

Wickstrom had been born in Illinois, in a town where his dad was a newspaper columnist. After trying newspapering and then putting in a brief stint as a legislative aide in Tallahassee, Wickstrom started his magazine in 1969. His first desk was a door across two filing cabinets. But soon the advertisers flocked to him, packing each issue with color ads for the latest boats and motors.

Wickstrom—working hand in hand with Ted Forsgren—used his magazine to lead a campaign to convince the public to pass a constitutional amendment banning commercial gill-net fishing in 1994. His opponents in the commercial fishing industry branded him "Herr Karl," because they regarded him as a dictator. But there was no denying his power to persuade.

His magazine had a circulation of more than one hundred thousand readers statewide, and the sales staff boasted that it actually reached three times that many. Eighty percent of his subscribers owned a boat, and more than 40 percent owned two. All but 1 percent were male. Only 35 percent had graduated from college.

Wickstrom had sold his magazine to Primedia Inc., a New York company that published *Seventeen*, *Modern Bride*, and *New York* magazines, but "Herr Karl" still ran it as if he were Citizen Kane. It wasn't just a publication. It was a bullhorn for shouting his views at the world. It didn't hurt that his views happened to coincide with those of his advertisers in the marine industry.

Now the sixty-five-year-old Wickstrom—a founding member of the Coastal Conservation Association of Florida, and still one of its major supporters—

began running stories and editorials in his magazine and on his Web site criticizing the new manatee protection rules.

"Creepy Crawl extreme slow zones that may ruin countless traditional fishing trips, while not appreciably affecting Florida's manatee population, are scheduled to be imposed by federal bureaucrats in weeks just ahead," the magazine editorialized at one point. "Only a continuing protest can stop the unjustified zones. Unfortunately, many anglers know little or nothing about the impending putt-putt proposals, so it's up to the rest of you to carry the flag of reason and common sense. What's essential at this point is for boaters to contact as many officials as possible." That item ran under the headline "Manatee Madness."

*Florida Sportsman* frequently targeted the Save the Manatee Club, accusing it of "ringing the extinction bell without letup, while raising many millions of dollars to do so."

Wickstrom said he had actually supported the Save the Manatee Club back when its purpose what he called an "awareness campaign" and it didn't advocate regulations on boating. However, he also contended—admittedly without a shred of evidence—that Jimmy Buffett had agreed to help Bob Graham start the Save the Manatee Club only "as part of a public service by Buffett in mitigation of a drug case."

Wickstrom and his writers encouraged their readers to rely on *Florida Sportsman*, and only *Florida Sportsman*, for the straight story about the whole sea cow situation: "As the Manatee War rages on this and other fronts, there are continually new developments that readers can follow on floridasportsman.com and some other sources. Unfortunately, typical general media sources have been anti-boating and biased toward manatee enthusiasts who managed to obfuscate the fact that the manatee population is flourishing as never before in modern times."

Now—in addition to having a united boating and development industry front working with Wade Hopping, a pair of grassroots activist leaders in Jim Kalvin and Ted Forsgren, and a legislative leader in Lindsay Harrington to push new laws—the lineup opposing the federal settlement had gained a media outlet to stir up the base. If an anti-Frisch had pulled together a mirror-image version of the lawsuit coalition, this would have been the group she would have assembled.

Wickstrom didn't confine his opposition to the printed word, either. Not long after the state settlement was announced, Governor Bush was scheduled to release the first redfish from the state's own hatchery into the Alafia River. Bush, always game for a photo op, donned a pair of rubber boots to wade into the river and dump out the fingerlings. Waiting on the riverbank stood Wickstrom, impatient to buttonhole the governor.

As Bush mugged for the TV cameras, still standing in ankle-deep water and cracking jokes, the publisher suddenly called out to him. Wickstrom said they needed to chat about the new manatee rules. Bush, dropping his jocularity, promised Wickstrom he was working on it. When he waded ashore, the two men sidled away from reporters to talk.

Because of his work on the gill-net issue, Wickstrom usually counted himself as a friend of environmental groups. In fact, a few years later he would wind up on the board of the Everglades Foundation, promoting the restoration of the River of Grass alongside Jimmy Buffett.

But Wickstrom told a reporter that what the Save the Manatee Club was doing was "a terrible thing. They are using a lovable animal as a tool to stop growth. That's really not fair. It's largely dishonest. The truth is there are more manatees than there ever was before. . . . The boating industry is going to suffer from these manatee zones. And the general public doesn't know it's been tricked by this extinction stuff. The extinction threat is one of the most valuable things you can use in fund-raising. These people don't boat themselves. They are anti-boating."

Wickstrom's readers responded to his editorials by making even stronger comments on *Florida Sportsman*'s online message boards. On the largely anonymous board, rumors and bad jokes flew back and forth at a dizzying pace. Some comments suggested manatees were actually bad for the environment: eating so much sea grass that they were more destructive than boats, and pooping so much that they polluted more than a sewage plant.

There were jokes about wishing Jimmy Buffett would "fall down a long flight of stairs," and there were declarations of pseudo-fatwas: "Death to Eric Glitzenstein!" When the Save the Manatee Club hired a new employee to open an office in southwest Florida, angry boaters posted what they thought were pictures of her house on the online message boards, and someone vandalized the place. Then it turned out they had targeted the wrong house.

One day someone named Captain Chris from Jacksonville asked whether any of the eight thousand members of Wickstrom's online chatterers had ever run over a manatee and would be willing to admit it. Several of them said yes.

"I was running a channel and saw the boil in front of me," wrote one called

Mexico, who was from Stuart. "Put it into neutral but still ran right up its back. Put about a four-inch gash in it. Felt horrible about it."

"I've hit only one in my years on the water here," wrote someone called Fatback from Fort Myers. "Pretty hard, too. I think he became a statistic. He . . . was out of his zone. Maybe we should put the manatee zone signs underwater where they can read them."

"Had the trolling motor get rammed by a charging manaturd one day," wrote someone called Storyteller. "He refused to yield. Come to think of it, he had the same look in his eye as Moby Dick."

Several more boasted that they had never hit one, nor even seen one with a scar. But someone called FlatsTime from Cocoa—who admitted hitting two— said he had seen "hundreds of manatees with prop scars, and I see boats flying through the manatee zone at the Port St. John launch ramp almost every time I launch from there on the weekends. I doubt most of those boaters would even know if they hit one at the speeds they were traveling."

Then someone cracked that manatees do taste good, and someone named Deepfish chimed in: "Yeah but a bitch to clean, really muck the chainsaw up."

•

While his aide was cutting deals in Orlando, Bush was pushing the legislature to come up with money to hire twenty-five more law enforcement officers to patrol Florida's waterways. The lawmaking body had changed a lot since the Manatee Sanctuary Act passed in 1990. Now legislators regarded with suspicion anything benefiting manatees.

"How many manatees does it take to get off the endangered list?" asked one Democratic lawmaker.

"Where is that number?" agreed a Republican committee chairman. "Why don't we already have that number? People are tired of this."

Still, the legislature rarely said no to Governor Bush. Two competing bills offered a way to raise the money he wanted. One, patterned after John Sprague's proposal, called for setting up a steady source of funding by tacking a charge on boat registrations. The size of the charge depended on the size of the boat: five dollars for boats under twelve feet long, ten dollars for boats between sixteen and twenty-six feet, and fifteen for boats between twenty-six and forty feet.

The other bill called for simply tapping the state budget for money that was already on hand and letting next year's legislature worry about finding the money to keep the increased law enforcement going. Bush liked that one, so that's what passed.

Now, with the state settlement in hand and the legislative money set, Bush took his next step. On May 29, 2001, he wrote a letter to the regional boss of the Fish and Wildlife Service in Atlanta urging him to back off the settlement with the Save the Manatee Club.

Bush noted that the federal agency had recently released a draft of its interim guidelines for permitting dock and marina projects in areas with manatee habitat. The new rules called for charging dock builders an extra fee to pay for boosting law enforcement, and to allow some marina owners to pay directly for increased patrols. Bush said he didn't like that.

"I, as Governor of the State of Florida, wish to advise you of several concerns I have with this approach, and recommend a more comprehensive solution to your agency's mandate to provide additional protection for manatees," Bush wrote.

He called the federal approach "a patchwork," while boasting that the state's strategy was more comprehensive. As proof, he cited the Sarasota Yacht Club vote by the cabinet—without mentioning that he and the cabinet had relented a few months later. He noted the funding for twenty-five new officers, though without spelling out whether they would all be patrolling full-time. He pointed out that the wildlife commission had agreed to settle its lawsuit, not mentioning that manatee advocates regarded the state settlement as far weaker than the federal one.

Since the state was doing such a good job, Bush said, the feds should get out of the state's way: "I respectfully request that the said guidelines be withdrawn from consideration and that the U.S. Fish and Wildlife Service allow the State of Florida to implement our pending settlement agreement as opposed to additional or expanded federal manatee refuges or sanctuaries."

That was good enough for Norton's Fish and Wildlife Service, which agreed to toss out the $542 fee. The service "believes that the state's initiative removes the need for implementation of the contributions for increased law enforcement," its notice stated. "Therefore we have removed the contributions for law enforcement."

Meanwhile, again and again, the Fish and Wildlife Service requested delays in its deadline for designating the refuges and sanctuaries that it had agreed to.

"They kept saying they had to coordinate with the state," Glitzenstein said.

"Not only were they not obligated to do that, ultimately coordinating with the state meant capitulating to Jeb Bush's political calendar."

The delays stretched out further and further. Some of it might be blamed on the tragic events of September 11, when terrorists who had trained in Florida hijacked commercial jetliners and forced them to crash into the World Trade Center and the Pentagon. Wildlife officers from both the state and federal agencies were pulled off manatee zone enforcement duty and put to work guarding Florida's ports against an attack from the sea.

But a lot of the delay, Glitzenstein concluded, resulted from old-fashioned politics. Despite Governor Bush's professed love for his favorite mammal, Glitzenstein became convinced that Bush was more concerned about his reelection in 2002. Because Bush wanted to take the lead on manatee protection, not simply take dictation from a bunch of biologist-bureaucrats in Washington, Norton's staff gladly bowed to the governor's wishes, the lawyer believed.

Glitzenstein was right, according to a top Interior Department official.

"Governor Bush very much wanted the state to take the lead," recalled Craig Manson, a former California judge who in late 2001 became Norton's assistant secretary overseeing fish and wildlife. "There was a feeling around Interior that it might be worthwhile to let them do that and hope they would do the right thing."

With Norton's department kowtowing to Bush, Glitzenstein could see the hard-won settlement slipping away. By late September the Fish and Wildlife Service had yet to designate a single refuge or sanctuary. Instead, it published a *Federal Register* notice stating it was suspending that effort, except for a pair of spots in Brevard County, and noted that it had been "coordinating closely" with the state wildlife commission ever since the settlement had been announced "to determine which sites are most appropriate for state designation and which are better suited for federal designation."

The best the federal wildlife service could promise would be to look at the results of the state's effort in December 2002 and then decide if any more refuges or sanctuaries might be needed.

Governor Bush praised the agency's decision, calling it "a balanced approach to protecting manatees while respecting the rights of Florida boaters."

However, Glitzenstein noticed that December 2002 happened to be a month after the gubernatorial election was over. Delaying any federal action until then, he concluded, played into Jeb Bush's campaign for reelection.

"It was designed to let Jeb Bush claim he kept the federal government off the backs of the people," he said.

On October 24, 2001, Glitzenstein wrote a blistering twenty-one-page letter to the Justice Department. In it, he slammed federal officials for what seemed to him to be an organized campaign of foot-dragging that placated the president's brother but failed to provide any help for manatees. The plaintiffs, he wrote, "believe that the federal government is blatantly violating the agreement in several critical respects."

The letter took particular note of the situation in Lee County.

"So far this year an overwhelming and record-setting 19 manatees have been killed by boats in Lee County—more than any other single county in Florida, including five more such deaths in the Caloosahatchee," he wrote. "Yet as the service knows, the state of Florida has made no firm commitments to address the crisis conditions in this deadly waterway or any other specific area of Lee County."

In fact, he noted, "the service has, inexplicably, yet to even propose any refuges or sanctuaries in six of the ten highest mortality counties in Florida."

It didn't stop there. As a result of the settlement negotiations, the Corps and the wildlife service had agreed to a carefully crafted set of interim guidelines for waterfront permitting. Yet before the ink was dry on the settlement, Glitzenstein wrote, the Corps and the service were cranking out permits that violated that interim guidance.

Since the settlement had been signed, he wrote, the Corps and the wildlife service had approved at least fourteen hundred new boat slips in counties the wildlife service had designated as being high or medium risks for manatees. When Glitzenstein asked the wildlife service for an explanation, he got no reply, he wrote.

Glitzenstein saved his harshest words for the feds' decision, at Governor Bush's request, to drop the $542 fee for new boat slips built in manatee habitat. The service had declared that the state's new enforcement initiative would be enough to resolve any problems with making sure speed zones were obeyed.

"In reality," he wrote, "under the service's own analysis of the asserted enforcement increase, many high and medium risk counties will receive no new officers whatsoever."

Once again, he focused on the situation in Lee County to illustrate what he called "the facial absurdity" of the wildlife service's claims. Ten officers patrolled the waterways of Lee County on a regular basis, yet Lee regularly vied with Brevard as the county with the worst manatee mortality in Florida. But the wildlife service had declared manatee protection measures "adequate" in the entire Caloosahatchee River for the purposes of permitting new boat slips and docks, Glitzenstein noted.

The state's plans called for adding two new officers there—which according to the wildlife service would not only alleviate the ongoing problems with speed zone enforcement there but would also justify allowing the construction of four thousand new boat slips in Lee County and another seven thousand new slips in nearby Collier County.

"If, as the service's own data reflect, the 10 existing officers in Lee County have not been adequate even to stop the already intolerable situation in Lee County from spiraling out of control, then it is impossible to fathom how the service could seriously maintain that the addition of two new officers will completely resolve the current enforcement situation in Lee County," he wrote.

Using those two new officers to justify adding thousands of new boat slips to southwest Florida's waterways was a "nonsensical position," he concluded.

In his closing pages, Glitzenstein accused the Fish and Wildlife Service of sacrificing manatees on the altar of politics. Noting the December 2002 date the wildlife agency had picked for designating any new federal refuges or sanctuaries, he wrote: "The conclusion seems inescapable that the FWS [Fish and Wildlife Service] has jettisoned its settlement obligations so that the final federal refuge designation—if any—can occur after the Florida governor's race, irrespective of the number of manatees who needlessly die and suffer terrible wounds in the meantime."

In short, he said, unless something changed and changed fast, the plaintiffs would be hauling everyone back into court to let a judge sort it all out.

If the federal agencies were worried about Glitzenstein's threat, they didn't show it. A month after Glitzenstein sent the letter, the Fish and Wildlife Service and the Corps allowed the Gulf Harbour Marina in Fort Myers to expand its slips for powerboats from 65 to 190 slips. Gulf Harbour, near the mouth of the Caloosahatchee, belonged to one of the largest developers in Florida, WCI Communities. WCI's CEO just happened to be Al Hoffman Jr., a major fundraiser for both Bush brothers who had recently been named the Republican National Committee's finance chairman.

When the Save the Manatee Club sent out a press release to denounce how the federal government had sloughed off its responsibilities under the settlement, Dave Hankla told reporters that he didn't understand all the fuss.

"I think we've met the terms of the settlement agreement," he said. "We're giving them what's in that agreement." Since Florida had agreed to take the lead on manatee protection, he said, "there is no point in providing duplicate protection."

However, the state hadn't exactly leaped into action, either. That made the Fish and Wildlife Service decision to defer to Governor Bush seem suspect to Glitzenstein. Assistant Secretary Manson said it was the state's fault for squandering its opportunity to lead.

"Florida had a contrarian Fish and Wildlife Conservation Commission," said Manson. "The commissioners seemed very contrary and mercurial. It was not easy for them to do what they needed to do."

•

The state's wildlife commissioners were all appointed by the governor. Traditionally, dating back to the days of Earle Frye, when it was the Game and Fresh Water Fish Commission, the seats had been handed out as political plums. Governor Bush treated the wildlife commission the same way as his predecessors. In September 2001, he appointed as a new wildlife commissioner a Miami lobbyist and developer named Rodney Barreto to become the board's first Hispanic member.

In Miami-Dade County, anyone who wants to do business with local government—the city, the county, the airport, and so on—has to hire a lobbyist to grease the skids, and Barreto was one of the best. A beefy, red-faced man with a hearty manner, Barreto sported a thick mustache and a head of hair that boxing promoter Don King would have envied.

Unlike other new commissioners, Barreto had some familiarity with manatee issues. His firm's clients included two marina operators, a boatyard, an outboard shop, and a condominium developer trying to rewrite the county's manatee protection plan to allow more powerboat slips in Biscayne Bay.

Despite those apparent conflicts, Barreto had one overriding qualification for the job: he had raised money for the governor's election. It didn't hurt that he had lots of political contacts in Bush's hometown.

Barreto, like many of his fellow wildlife commissioners, enjoyed boating and sportfishing. He earned enough money to pursue his hobby in style. He had a house in Miami and a second one in Key Largo, where he docked his twenty-seven-foot Contender. (Five years later he had traded up to a thirty-six-foot Contender, as well as a twenty-one-foot Hewes Redfisher, and even employed a full-time captain.)

"I'm not anti-manatee," Barreto said during one wildlife commission meeting. "I have manatees behind my house in Key Largo. I don't wake up in the morning and say, 'Let's get in a boat and go out and kill a manatee.'"

Barreto's passion for fishing couldn't hold a candle to that of a commissioner from Pensacola, chiropractor Edwin Roberts. Roberts was such an avid sportfisherman that he had twice served on the board of the predecessor to the Coastal Conservation Association of Florida—the same organization now questioning whether manatees really were endangered. In 1994, Roberts served as its president.

Another commissioner appointed by Bush, Jacksonville apartment developer John Rood, had earned his seat the same way Barreto did: by raising hundreds of thousands of dollars in contributions for Governor Bush and his brother. He had also served on the board of Bush's Foundation for Florida's Future.

Rood's boyish demeanor made him resemble a blond version of J. Pierpont Finch from *How to Succeed in Business without Really Trying*. Among the commissioners he enjoyed the closest ties to Bush, so he often took the lead in discussions about manatees. Like Bush, he was convinced the state settlement was far superior to the federal one. At one meeting, a closed-door session to discuss some legal complications after the settlements, Rood described his view of the situation this way: "My summary is the state is smooth, the federal is a disaster, and the federal is where we are going to have riots pretty quick."

When voters approved the creation of the Fish and Wildlife Conservation Commission, the name suggested a new tack for an agency that had previously been concerned only with hunting and fishing. This new agency was supposed to have as its primary purpose conserving the state's fish and wildlife. But that wasn't the attitude of Rood and the other wildlife commissioners, who saw themselves fulfilling the same role as the old game commissioners.

"We need to represent the recreational interest in this state in all federal actions," Rood said in the closed-door session. "In other words, there is recreational interest, whether it is waterskiing and associated interest, dock building, marinas, boating, fishing, those interests need to be represented in . . . rule-making and in the speed zones by our agency and defended."

A staffer reminded Rood that the commission's job was actually to look out for the state's wildlife. Rood just said, "Okay."

Even when the state wildlife commission did try to establish a new regulation, the commissioners' actions could be slowed down or even overturned by an administrative challenge. That's what happened in Brevard County when the commission tried to set up its first new speed zones under the settlement.

Citizens for Florida Waterways filed a legal challenge to the new Brevard zones. Jim Kalvin joined in, as did Sea Ray boats and a pair of cities, Titusville and Cocoa Beach. One of the provisions of the state settlement called for the Save the Manatee Club to help defend the state against any challenge, so David Guest trekked down to the courthouse in Titusville for the trial. It became "one of the greatest circuses that I've ever been in," Guest recalled happily.

The challengers held frequent rallies outside the courthouse, drawing up to two hundred people "ranting and raving and acting pretty crazy," Guest said. "They were of the mind-set that we were devils."

One day the devilish Guest decided to have some fun. He waded through the crowd, found Ron Pritchard—soon to be elected a Brevard County commissioner—and shook his hand. Pritchard looked "like someone had handed him a live rattlesnake," Guest said.

Guest told Pritchard that his clients were not a bunch of killjoys trying to ruin everyone's fun on the water. They were acting in good faith, trying to keep an ancient species around for a few more generations, he said. At that point, Guest said, the crowd around him "started this growling again," so he got to his point. He solemnly promised Pritchard that, on the day manatees really were no longer endangered, "I would eat a manatee with him."

Afterward, a chuckling Guest informed his clients about his stunt.

"The clients were, shall I say, disappointed," he said. "*Real* disappointed."

In the courtroom, the pro-boating plaintiffs represented themselves, doing their best to mimic the attorneys on *L.A. Law* and *Law and Order*. But they pursued an odd strategy in the eleven-day trial: attacking the science on which the policy decisions had been based.

For instance, they argued that the state's proposed speed zones would not work because manatees had trouble hearing boats going slow. Their evidence: a study by Dr. Edmund Gerstein and Dr. Joseph Blue of the hearing capabilities of two manatees that had been undergoing rehabilitation at the Lowry Park Zoo. Gerstein and Blue contended that scientists should try to come up with a warning device that could be attached to boats to warn manatees to get out of the way. To the members of Citizens for Florida's Waterways, Gerstein and Blue were visionaries on a par with Albert Einstein, and anyone who disagreed was part of a vast conspiracy—a Manatee Mafia, as one of them dubbed it.

However, manatee biologists didn't buy Gerstein and Blue's conclusions. The Manatee Technical Advisory Council, after conducting two workshops on the subject, concluded that Gerstein and Blue were wrong because "manatees can hear sounds in the frequency range that boats make." As for the Gerstein-Blue warning device, the MTAC reported, "It is not at all clear that wild animals in a natural setting have the cognitive ability to recognize a particular sound as a danger or determine how to escape."

One of the major flaws with the warning device that Gerstein and Blue had proposed involved simple logic. Before manatees would learn to associate the warning signal with danger, biologists pointed out, they would have to be hit by a boat after hearing the signal. If that one hit didn't kill them, then maybe they would learn what the signal meant. However, it might take repeated clobbering. It was like training convenience-store clerks how to deal with robberies by allowing robbers to shoot them a few times.

Even then, there was no assurance manatees would know where the warning signal was coming from, given how sound travels underwater. Nor would they automatically know which way to swim to get out of the way.

"The animals sometimes dive or appear to move toward deeper water when approached by vessels, but have also been observed to turn or move toward an approaching boat," the MTAC report noted.

In a 1994 study in Tampa Bay, scientist Brad Weigle—before he became fascinated by blimps—filmed manatees' response time to boats traveling toward them at various speeds. Manatees in the wild generally reacted to the sound of an approaching boat when it was 165 to 190 feet away, no matter what its speed. Of course, the faster the boat was going, the less time both the boater and the manatee would have to take action to avoid each other.

During the trial, "we went through it in excruciating detail," said Ross Burnaman, the state wildlife commission's attorney. "There's no question that slowing boats down is better for manatees."

Ultimately, the judge agreed with the wildlife commission. Although he clearly sympathized with the fishing guides who testified they might be put out of business, Guest said, the judge recognized that the legal standard for the rules had been met. They were based on science.

But by then, a year had passed since the state had first proposed the new speed zones. Then some of the plaintiffs appealed (they lost again). That dragged out the process even more.

Kalvin was ready to bail out long before the case was over. Although he didn't say so publicly, the contingent from Citizens for Florida's Waterways played too rough for his tastes.

"They were too abrupt," he said. "They were too confrontational." But their tactics did succeed in postponing state rules they didn't like.

The state's rule-making process wasn't just hampered by legal challenges. It could be hamstrung by the legislature, too.

In October 2001, the devastating economic losses that followed the September 11 terrorist attacks forced Bush to convene an eleven-day special session to slash the budget the lawmakers had just approved a few months before. During that special session, Representative Harrington sponsored a bill to forbid the state wildlife commission from imposing any new manatee protection rules on any county unless the rules had first been vetted by a committee of local residents.

Harrington—who in one Standing Watch meeting managed to link the Save the Manatee Club to terrorist Osama bin Laden, unaware that a club member had snuck in—tried to tie his bill in with the patriotic fervor of the time.

"What better freedom do we have than using our waters?" Harrington said. The bill went nowhere. But when he brought it back up the following spring, the legislature passed it.

While the state's efforts at setting new rules got bogged down by lawyers and lawmakers, the U.S. Fish and Wildlife Service had not exactly been idle. On Halloween, the wildlife agency unveiled the new manatee recovery plan.

The recovery plan had been greatly altered from what the nineteen scientists who worked on it had recommended. Instead of a 94 percent adult survival rate—which would mean the population would be growing by 4 percent a year—the plan called for a 90 percent rate as the standard for taking manatees off the endangered list.

In other words, the federal wildlife agency had concluded that 10 percent of the estimated manatee population—between two hundred and three hundred—could be killed every year without jeopardizing the species' future. Manatees could have zero population growth and the species could still be classified as recovered.

Hankla said the agency made those changes because his staff needed more "flexibility." He said the recovery team's recommendations had called for ideal conditions, not for the minimum threshold allowed by law. Besides, he contended, that 94 percent rate had not undergone peer-reviewed publication in a scientific journal, so it couldn't really be a factor in the plan.

Buddy Powell snorted when he heard that one. As far as he was concerned, this was all just an excuse by the Fish and Wildlife Service to loosen the science-based standards and make it easier to knock manatees down lower on the endangered list.

•

Early the following year, Glitzenstein filed a lengthy motion to haul the Fish and Wildlife Service and the Corps back before Judge Facciola. He said they had made "material" changes to the settlement agreement.

Facciola, the sailing magistrate, agreed. His ruling set the stage for a new round of courtroom battles over a lawsuit that was supposed to be over. But this time, the government wouldn't be quite so inclined to be agreeable with the environmental and animal-welfare groups the way it had been under President Clinton.

Now the battle moved to a new arena, the courtroom of U.S. District Judge Emmet G. Sullivan. A native of Washington, D.C., Sullivan earned both his undergraduate and law degrees from Howard University, the most prestigious black college in the country. He landed a position with one of the city's most prestigious law firms, one where nine previous associates had been named to the bench. Sullivan soon followed suit.

Because the District of Columbia is not a state or a county, the person who picks its local judges is the president. President Reagan selected Sullivan as a district court judge, and then President George H. W. Bush named him to the local appellate bench. Then in 1994 President Clinton elevated him to a federal judgeship—a rare show of bipartisan agreement about his qualifications.

On April 17, 2002, in press conferences in Washington and Florida, the Save the Manatee Club and its allies announced they were filing a formal motion asking Judge Sullivan to enforce the terms of the settlement.

The Florida press conference, held in an open field at Boyd Hill Nature Park in St. Petersburg, featured the president of the Defenders of Wildlife and Save the Manatee Club co-chairwoman Helen Spivey. Both blasted the Bush administration for not just the manatee case but also for what they viewed as a wholesale assault on the Endangered Species Act.

They were, however, literally overshadowed by a minor player. Tethered tightly between two oak trees behind the speakers' portable lectern, looming above the two environmental activists, was a Macy's Parade–size balloon shaped like a manatee. Its name was Tallulah.

Had it been functional, blimp fan Brad Weigle would have loved it. Actually it was just a big prop. The idea for Tallulah sprang from the fertile brain of Susannah Lindberg, an athletic, blond woman with a pugnacious set to her jaw. Lindberg grew up in Orlando but didn't see any manatees before she visited Disney World's "Living Seas" exhibit. An avid horseback rider, mountain biker, and skier, Lindberg was a big fan of Carl Hiaasen's anti-developer Florida novels. But her favorite quote is attributed to the poet Dante: "The hottest places in hell are reserved for those who, in time of great moral crisis, maintain their neutrality."

Lindberg had learned how to knock on doors while she was still a student at Florida State by volunteering for the Florida Public Interest Research Group, an organization that battled everything from nuclear plants to offshore drilling. Glitzenstein hired her in 2001 for his Wildlife Advocacy Project, specifically to work on the political side of the manatee case. Her job was to do grassroots organizing, as well as to drum up media interest in the issue.

Most of the time that meant making phone calls, trying to turn out the right kind of audience for public hearings, organizing press conferences, and making speeches. Lindberg had no budget for advertising, so she tried to target specific regions where powerful legislators lived—for instance, giving a Power-Point slide presentation on manatees to the Kiwanis Club in rural, landlocked Plant City, because that was the hometown of the incoming speaker of the state House of Representatives.

Sometimes, though, her job called for something more colorful. One Halloween she dressed like a grinning Grim Reaper and set up a "manatee graveyard" at the University of Central Florida campus to show the death toll from government inaction.

"Those tactics were fun!" Lindberg said. "We tried to do things like that to jolt people awake."

Another time she unleashed a squad of college students to deliver body bags—purchased from a medical supply house and labeled as if they contained manatee carcasses from Lee County—to Wade Hopping's Tallahassee law office.

"We thought that was a riot," she said. Hopping came out to talk to the pro-

The Humane Society spent eight thousand dollars on this balloon so "Tallullah" could serve as a prop for press conferences like this one, featuring Save the Manatee Club co-chairwoman Helen Spivey and Defenders of Wildlife President Roger Schlickheisen. Photo courtesy of the *St. Petersburg Times*.

testers, "which was a huge mistake on his part because that legitimized it," she said.

Props like the body bags helped drive home the Manatee Coalition's points, as well as ensuring a good visual image for the TV cameras, Lindberg explained. That's why she came up with Tallulah, a prop that Frisch said cost the cause eight thousand dollars.

"I convinced this guy at the Humane Society to shell out an ungodly amount of money for this inflatable manatee," she said. "It was just a beautiful creation. I drove around with it in my car, and I would take it out and inflate it whenever we wanted to do a press conference."

Helen Spivey frequently took Tallulah along when she set up tables outside Buffett's concerts to collect signatures on Save the Manatee petitions. The balloon would attract lots of attention among the Parrotheads, she said, although usually the various substances being consumed by Buffett's fans meant that their signatures, when examined later, were impossible to decipher.

Another of Lindberg's initiatives proved to be far less successful. Ever since Fran Stallings first proposed the lawsuit, there had been talk of starting a "Boaters for Manatees" group as a way to counteract the expected opposition from that quarter.

Lindberg did manage to pull together a small group of boaters from Brevard County who could balance out whatever Citizens for Florida's Waterways might say. She even found a few dock builders in Lee County who just wanted everything to calm down so they could get back to work.

She had hoped the organization would spread statewide just like Standing Watch. But her counter-movement sputtered out while the backlash to the settlements continued to gather steam.

"We recognized it would not be smooth sailing" after the settlements, Glitzenstein said. "To me that's the reason why the coalition was put together. It was designed to develop a full range of tools to fight a battle like this one: media, law, lobbying, grassroots. Were we fully prepared for the onslaught we triggered? No."

The passions involved in the boater backlash mingled with the heightened sense that freedom was under assault in the months after the September 11 attacks.

"I got called 'Osama bin Laden with a sex change,'" Lindberg said. People like Kalvin talked about the freedom to use their boats in the same tones as the freedom of speech and the right to assemble, she said, and it frequently drew a strong response from the audience at public hearings.

Lindberg became so frustrated with the influence of the boaters and developers that she suggested a desperate countermeasure. She told some fellow activists that at the next public hearing, "they should beat me up in an alley and then I would run in and say, 'One of these boaters beat me up!' It would undercut their credibility. But nobody would ever beat me up."

•

Tallulah's appearance marked the start of a surreal summer in the battle over manatee protection. On the Fourth of July in 2002, football star O. J. Simpson, the most famous murder defendant in America, got busted for violating a manatee speed zone.

Simpson had been acquitted of charges he fatally stabbed his ex-wife and another man in Los Angeles in 1994 in what had been dubbed "The Trial of the Century," but he lost a civil suit filed by the family of one of the victims. The jury in the civil suit ordered him to pay $33.5 million. Although Simpson had publicly vowed to dedicate the rest of his life to tracking down the true culprit, he moved to Miami and played a lot of golf.

Then, on Independence Day, while "The Juice" was joyriding in his thirty-foot powerboat with his latest girlfriend and another couple, a wildlife commission officer ticketed him for creating a wake in a manatee zone. Simpson, who continued to maintain his innocence in the double murder, refused to plead guilty to the ticket either, even though it would involve a fine of just sixty-five dollars. Instead, he filed a plea of not guilty.

Unfortunately, he filed his plea five days after he had been ordered to appear in court. A judge issued a warrant. There were headlines and smirking jokes.

"He was chasing the real killers," cracked one newspaper columnist, while another joked, "Have you ever seen the back of the average manatee? It's a patchwork of propeller gashes that look like the handiwork of somebody with . . . er, a big knife."

Finally, in November, Simpson paid the fine, which by then had doubled.

Simpson wasn't the only football star tripped up by manatee protection rules that summer. The biggest game of the year was always the Super Bowl, and the host city spent years planning ahead to make the most of it. Jacksonville had won the right to host Super Bowl XXXIX in 2005. City officials expected to spend the next two years working with developers to transform the rundown waterfront around Alltel Stadium into a shimmering downtown skyline they dubbed the "Billion-Dollar Mile."

But because of the scrutiny that came with the federal settlement, the Fish and Wildlife Service took a tough stance on the Super Bowl plans. Hankla's staff said the Duval County speed zones through the St. Johns River failed to offer sufficient protection to manatees. Therefore, crucial permits for those waterfront developments and their marinas were put on hold.

"It should not be this contentious to protect the manatee," grumbled one city official who had apparently not been paying attention to the events of the past two years.

Eventually, though, Super Bowl organizers were able to work everything out. In fact, the official mascot of Super Bowl XXXIX wound up being a guy dressed in a manatee costume who wandered around interviewing celebrities.

While O. J. Simpson tangled with the legal system and Super Bowl organizers tried to juke their way past the permitting problems, some Hollywood movie producers showed everyone how to get around the manatee protection rules. All it took was a lot of money and some political clout.

In 1995 actors Will Smith and Martin Lawrence teamed up for a movie about a mismatched pair of Miami police officers who crack jokes and shoot their guns a lot while catching a ruthless villain. *Bad Boys* did so well at the box office that in the summer of 2002 Columbia Pictures wanted to film a sixty-million-dollar sequel in Miami. The studio's ability to flash around cash helped the producers win permission to shut down the MacArthur Causeway for four days for one chase scene, diverting ninety thousand commuters.

The script for *Bad Boys 2* called for a boat chase through Biscayne Bay and the Miami River—the same area where Simpson had been ticketed. The producers sought an "emergency waiver" of the speed zones along the route of the chase scene. Initially, the state wildlife commission staff said no. To overturn the decision, the producers hired a high-powered lobbyist for help: Ron Book, the Bob Graham aide who had helped set up the Save the Manatee Club.

"To not approve this variance or waiver will create significant economic hardship to the city of Miami (now officially designated as the poorest big city in America)," Book wrote in an appeal. Meanwhile, he arranged for one of the movie's producers to meet with Governor Bush.

Two days later, the state wildlife commission's director, Ken Haddad, reversed his agency's decision. He allowed the filming of the chase scene to proceed so long the producers posted a team of observers in the air and on the riverbank to watch for manatees. The producers agreed to shut down if any were spotted. Haddad insisted that no one pressured him.

"This is really unprecedented," Patti Thompson told the *St. Petersburg Times*. "I've never heard of any emergency waivers for manatee rules, period."

However, Haddad pointed out that he had checked with the club's own lobbyist, Pat Rose, and got his approval of the deal. Rose said that with all the observers keeping watch, "manatees are likely going to be pretty safe there."

Sure enough, during the filming, manatees popped up seven times, forcing the filming to halt each time. But no manatees appeared to be injured or killed.

Although *Bad Boys 2* offered more explosions, there was plenty of real-life drama in Washington, where a July 2002 hearing showed just how weird things were about to get with Judge Sullivan. With a new administration in the White House, a new Justice Department lawyer named Wayne Hettenbach took over the manatee lawsuit.

During the hearing, Glitzenstein talked for a bit about the number of manatees killed so far by boats. Then he held up a photo of a manatee with twenty-two propeller scars down its back.

"Deaths are the tip of the iceberg," he told the judge. "This is a photo, a typical photo, of a manatee that's been scarred repeatedly by propellers."

Suddenly, Hettenbach was on his feet. "Your Honor, I would object," he said. "It's inflammatory. It's not relevant. It's a picture of a manatee being hit by a propeller. What relevance does that have to the issue before the court?"

An objection might have been proper during a trial in front of a jury—but this was a motion hearing in front of a judge. Sullivan had already mentioned being frustrated, and now the Justice Department was objecting to pictures?

"Sullivan fixes him with a steely gaze," Glitzenstein recalled, "and says, 'Sir, this *is* what this case is about.' It's almost like they set up a strategy to get the judge as upset as possible."

Initially the federal agencies' defense was to claim that, despite appearances to the contrary, they were doing precisely what the settlement agreement required—and besides, a delay didn't harm anyone.

Judge Sullivan didn't buy it.

"The whole purpose of this lawsuit is to what? Save the manatee," he said. "And for the federal government to say delay doesn't hurt anyone because humans aren't being affected? Well, the humans weren't the subject of the lawsuit. It's the manatees that are the ones dying in record numbers. It's totally insensitive of the federal government to make that argument."

He ruled that pleasing the president's brother was not a valid reason for a federal agency to violate a legal agreement "regardless of the political ramifications." Then Sullivan ordered the wildlife agency to come up with a series of actions to comply with the agreement no later than August 10, 2002.

An editorial in the *St. Petersburg Times* noted the coincidence of one Bush brother helping movie producers get around manatee protection rules while the other dragged his feet on living up to a settlement on protecting manatees.

"Given the Bush brothers' apparent indifference to manatee safety, we wonder if the governor and the president might have been better cast in the roles Will Smith and Martin Lawrence play in this comedic action sequel," the editorial concluded. "Call them Bad Boys, Too."

For his next trick, Hettenbach came up with an unusual new argument. He said the settlement agreement was illegal because it had been signed by a previous administration. Therefore the Fish and Wildlife Service did not have to abide by it.

"They had found an old memo written by someone high up in the [Justice Department] during the Reagan administration that said one administration could not bind future administrations," Glitzenstein said. "Somehow it was unconstitutional. They had dusted that off and were relying on that."

Of course, administrations are constantly binding the ones after them to comply with legal agreements—peace treaties, for instance, or contracts for military supplies. Sullivan blew up at Hettenbach for raising such an excuse.

"The thought that this agreement is now illegal is ludicrous and preposterous," Sullivan snapped. "The government can't pick and choose when it complies with court orders. The government is not above the law."

Now the judge put the federal agencies on a tight leash. He told them that they had to complete all the rulemaking they had promised to do the year before and have everything published for public comment in the *Federal Register* no later than November 1, 2002—four days before Florida's gubernatorial election.

"For the last time, just comply with the order. Just comply with the settlement agreement. This is nothing new," Judge Sullivan told the government attorneys. "It's about saving the manatees. That's what we're talking about."

Then he issued what's known in legal circles as an "order to show cause." It means he demanded the Justice Department lawyers show him why he should not hold Interior Secretary Gale Norton in contempt of court for failing to comply with his orders. If found in contempt, Norton could face jail, although a more likely outcome would be a fine levied against her agency for every day it failed to comply with the judge's order.

Sullivan also told both sides to sit down and figure out if the wildlife agency could issue emergency rules to increase protection of manatees in places like the Caloosahatchee River.

Outside the courtroom, Hettenbach continued making Alice-in-Wonderland arguments, denying that all the missed deadlines meant that the agreement had been violated.

"We don't believe there was a delay," he told reporters with a straight face.

And when the two sides sat down together, Glitzenstein said, federal officials "adamantly refused to designate emergency refuges or sanctuaries at even a single area where manatees have been killed or injured by boats in large numbers."

Yet Norton, breaking her silence on the case for the first time, told a reporter for the Gannett newspaper chain that Judge Sullivan had no reason to be concerned about her staff.

"We believe very strongly in restoration of the manatee population," she said. "We have been working with the state, and we are moving forward with the process of reviewing designation of [manatee] sanctuaries and refuges."

Then she blithely suggested that Florida ought to do a better job of educating its boaters about how to behave on the water.

The day after Sullivan's ruling came out, Governor Bush happened to be making a campaign stop to greet supporters at the Iguana Mia Mexican restaurant in Cape Coral. He was accompanied by Representative Jeff Kottkamp of Cape Coral, who, like Bush, was seeking reelection. When reporters asked about the judge's ruling, Bush condemned it as "overreactive and over-the-top."

Then Bush made some comments that didn't quite jibe with his previous contention that he only wanted the feds to back off so the state could take the lead in manatee protection.

"We've tried to slow down the federal process so we can have more buy-in from boaters and groups here concerned with the manatees and to build some common-sense solution," he said.

This marked the first time Bush had ever mentioned trying to slow down the new federal regulations just to accommodate boaters' wishes to go fast.

Bush acknowledged that Norton would probably have to comply with the judge's order, but he added that he hoped Norton would appeal.

"These decisions should be more local and state as opposed to from on high," he insisted, blaming the judge and not the parties who had agreed to a settlement he didn't like.

Instead of appealing, Norton's agency dropped the ball again. Instead of doing exactly what Sullivan ordered, the Fish and Wildlife Service submitted the new rules to the *Federal Register* on the day the judge had said the rules had to be published. That meant they would not make it into print until three or four days later—after the election.

Sullivan was furious. "The order couldn't be clearer," the judge told Hettenbach during a hearing on November 5, the day voters turned out in droves to reelect Jeb Bush governor. "This means to any rational human being that all steps (to publish) will be taken well prior to Nov. 1."

Hettenbach tried to weasel out of the situation by pointing out that the Fish and Wildlife Service had in fact "published" the rules by posting them on the agency's Web site and sending out a press release.

"That's just absolutely ridiculous," the judge barked. "That's a ridiculous interpretation of the court's order."

Sullivan then issued a second order to show cause, meaning Norton faced a big fine or jail time, times two. He scheduled a December 19 hearing to decide whether to hold Norton in contempt.

This was where Craig Manson stepped in.

"If there's one rule in Washington," he explained, "it's that you don't want your boss held in contempt."

•

Manson had been a judge himself in California. At several previous hearings, he had quietly slipped into the back of Sullivan's courtroom to keep an eye on the proceedings. As assistant secretary of the Interior Department, the Fish and Wildlife Service answered to him.

He knew the manatee case had been heating up. His Blackberry told him that. It buzzed whenever he got a new e-mail, and lately—ever since one of the environmental groups had gotten hold of his e-mail address—it had been buzzing all the time. It buzzed while he drove in his car, while he ate dinner in a restaurant, even when he was home.

"My wife was upset about that," Manson said. "I had it on in the bedroom."

Now he had to do something to work his boss out of the jam she was in with Judge Sullivan, yet also deal with the political ramifications in Florida.

"The whole situation was tense," Manson said. "In Florida it was tense. In the courtroom it was tense. There was tension with the governor's office."

Manson's first step might seem minor, but he says it immediately yielded results. At the next hearing, instead of taking his usual seat back in the gallery, the courtly ex-judge sat at the defense table with all the other government attorneys. That brought an immediate change in the judge, said Manson, who, like Sullivan, is black.

"The lawyers introduced me to the judge," Manson said. "He saw another African American face in the courtroom, and you could see his eyes light up. Something about his look. And I think he softened his approach after that."

Glitzenstein, however, is convinced that Sullivan brightened up for a different reason: Manson's presence meant that Gale Norton had gotten the message and now Interior would be taking the case a lot more seriously.

Manson's involvement in the case "was the turning point," Glitzenstein said. "Obviously, at the highest levels of the administration, orders had been issued to get this thing resolved."

As with all of the Bush administration appointees, environmental groups had not been happy to see Manson put in such a high position in the Interior Department. They worried about whether he would undercut endangered species protection. He had once argued that no human being could tell whether extinction was really a bad thing for every species—a position that, while logical, failed to reassure environmental groups that he would try to stop species like manatees from going extinct.

But Manson now threw himself into trying to work out a cease-fire in the manatee war. He even traveled down to Cape Coral to meet with city officials, who had been talking about filing their own federal lawsuit to free up more dock permits. He scheduled a sit-down with the city manager at city hall. To his surprise, the police chief showed up too.

"I have no idea what the *hell* he was doing there," Manson said. "They started off from the get-go very aggressive and very hostile, and it took us a while to get them calmed down."

He and several high-level officials from the Fish and Wildlife Service also took city leaders and reporters out on a boat ride "to show them what twenty-five miles per hour mph looked like and what it would feel like going out to the ocean," he said. "We thought it would calm them down. It did not work."

Meanwhile, Manson now took the lead in negotiations with Glitzenstein and the attorney for the developers and boaters. Soon they had a deal. They announced several new refuges and sanctuaries, and promised to write new rules for the "incidental take" of the manatees due to new boat docks being built.

Judge Sullivan, satisfied at last, dropped the contempt threat. Manson himself got to deliver the news to his boss.

"She was pleased, I'll say that," Manson said. "She was not one to give an overly expressive display of emotion, but she was happy."

But instead of ending the war, Manson had only resolved it on the legal front. Down in Florida, the fight had turned ugly. While the Fish and Wildlife Service was finally putting out new regulations to protect the endangered manatee, the state wildlife commission had decided it might no longer be endangered.

15

# Down with the Manatee

TED FORSGREN'S LOVE AFFAIR with the water began when he was just a boy growing up in Tampa. His mother worked in a bakery and his dad worked at the phosphate plant in nearby Ruskin. When his dad's work schedule allowed him a weekend off, they would grab their fishing poles and head for one of the many bridges or piers around Tampa Bay.

"Sometimes we'd put a chicken leg on a stick and catch crabs," Forsgren recalled.

Eventually, Forsgren didn't wait for his dad. "When I was a teenager, every summer day I would ride my bike down and fish off the catwalk off the Gandy Bridge" over Tampa Bay, he said. "I'd catch sheepshead and croker. I had a Zebco 202 rod and reel."

Casting his memory back to those days in the mid-1960s, to those endless summer days spent reeling in fish as the cars and trucks roared past him, Forsgren noticed something missing.

"I *never* saw a manatee," he said.

Forty years later, Ackerman's aerial surveys had found some three hundred or so manatees that called Tampa Bay home. To Forsgren, that seemed proof enough that the Fraser report was right on the money.

"There's no doubt there's been a tremendous increase in the number of manatees," he said.

In fact, Forsgren was convinced that the only thing keeping manatees on the endangered list was the environmental group dedicated to protecting them.

"If manatees are already saved," he frequently asked, "then what is the Save the Manatee Club going to do?"

Although Forsgren had a degree in natural resources management, his expertise had nothing to do with manatees. In the early 1980s he worked for the DNR overseeing the state's aquatic preserves. Then in 1985 the founders of what would become the Coastal Conservation Association of Florida—among them magazine publisher Karl Wickstrom—hired him as the fledgling organization's first executive director.

Forsgren would go on to hold that job for more than twenty years. During that time he frequently stood before the wildlife commission and its predecessor organizations, the Game and Fresh Water Fish Commission and the Marine Fisheries Commission, to talk about issues important to anglers. Because of whom he represented, and because he knew how to talk to them, when Forsgren stepped to the microphone and began to talk in his slow and measured baritone, the commissioners paid attention, and they usually agreed.

People who deal with fisheries are used to dealing with stock assessments of game fish species—redfish, for instance. That means picking a population goal and tailoring the fishing regulations to reach it—in effect, managing the species to benefit recreation.

"You tell us what the resource goal is, and when we get to that goal, you don't have to continue adopting regulations," Forsgren explained. "If they're being achieved or exceeded, that should mean that the regulations are doing the job."

To Forsgren, manatees should be handled no differently, no matter what the Endangered Species Act or the Marine Mammal Protection Act might say about protecting every single one of them. If their population had grown, then it was time to declare success and stop slapping new regulations on the state's waterways.

So on August 20, 2001—the same day the U.S. Fish and Wildlife Service unveiled the recovery plan in which Hankla had rejected the scientists' recommendations in favor of something more "flexible"—Forsgren handed the wildlife commission a petition asking that manatees be declared no longer endangered.

"Environmental and animal rights groups continue to state that manatee populations are in serious trouble and declining toward extinction," Forsgren wrote. "We believe that all the available state and federal scientific information shows a completely different picture."

Forsgren made his intent plain: use this attack on the manatee's status as a lever to upend the push for more regulations.

"Our concern is that, is there really a need for all of these Draconian measures that are being proposed throughout the entire state?" he told reporters.

Patti Thompson strongly disagreed with his petition. To her, it seemed likely that there had always been three thousand manatees and that Bruce Ackerman's synoptic surveys had just missed a lot of them. After all, as Ackerman frequently reminded everyone, whatever his scientists spotted should be regarded as only a minimum number, not an actual census.

A student of history might also point out that manatees had not been put on the endangered list because of their numbers. Craig Phillips had specifically cautioned the federal committee picking endangered species about the difficulty of counting manatees. Instead, they were put on the endangered list because they had lost habitat and kept being hit by boats—two threats that had not gone away in the thirty years since Walter Gresh first pushed for them to be added to the list.

Still, manatee biologists said that Forsgren's argument about the increased population could be on the mark. When Ackerman's 2001 survey results came out, some scientists did a little back-of-the-napkin figuring and came up with the same answer Forsgren did.

"Say you start with a thousand manatees," said Bob Bonde of the U.S. Geological Survey, one of the pioneers of manatee necropsies. The estimate of a thousand manatees statewide came from Blair Irvine's first aerial survey in 1976, twenty-five years before, and seemed somewhat more defensible than Woodie Hartman's guesstimate.

"Given what the necropsies have found, it seems perfectly reasonable to conclude that they're 50 percent male and 50 percent female," Bonde said. "So now you've got five hundred females. A conservative approach to this would say that two-fifths of those are immature. . . . So let's say three hundred adult females. They have one calf every three years, and the gestation period is one year long, and there's one calf born to each female. So out of a thousand manatees you would get one hundred calves a year. So now you have eleven hundred. Subtract the mortality, and you'd come up with a little net gain."

In a few years—1996, the year of the Red Tide epizootic, being the prime example—the manatee population might lose more adults through various causes of death than it gained, he said. But eleven hundred manatees a year would soon become twelve hundred, and so on.

"Keep going, and by the early 2000s you would end up with about thirty-five hundred manatees," Bonde said.

Bear in mind, too, that since the day Joe Moore first stood on a bridge in Miami and spotted a prop scar, people have done quite a lot to cultivate an increased population of manatees, said Bruce Ackerman.

"Over the last fifty years . . . we've done a lot of positive things for manatees," Ackerman explained. "Fifty years ago we built these power plants so they have these reliable sources of hot water in the winter. . . . I think people hunting them somewhat dwindled down. I think thirty years ago there were no protected areas at Blue Spring and Crystal River. . . . There was a groundswell of public awareness that manatees are important and should be protected."

The state also took steps to protect sea grass beds and to clean up rampant water pollution, he pointed out. And then there were all the speed zones that had been established through the 1990s. Even without heavy-duty enforcement, they still made the more conscientious boaters slow down, he said.

Put all those factors together, Ackerman said, and "to me it's believable that the population slowly increased." Compare the numbers to money, he said: "If you once had six hundred dollars in your savings account, and now you've got three thousand, I'd consider there's hope."

On the other hand, Ackerman said, "I don't think it can get any better than now. The power plants may go away. The water quality may get worse. My guess is we've done most of what is going to get done." And in the meantime, he pointed out, "the number of boaters is increasing steadily, faster than the number of people living in Florida."

That means that however many manatees there are, they are likely to continue getting clobbered, their tails shredded by propellers, their ribs shattered by the hulls and skegs. Even if the boat strikes don't kill them, the odds are they will be maimed repeatedly, which could limit their reproduction.

One study, done by Tom Pitchford's wife, Meg, looked at the ages of the dead manatees brought to the necropsy lab from all over the state. Although manatees can live into their sixties at the least, and can start reproducing by age five, she found that nearly three-fourths of the dead females had not lived long enough to have more than one calf.

And what if another Red Tide epizootic hit the manatee population? As Governor Chiles had pointed out, knowing the cause of so many manatee deaths did not mean anyone would be able to stop it from happening again.

During one wildlife commission meeting, the commissioners found out that if they divided the number of deaths from all causes by the number of counted live manatees, the number that results is 3 percent. To some of the commissioners, 3 percent didn't seem like much.

"None of those people on that commission are trained biologists," Ackerman said with a shrug.

However, he contended, even a layperson should be able to see what's wrong with that figure. Go to one of the big grocery chains like Publix, he said, "and ask them, suppose the shoplifters took 3 percent a year. Oh, that'd be huge!"

Bear in mind, he said, how slowly manatees reproduce even under ideal conditions.

"Three percent is the most they can grow in a year," Ackerman said. If 3 percent of the population dies every year, "you're taking away their ability to grow. It's like living on a fixed income. You know that your income is constant. But your expenses keep going up. You'd be worried. There comes a point where you can't make it anymore. If the number of carcasses increases 6 percent and the population is growing 3 percent, then the prudent thing is to take some action to fix that problem."

Anyway, three thousand manatees still isn't a lot, Ackerman said.

"There are a number of endangered species where there are more than that," he pointed out.

For instance, Asian elephants are on the endangered list, and there are an estimated thirty to fifty thousand of them. Or look at another Florida species, the Cape Sable seaside sparrow, a small brown bird that lives nowhere but the Everglades. In 2001, the same year Forsgren filed his petition seeking to have the manatee removed from the endangered list, scientists counted 3,264 Cape Sable seaside sparrows. Throughout the 1990s, the official count ranged from a low of 2,624 in 1996 to a high of 4,048 in 1997. Yet nobody proposed taking them off the endangered list. But then, those species haven't stirred quite the same degree of controversy, or angered quite so many powerful people.

After Forsgren turned in his petition, he got a chorus of amens from the

Marine Industry Association of Florida, the Florida Council of Yacht Clubs, the Water Access Task Force, the Florida Guides Association, and Standing Watch.

That fall, meeting at a resort hotel in Key Largo, the wildlife commission voted to accept the petition and told Ken Haddad's staff to proceed to the next step: launching a full-fledged review of the manatee's status.

"There really is nothing wrong with having a process to look at where the manatee is—it's hard to argue against that," said Commissioner Barreto, who made the motion to conduct the study. "I know this has been a very controversial issue in the past. I want them to be deliberate, methodical, take their time and review all the information."

One of the first stops for the petition was the wildlife commission's own outside group of expert advisers, the Manatee Technical Advisory Council. Dan Odell, who had pioneered manatee carcass recovery and necropsies while at the University of Miami, sat on the MTAC, and he cast a skeptical eye over Forsgren's petition.

Odell had read what the rules said about such petitions. "The petitioner had to provide sufficient biological information in the petition to justify the evaluation," he said. So he checked Forsgren's petition to see if it measured up and, in his opinion, it did not come close to that threshold.

"Well, it's real short. There are four references. Two are from popular literature that's out of date. One is the Fraser report, which they paid for. And there was one more," he said.

Odell asked the commission staff who had determined that the petition contained sufficient biological information to justify even being evaluated.

"The answer was: The lawyers," he said.

The fact was, when it came to the subject of endangered species, the wildlife commission was a bit gun-shy.

•

To understand why, turn back the clock to 1993, before the game commission became the wildlife commission.

A University of Florida professor had become concerned about a wading bird called the white ibis. A typical ibis stands about two feet tall and has a long, downward-curving bill. Treasured by Egyptians as a symbol of wisdom, the ibis became a common menu item for Depression-era Floridians, who nicknamed it the "Chokoloskee chicken." Although the ibis survived the Depression, between the 1970s and the 1990s the population declined dramatically. The reason: developers wiped out thousands of acres of wetlands where they lived.

The ibis population in the Everglades declined 90 percent. John W. Fitzpatrick of the Archbold Biological Station called the decline of the ibis "as precipitous as that of any species recorded in this state. This tells us the underlying environment is potentially endangered—not just the species itself."

As a result, Professor Peter Frederick petitioned the game commission to add the ibis to its list of protected species. There were still an estimated sixty-five thousand ibises across Florida, but Frederick said he wanted the commission to take action before the situation became worse.

At that time, the game commission's biologists had the final say over whether a species belonged on the state's list of species in peril. They had three possible classifications to choose from. The animals closest to going extinct were considered endangered. The ones close to becoming endangered were called threatened. Those matched up pretty closely to what the Endangered Species Act called for on the federal listing.

But Florida also had a third classification: "species of special concern." That third category was for wildlife that wasn't quite at the threatened stage, but could get there soon.

Frederick asked the commission's biologists to classify the ibis as "threatened." But business groups and the state's agriculture industry objected, particularly the state's cattle ranchers. Florida has the biggest cattle industry east of the Mississippi River, and the cattle ranchers have long enjoyed a strong influence over the state's political establishment. The ranchers feared that listing the ibis could limit the use of their land. So they complained that the ibis decision would be made by a bunch of biologists rather than by duly elected or appointed public officials.

To placate the protesters, the state biologists put the ibis on the lowest rung of the protected-species ladder, classifying it as a species of special concern. The staff then wrote to local governments in the sixty-seven counties, "advising them not to overreact to the listing with a lot of land regulatory restrictions," said the commission's attorney.

Just to be helpful, the commission's staff drew up some nonbinding guidelines for property owners, to help them avoid disturbing ibis nests. But the guidelines, when they came out in draft form in 1995, caused an even bigger uproar than the listing.

"All on-site potential white ibis foraging habitat within 15 kilometers (9.3 miles) of an active or recently active colony should be protected," one part of the guidelines read. "The foraging habitat protection areas should be maintained as natural wetland systems."

The guidelines "need not apply after a colony has not been used by white ibises for more than 10 consecutive years," the draft said. "However, permitting or regulatory agencies may have to be contacted prior to alteration of the site."

Although the guidelines were strictly voluntary, the state's cattle ranchers erupted with anger. They called the game commission "a runaway agency."

Then the ranchers decided to do more than just complain. Shortly thereafter, two state senators who were friendly to agriculture announced that they would strip two million dollars out of the game commission's fifty-nine-million-dollar budget. That happened to be the exact amount needed to pay for the forty-five biologists who monitored wildlife on the state's list of imperiled species.

One of the senators who co-sponsored stripping the money out of the commission's budget was a big, beefy rancher named Charles Bronson, a Republican from Satellite Beach.

"This isn't about the ibis," Bronson drawled. "It's about property rights." The guidelines the game commission had proposed were "drastically going to affect the economics of the state of Florida," he warned. "Lands are going to be tied up."

When pressed, Bronson could not name a single instance in the previous two years where any project had been tied up by protection for the ibis. Commission staffers explained that putting the ibis on the list as a species of special concern actually offered the birds very little in the way of regulatory protection, except for making it illegal to shoot them.

People outraged by the senators' actions started wearing "Save the Ibis" buttons around the capitol. People who agreed with the senators responded by wearing buttons that said "Kill and Eat the Ibis."

The Speaker of the House vowed to make sure the two million dollars stayed in the state budget, no matter what the Senate did. Meanwhile, Bronson showed up on the floor of the Senate one day wearing a peculiar helmet. He said it was in the shape of an ibis, although the purpose of his unusual headgear remained as obscure as its form.

In the end, the legislature put the money back, but the game commission got the message. It suspended adding any new species to the 118 already on its imperiled list. In the meantime, the commission launched a complete revamping of its listing process to make sure nothing like the ibis situation ever happened again.

The rewrite took four years. In 1999, the newly minted wildlife commission approved the new process. No more would the final listing decision be made by its own biologists. Now the process would require two steps.

First, after a petition had been accepted, the biologists would spend about a year reviewing the species' status, then make a written report. The report would include a recommendation on whether the species should be listed, and what the listing should be. Among the factors to be considered would be the economic impact on landowners and business.

That report would then go to three scientists who were experts on this particular species. They would comment on whether the staff had gotten their facts straight. Then the report and the comments would go to the commission to vote on the listing.

Next came the second step: the commission's biologists would write a management plan for the species, a process likely to take another year. The management plan would include the actions that everyone should take to help the species recover. Until the wildlife commission voted to implement that management plan, its listing decision from step one would not officially take effect.

The wildlife commission made one other significant alteration—the most significant one of all.

The new listing process included new criteria for each one of the three levels of imperilment. Wildlife commission officials said they did not want to simply mimic the criteria on the federal list because they believed Lee Talbot's wording to be too vague.

Instead, they took the new criteria from Talbot's old agency, the Switzerland-based International Union for Conservation of Nature. After all, the IUCN had virtually invented the whole idea of the endangered list back when Talbot worked there. Then when Talbot moved to the Nixon White House staff he had used the lessons he learned at the IUCN in writing the Endangered Species Act.

But the way the state wildlife commission applied the criteria didn't quite match up with the IUCN. The IUCN has four, not three, rungs on its ladder. The species in the biggest trouble is classified as critically endangered, and then comes endangered, threatened, and vulnerable.

For the wildlife commission to exactly match those four categories would have required asking the legislature to change state law. The wildlife commission did not want to take this issue back to the same place where the agency had nearly lost a chunk of its funding. Instead, the commission shoehorned the IUCN's criteria for four categories into its preexisting three categories. That meant that the IUCN's endangered and threatened categories got crammed together into the single Florida category of threatened. The IUCN's definition for "critically endangered" wound up converted into the definition for any endangered species.

So now, to rank as endangered, a species would have had to lose at least 80 percent of its population over the previous ten years. To qualify as threatened, a species would have had to lose at least 50 percent of its population during the previous decade.

"When I saw those criteria," Patti Thompson said, "the hair on the back of my neck stood up."

Manatees could not meet such a high standard to stay on the state's endangered list. In fact, those criteria were so strict that not even the Florida panther—with a population that had slightly increased over the previous decade but which still totaled about one hundred—could meet the standard.

Environmental activists from Audubon, Defenders of Wildlife, and the Florida Wildlife Federation all protested. Under the new system, they said, a species would have to be dead as the dodo before it could be called endangered.

Although being on the state's endangered list did not confer the same strong legal position as being on the federal endangered list, the state's listing decisions were no mere academic exercise. For one thing, a species' status granted it different levels of legal consideration from local governments. A project that might hurt an endangered species would face more hurdles in getting a zoning change from city or county officials than one that might hurt a threatened species or a species of special concern.

Then there was the matter of funding. According to a study by the Florida Ornithological Society, animals on the state's endangered list tended to get three to five times as much tax money as other species. The endangered few stood first in line for state funds in scientific research and for the purchase of habitat.

The Florida Ornithological Society did its study because, at the suggestion of one of the commission's own biologists, the commission had launched into a study of reclassifying another species on its endangered list, the red-cockaded woodpecker.

About 12,500 red-cockaded woodpeckers were scattered through forests across the South. Florida had the largest single group, living in the Apalachicola National Forest near Tallahassee. Nearly 97 percent of the South's red-cockaded woodpecker population had disappeared over the previous century because logging wiped out the old-growth forests the birds favor. However, because the population had not dropped by 80 or even 50 percent in the previous decade, this woodpecker seemed likely to be reclassified at the lowest rung on the state's ladder, as a species of special concern.

Species of special concern didn't get much protection at all. One animal on Florida's special concern list, the gopher tortoise, tended to dig its burrows in areas that also happened to be the kinds of places where developers liked to build subdivisions and shopping centers. So the state devised what became known as the "pay-to-pave" program: developers wrote a check to a state fund to buy gopher tortoise habitat somewhere else, then simply paved over the burrow, sealing the tortoise inside, alive. Thousands of them suffocated and died that way.

Despite the strong protests of the environmental activists and the ornithologists, state wildlife commission officials said they intended to stick to their new criteria, at least for now.

"I believe we should let this play out and see what results we get," said Frank Montalbano, a bear-sized bureaucrat with a thick country twang who headed up the state's wildlife division.

Yet not even the U.S. Fish and Wildlife Service wanted to see Florida downgrade its listing for the red-cockaded woodpecker. Reclassifying the bird based on those criteria could "reduce the management attention that is given the species, particularly on private and state-owned lands in Florida," federal officials complained to their state counterparts.

Even as the federal wildlife service protested about the woodpecker, though, the same agency was unleashing a set of regulations to protect manatees that would set off the biggest round of controversy yet.

•

The law that Woodie Hartman had endorsed thirty years before, the Marine Mammal Protection Act, kept giving Dave Hankla fits.

In order to process all the Florida dock permits that had gotten backed up, he needed to authorize the "incidental take"—the unintentional killing—of a certain number of manatees under the MMPA. Under the MMPA, incidental take can be allowed if the amount of dead animals would have no more than a negligible impact on a population or stock.

But nobody knew how many manatees could die without sending the population into a tailspin. As a result, there was no way to figure out how many could be killed by boats each year without any consequences for the species. Thus Hankla had no easy way to set up regulations for incidental take.

"There's really no clear guidance on how to do that," he said. The one region of the service that had dealt the most extensively with incidental take, the Alaska office, "had never addressed lethal take," he said.

Hankla's staff looked at fisheries management, consulted with manatee experts from other agencies, and compared the results of various formulas to what they were already doing. Nothing seemed to work exactly the way they wanted it to, Hankla said.

"The issue we have wrestled with over time is, 'What do you do if you set a number, and by May the number of manatees killed by boats is that number plus one?'" he asked. "Then what do you do? Stop all dock construction? Deny it? I'm not sure that works."

The discussions and debate "went around and around" among the field station staff in Jacksonville, the regional office in Atlanta, and officials in Washington of both the service and the Interior Department, Hankla said.

"There were lots of starts and stops," he said. "We had to bring everybody in and pound out a solution. The end result of that is what we all agreed on. And we put it out there and everybody hated it."

On November 6, 2002—the day after the disastrous hearing in front of Judge Sullivan that led Craig Manson to step in—the Fish and Wildlife Service unveiled a new rule that led to the biggest explosion yet in the Manatee War.

The new rule "would authorize for the next five years the incidental, unintentional take of small numbers of Florida manatees . . . related to watercraft and watercraft access facilities within three regions of Florida."

The service split the state's manatee population into regions because manatees seldom migrated from one of those regions to the other. They stayed apart, in distinct subpopulations. That was why the Red Tide epizootic affected only manatees in one part of the state, and not the entire population.

The three regions where the wildlife service said it could authorize a small amount of take were the upper St. Johns River, defined as Palatka southward, including Rick Rawlins's stomping grounds in Volusia County; the northwest, which included the manatee-mad town of Crystal River; and the Atlantic coast, which included Brevard County's deadly waterways.

In two of those regions, the upper St. Johns and the northwest, the adult survival rate topped 96 percent, so any additional deaths of manatees from new boat slips built there "would have a negligible impact," the proposed rule said.

In the third region, the Atlantic coast, the adult survival impact measured out around 94 percent. But with a few "additional mitigating measures," this region could rate a "negligible impact" finding too. That meant adding more speed zones, increasing enforcement, educating boaters about manatees, and trying to minimize the impact of new docks on manatee habitat.

As a result, three-fourths of the state could breathe a sigh of relief. But not the southwest region, defined as everything from the Ten Thousand Islands north to Tampa Bay, which would include boat-obsessed Cape Coral in Lee County. More than 40 percent of the state's manatee population lived there, and constantly risked being maimed or killed by boats, losing habitat to new development, or dying from another Red Tide epizootic. Based on the adult survival rate—90 percent, exactly what was in the recovery plan—the wildlife service concluded that "it is likely that this stock is currently declining or is, at best, stable."

As if to underline the point, Lee County was now leading the state in manatee mortality, with fifty-one dead, thirteen from being hit by boats—and the year wasn't over yet. Yet somehow, thirteen years after it had been ordered by the governor and cabinet, Lee County still had no manatee protection plan.

Given those circumstances, the wildlife service declared: "For the Southwest stock, the best available information indicates that these activities would have more than a negligible impact on the stock and, therefore, we are not proposing to authorize incidental take for this stock."

What did that mean? A five-hundred-page impact statement from the wildlife service spelled it out in hard, cold numbers. For the next five years, people in southwest Florida would face tougher scrutiny of dock permits, it said.

About 37 percent would be rejected because they would put too many boats into areas where manatees were already getting hit too frequently.

The slowdown in dock permits, combined with rejection of more than a third of them, would probably drive down the value of waterfront property, the impact statement said. That would affect a wide variety of development-related businesses, which could result in losses estimated to range from $87 million to $175 million. The number of lost jobs could reach nearly a thousand over the five years.

To further complicate matters, the Corps had been sitting on about five hundred Lee County dock permits for the past year because of the lawsuit. Until May 2003, when the final version of the rules for incidental take took effect, that freeze would continue.

The two things became merged in the public mind. The result was a widespread belief that the Save the Manatee Club had somehow bewitched those bumbling federal bureaucrats into slapping a moratorium on all new dock permits as a sneaky way to stop growth.

Jim Kalvin quickly condemned the new rules for incidental take and blamed the club: "We knew all along that they were going to fight every single-family boat access. They're using voodoo biology to destroy a $100-million economy."

Cape Coral's city manager, Terry Stewart, agreed that the whole thing must be based on "bad science." The city rushed to hire a Washington law firm to overturn the new rules, agreeing to spend up to one hundred thousand dollars lobbying lawmakers and federal agency bosses.

Although the wildlife service repeatedly said the regulations for incidental take had been a response to the lawsuit, Glitzenstein and other representatives of the Save the Manatee Club insisted that what the service had proposed had nothing to do with what they wanted. Besides, Glitzenstein complained, the new regulations seemed so vague they were "a nothingburger."

Given what happened as a result, Patti Thompson wondered years later if this was all part of a crafty plan by the Fish and Wildlife Service to hurt the Save the Manatee Club.

"They did that on purpose," she said. "It was quite a brilliant stroke on their part. No one asked them to do that. That did seal a backlash."

But Hankla contended that the rules for incidental take were actually a stab at something the club had asked for: assessing the cumulative impact of the permits the Corps had been issuing.

The effort was doomed from the beginning, he said, because of the number of manatees already being hit and killed.

"There was no way to authorize incidental take at a level that would work and still meet the standard of the law," he said.

Representative Harrington once observed that "if you want to turn out a crowd, all you've got to do is mention manatees and boating speed limits." Limiting dock building proved to be even more powerful an attention-getter.

On November 23, 2002, about a thousand people crammed into Jaycee Park, on the banks of the Caloosahatchee in Cape Coral, for what was billed as a "Moratorium Madness" rally. The *Fort Myers News-Press* described the crowd as "real estate agents, boat dock builders, waterfront property owners, boaters, and other residents." They chanted "Unlock our docks!" and lined up to sign letters urging President Bush to help them.

"We all need to say, 'Hey Washington, it's about people too,'" City Manager Stewart told the crowd. When he asked if everyone was "on board," they cheered his nautical metaphor.

"We really have a fight on our hands," Representative Jeff Kottkamp told the crowd.

Two weeks later came the first public hearing on the new rules for incidental take, when three thousand people showed up at the Harborside Convention Center in Fort Myers to howl at Hankla. They toted signs that said "Save Our Jobs" and "Rescue Our Property Rights." A bus from Hooters—a chain restaurant popular for its chicken wings, double entendres, and scantily clad waitresses—parked out front, decorated with a banner that proclaimed, "Docks Don't Kill Manatees."

The air was thick with tension and unintended irony. The hearing occurred on the banks of Florida's deadliest waterway for manatees, on a day with the kind of nippy weather that would drive them to swim upriver to warmer spots like the Florida Power and Light outfall.

The cavernous meeting hall filled up quickly, with every chair occupied and knots of people milling around the edges. Sitting with Hankla at the front of the room were two other wildlife service employees, a court reporter to take down what everyone said and pinstriped lawyer named Roger Babb, who had been hired by the service to conduct the hearings.

At 6:07 p.m. Babb announced, "Ladies and gentlemen, the appointed hour has arrived." When he explained that he was not an employee of the wildlife service, the audience applauded and whistled.

Babb then asked everyone to take down their banners—a request no one bothered to comply with—and urged the crowd to provide "thoughtful, persuasive comments." He reminded them of September 11, noting that "we as Americans have more in common than what divides us."

Then came Hankla's turn. He tried in vain to explain the regulations in a way that would make sense. Watercraft deaths among southwest Florida's manatees were increasing faster than the estimated population growth rate, he said. The situation demanded action, but that could change, he said. Although the regulations were supposed to last for five years, he said, "we do not have to wait for five years to reevaluate the stock."

Despite what everyone else was saying, he told the crowd, what was being proposed "does not equal a moratorium." They responded with gales of derisive laughter.

Hankla said the agency would continue to evaluate permits on a case-by-case basis. Approval depended on their proximity to manatees and the possible impact on them. He then urged everyone to work with the government. He might as well have urged them to flap their arms and fly around the room.

Babb then announced that, as a courtesy, elected officials would be allowed to speak first during the public comment portion of the hearing. The first one up, Representative Harrington, got the crowd roaring with his comment about the new regulations going too far. He went on to complain that the regulations were "going to stress this region to the breaking point. . . . Loss of homes, loss of jobs, loss of lifestyles!"

After him came Kottkamp, Cape Coral's state representative, who said he wanted to talk not about the manatee population but about "the human population—we call 'em taxpayers here in southwest Florida." That drew cheers.

"Certainly manatees are killed when they come in contact with boats, but I've never heard of a dock killing a manatee," Kottkamp added, echoing the banner on the Hooters bus. People in the crowd shouted "Yeah!" as if he'd made a first down with goal to go. Emboldened, Kottkamp went for the touchdown: "This moratorium is essentially a death sentence for five years on our local economy." More cheers rewarded his rhetorical excess.

Next up: Cape Coral's mayor, Arnold Kempe, a diminutive man in a snappy khaki suit who wore his white hair in an elaborate wave. He began by explaining a quirk of the Rosen brothers' development process.

"Docks," he explained to Hankla, "are a needed extension of our almost nonexistent backyards in Cape Coral." Disregarding Hankla's promise of no moratorium, Kempe called it one anyway: "This moratorium will have a devastating impact."

As Kempe spoke, the red light on the lectern flashed, indicating that he had reached the time limit for speaking. The mayor ignored it and kept going, minute after minute after minute. Finally, he got to his punch line, his voice rising as he said, "The moratorium must *cease!*" Nearly the entire crowd rose to give him a lengthy standing ovation.

Babb, sensing at last that his control of the meeting had slipped out the door and run off down the street, warned the crowd about too much clapping.

"Deal with it!" somebody shouted.

"Are we allowed to breathe?" called out one wag. Another replied, "Yeah—in five years!"

Speaker after speaker railed at Hankla, bringing up everything from the Civil War to Spanish land grants as a reason to disobey the government. Andy Coy, a Lee County commissioner, complained that Hankla was "asking us to give up the Constitution, to give up state's rights . . . to more or less be chattel for the slaughter." Outlawing docks in Lee County, he said, "is like outlawing cabins in North Carolina or outlawing basketball in Indiana or outlawing Mickey Mouse in Orlando."

Many of the already angry people in the crowd grew even more upset because Hankla and his staff sat at their black-draped table taking all the abuse and not responding. They wouldn't answer questions or react to the most outrageous comments. They were as responsive as the statues out front, a living embodiment of the unfeeling bureaucracy.

Hankla felt equally frustrated. What the audience didn't understand, what no one had explained, was that the wildlife service's rules for conducting a hearing like this required that he remain mute. He wasn't allowed to respond, not even to attempt to correct inaccurate statements.

Next came Jim Kalvin's turn to blast away. Instead of identifying himself as the president of Standing Watch, he said he represented a new umbrella group, the Florida Water Access Coalition. This group combined boaters with waterskiers and the Marine Industry Association. With 250,000 members statewide, it surpassed the Save the Manatee Club's worldwide membership.

Kalvin urged the wildlife service to do more research on manatees. However, his proposals for study sounded like they had come from the *Florida Sportsman* message board: "What's attracting them here? What's causing them to degrade our estuaries?"

Then he called on Hankla and his bosses to take a drastic step.

"Abandon the settlement agreement with Save the Manatee Club and take 'em to court!" he said, drawing shouts of "Yeah!" from the crowd. Just as Babb did, Kalvin made reference to the terrorist attack of September 11, an attack on the freedoms that Americans hold dear. But he flipped the reference on its head by adding, "We're dealing with a plaintiff organization that goes to court to circumvent those freedoms!"

After Kalvin sat down, a Fort Myers boat-lift manufacturer named George Becker tossed in a lightly veiled threat, telling Hankla, "Sure, we'd like to keep the manatee as our friend here, and not have to look at it as a food source."

Then, at about 7:30 p.m., an hour after the public comment part of the hearing began, a woman from Punta Gorda named Debra Highsmith stepped up to the mike. Employing a line made popular by the 1970s comedy show *Monty Python's Flying Circus*, Highsmith announced, "And now for something completely different."

She talked about visiting Blue Spring, where crowds of people were spending four dollars a carload to see manatees. She went on to point out that the state was spending money on educating boaters and rehabilitating manatees "while we're tearing apart and grinding up manatees with 225-horsepower motors."

At that point there were shouts of "Yeah!" from people in the crowd who apparently relished the thought of using a boat motor to chew up the flesh of a wild animal. Others angrily shouted, "Tree hugger!"

"I won't tolerate this form of expression!" Babb sputtered, but no one paid him any attention.

Over the next few hours, from time to time, another speaker would stand up who, like Highsmith, admitted liking manatees. That person could count on being booed and shouted down. When one speaker mentioned that manatees were endangered, there were cries of "No they're not!" When that speaker's red light went off, the crowd shouted, "Hey, his time is up! Get him out of there!"

The crowd had its favorites. One was Jerry Geyer, a recreational boater in a khaki shirt that said Cape Coral Tarpon Hunters Club. Geyer said he was on the water two hundred days a year, so he knew what he was talking about. In a strong Noo Yawk accent, he accused the Save the Manatee Club of what he called "fraaawww-ud" and said of manatees in general: "If in fact they were relocated or eradicated, the overall environment of southwest Florida would probably enjoy an overall positive effect."

Then, to gales of laughter and wild applause from the audience, Geyer told Hankla: "These rules prove that the Three Stooges and the Wicked Witch of the West did in fact get together and produce offspring."

Finally, at 9:10 p.m.—ten minutes after the public hearing was supposed to be over—the only official representative of the Save the Manatee Club in attendance got a chance to speak. When she announced the name of her employer, she was greeted with so many hisses it sounded as if the room had suddenly sprung a leak.

She had curly brown hair, a sparkly burgundy sweater, and a black skirt. Her name was Laura Ruhana Combs. She was part Arab, a fact about herself that she seldom mentioned in this post-9/11 milieu. All the comments about her group being a bunch of terrorists tended to unsettle her.

A Detroit native with a master's degree in urban and regional planning, Combs had worked for Pat Rose in his final years at the Department of Environmental Protection, reviewing waterfront development permits. She recently had been hired by the club to open its first southwest Florida office, an assignment akin to opening a New York Yankees souvenir shop in the shadow of Boston's Fenway Park.

Combs was visibly pregnant, which is probably all that discouraged some people in the crowd from assaulting her on the spot. Still, compared to all the hyperbole that preceded her, Combs's speech to Hankla seemed dry and matter-of-fact.

She began by saying all the problems could be resolved if everyone would sit down and work together. She contended that, to satisfy the wildlife service, Lee County needed improved speed zones, more law enforcement, a truly protective manatee protection plan, and extensive public education about how to avoid manatees.

She pointed out that Lee County hadn't bothered to complete its protection plan for thirteen years, while the wildlife service didn't get around to the MMPA regulations for incidental take until thirty years after the law had passed. She didn't quite say it, but she strongly implied that it was their own fault that everything about manatees was now such a mess.

When Combs was done, exactly two people clapped. Far more booed. Afterward, as she stood chatting outside, she was accosted twice by people who yelled at her for what the club was doing.

"They would ream me out," Combs said. "My husband was standing there. They were just *yelling,* and I said, 'Is there any response that I could give you that you'd be willing to listen to?' They said, 'No!' and they stormed off. The second one was a woman. She said, 'You're ruining people's lives! Do you even understand what you're doing?' I was pretty flummoxed by that."

By then, people had begun trickling out of the hearing, their spleens vented for the moment. At last a few more of the club's allies got to speak. One was an extremely jittery Cynthia Frisch, speaking very, very fast. She was convinced that the people in this crowd could not comprehend the peaceful role she saw for manatees.

"It's not within their realm of understanding," she said later. "They just can't stretch their consciousness enough. To them it's like thinking a black person is subhuman."

In her brief turn at the microphone, Frisch urged better law enforcement and better speed zones, then sat down. Nobody in the crowd knew what the Pegasus Foundation was, or Frisch's role in pulling together the lawsuit, but that didn't stop them from saying things that she found intimidating.

"People were very threatening, and I got a police escort out to my car," Frisch said.

Next up, though, was Susannah Lindberg, the erstwhile "Grim Reaper," the woman once tagged as "Osama bin Laden with a sex change." While Frisch had been visibly nervous, Lindberg remained in control. She liked to joke with Frisch that she possessed "ovaries of steel."

Lindberg dispensed with the can't-we-all-get-along lines of previous manatee advocates. She spelled out what she viewed as wrong with Lee County, and why it needed special sanctions from the wildlife service to ensure manatees got better protection: "Lee County is responsible for more watercraft deaths than any other county in Florida. Lee is responsible for more *human* watercraft deaths last year than any other. *No* new watercraft access facilities should be permitted until manatees are adequately protected. It's ludicrous that Lee County could not implement an MPP [manatee protection plan]."

When she finished, the people sitting in the front row shouted, "'Good night! Good night! Good night! Go hug a tree!'"

The meeting meandered along until close to 11 p.m., two hours past its scheduled deadline. It ended with a whimper, not a bang. Afterward, in the litter the crowd left behind, one of Hanka's assistants found a placard and presented it to his boss. It said "FED UP WITH THE FEDS" and featured four very authentic-looking bullet holes.

The following night, at the second hearing, Hankla faced a smaller and much more orderly crowd in a hotel meeting room in Tampa. Among the 250 people who showed up to speak to him there, though, was none other than Wade Hopping himself.

Wearing a suit and a smirk, Hopping insisted the impact on the region's economy would be even worse than the wildlife service had predicted. Then he suggested a solution he said would make much more sense: capture every manatee in Florida and implant a device that would alert boaters to their presence anytime one got too close. Nobody took him seriously.

The rest of the hearings rocked along in a similar vein until the final one, held at the Renaissance Hotel in Fort Lauderdale. It drew just fifty people, among them a marine construction company owner who accused the Save the Manatee Club of being "full of bigots and anti-growth wackos."

But that's the meeting where the opposition to the rules for incidental take picked up a powerful ally. An aide to Governor Bush stood up and read a letter from the chief executive that said: "The rule could lead to a moratorium on dock permitting in that region and make it significantly more difficult to register vessels and operate boats."

The letter went on to say that Bush wanted to meet with Interior Secretary Norton to convince her to ditch these new rules. A month later, on January 24, 2003, Bush flew to Washington for his sit-down with Norton. He reiterated the letter's message: the new rules on dock building would cause great economic hardship on booming southwest Florida, and therefore they should be dropped.

By then, though, Judge Manson had worked things out to satisfy Judge Sullivan. Because she faced a potential contempt charge, Norton no longer leaped to do everything the president's brother asked.

After the meeting, Governor Bush didn't speak to the press. Instead, a spokeswoman said he and Norton had simply agreed to keep talking. The spokeswoman said the governor might try to call a meeting to talk to everyone involved—sort of like his manatee summit two years earlier, although she didn't mention it—"to move forward in a way that protects manatees as well as the rights of boaters and property-owners."

The tension between what Governor Bush wanted and what Secretary Norton could do made the two of them "like two neighbors who had gotten along so far but now one of their dogs has pooped on the other one's lawn," said Manson.

Bush's demand for fewer regulations to protect manatees arrived at a bad time, not just because of Norton's legal entanglement but also from a publicity standpoint. Tom Pitchford's staff had just announced that in the year just concluded—a year in which, because of the lawsuits and attendant controversy, manatees got far more air time and ink than they had in any year since 1996—boaters had still managed to kill ninety- seven of them, a new record.

Nevertheless, a week after Bush met with Norton, a new politico joined the anti-regulation side: U.S. Representative Porter Goss, a Republican from Sanibel whose district included Fort Myers and Cape Coral.

Goss had once been a spy for the Central Intelligence Agency. When he retired he joined a coterie of ex-CIA men who had settled in Sanibel, an island near Fort Myers that they had discovered while training for the ill-fated Bay of Pigs invasion. Although they failed to seize control of Cuba, the ex-spooks succeeded years later in taking over Sanibel. They started the island's first newspaper, led the charge to incorporate as a city, then got one of their own—Goss—chosen as the first mayor. Sanibel won plaudits for its tight rules on development, designed to maintain the island's quaint charm.

From there Goss had climbed the ladder to county commissioner and then congressman, and soon President Bush would select him to lead the CIA. Despite his dashing background, Goss preferred the conservative approach to everything. Once, on the campaign trail, he boasted to a reporter that he wore both a belt and suspenders, then showed them off as proof.

Yet now Goss, hearing the howls of outrage from his constituents (not to mention his campaign contributors), announced he wanted to take a more radical approach to the manatee-versus-dock problem. He said he wanted to amend the Endangered Species Act and the Marine Mammal Protection Act to eliminate these conflicts.

Goss met with Manson and with Hankla's boss in Atlanta, Sam Hamilton, to let them know they now had bigger problems than satisfying the Save the Manatee Club. They had Congress to deal with.

"The idea of not allowing the building of docks in Southwest Florida is like saying the building of garages is responsible for road kill," Goss told a reporter after the meeting. The ex-mayor had apparently forgotten the fact that when traffic gets too dangerous on a highway, the government will usually impose new rules on developers that may limit what gets built—say through charging higher impact fees or requiring the developer to build a new turn lane.

"Secretary Norton and I met with Goss together on one occasion and I met with him probably twice more," Manson said. "In the first meeting, I did most of the talking. . . . Goss was a bit gruff, but not in an overly unpleasant way. When I met with him twice more, I found him receptive to the process of making the regs, but a bit impatient with the time it was taking."

Meanwhile, the U.S. Marine Mammal Commission—Lee Talbot's designated watchdog to make sure the MMPA didn't get off track—weighed in on the controversy with an eight-page letter that also said the regulations didn't make sense. But the commission took that position because the numbers didn't add up.

The commission's executive director, David Cottingham, wrote to Hankla that "the basis for the Service's conclusions regarding negligible impact levels is difficult to assess and seems questionable." Then he went on to show exactly what was wrong with the math:

> Given the death of at least 95 manatees by watercraft in Florida in 2002, the net productivity of manatees in Florida would need to be 950 manatees per year for watercraft-related deaths to be considered a "small portion" (i.e., no more than 10 percent) of the total stock's net productivity. The maximum net productivity rate adopted by the Service in its Florida manatee stock assessment report is four percent. Assuming this rate is correct, and using a minimum abundance estimate of 3,276 for the total Florida manatee population (the best available estimate of the minimum population size), the current maximum net productivity level for the statewide population should be about 131 manatees per year. Thus, to consider watercraft deaths in 2002 to be negligible, the overall maximum net productivity level would need to be more than seven times higher than what reasonably might be estimated to be the current net productivity level. Unless the proportion of manatee deaths due to watercraft was disproportionately low by a considerable margin in the three regions covered by the proposed rules and most watercraft deaths were concentrated in the southwestern Florida region, recent watercraft-related mortality levels have exceeded negligible levels in all three regions in recent years and may have far exceeded negligible levels in the Atlantic coast region.

That wasn't all. In the letter, which also went to Manson, Cottingham pointed out that the MMPA defines "take" to include harassment and non-fatal injuries as well as death.

"Virtually every adult manatee in Florida has multiple scars on its back," he wrote. "Accordingly, the Service should include its rationale for determining that non-lethal harassment and habitat degradation associated with increased vessel traffic would be dealt with under the rule."

The Marine Mammal Commission did more than simply write a letter. Because it exists to advise Congress, its leaders also made sure to notify congressional leaders on Capitol Hill about what was going on.

"Behind the scenes, they were working the Hill and interest groups rather intensely for a government agency," Manson said.

Three months later, word came of a new scientific study that spelled out just how badly the regulations for incidental take had missed the boat.

•

In an effort to shore up the scientific basis for the new rules for incidental take, wildlife service officials had asked a scientist named Michael Runge to gaze into his version of a crystal ball and predict the future of the species.

Runge worked for the U.S. Geological Survey in Patuxent, Maryland. He was a man of wide interests. He had earned his bachelor's degree from Johns Hopkins University while majoring in both biology and philosophy. He got his master's while majoring in secondary education and biology. In 1999 he earned a Ph.D. from Cornell in natural resources management. But his work on natural resources took him indoors far more often than out to the field.

A slender man with a bus-station grin and fly-away hair, Runge had become one of the nation's premier experts on creating population models for various kinds of wildlife.

Biologists use computer-created population models to figure out how an entire species will react to different events: If this happens, will the population increase? If we try this strategy, will the population decrease? What if this second variable happens too? How will that affect the future?

Grad student Miriam Marmontel had used a computer program called VORTEX to create a population model for manatees in 1994. But VORTEX was a package of preset software that worked sort of like a TurboTax computer program. A biologist answered the program's questions and set the parameters for the study, and then VORTEX spit out the answer. Veteran programmers said VORTEX lacked flexibility. It could not be made to account for every variable. So experts like Runge had figured out how to create a custom-made population model that would handle more variables.

In 2001, Runge began collaborating with Cathy Beck and her colleagues at the U.S. Geological Survey office in Gainesville to create a population model that they presented at a conference in 2002.

Although he had never studied them before, Runge said, "manatees are not a particularly difficult species to deal with from a population modeling standpoint. There's a *ton* of data. They're not like blue whales, which live a mile deep in the ocean where they're completely inaccessible to humans. Manatees—they're right there. They're where the people are."

Thanks to Ackerman's synoptic surveys, Pitchford's crew at the path lab, and Beck's scar catalog of the wounded, he had a lot to work with.

"Manatees," he said, "have more data than any other marine mammal."

Runge primarily based his calculations on data from Beck's catalog of photos of scarred manatees that dated back to the 1960s, thus building his model on the pioneering work of both Joe Moore and Woodie Hartman. Using the scar catalog, Runge could calculate how often the same manatees appeared over and over again, helping him to plot reproduction and survivability. Using that information, the model could predict the population's growth rate based on different potential scenarios for the future.

After seeing Runge's work on that initial population model, Hankla and his staff asked him to modify it to help them with the regulations for incidental take. Doing that required tackling a different question than the one addressed by the original model.

"The question under the MMPA was: could you authorize take on the order of one hundred manatees a year statewide?" Runge said. "Does that rise above the level of 'negligible'?"

To reach an answer, Runge had to tinker quite a bit with the 2002 model. That one focused exclusively on female manatees, so he added males into the mix. He added in other variables—"a potential disease catastrophe," for instance, as well as another Red Tide disaster like the one from 1996. But he grounded everything in the numbers produced by Pitchford and his colleagues at the path lab for the minimum number of manatees killed each year by boats.

Runge said he focused on three questions: "What do we think are the ongoing impacts of watercraft take? Is the current level of take legal? Could you authorize take at that level?"

The answer Runge came up with pulled the rug out from under the whole process of incidental take.

He found that the maximum number of manatees that the wildlife service could authorize killing via boat was 5.6 a year in the Atlantic region, 0.6 a year in the St. Johns region, 1.5 a year in the northwest region, and 5.5 a year in the southwest region. Any more than that would have too great an impact on the future of the species, and thus could not be classified as "negligible."

"I think people were hoping for something a lot closer to what was happening," Runge said. "But the take that was occurring was *way* above what we defined as negligible."

For instance, for manatees in the Atlantic region—one of the three regions the wildlife service had said seemed to be stable—the number of manatees that Runge said could be killed was thirty-two fewer than the yearly average for the previous five years.

Runge also found that the statewide manatee population did indeed appear to have grown over the previous fifteen years. But the manatees were far from overcrowded, based on his estimates of the carrying capacity—the number of animals that could be supported by the resources available—for the four regions. He estimated that the state could comfortably support about 5,025 manatees, primarily based on the availability of power plants and springs that provided a warm haven from cold winter weather.

However, he noted, several of those springs—Homosassa Springs in Citrus County being one example—had seen a sharp reduction in the amount of water being produced because of overpumping by nearby wells. That threatened to limit the number of manatees that could use those sites.

Runge found the biggest danger sign in the number of watercraft-related manatee deaths. Contrary to the assertions in the Fraser report and the arguments put forward by everyone from Ted Forsgren to Wade Hopping, Runge said that the number of deaths did not match up with the growth rate. Instead, the percentage of manatees being killed by boats between 1990 and 2002 in most of the state had increased at a faster rate than the manatee population had grown in those areas.

"In the Atlantic and Southwest regions, the rate of increase in watercraft-related mortality over that period far outstripped the estimated growth rate of those populations (by 8.5 percent in the Atlantic and 10.6 percent in the Southwest)," Runge wrote, echoing the Manatee Technical Advisory Council's findings on the Fraser report.

Part of the problem with the southwest region, he wrote, was that the population there appeared to have declined since 1990, not increased. Conditions were so bad there that even if the wildlife service could halt all boat-related mortality, he wrote, "the growth rate over the next 20 years is not expected to be positive." Add in the watercraft mortality figures, and the future looked far worse.

So in the summary printed on the first page of his report, Runge included one fateful sentence: "In the absence of any new management action, that is, if boat mortality rates continue to increase at the rates observed since 1992, the situation in the Atlantic and Southwest regions is dire, with no chance of meeting recovery criteria within 100 years."

The Runge report, titled "A Model for Assessing Incidental Take of Manatees Due to Watercraft-Related Activities," was released on April 4, 2003—but not with any fanfare whatsoever. Instead, Hankla's office merely included it as an attachment to the wildlife service's lengthy environmental impact statement (EIS) on its proposed rules for incidental take.

But it was impossible to hide something this momentous.

"I am reading it now and all I can say is HOLY SEA COW," Patti Thompson wrote in an e-mail to a reporter. "I need to look through this and the rest of the EIS very carefully but it appears some of the assumptions made on the part of FWS [Fish and Wildlife Service] . . . are clearly flawed."

She wrote that she could not imagine how the bureaucrats would get around Runge's findings, "but they will surely try. It is what they do best—weasel out of their responsibilities under the law."

The Save the Manatee Club decided to trumpet Runge's findings. It quickly posted his report on the organization's Web site with a press release that did everything with the word "dire" except put it in 72-point all-caps.

"Long Term Prospects for Manatee Recovery Look Grim, According to New Data Released by Federal Government" blared the headline atop the press release, which the club's staff then faxed and e-mailed to reporters across the state.

"The Runge report is going to change the face of this whole debate," Judith Vallee predicted in an interview at the time. "It's really 'dire.' That's his word. It does show that the manatee is not doing well."

Glitzenstein told reporters that the Runge report should spur the wildlife service to delay its rules for incidental take so they could be completely revamped.

"This obviously has enormous bearing on whether the federal government should allow any incidental take of manatees," the lawyer said. "If you want to save manatees, you have got to bring that watercraft-related mortality under control. If not, it's a prescription for disaster."

When the Associated Press reported the story, the first sentence said: "Manatees in Florida face a bleak future, if not outright extinction, unless regulators crack down on watercraft, according to a report by the Patuxent Wildlife Research Center."

Years later, Runge said he regretted using the word "dire" because "people think they're going to die." He also wasn't thrilled with the way Patti Thompson and her colleagues capitalized on that sentence, complaining that "the Save the Manatee Club essentially stripped off the 'if' clause and left the 'dire.' That's probably the one word choice, out of all the things I've written, that I'd like to take back."

Obviously, new "management actions" were being deployed all over the state—all the new speed zones and new refuges and sanctuaries called for by the two settlements. Those offered the hope of turning around the "dire" situation.

Also, Runge pointed out, there's a big difference between not meeting Hankla's watered-down recovery criteria and disappearing forever from the Earth, which was what the club's release suggested might happen.

"They're *not* going extinct," he said.

While environmental advocates were touting Runge's report as the latest in manatee science, his conclusions drew snorts of derision from boating advocates. They contended Red Tide and habitat loss should get more attention from regulators than all those boating-related deaths.

For instance, *Tampa Tribune* outdoors columnist Frank Sargeant, who consistently backed the boaters' positions, labeled Runge's conclusions "bizarre" and said the evidence of a growing population from Ackerman's synoptic surveys was "so obvious that even a biologist in Maryland could be expected to understand it."

Although the Fish and Wildlife Service had asked Runge for his study, a service spokesman said that, now that the agency had it, the report would not be used. It could not be allowed to have any effect on shaping the rules for incidental take because Runge's computer model had not yet been peer-reviewed, an essential step in ensuring no mistakes had been made. It was the same argument Hankla had made for not accepting the scientists' recommendations for the new recovery plan.

That was just for public consumption, though. Behind the scenes, Runge's report had thrown the wildlife service into turmoil, according to Manson.

Runge had done more than show that the draft rules allowed for too many manatees to be run over by boats, and that the boat-related deaths were becoming a bigger problem all the time. He also created a conflict between federal biologists and lawyers.

The Fish and Wildlife Service's biologists believed that Runge had answered the question of what constituted negligible take. But the lawyers for the Interior Department believed that Runge's work answered a very different question, Manson said. Because his work talked about the carrying capacity of each region, they thought he was defining a legal term called the "Optimal Sustainable Population" for manatees.

Faced with these conflicting interpretations, Manson tried to sort it out by convening a day-long meeting at the Interior Department's training center in Shepherdstown, West Virginia, a few miles northwest of Washington. He heard from Runge, who found it "a heady experience" being called in to talk to such a high-ranking official. Manson then listened to presentations from everyone else involved. The more he listened, the more he realized what a tangled mess the department had blundered into.

Finally, he threw up his hands. He decided he couldn't decide.

"I listened to each group present its interpretation and then came to the conclusion that they were answering different questions and that it was not up to me to resolve the differences," Manson said.

Instead, he dumped the decision back in the laps of the people who most needed an answer from above: Hankla, his staff in Jacksonville, and Hankla's bosses in Atlanta.

Manson's failure to make a decision about the Runge report added to the tremendous pressure being brought to bear on the Jacksonville office of the wildlife service. Politicians and developers and dock builders and environmental activists had all been sniping at the biologists there. Meanwhile, the strain of trying to meet the deadlines the agency's attorneys had agreed to had taken a tremendous toll on the staff. In addition to trying to cobble together the new regulations, they also had to brief agency officials in Atlanta and Washington on what was happening. Sometimes staffers burst into tears for no apparent reason. Hankla said he felt lost and angry too.

"I was mean to my wife and my kids, and if we had a dog he would've been in trouble," he said.

Hankla took a day off to get away from all the stress, but he couldn't put it out of his mind. The deadline for making a final decision regarding the rules for incidental take loomed, and he kept thinking about it, turning it over and over. Finally, Hankla said, he called his deputy and told him he had come up with the only possible solution: withdraw the rules. Just drop them. Forget they had ever been proposed.

According to Hankla, his assistant's reply sounded like this: "AAAAAAAA AAAAAAAAAAAAAAAAAAAAAAAAughhhhh!!!!!"

When the assistant stopped screaming, Hankla went through his reasoning for ditching the rules: "Nobody likes [them]. There's almost no reason to move forward. We will be sued and probably lose. So withdraw them—that satisfies the terms of the settlement."

At first his bosses in Atlanta called him crazy, Hankla said, but finally they agreed he was right. When Hankla's recommendation reached Manson, he approved the decision.

"Without agreement on the science and the law, it was impossible to go forward," Manson said. "The problem was that the biologists and the lawyers were both right—they just were speaking different languages. It's hard enough in most environmental issues to keep science and law and policy on the same track. It's even more difficult with manatees."

On May 5, 2003, the day the wildlife service had scheduled the announcement of the final version of the rules for incidental take, Manson instead announced the agency would be withdrawing the rules. Although no one mentioned Runge, he was the reason.

"The decision was based on information from scientists . . . that called into question what the service was using for data," Manson told reporters.

In other words, the rules that everyone in Lee County considered too restrictive actually weren't restrictive enough—so instead there would be no rules at all.

Although the service's announcement talked of refining the regulations and trying again, the agency just dropped the whole matter. Five years later, all the boat-related deaths—not to mention the non-fatal boat strikes that leave all those scars—remain "unauthorized take" under the MMPA.

"There was nothing we could authorize that was going to be a workable program," Hankla said.

Yet they went back to issuing permits anyway.

"What they have now acknowledged is that they're not allowed to approve any project at all for manatee habitat," Glitzenstein said five years later. "So now in their biological opinions, they've contorted the rationale for why it won't result in take; 'Are there speed zones in place? Then it will not result in take taking place.'"

Yet everyone knows enforcement of the speed zones is sorely lacking, so that means the biological opinions allowing new docks are just as nonsensical as ever, he said.

"Legally they're in a more precarious position," the lawyer said. "You've got a federal agency that's admitting they cannot do anything that results in a take of manatees, yet they *are* issuing permits. So what the agencies are doing is illegal, blatantly illegal."

In the end, Glitzenstein said, the lawsuits that at first seemed like a grand slam had turned out to be a half-win. The Save the Manatee Club and its allies got a lot of new speed zones and sanctuaries and refuges to protect manatees.

"I do think that [because of] the protections we put in place, the species is better off than it would've been had we not done anything at all," he said.

But they failed to get the cumulative impact study they had contended was necessary before any more permits were issued. As a result, waterfront permitting continued just as it did before the lawsuit, with everything handled on a case-by-case basis.

"I don't think we were ever able to come up with anything that would be effective as a cumulative impact analysis," Glitzenstein conceded.

•

The end of the year brought an odd postscript to the Runge study and its warning about the ever-increasing number of watercraft mortalities.

The pathology lab reported that out of 361 manatees that had died in 2003, 70 had been killed by boats—a big drop from the previous year's record-setting high of 95. It marked the first time in five years that deaths from boats had declined.

Pro-boating forces contended that the drop showed it was time for all those new boating speed zones and restrictions on building docks to be scaled back.

But Kipp Frohlich saw it as a sign that all those new regulations might actually be working.

"There's a certain amount of probability to have a boat and a manatee in the same place at the same time," he said. "We'd like to think that boaters are doing a better job of knowing where the speed zones are and that compliance is better. We'd also like to think that overall conservation measures are working better this year."

Bruce Ackerman, ever the numbers man, put it all into perspective: "It boils down to whether you're an optimist or a pessimist. Seventy is still a lot. That's almost 3 percent of the population. If 3 percent of humans died of one thing, that would be considered a pretty big deal."

There was also one last act in the dock drama (or farce, depending on your viewpoint).

A week after the regulations for incidental take had been withdrawn came another startling announcement from the wildlife service. Because Lee County had finally produced a manatee protection plan, and watercraft mortality had dropped, Hankla's boss in Atlanta announced the service would no longer stand in the way of issuing dock permits in most of the county.

The moratorium that had never existed was now over, sort of. Congressman Goss and Cape Coral's leaders all hailed the decision, while Patti Thompson protested that a decision that had taken into account twenty years of information had just been overturned based on six months of new data.

The decision did little to mollify angry boaters, however. The wildlife service was still pushing forward with proposals for new refuges required by the lawsuit settlement, including in the Caloosahatchee. And once again, the first public hearing was in Fort Myers, in the same convention center as the raucous hearing on incidental take.

"The walls of Harborside Convention Center in Fort Myers reverberated with applause, again and again, as citizens decried federal intervention in what has become the Great Manatee War," Karl Wickstrom's *Florida Sportsman* magazine reported.

About two thousand people attended the hearing, many carrying the same signs they carried for the hearing on incidental take: "Docks Don't Kill Manatees." The magazine quoted Jim Kalvin asking: "At what point will we reach a status quo when people can relax and not feel like we're being railroaded off our waterways?"

The dock-building fight wasn't over either. Permits began trickling out, but slowly. Without regulations governing incidental take, the wildlife service had to scrutinize each one instead of simply wielding a rubber stamp.

In August 2003, both the Florida Marine Contractors Association and the city of Cape Coral filed suit against the Fish and Wildlife Service over the continued delays. The lawsuits hit a delay of their own, however, when the only federal judge in Fort Myers had to recuse himself. It turned out his wife had applied for a dock permit for the couple's home the day after Cape Coral filed its suit.

Soon the manatee madness had spread to other parts of the state, including, of all places, Manatee County. Manatee County lay just south of Tampa Bay, and thus was part of the southwest region where Runge said the population of manatees was in trouble even without boats hitting them. When the county commissioners proposed establishing speed zones that would go up to thirty miles per hour—higher than the twenty-five miles per hour that was the usual top speed allowed in manatee zones—the wildlife service said that wasn't good enough and suspended about two hundred pending dock permit applications.

Angry Manatee County commissioners began talking about filing their own lawsuit. One commissioner blasted Hankla and his staff for making "unreasonable" demands that put the county in "a hostage situation." Another contended that there was no need for making boaters slow down anymore because "the data doesn't show that there's wholesale slaughter of manatees in Manatee County."

But when a *Sarasota Herald-Tribune* reporter talked to a homeowner named Gene Marks whose dock permit on the Manatee River had been held up, Marks blamed the saber-rattling county commissioners for his plight. The commissioners passed tough boat speed restrictions in 1999, he said, but in the face of boater anger the county had never tried to enforce them.

"If they did what they said they would do in 1999, this problem wouldn't exist," said Marks, a riverfront homeowner for twenty-four years. "They need to get off their butts and do something."

In some places the problem originated even earlier. Sarasota County, for instance, still hadn't pulled together the manatee protection plan it was supposed to have begun working on in 1989. It had been given a second chance in 2000 when Governor Bush and the cabinet approved the Sarasota Yacht Club expansion based on the county's promise to apply for a grant to pay for a plan.

Yet four years later, Sarasota County's plan still remained in limbo. Even though the wildlife commission had pretty much written the plan for Sarasota County, the county commissioners decided at the last minute to throw in a bunch of "variances" from the rules. Those loopholes, the state and federal wildlife agencies agreed, would "reduce protection for manatees." So Sarasota County faced a suspension of dock permits too.

In Lee County, the county officials' resistance to rules led to the dock permitting slowdown becoming a freeze again. It was all thanks to court administrator Doug Wilkinson and his legal eagle fishing buddies.

When the Wilkinson case resulted in a judge rejecting Bruce Ackerman's expertise and overturning five speed zones in February 2004, the decision meant those state speed zones no longer could be enforced. In fact, one of Wilkinson's attorneys urged every boater who had gotten a ticket to go to court to contest it.

Because the zones had been tossed out, though, Lee County's waterways were once again an "area of inadequate protection" in the eyes of the wildlife service. That meant dock permits had to be withheld once again until new speed zones could be put back into place—regardless of Wilkinson's constitutional right to ride around in his boat.

Ironically, a week later, in one of the areas the judge had ruled wasn't frequented enough by manatees to warrant a speed zone, the carcass of a dead manatee washed ashore. Necropsy results showed it had been killed by a boat.

•

Rather than condemning local governments for failing to live up to their obligations, Congressman Goss started making angry phone calls to Gale Norton again.

"Cape Coral has been extremely patient and has jumped through every hoop and fulfilled every request made by the U.S. Fish and Wildlife Service to them," Goss told a reporter. "My message to the Secretary: this is one train wreck she doesn't need to have."

In October, Goss joined other Republican members of the Florida congressional delegation in meeting with top federal and state wildlife officials to discuss a proposal to put an end to the dock-building holdup.

The proposal came from Ken Haddad, executive director of the state wildlife commission. With his balding pate and gingery beard, Haddad looked like he might be an Amish farmer. He had originally planned to be a dentist, "because I come from a long line of dentists on my mother's side."

The son of a Presbyterian minister, Haddad had been born in Minnesota and sounded like it. His family moved to Florida when Haddad was five, and he grew up in Ormond Beach, "always on the water, I loved the water." While he was in college he worked for a dentist and "decided I didn't want to spend my life sticking my fingers in people's mouths." So he switched to marine biology.

Haddad had been in charge of the state marine science lab when Pat Rose had worked there, and when Tom Pitchford found all those manatees dead from Red Tide. Now he ran the entire wildlife agency—although he served at the pleasure of the pro-boating, pro-fishing wildlife commissioners.

Haddad's suggestion to Congress: change the MMPA so its "negligible take" provision no longer covered manatees. Instead, they would be covered only by the Endangered Species Act, which could be construed to allow for both fatal and non-fatal "take."

Haddad's proposal failed to draw enough support, but now even more congressmen piled onto the fight. Fourteen members of Congress from Florida signed a letter to the White House Office of Management and Budget that said the wildlife service's limits on dock building in southwest Florida would have a "substantial economic impact on the state of Florida."

At this point the Manatee War became one particularly active theater in a nationwide conflict over the future of the Endangered Species Act. Ever since the snail darter controversy, conservatives in Congress had been trying to curb what they viewed as the law's excesses. The push to rein in the act had gained momentum in the 1990s, helped along by conservative radio show hosts like Rush Limbaugh, who, during the controversy over saving the Northern spotted owl from logging, argued, "If the owl can't adapt to the superiority of humans, screw it."

Libertarian law firms like the Pacific Legal Foundation showed up with a friend-of-the-court brief every time someone sued over the Endangered Species Act. And pro-property rights think tanks like the Property and Environment Research Center in Montana cranked out studies showing the superiority of offering landowners economic incentives to save imperiled species, rather than forcing people to obey a law they didn't like.

With Republicans running the lower chamber of Congress and a sympathetic administration in the White House, the movement had reached its peak of power. Leading the charge to scale back the Endangered Species Act was a California congressman named Richard Pombo. The head of the Property and Environment Research Center declared him "a breath of fresh air."

Pombo was a rancher with a pencil-thin mustache who often posed for pictures wearing a cowboy hat. He chaired the House Resources Committee. Under his direction the committee had proposed selling off land in fifteen national parks, easing restrictions on logging in national forests, and allowing oil and gas drilling within 125 miles of the Florida coast. As it happened, his biggest campaign contributor that year was the oil and gas industry, and he also raked in big contributions from development interests, mining, and utilities.

Like Jim Kalvin, Pombo had a personal story to tell about the Endangered Species Act. He told people he ran for Congress because the Fish and Wildlife Service had declared his ranch to be critical habitat for the endangered San Joaquin kit fox. He said protecting the fox had devalued his land and forced him to run the ranch "with an unwanted, unneeded, un-silent partner—the federal government."

But when the *Los Angeles Times* checked his story, it turned out to be a lie. The Fish and Wildlife Service had never designated any critical habitat for the San Joaquin kit fox. Nor had it limited the development of his property. When confronted, Pombo at last admitted that having an endangered species on his land "didn't prevent me from doing anything."

In April 2004, Pombo convened his committee to hear about flaws in the Endangered Species Act's treatment of critical habitat. His staff decided to get some testimony about the whole manatee mess. They could have chosen from a long list of people to talk about the complex struggle over manatees—a bureaucrat like Dave Hankla, a scientist like Buddy Powell, perhaps someone from the Marine Mammal Commission, even a state official like Ken Haddad. The committee could have called a witness from one of the counties suing the federal government, a group that had now grown to include Duval and Clay counties in north Florida.

Instead, as its sole witness regarding manatees, the committee heard testimony from the executive director of the 140-member Florida Marine Contractors Association, one Steven Webster. In a nice coincidence, Webster also happened to be a vice-president of Citizens for Florida's Waterways, the group that even Jim Kalvin thought was too radical.

Webster blamed the whole dock permit holdup on two people: Eric Glitzenstein and Judge Sullivan. He told Pombo's committee that "instead of science-based rules, the Washington lawyer and a Washington federal judge are now in charge of manatee protection in Florida. The lawyer has made bagfuls of money suing the Fish and Wildlife Service, and the judge—well, he's wrong. He's terribly wrong."

Webster complained that Glitzenstein's clients "have used the [Endangered Species Act] to close down factories, shut down permitting, wreck boating, endanger our kids and sacrifice jobs"—without citing any specific examples. "They haven't reduced the rate of manatee mortality. They haven't found a way to count manatees accurately. They haven't helped reduce increasingly frequent manatee deaths from disease. They have blocked important scientific research and they do hamstring state programs. They wouldn't know science if it kissed them on the lips, and if it did, they'd accuse science of being a whore."

That last line brought a big guffaw from Pombo and his committee members. But in that fall's elections, the Democrats wound up with as many seats as the Republicans in the Senate. As a result, Pombo had no chance to make any changes to the Endangered Species Act before his California district voted him out in 2006 amid questions about his ties to a shady lobbyist named Jack Abramoff.

Rather than loosening the manatee protection rules, the wildlife service's crackdown was slowly forcing the adoption of new speed zones throughout the state, sometimes over the objections of the state agency to which Gale Norton had once deferred.

For instance, after the state wildlife commission voted for new speed zones in the Peace River that offered a compromise between manatee protection and boater access, the federal wildlife agency slapped on far tougher rules. One wildlife commissioner complained that every new rule was based entirely on what he termed the Save the Manatee Club's "horse hockey."

Even as Manatee County officials were petitioning U.S. Representative Katherine Harris to convene a meeting with federal wildlife officials in Washington to end the dock slowdown, the wildlife commissioners felt pressured to impose new rules just to satisfy the federal agency's demand for tighter regulations.

"The feds are holding this over our heads to bring the counties to the table," grumbled wildlife commissioner Rodney Barreto. He said that "developers are beating down my door" to get the new rules in place so dock permits could start flowing again.

This form of practical extortion, as effective as it was, won the Save the Manatee Club few friends. Byron Stout, the boating columnist for the *Fort Myers News Press*, wrote that "it is a stretch to make a direct comparison between Saddam Hussein and the Save the Manatee Club, but there are similarities."

During a closed-door meeting in March 2003, one of the wildlife commissioners, apartment developer John Rood, told his colleagues that it was time they struck back at the Save the Manatee Club for causing them so much grief. Where cooperation once reigned, there would now be enmity.

"We are getting them off all our material, off our Web site, off our signage," Rood ranted. "We are not doing anything with Manatee Club because they are the enemy right now."

Rood, who had been busy raising money for President Bush's reelection campaign, told his colleagues that he was convinced there was more than just manatee protection at stake.

"This is about the upcoming presidential election," he said. "It is about politics, national politics, and they're going to use environmental issues against George Bush and they don't care if it is right or wrong, they're going to use them."

As a result, Rood said, he would have a hard time even listening to Pat Rose, Patti Thompson, and the other club employees the next time one of them stood up to speak.

"I have spent a lifetime listening to them," he complained, "but it hasn't done a lot of good."

It didn't take long for the commissioners' disdain for the club to extend to the species the club wanted to protect. During a discussion of the need for new speed zones in Tampa Bay, several speakers objected to any restrictions that would benefit manatees while hampering human enjoyment of the water. A well-known Tampa fishing guide named Dave Markett contended that no waterway should be restricted just because manatees had been killed by boats there. He compared the situation to highways where children had been hit by cars or trucks: "You don't close down a road just because a child got struck there."

Kipp Frohlich rattled off some statistics to explain why the zones were needed. Between 1976 and 2003, he said, boats killed sixty-eight manatees in Tampa Bay, nearly all of them in the past dozen years. Since 1990 the number of manatee deaths in Tampa Bay attributed to boats had risen by more than 12 percent a year, a higher percentage than the growth of the manatee population and a higher percentage than the increase in deaths from other causes.

"Statistics, statistics," snarled one wildlife commissioner, a Tampa mall developer named Richard Corbett. "Frankly . . . there are a lot of people who feel there are way too *many* manatees."

Yet, somehow, the wildlife commissioners couldn't quite bring themselves to vote on taking manatees down a peg on the endangered list. Not at first.

## Political Science

IN JANUARY 2003, the state wildlife commissioners met for three days in Fort Myers. They gathered in the oak-paneled Lee County Commission chambers beneath an imposing portrait of General Lee. The general was wearing his full-dress uniform and a rather vexed expression that suggested he was unhappy with how his war turned out.

The agenda said that on the first day they would vote on Forsgren's petition to downlist manatees. Because the meeting had been scheduled for the city where, just a month before, three thousand people had screamed at Dave Hankla, the chances that the vote would go the way the Save the Manatee Club wanted lay somewhere between slim and none.

"The manatees . . . according to every research document I've ever seen . . . are healthier than they've ever been," said wildlife commissioner Ed Roberts, the Pensacola chiropractor who had once been on Ted Forsgren's board. "While there are a lot of boaters, there are a lot of new programs being introduced to protect the manatee."

Roberts also made it clear he was no fan of the Save the Manatee Club and its many letter-writing members who were constantly bothering him.

"We all run businesses," the chiropractor told the Fort Lauderdale paper. "Especially the manatee club has been inexcusable in how they've handled this issue. All these e-mails and letter-writing campaigns—in the end, they do themselves a disservice because no one can get to it all. I'm certainly interested in protecting the manatee, but the boaters and CCA [Coastal Conservation Association of Florida] have brought reasonable proposals to the table."

The wildlife commission staff contended to reporters that changing the classification wouldn't really matter. They were recommending moving manatees down one step on the ladder, to "threatened," not taking them off the list altogether. The state would take just as good care of a threatened manatee as it did an endangered one, they said, despite that Florida Ornithological Society report.

Of course, the Save the Manatee Club argued that the state had actually done a poor job with the animal while it was classified at the top of the imperiled species list. Taking it down a notch had to be worse.

Yet taking the manatees down to "threatened" still wasn't enough for some boating activists. On the Standing Watch Web site, one of Jim Kalvin's more radical acolytes urged every member to show up for the meeting. He urged them to push not just for downlisting but for the complete delisting of the manatee—and not in a please-and-thank-you way, either.

"If ever there was a time for civil disobedience, this might be it," he wrote. "Let your conscience be your guide."

Before the meeting, the commissioners got a report from the state's marine science laboratory that predicted the manatee population could drop by half over the next forty-five years. That, the scientists said, was not sufficient under the state's listing criteria for them to qualify as endangered. Because the study found they would not become extinct within one hundred years, manatees would indeed qualify under the new system as merely "threatened."

In accordance with the state's new listing process, the marine lab then sent its report out to a panel of three experts for review. Two of the three didn't like it. One in particular, Solange Brault, associate professor of biology at the University of Massachusetts, said she was "disappointed" with what she called the "overly optimistic" projections regarding how many manatees might be killed by boats.

The wildlife commission's report assumed that boating deaths as a proportion of the population would remain constant even if manatee numbers started to decline. But the number of boats seemed likely to continue increasing, Brault pointed out, thus increasing the chances that manatees could be hit.

Then, if manatee numbers declined, a constant number of deaths would amount to a higher percentage of the total population, she wrote in her review. Her conclusion: "There are too many uncertainties to downlist it."

Ken Haddad, the preacher's kid, had to admit that the state's data were shaky. One some things, he said, "We just guessed."

That was hardly a good foundation for a decision likely to be challenged in court by the Save the Manatee Club and Eric Glitzenstein. So Haddad counseled the wildlife commissioners to postpone the vote.

"We don't want this to be a polarizing decision," he said, as if it were possible to come up with a decision both sides would support.

Because of the recommended delay, only one hundred or so people turned out for the Fort Myers meeting, none of them ready to ready to chain themselves to Haddad or commit any other acts of civil disobedience. For the ones who did attend, though, the wildlife commission meeting turned into a shooting gallery, with science and scientists as the targets.

Ted Forsgren told the commissioners they should quit stalling over science questions and make a decision about how many manatees the state needed, period.

"There's no evidence there's ever been any declines in the manatee population in this state," he said, ignoring the 1996 epizootic.

Jim Kalvin challenged just about every aspect of manatee science. He started off questioning why biologists had divided manatees into four separate subpopulations.

"We're certain the animals migrate back and forth," he insisted, despite research that said otherwise. "It seemed to us that this is something that was drawn up just to make it more difficult to recover the species."

Then he questioned the use of Cathy Beck's scar catalog, suggesting that using the photos of repeatedly injured manatees as the basis for any study was just a sneaky way to lowball the predictions about the species' future. Instead, he said, "we would like to base our population on the healthy stock." He was apparently unaware that finding a stock of unscarred manatees might require importing some from Belize.

Next, Kalvin asked why the state kept wasting money on Ackerman's synoptic surveys if the results couldn't be trusted.

"If the synoptics are not the way, then why are we still doing them?" Kalvin inquired. Finally, he got in a not-so-subtle dig at the Save the Manatee Club: "There's one group of people here at this meeting who could, with one phone call, take this issue out of the federal courts and put it back with this commission where it belongs." But no one took him up on it.

Then up popped an unlikely ally for the boating groups. John Reynolds, once one of Dan Odell's students, had studied manatees for thirty years. Now, looking more like a prosperous banker than a biologist, he worked for Mote Marine Laboratory in Sarasota and chaired the U.S. Marine Mammal Commission. Like Haddad, Reynolds urged the commission to hold off taking a vote.

But then, out of the blue, he told the state wildlife commissioners, "Based on the numbers I could support downlisting manatees to threatened under the federal criteria." However, Reynolds quickly added that he would also be reluctant to do so "because of the growing threats" from things like speeding boats.

Buddy Powell, wearing a gray jacket and khakis, took the mike next. He was still short and slender and bearded, just like back in the 1970s when talking up a manatee refuge in Crystal River got his tires slashed. But now he wore reading glasses, and his beard was flecked with gray.

Powell complained that the state's science appeared to be "plagued with many assumptions." Like his former boss Haddad, he recommended delaying the vote so the wildlife commission staff could make sure biology, and not politics, drove the decision.

Wade Hopping followed, his thick eyebrows so wild they looked like they were squirming away from his face. At first, instead of talking about science, the master lobbyist talked about spin. He warned the commissioners that a delay could be misinterpreted by the Fish and Wildlife Service as a withdrawal of the decision. He urged them to plunge ahead and not only declare that manatees were doing better but to pop open some champagne to salute the fine work the state had done saving the species.

"Every now and then, we need to celebrate good news," Hopping said blithely.

That struck a chord with the commissioners. "We *do* have reason to celebrate," agreed Commissioner Rood with a boyish grin.

But then Hopping zeroed in on the science question too. He contended that the state's computer model was flawed. He wanted one that showed there were now so many manatees that the species could be taken off the endangered list completely.

"You need to have a model where, if you feed it information of population success, it predicts recovery," the uber-lobbyist told the commissioners. "This model is too pessimistic."

Hopping's appeal failed to move the commissioners to take a vote, though. The shaky science was strike one. The lack of support from either side of the debate was strike two. Strike three was the timing. Governor Bush was on his way to meet with Interior Secretary Norton to try to persuade her to ease the dock-building slowdown.

"I think downlisting in haste, without good solid science and buy-in, is very dangerous," Rood said. "I wanted the federal government to understand that we take our responsibility for manatee protection very seriously."

Rodney Barreto, the Miami lobbyist, agreed: "We need to make sure it's sound. We don't want the feds to say, 'The state of Florida screwed up. They can't even get their science straight.'"

He even suggested convening a second manatee summit to work out everyone's differences, explaining, with a reference to a song popular at Sunday schools and other peaceful gatherings, "It's important for us all to come together and do a little *Kumbaya.*"

So the wildlife commission agreed to postpone the vote. In the meantime, manatees would still be classified as endangered.

Pat Rose, still not completely recovered from his series of illnesses, made up for his physical weakness with rhetorical bombast. He wrote the state's papers, blasting the wildlife commissioners for even considering the notion of downlisting.

"We cannot eliminate poverty and save starving children by lowering the definition of poverty," Rose complained in an op-ed piece published in the *Jupiter Courier* and a few other papers. "Nor can we recover an endangered species by raising the standards for it to qualify as endangered. Yet this is just what the state of Florida has done. . . . It should be a wake-up call for everyone who loves manatees that their protected status under Florida law presently hinges on a question of semantics."

•

As Buddy Powell had feared, the legal struggle over manatees and now dealing with the downlisting controversy had begun taking up virtually all of the scientists' time at the state marine lab.

"It's killing us," Haddad said. "The impact on the scientists dealing with this thing is huge. We're not getting the data we should be getting. We could be out getting adult survival information. We could be doing more aerial surveys, so we could get how the regulations should be applied."

But the legislature had plans of its own for the state's manatee scientists. A bill sponsored in the House by Lindsay Harrington called for diverting $2 million of the $3.8 million Save the Manatee Trust Fund away from manatee research and instead spending it on putting more wildlife officers into the field. Among its fans: Wade Hopping.

"Everyone agrees we need more on-water law enforcement," Hopping said. He estimated the bill would put twenty-five new officers on patrol. Cutting research funding would force state officials to set better priorities, he contended.

"There should be a lot of scrutiny for what people are doing and why they're doing it," he said.

The Senate version of the bill went even further than Harrington's version. It would shift every penny from research to enforcement, which suggested where the legislature's priorities lay.

The sponsor was a Manatee County state senator named Mike Bennett, a feisty politico with a crooked grin and a skeptical squint. When he wasn't in Tallahassee, Bennett ran an electrical contracting firm, making his living off the building and development industry just like Harrington did. He was also amazingly successful at collecting contributions from developers, both for his own campaign and for his political action committee.

In sponsoring this bill, Bennett made it clear his motivation had a lot to do with the slowdown in dock permits for new development in his county. He said he had offered to amend his bill to satisfy any objections from Pat Rose—but only if Rose's employer offered something substantial in return.

"I told the Save the Manatee Club people that if they would write a letter . . . that they have no objections to personal docks at people's homes, I would be more than happy to revisit my bill," he said. "If not, I think we need some serious research money to see how many manatees are running into docks and killing themselves."

Bennett's bill ran out of steam before it could siphon off all the money from manatee research. Instead, the legislature passed a measure that diverted a small percentage of gas taxes collected at marinas to pay for twenty-nine new wildlife officers. But it wouldn't be the last time lawmakers used legislation to send a message to the commission about manatees.

•

Although they had promised to delay the vote until November 2003, the wild-life commissioners changed their mind. The problem was that Barreto's *Kum-baya* meeting had come up empty-handed.

Haddad had arranged for two meetings in February and March that brought together state and federal officials, boaters' groups, and environmental activists in a process called "conflict resolution." It turned out to be all conflict and no resolution.

At the two meetings, the first one in Tallahassee and the second in Orlando, Patti Thompson and Judith Vallee represented the Save the Manatee Club, while Ted Forsgren and Jim Kalvin represented the anglers and boaters.

To Thompson's surprise, Forsgren and Kalvin insisted they would not negotiate unless the Save the Manatee Club agreed to end the dock-permit slow-down, delay the regulations on incidental take, and postpone the designation of three federal manatee refuges, one of them on the Caloosahatchee River.

"We were like, 'Whoa-ho! Nobody told us there would be pre-conditions,'" Thompson said.

Although Thompson and Vallee said they had no problems with the first two demands, they refused to give up the refuges they had fought so hard to get. With neither side willing to compromise, the talks broke off.

So in May 2003, the wildlife commissioners again wanted to vote on down-listing. This time they would meet in a hotel ballroom in Kissimmee, not far from Walt Disney World.

Buddy Powell, disgusted by what he'd already seen, refused to attend.

"Why should I?" he wrote in an e-mail to a reporter. "The [Fish and Wild-life Conservation Commission] has shown their colors by reconsidering their previous decision to postpone until better information is available (the right decision). . . . I cannot tell you how discouraged I am. It sends a powerful and wrong message to the people of Florida by the stewards of our wildlife and environment."

Powell blamed Forsgren's group for pressuring the wildlife commission to move up the vote. But he also complained about the Save the Manatee Club's refusal to compromise on any of its hard-won gains in federal court. All in all, he concluded, "politics and interest group pressure is driving this process, while good or better science is left behind."

But the amiable Forsgren showed up at the meeting just as he always did, wearing a vented fishing shirt the color of celery, this time with a red, white, and blue fish on it. When the commissioners took up the controversy over their listing criteria, Forsgren told them there was nothing wrong with the criteria.

"The problem comes when someone's particular animal doesn't come out where they want, they pitch a tantrum," he said.

However, at Haddad's urging, the commissioners again postponed making a decision on the listing process, giving their staff more time to sit down with the various interest groups to try to work out a compromise. So far, though, it didn't look good. "It's fifty-fifty," Haddad said.

When the commissioners announced they would next take up the subject of manatees, the throng of television camerapeople lounging along the sides of the room leaped into action, switching on their cameras and swinging around to get shots of the crowd. If they expected the kind of wild action that occurred at Hankla's hearing on incidental take, though, they were disappointed.

One of the first speakers, Forsgren, urged the commissioners to go ahead and take the leap—and he was very candid about why he wanted them to do it.

"We think it's very important that this commission makes a strong statement that the manatee is not in trouble or we just think we're going to be crushed" by new regulations, he said. "We need you as a state agency to say: 'We don't have a crisis with the manatee population in this state.'"

John Sprague, the Lake Okeechobee marina owner, told commissioners they should put manatees down even lower on their list—not just calling them threatened but classifying them as a species of special concern. Anything higher just didn't fit reality, he said.

"We need to stop telling people they're eating steak when we're feeding them hamburger," he drawled. "Does anybody up there really believe this animal is *ever* going to go extinct?" Also, he added, "The proliferation of zones—we need to stop it."

Jim Kalvin showed up late, explaining that he'd driven five hours to get there.

"The boating public already knows the manatee is not an endangered animal," he said. Changing the manatee's classification would be good for the wildlife commission, he contended, "because it's going to free up some resources, logistical and tactical" that could then be spent on something other than manatees—thus undercutting the commission's argument that changing the designation would not mean anything.

Wade Hopping prowled the rear of the room, a rusty dab of blood on his shirt collar, one side of his button-down collar undone and flying at half mast. When his turn came at the microphone, he slipped and called his audience the "game commission"—a sign that he wasn't at the top of his game.

Hopping could tell that his downlisting initiative had run aground, and now he tried desperately to get it afloat once more with a tried-and-true lobbying device: the sunset review. He suggested that any listing decision that the commissioners made could be reviewed again in five years, or even three. If it turned out something was wrong, the commission could fix it.

Then Hopping slipped up, letting his desperation show.

"The numbers show that manatees ought to be brought down to species of special concern—today! Now!" he shouted. Then he sat down, spent.

One of Doug Wilkinson's attorneys, a beak-nosed man with a ponytail and a thick mustache, seemed to be auditioning for the role of Hopping Jr. Just like Hopping, he focused on the synoptic survey numbers, arguing they showed a huge population boom.

"Ever since you folks have been counting these things, there's been more and more and more and more," said the attorney, whose name was Hal Stevens. Then Stevens focused on something so bizarre that no one else had ever thought of it. He called for shutting down the warm-water outfalls from all the power plants in Florida. The utilities' warm-water discharges were guilty of altering manatee behavior, he contended. Instead of pampering the manatees and thus altering their migration patterns, he said, the animals should brave the cold water with no help from mankind "and let these creatures propagate on their own."

Corbett, the mall developer, kept frowning. He was a short, skinny man with a high, wrinkled forehead and a high-pitched voice. If he had been cast in a Western, he could have played the bank teller who gets robbed. He had been president of his class at Notre Dame in 1960, and in 1964 he earned a master's in business administration from Harvard Business School. Now, in addition to building shopping malls, he and his wife managed a quail plantation near Tallahassee. He tended to see wildlife in terms that Earle Frye would have understood.

When Corbett finally spoke, he didn't want to talk about how few manatees there were. He wanted to talk about how many extra ones might be clogging up Florida's waterways.

"What if we woke up this morning and said, 'There's too many'?" Corbett asked. "What is the effect of too many?"

Answering that question fell to the newly hired boss of the Florida Marine Research Institute in St. Petersburg, a soft-spoken scientist named Gil McRae. McRae stood about five foot seven and had bristly black hair that stuck up above his forehead like the edge of a knife. Before the meeting, when a reporter joked that the M in FMRI now stood for Manatee, McRae said if he ever saw that the sign on his building had changed like that, "I would keep on driving."

Quietly, calmly, with no sign of impatience, McRae explained to Corbett that if there were ever too many manatees occupying the state's waterways, "we would see a large number of cold-killed manatees each year. And we're not seeing that."

Instead, the newly released Runge report, with its "dire" projection of the future, stood in the way of the state's saying they weren't endangered. McRae strongly endorsed Runge's findings and said his staff was now working with Runge to come up with a computer projection of their own.

So the commissioners postponed their decision again. Hopping made it plain he wasn't happy.

"One of these days," he grumbled, "they're going to figure out that it doesn't matter how long you study it, at some point you're going to have to make a judgment call."

Regardless of what the Runge report said, though, some commissioners made it obvious what side of the "judgment call" they would pick.

"We do not see any evidence that the manatee population is in immediate jeopardy," Barreto said.

To Cynthia Frisch, the attitude of the wildlife commissioners seemed rooted less in science than in a desire to let boaters keep plowing through the state's waterways at full throttle.

"Should Runge make a difference?" she asked. "Logically it should. But are we in the realm of logic? No." She predicted the Runge report would make no difference to the downlisting because "it's just too inconvenient to have an endangered animal that affects their lifestyle."

•

In September 2003, while meeting at a motel on Pensacola Beach, the commissioners took a fateful step that did not directly involve manatees. They voted four to three to downgrade the red-cockaded woodpecker from threatened to a species of special concern, despite the objections of the U.S. Fish and Wildlife Service.

The feds warned the state wildlife commissioners that the numerical requirements in the state's listing guidelines were so strict now that they would no longer allow listing the Northern right whale, which had a population of just three hundred. The state Department of Forestry, the Treasure Coast Regional Planning Council, and the South Florida Water Management District also said the change suggested the bird no longer needed any legal protection, which they said was just plain wrong.

Even Haddad tried to get his bosses to hold off, warning them that the vote would be viewed by the public as a sign that "we're not taking this species as seriously as we should." Commissioner Rood agreed, telling his colleagues: "If we do something and it's incorrect, it's going to be hard to undo it."

But the commission's chairman, Edwin Roberts, insisted it was time to "bite the bullet and move forward." So they did.

Then, in November 2003, the wildlife commissioners tried again to downlist manatees. Just before a scheduled meeting at a resort in Duck Key, near Marathon, Chairman Roberts said once again that he was likely to vote yes.

"I would like to move us along," he said. "I think the biology is there to support downlisting."

Rood agreed: "The reality is the manatees are flourishing. They're doing great."

Rood's blithe comment ticked off one of the most influential writers in Florida.

"In a sane place, someone so stunningly clueless would have no say in the future of an endangered species," griped the *Miami Herald*'s popular columnist-turned-novelist, Carl Hiaasen. Take manatee off the endangered list, he warned, and "you might as well paint a bull's-eye on its rubbery, bucket-shaped noggin."

Because of what had happened with the red-cockaded woodpecker, Haddad arranged for the wildlife commissioners to attend a daylong workshop about all the problems with their new listing process. By focusing so intensely on one topic, they finally understood what all the environmental groups had been yelling at them about.

"Any time we are this confused, and the public is this confused, we have a problem," Rood said afterward.

Only after fixing the flaws in the listing process could the commissioners make a sound scientific decision on the manatee's status, Rood conceded.

Meanwhile, manatee deaths were again on the upswing. The increase was driven not by boats this time but by Red Tide. The poison killed ninety-eight of them, second only to 1996's epizootic.

So the commission voted to postpone downlisting again—this time for a full year, until November 2004. Not only that, they voted to delay making any further changes in their listings for any species until the staff could recommend a better system.

The blue-collar boating activists who had driven down to the ritzy Hawks Cay resort for the meeting were livid. Some accused the commissioners of putting off the decision for a year so it would not be an issue in President Bush's reelection.

"It's not a scientific decision. It's a purely political decision," contended Tom McGill from Citizens for Florida's Waterways.

Only months earlier, Rood had accused the Save the Manatee Club and its allies of using manatees to attack President Bush while he was running for reelection. Now, faced with an accusation that he and his fellow commissioners were protecting the governor's brother from those attacks, Rood insisted the presidential election had nothing to do with it.

"We never even thought of that," he said.

During the year delay, the legislature came roaring back into the fray. Senator Bennett and Representative Harrington teamed up on a new version of the previous year's drain-the-brains bill. This time, the money intended for manatee research would be taken away from the state's marine science lab and instead handed over to John Reynolds's employer, Mote Marine Lab, which just happened to be in Bennett's own district.

But they didn't stop there. Bennett and Harrington also wanted to set new limits on the state's authority to adopt speed zones to protect manatees. Their bill ordered the wildlife commission to set "measurable biological goals" for manatees and said that when manatee populations reached those levels, regulations such as boat speed limits would not be needed.

Ted Forsgren especially liked that part.

"Once you achieve [the goals], there should be a reward for everybody involved, not more regulation," he said.

The bills also called for broadening the wildlife commission's mission. Instead of just promoting conservation, the state agency would be required to maximize opportunities for recreational boating.

Outraged environmental advocates accused Bennett and Harrington of setting the stage for more manatee deaths. Hogwash, replied Bennett.

"People say we're killing manatees," he told a Senate committee hearing. "We've not named manatees the other white meat, so I don't know how we're doing that."

He accused the Save the Manatee Club of using "lies and innuendo" to stop the bill, and he mocked their concerns about its impact: "What? Are we gonna start shooting manatees in the morning? I don't think so."

Senator Bennett said he suspected even the state's marine scientists of having some hidden, anti-boater agenda. After all, he pointed out, look at the most recent synoptic survey. Ackerman's squadron of spotters had found 2,568 manatees, a big drop from the 3,276 found in 2001. Although Ackerman blamed the warmer conditions, Bennett saw a conspiracy afoot.

"I think the manatee counts are being controlled by the Save the Manatee people, the no-growth people," the senator complained, apparently unaware of how much the boating industry relied on the survey's numbers for its arguments. "I question their funding sources, and I question their knowledge. We've got to find a better way to count."

Bennett said what he really wanted to know was how manatees affected the state's sea grass beds. "What I want to do is have some true, unbiased research as to how big a population will the grasslands support," he said. "The more grass they eat, the less is available for the rest of the ecostructure." (He meant "ecosystem.")

Had Bennett checked, he would have learned that such research had already been done. Buddy Powell, among others, had looked into the question. Manatees are like lawn mowers, not garden tillers, he told the *Palm Beach Post*.

"They eat the leaves of grass, and don't generally eat the roots," Powell said. "Usually, grass grows better where they have grazed."

Bennett's bid to siphon off money from the state and hand it to Mote Marine Lab failed. But the other bill, the one calling for measurable biological goals, passed. However, money that had been allotted to pay for the additional scientific studies was pulled from the budget at the last minute. The wildlife commission would have to pay for the extra work by cutting somewhere else.

Most of the state's editorial boards and all of the environmental groups lined up to urge Governor Bush to veto Bennett and Harrington's bill. Instead, Bush signed it into law, insisting it would not hamper the authority of the wildlife commission. All of the high hopes that the Save the Manatee Club had for Bush being the next Bob Martinez had now evaporated.

In the meantime, as members rotated off, Bush had injected some new blood into the wildlife commission board. In keeping with his anti-government bent, Bush picked people who were ideologically opposed to government regulation—an interesting choice for people to be in charge of a regulatory agency.

To replace chiropractor Edwin Roberts, Bush appointed Brian Yablonski, who had closer ties to Bush than even John Rood. Yablonski had grown up in a union family in suburban Washington, D.C. His great uncle Jock, as well as Jock's wife and daughter, had been assassinated in 1969 in a dispute over the presidency of the United Mine Workers. Yablonski liked to joke that in his pro-union family, "I'm the black sheep."

He was a child of the Reagan years, he explained, "and I went to work as an intern for a congressman who happened to be a Republican."

That internship led to the most fateful event of his life. He became a staff assistant for President George H. W. Bush and met the family, which led to a job with Jeb Bush's Foundation for Florida's Future after Bush lost his 1994 bid for governor. When Bush won in 1998, Yablonski became his deputy chief of staff.

Yablonski left Bush's staff in 2003 to become a lobbyist, but he didn't stay a hired-gun persuader for very long. In 2004 he became vice-president of public affairs for the St. Joe Company. For decades a timber company, St. Joe had turned itself into Florida's largest private landowner and the most ambitious developer to hit the state since Henry Flagler. The company was busy redrawing the map of the Panhandle, turning vast expanses of forest and beachfront into new subdivisions, shopping centers, hotels, golf courses, even successfully lobbying for an airport bigger than Tampa's, to be built by the taxpayers in the middle of St. Joe property near Panama City.

St. Joe's executives believed boat sales could drive home sales, so they frequently hit the big boat shows in Fort Lauderdale and Miami to promote their projects. They even partnered with a company that operated marinas "to create a superior boating and waterfront experience" at their developments.

In *Florida Sportsman*, Karl Wickstrom lamented Bush's decision not to reappoint Roberts, noting that a "powerful sportfishing advocate" had been re-placed by someone who "reports enjoying hiking, kayaking and fishing." While Yablonski lacked the connection to Ted Forsgren's fishing group that Roberts had had, the new commissioner had another intriguing association: He was an adjunct fellow at the Property and Environment Research Center in Montana, one of the more vocal opponents of the Endangered Species Act.

In mid-2004 President Bush named John Rood ambassador to the Baha-mas, ending the apartment developer's stint on the wildlife commission. To replace him, the governor picked Kathy Barco. Although her blond hair and thousand-watt smile gave her the look of a faded starlet, Barco was president of Barco-Duval Engineering, a heavy construction company in Jacksonville. Her company's motto was "We Move the Earth for You." She loved hunting so much that she belonged to the Safari Club, the big-game organization that showed no love for endangered species laws.

More troubling for environmental groups than Barco's development con-nections or her Safari Club membership was the fact that, since 1995, she had served on the board of trustees of the Southeastern Legal Foundation. The foundation was an Atlanta nonprofit law firm that had spent nearly thirty years fighting against government regulation of private property rights, affirmative action programs, minority business set-asides, and gay rights. Atlanta's mayor compared the foundation to the Ku Klux Klan, but executive director Matthew Glavin boasted that it had actually become "the liberal establishment's worst nightmare."

Barco's foundation garnered national headlines in 2000 when it succeeded in getting the Arkansas Supreme Court to recommend President Clinton's dis-barment for lying under oath about an affair. The foundation gained national notoriety a few months later when Glavin was arrested for fondling himself and an undercover officer in a park known to be a hot spot for gay cruising. Glavin's arrest—his second for the same crime in the same park in six years—launched a thousand smutty jokes on liberal blogs and alternative newspapers. Glavin handed in his resignation to Barco, who by then had become the foun-dation's chairwoman, and then pleaded guilty. The damage to the foundation's reputation took years to repair.

When Governor Bush appointed her to the wildlife commission, Barco promised she would not base her decisions solely on the ideology that drove her foundation's legal battles.

"I base my decisions on facts," she said. "Everything is a balance. There's somebody way to the right, and somebody way to the left, and I listen to all the facts and make an educated decision."

While Bush dispatched new soldiers to the front lines of the Manatee War, an act of God pulled one out.

A month after the end of the legislative session marked the start of Florida's traditional hurricane season, which runs from June to November each year. The 2004 hurricane season would be the least traditional in history. Four major hurricanes slammed into the state between August 13 and September 26. Never before had nature vented so much fury on Florida in such a short space of time. Hurricanes Charley, Frances, Ivan, and Jeanne left multiple paths of destruction etched in the state's landscape.

The first one, Charley, made landfall in August on a Friday the thirteenth, roaring ashore just north of Fort Myers. Instruments at the Punta Gorda Airport registered a wind gust of 111 miles per hour before they blew away. The hurricane, a Category 4, killed at least sixteen people and caused some ten billion dollars in damages.

Among the collateral damage: Standing Watch. The hurricane badly damaged Kalvin's home and sank his dock-building barge in Port of the Islands. Many of Kalvin's members lost roofs, cars, tools, appliances, boats. They became so focused on recovering from their hurricane losses that they lost interest in Standing Watch.

"When things are good, people are concerned about their rights," Kalvin said. "When things aren't good, people are more concerned about getting their electricity turned on."

As Standing Watch's members became absorbed by their own day-to-day struggles, Kalvin's ability to mobilize thousands of angry boaters at a moment's notice dwindled noticeably. He faded from the manatee debate just as one of the goals he had worked toward seemed about to fall into his hands.

•

One of the groups that had been critical of the state's actions on downlisting was its own science advisory group, the Manatee Technical Advisory Council. Ken Haddad responded to the criticism by disbanding MTAC.

In its place, Haddad and officials from the Fish and Wildlife Service put together a new group made up, not of experts or scientists, but of a bunch of people who had a stake in how things turned out. They called it the "stakeholders group," but as time went on it became known as the Manatee Forum.

More than forty of the stakeholders convened for the first Manatee Forum on July 9, 2004, at the Florida Marine Research Institute on St. Petersburg's waterfront. It was, Haddad wrote later, "the first step in a proposed long-term process to improve communication, cooperation, and trust among stakeholders and conservation agencies."

The Manatee Forum, which met twice a year, included Ted Forsgren and John Sprague, as well as Patti Thompson and Judith Vallee from the Save the Manatee Club. The only scientist was Buddy Powell, who didn't want to be seen as favoring either side.

"We had a U-shaped table and it always divided right down the middle, so I purposely sat in different places around the table," Powell said, chuckling.

The whole point of those Manatee Forum meetings, Powell said, was "to keep people out of court." Each session was conducted by a professional facilitator whom Haddad had hired for his expertise at helping groups reach consensus. But now that Fran Stallings was gone, the Save the Manatee Club wasn't as combative as before. The staff was weary from all the battles over the results of the lawsuit settlements. Judith Vallee said the time was right for the club to adopt a more conciliatory tone.

"We're trying to put the past behind us," she said. "We're going to have to build new bridges, and so is the government."

Helen Spivey said she was concerned about how the war over manatee protection had hurt the public's perception of the club's favorite animal.

"Anytime you're made the scapegoat in something, people don't look at you the same way," Spivey said. "A lot of people were once awed by the manatee, but now a lot of boaters view them as a pest."

However, the Manatee Forum failed to deliver any actual consensus. Each meeting began with a presentation about some aspect of manatee research or protection. After that, Patti Thompson said, the meetings "quickly morphed into an ongoing, no-end-in-sight bitchfest. . . . At every meeting, once the presentations were done, the inanity would begin and certain individuals on both sides would just pontificate endlessly. It should have been called the 'I love to hear myself talk' forum. More than once I thought my head would explode."

While the Manatee Forum tackled the larger issues of manatee protection, another committee of stakeholders had been meeting to discuss the problems with the species listing process. Like the Manatee Forum, they split right down the middle.

By December 2004, Haddad and his staff had given up trying to find a compromise on the listing process. Instead, with the paid assistance of a Florida Museum of Natural History expert on crocodiles and sea turtles named Perran Ross, they recommended the commissioners make a few minor tweaks, and that was that. The wildlife commission scheduled a vote on it for April 2005.

In the weeks leading up to the vote, Haddad toured the state's newspapers, sitting down with editorial writers to try to put their version of what was going on into play before the Save the Manatee Club and other environmental groups could gain control of the storyline. But Haddad lacked the skills of a true spinmeister like Wade Hopping. The minister's son tended to give overly honest answers to the journalists' questions.

For instance, while talking about the controversy over manatees, he admitted he had never expected to see such a furor.

"We're getting people that *hate* the manatee now," he told the *St. Petersburg Times* editorial board. "That was unheard-of fifteen years ago." He compared the rapidly expanding dislike for the state's official marine mammal to "a kind of a little disease that starts to spread. . . . Then the politicians get involved."

As the April 2005 meeting date drew near, environmental groups galore had signed up to speak against approval of the listing process. Among them was one of the staunchest members of the lawsuit's Manatee Coalition, a national group called Defenders of Wildlife. Though it was better known for campaigns to protect the wolves of Yellowstone National Park and the caribou of the Alaskan National Wildlife Refuge, Defenders had an office in St. Petersburg where employees toiled away on such Florida-centric causes as saving the panther.

One of the Defenders of Wildlife employees in Florida, Elizabeth Fleming, had spent nearly a dozen years working in Europe with TRAFFIC, a wildlife trade monitoring program co-managed by the World Wildlife Fund and the IUCN. An imposing woman with straight blond hair and the pitiless gaze of a veteran prison guard, Fleming had conducted countless investigations of wildlife smuggling across twenty countries. She knew the laws on wildlife protection backwards and forwards. She knew that this was the first time the IUCN's listing criteria had ever been adapted to a state level, and she knew it didn't match up.

Yet whenever the environmental groups would point out the misalignment, the wildlife commission and its staff members kept saying it didn't really matter, it was just semantics.

"For us it was just so frustrating because we knew we were right," Fleming said.

Fleming started sending out e-mails and making phone calls to her old IUCN contacts. Maybe, she figured, if the commissioners heard from the IUCN's own experts about what was wrong, they would finally see the problem.

She discovered that many IUCN scientists didn't want to get involved in a dispute that involved state politics and not some global threat. "I let them know that silence on the part of the IUCN would be interpreted as approval," she said.

One of the experts she contacted was Russell Lande, a biology professor at the University of California, who had co-written the IUCN's own species criteria—the criteria that Florida's new system was supposed to be based on. Lande already had a low opinion of Florida's listing process. When the commissioners had been considering downlisting the red-cockaded woodpecker, Lande wrote an article for the Florida Ornithological Society's magazine criticizing the state for even thinking about doing such a thing. He wrote that the listing system the wildlife commission had set up "contradicts both common sense and plain English."

Since his paper had had absolutely no effect on the wildlife commission, Lande now agreed to show up and make his arguments in person to the commissioners.

Of course, the listing criteria still drew strong support from a few organizations: the Florida Chamber of Commerce, the Florida Home Builders Association, the Association of Florida Community Developers, the Florida Farm Bureau Federation, plus Ted Forsgren's Coastal Conservation Association of Florida. With the exception of Forsgren's group, none carried much of a reputation for being friendly to environmental causes. But they were all groups that the legislature listened to. Because the legislature set the commission's budget, those groups had the wildlife commission's attention as well.

On April 14, 2005, the commissioners assembled at a Ramada Inn in Tallahassee. They listened politely to Russell Lande, as well as Cynthia Frisch, Elizabeth Fleming, Laura Combs, Patti Thompson, Pat Rose, and more than a dozen other environmentalists and animal-welfare activists.

Lande's criticism of the commission's listing process had as much effect in person as it had in print—none, in other words. The commissioners voted seven to zero to approve the listing process, the two new commissioners marching in lockstep with the five veterans.

One of the new commissioners, Brian Yablonski, said he was sure the new process would actually provide *more* protection for the state's wildlife, not less. And Commissioner Corbett, echoing Wade Hopping's previous argument, said that even if the commission messed up, it was no big deal to fix it sometime down the road.

"We have been talking about this and talking about this," Corbett said. "If we make a mistake, we'll go back, revisit it, and correct it."

A few days later, in an e-mail to Perran Ross, the furious Lande called the meeting a "fiasco." He wrote that he had decided the commissioners, the staff, even Ross himself, "do not deserve a single shred of respect for intellectual or scientific honesty or capability, and that wildlife conservation in Florida is in a steep downward spiral from which it will never emerge."

Lande wrote that after the meeting he spent some time chatting with several commissioners, and one of them explained that "the ultimate reason why such deference was given to developers while completely ignoring independent scientific criticism is that if developers become too unhappy, the state legislature will cut the budget for the commission. The commissioners as a group do not understand that maintaining viable populations has absolute limits which cannot be subject to continual political compromise."

Like Buddy Powell, Lande had had enough in trying to deal with Florida's wildlife commission. He wrote to Ross: "I am not going to waste any more of my time on these people, who are severely impaired by various combinations of abysmal ignorance, mediocre intelligence, political temerity, and intellectual dishonesty. You will have to find another scientific sucker to provide a veneer of respectability to the Extinction Commission."

The commissioners didn't stop at approving the controversial listing process, though. They also took a vote on new boat speed restrictions in Lee County. Before the vote, Kipp Frohlich told commissioners that his recommended zones resulted from a delicate balancing act—on one hand, trying to be protective enough that the Fish and Wildlife Service would back off some federally imposed zones it had slapped on the region after the Wilkinson case, and on the other, trying to keep the Lee County Commission happy. He also reminded them that Lee County was part of the southwest region, where Runge had predicted a decline in the future manatee population.

Despite his explanation, the commissioners wound up approving zones that were more lenient than what Frohlich had recommended. Corbett said they were trying to provide Lee County's boaters with "relief" from those burdensome regulations. The zones the commissioners approved were so lenient that on the second day of the meeting, Haddad persuaded them to revisit the issue and back off the most outrageous changes they had made.

The news got worse for Glitzenstein's clients—and better for Hopping and Forsgren and Wickstrom. The same day the wildlife commission vote to approve the new listing process, Dave Hankla announced that the U.S. Fish and Wildlife Service would be launching a five-year review of the manatee's status on the federal endangered list.

Although such five-year reviews were required under federal regulations, the wildlife service had seldom gone to the trouble of doing one, Hankla said. But Bush administration officials, who had added to the endangered list fewer species than any previous administration, had decided to begin enforcing that part of the rules. The decision pushed Hankla's agency to reconsider the status of a lot of animals and plants.

"If after reviewing all the information, we determine nothing has changed, the manatee's status will remain federally listed as endangered," Hankla told a reporter for the Fort Lauderdale paper. "However, if the data substantiates that a reclassification or de-listing is warranted, we could recommend either."

Now the stage was set for what Hopping had sought back in 1999, on the eve of the Manatee Coalition lawsuit: a vote by the wildlife commission to knock the manatee down a notch on Florida's imperiled species list, leading to a similar decision by the U.S. Fish and Wildlife Service regarding the federal endangered list. Surely that would at last halt the march of new regulations across the state's waterways.

•

Now that the wildlife commission had approved a new listing process, Ted Forsgren's petition for downlisting the manatee became active again. Under the just-approved listing process, the next step would be an assessment by Haddad's staff of what the species' status was, and how it matched up with the criteria.

Runge worked with the state to customize his modeling work—but he didn't look at whether the population had increased, which was the main concern of Forsgren and the other groups urging downlisting.

"That wasn't even a question we were trying to answer," Runge said. "The core biological model is a prospective model. The purpose is to make predictions. It doesn't answer the question of what happened over the past thirty years. . . . The concern is about the future status of the animal and will it ever go extinct."

But 2005 turned out to be the second-worst year in history for manatee deaths. At least eighty-one died from Red Tide, according to Tom Pitchford's necropsy lab experts, while eighty were killed by boats. That marked an increase in watercraft-related deaths after two years in which the number had dropped.

John Sprague suggested that the increase in watercraft deaths might be due to Hurricane Katrina, which swept across the Florida peninsula in August 2005 on its way to virtually destroying southern Louisiana and the Mississippi coast. The wildlife commission dispatched more than one hundred law enforcement officers to assist with cleanup in Florida and the other storm-battered states. That pulled them from their regular duties of ticketing speeding boaters, catching poachers, and enforcing fishing rules.

"There was definitely a loss of law enforcement on the water," Sprague said.

Two weeks after those numbers came out, the latest assessment from Haddad's staff hit the streets. As expected, it said manatees were doing so well that they could be downlisted to threatened on the state's list.

Patti Thompson contended the finding was the result of "a carefully calculated effort on the part of the people that manatees are in the way of." But given the state's listing criteria, no other outcome was possible.

Now at last it was time for the wildlife commissioners to vote on Forsgren's petition. The June 2006 meeting, held in a Marriott in West Palm Beach, drew about two hundred people. This wasn't the rowdy crowd that packed the Fort Myers convention center four years before. Instead, everyone just seemed frustrated and exhausted. To make matters worse, in the middle of the daylong meeting the air-conditioner conked out.

Haddad's staff had scheduled for that day a discussion not only of manatees but also of three other species that required listing action. The commissioners took eagles off their imperiled list completely, since the number of eagles had increased 300 percent since the 1970s. Then they raised the listing for both the Panama City crayfish and the gopher tortoise from species of special concern to the category of threatened. As it turned out, the gopher tortoise's decline had resulted from the commission's own "pay-to-pave" policy, which left thousands of tortoises entombed in their burrows, buried alive by developers who had written a check to the state and then cranked up the bulldozers. Within a year, the commissioners would vote to end that practice too.

About fifty speakers lined up to talk about the final of the four species, the manatee. Most of the speakers were the same people who had been to the mike countless times before to talk about the same issue, including Ted Forsgren, John Sprague, Judith Vallee, and Pat Rose, and they all said pretty much the same things they had said before.

One of them had a surprise in store, though. Virginia Splitt, a frail, rail-thin woman in red who sat on Save the Manatee Club's board, had attended many of the state and federal meetings concerning manatees, including the one in December 2002 in her hometown of Fort Myers. She usually spoke so softly that no one paid much attention to what she said. But this time Splitt carried to the lectern a small package wrapped in pink tissue.

Barreto, trying for a joke, asked, "It's not a bomb, is it?"

Actually, it was an antique porcelain cream pitcher. Splitt unwrapped her delicate package and set the pitcher on the floor. Then she raised one foot and stomped it to pieces.

That, she said, is what happens to a manatee's bones when it's hit by a boat. They're fragile. They shatter. Then she picked up her shards and sat down.

In the end, though, Splitt's crockery hara-kiri didn't matter. The commissioners at last voted to downlist the manatee. The vote was unanimous.

"Going from twelve hundred manatees a couple decades ago to thirty-two hundred today and calling them 'endangered' is confusing to me," said Commissioner Yablonski, taking the synoptic survey results at face value. And after all, "threatened" was still pretty dire, he contended: "When someone hears the term 'threatened,' it doesn't mean 'happy campers.'"

The vote, however, was still only a first step. The downlisting would not officially take effect until after the staff had written a management plan for the species and the commissioners approved it.

Over and over, Frohlich and Haddad had contended that what mattered wasn't the rank of the species on the list but what they put in the management plan. Pat Rose promised to push for "everything including the kitchen sink," in particular, new restrictions and greater enforcement of speed zones from Tampa Bay south to the Ten Thousand Islands. One of the commissioners suggested including a call for licensing for boaters—a proposal that went nowhere.

Meanwhile, John Sprague said the commission should put in something about reexamining all of its boating regulations in light of the manatee's new status.

"We need to tweak our speed zones," he said. "Some may be effective, but some may not be."

The downlisting vote brought the wildlife commission lots of unfavorable publicity. A *Lakeland Ledger* editorial snorted, "The problem is, simply, that manatees are not dying fast enough to suit the Florida Fish and Wildlife Conservation Commission. And since they aren't dying fast enough, boaters and waterfront developers might just as well speed up their activities."

Meanwhile, the same people who had pushed for the downlisting showed little patience with how long the staff now took in writing the all-important management plan—because, of course, the downlisting wouldn't count until after the plan had been approved.

"The plan is a thick stack of paper without force of rule or law," Steven Webster wrote in the Citizens for Florida's Waterways newsletter. "Let's get on with it already."

•

While Runge had been helping Haddad's staff with their modeling work, he was reworking his model yet again to aid Dave Hankla's five-year review of the manatee's federal status.

Once again, Runge didn't look at how much or how little the population had grown over the past thirty years. Instead he tried to use his computer to peer into the future.

At Hankla's request, he analyzed what might be the most serious threats facing manatees. However, one of the first decisions about how Runge would do the modeling would lead to questions about the whole process.

"We pretty quickly dismissed the existing federal criteria," Runge said.

So the controversial, watered-down version of the federal recovery plan criteria went out the window. No more discussion of 94 percent adult survival versus 90 percent. Instead of focusing on what the criteria might be for recovery, Runge said, they decided "we should focus more on the probability of extinction." That seemed more in keeping with what the Endangered Species Act required, he explained.

Runge ran his numbers and found the risk of extinction over the next century to be quite low. However, he found an 8.6 percent chance that over the next hundred years the population could fall to fewer than 250 manatees on either coast. Such a population would be so small that Runge called it "quasi-extinction" because "you would have essentially lost the population. Its functionality was lost."

In fact, Runge found, there was a strong chance that the statewide manatee population could dwindle over the next fifty years to just 500 on either coast.

"On the Gulf Coast, there is a fairly high probability (0.33) that the effective population could fall below 500 animals within 100 years under the status quo scenario," he wrote. "On the East Coast, the probability the effective population would fall below 500 within 100 years under the status quo scenario is 0.26, lower than on the Gulf Coast, but still fairly high."

Among the threats facing the species, he found that number one—the one with the greatest power to push manatees closer to oblivion—was the speeding boat.

Contrary to the contention of Wade Hopping and his allies, Runge found that boats held the key to the future of manatees. An increase in watercraft mortality could reverse all positive population trends for the species, he found.

"Watercraft-related mortality is the most important threat across all thresholds and all time frames for quasi-extinction," he wrote. On the other hand, if the government could eliminate all watercraft mortality, that would lower the risk of "quasi-extinction" to near zero, Runge found.

Runge himself drew no conclusions about whether those numbers added up to a species that still deserved to be called "endangered." He said it wasn't his place to turn his computer modeling into policy. It was up to Hankla and his bosses at the Fish and Wildlife Service to decide whether a 50 percent chance of a major population decline, and an 8.6 percent chance of quasi-extinction, seemed high enough or low enough to warrant keeping manatees on the endangered list, he said.

Hankla decided that Runge's findings meant it was time to downlist manatees to threatened, just as the state wildlife commission wanted to do. In fact, the report said that by 2009 the manatee could be taken off the endangered list entirely and protected only by the Marine Mammal Protection Act.

Hankla contended the five-year review provided results that were more scientifically valid than anything the agency had produced before, because "it was an opportunity for us to make a recommendation without the scrutiny of judges and attorneys."

By March 2007, the five-year review of manatees had reached the stage where Fish and Wildlife Service and U.S. Geological Survey officials could brief top

Interior Department officials on what it said and what Hankla's recommendation would be. By this time Judge Manson had resigned from his office to go teach college, so Runge faced a new set of Interior's upper-echelon leaders. Among them: Mark Limbaugh, the assistant secretary who oversaw the U.S. Geological Survey, and also happened to be Rush Limbaugh's cousin.

One newly hired Interior Department official, a dark-haired man with a Nixonian five o'clock shadow, walked into the briefing late, Runge said. But when it was over, he asked the most questions—and the best ones.

"He was really sharp," Runge said. "He asked some pretty astute questions. He knew a lot about endangered manatees. . . . I remember thinking, 'There's a young guy asking all the questions—who the hell is this young guy?'"

As it turned out, the "young guy" was Todd Willens, the deputy assistant secretary for fish and wildlife and parks. The reason Willens knew so much about manatees is that he had until recently worked as a top aide for Representative Richard Pombo. His job involved organizing such hearings as the one that brought Steven Webster to Washington to talk about dock permitting and whores. Willens quit his job with Pombo before voters turned the California congressman out of office, and he quickly found work with the Bush administration.

A year after the Runge briefing, investigators from the Government Accountability Office would name Willens as one of several Interior Department official who had tried to manipulate the science behind endangered species listings to suit right-wing political ends (Judge Manson was another, they said). However, both Willens and Hankla deny that Willens had anything to do with the outcome of the five-year status review of manatees.

"I was briefed—that's all," Willens said.

"There's been no Washington influence of any kind," Hankla said.

Someone inside the Fish and Wildlife Service thought Willens got more than just a briefing, though. That person leaked an internal memo to an activist group called Public Employees for Environmental Responsibility (PEER). PEER fed the information to a reporter from the *Washington Post*, hoping for a story that would make a big splash nationwide.

On April 9, 2007, the *Post* ran the story—but inside its A-section, not on the front page. The story quoted from the unsigned memo sent from the Fish and Wildlife Service's Atlanta regional office to the White House on March 26, but it made no mention of Willens.

"In Florida, manatees are exhibiting positive growth rates and high adult survival rates along the entire east coast and in the northwest region," the memo said. "There is still uncertainty about the status of manatees in the southwest region of the state. . . . Therefore the FWS [Fish and Wildlife Service] believes the proper status for the West Indian manatee is 'threatened' due to an improvement in population status and abatement of many threats associated with the species."

While the *Post* reported the memo's contents, the story failed to note the memo's curious omission. While the memo contended that there had been an "abatement" of "many threats," it did not spell out which threats had gone away. Runge's modeling results showed that watercraft deaths were still the biggest threat to the future of the species, something that hadn't changed since 1967. The "abatement" statement sounded more like wishful thinking than actual science.

Underlining Runge's results, Pitchford's crew at the path lab had just announced in January that the number of manatee deaths the previous year had hit a new record of 416—also not mentioned in the memo. That was one more than the previous record, set during the Red Tide epizootic of 1996. But there was no widespread epizootic to blame this time. Watercraft-related deaths hit 86, the most since the high of 95 in 2002. None of the other threats—Red Tide, loss of habitat to development, the closing of power plants, the loss of flow from springs—had gone away either.

So why would the memo to the White House say the threats had been abated? In a joint press release, both PEER and the Save the Manatee Club pointed the finger at Willens, contending the political appointee was shepherding the downlisting effort for the Bush administration and its campaign contributors.

"This is another case of the scientists being run over by the combined political weight of the Florida homebuilder, marina, and recreational boating lobbies," the executive director of PEER, Jeff Ruch, said in the release.

The results of the five-year review had been scheduled to be made public in mid-April. But because of the leaked memo, the announcement had to be pushed up, Runge said.

So on the same day the *Post* story hit the streets, Hankla's staff held a hastily organized phone-in press conference about the eighty-six-page report. Of course the recommendation of downlisting the species garnered the most attention, especially since Hankla could not really explain what it meant.

"We just believe it fits the definition of threatened better than it does endangered," Hankla told reporters. Just like the wildlife commission, though, he contended that a listing change would not alter any regulations, insisting: "This doesn't provide regulatory relief for anyone."

In fact, Hankla repeatedly emphasized that the report's recommendation would not automatically trigger a change in the manatee's classification. Instead, he said, that process might begin in a few months or sometime even later, depending on his office's workload.

However, Hankla's five-year report drew fire from more than just environmental groups. Respected scientists rolled their eyes at its rosy language, such as the line in the report that said "manatees are exhibiting positive growth rates." Buddy Powell said that line "sounds like a bit of an exaggeration."

And Lee Talbot's favorite watchdog, the U.S. Marine Mammal Commission, criticized it as well. The commission's policy and program analyst, David Laist, told reporters that, contrary to Hankla's assertions, "in the foreseeable future for manatees, there is a likelihood of a population decline."

The five-year status review lacked a lot in the specifics department. It recommended no new regulations or speed zones to cut down on the number of boat collisions. Nor did it recommend tightening controls on development of marinas and boat docks in manatee habitat. Quite the contrary. Hankla said his agency might begin relying on the report's findings about the manatee's improved status in reviewing permits for waterfront development—in effect, going the opposite direction from the MMPA "moratorium" debacle.

Most of the newspaper reports on the five-year review missed the strangest aspect of the five-year review's recommendation: the ditching of the recovery criteria.

Experts on the Endangered Species Act said it was not against the law for the agency to ignore the official criteria in a species' recovery plan in making a recommendation to downlist. But it was unprecedented for the wildlife service to talk about changing the status of a species that had not met a single one of its recovery plan goals. Never before had the wildlife service ignored a recovery plan in favor of the results of computer modeling. Instead of sticking to data from the present in judging whether the species had recovered, the wildlife service was ready to take a leap of faith that a prediction about the future would turn out to be accurate.

"It had as much science behind it as you're ever going to find," Hankla insisted. "It says what we think about the manatee more than any other product we've come up with." He said Runge was so good at predicting the future that "I think if Jimmy Buffett sat down with Mike Runge, he'd probably come away with a different perspective." And the computer modeling, he said, "set the template for how to do those reviews with other species."

Newspaper opinion-makers from around Florida called the wildlife service recommendation a blatant attempt to weaken protections. The *Bradenton Herald*'s editorial page headline spelled it out: "Doom the manatee: That's what new species status will do." A *Lakeland Ledger* editorial said that manatees were a slow-moving throwback to old Florida being sacrificed by the wildlife service to satisfy the modern need for speed, which "seems a perverse government policy indeed."

Stung by the widespread criticism, Hankla wrote an op-ed piece defending the five-year review's recommendation. He complained that "special interests have used the results to pick and choose the scenarios that best support their own agenda, doing an injustice to both the science and the manatee. . . . Twenty years ago few if any believed recovery of the Florida manatee was possible. But thanks to the contributions of many in Florida, recovery is now attainable."

The wildlife service's downlisting recommendation, he said, had been based on "a cutting-edge population model" that had been "developed by highly respected scientists."

In the end, though, what happened next depended not so much on "highly respected scientists" and their "cutting-edge" work but on political machinations so old-fashioned that Fred Morse himself would have recognized the creak of the gears.

# When Jimmy Met Charlie

IF A TEAM OF SCIENTISTS built the perfect politician, the end result would look something like Charles Crist Jr.: tall and athletic, his hair a distinguished white, his handshake firm and comforting, his liquid brown eyes brimming with empathy.

Crist even had a great backstory. His paternal grandfather, Adam Christodoulos, a Greek, emigrated from Cyprus to the United States around 1912 with an address pinned to his shirt. The immigrant Christodoulos shined shoes for five dollars a month. His son, Charles Sr., grew up to become a successful doctor, and shortened the family name so it would fit better on his shingle.

The doctor's son, whom everyone called Charlie, was born in Altoona, Pennsylvania. Four years later the family moved to Florida so his dad could set up his medical practice in St. Petersburg. This was in the early 1960s, when the town was a retirement haven in the winter and virtually deserted in the summer.

Dr. Crist bought a house in the upscale Snell Isle neighborhood. The place sat on a finger canal with its own backyard dock. Young Charlie spent every minute he could either near or in the water, swimming, fishing, and boating. When he grew up, he rented an apartment in the Bayfront Towers in downtown St. Petersburg. He could wake up every morning and drink in the sunrise across the watery mirror of Tampa Bay.

When Charlie Crist was ten, Dr. Crist ran for the Pinellas County School Board. The doctor's son went to a political forum and handed out leaflets for his dad. After that he was hooked. He played quarterback for the high school football team, but the sport he really lettered in was politics. In his senior year, Charlie Crist ran for class president and won. His course was set.

Crist earned a law degree, but the law was really just a stepping stone to public office. He spent six years as a Republican state senator, where his push for Draconian law-and-order measures earned him the nickname "Chain Gang Charlie." He then mounted a quixotic challenge to U.S. Senator Bob Graham. Although he got walloped at the polls, the campaign served its real purpose, raising his profile among voters statewide. Crist then ran for state education commissioner and won. Then he ran for attorney general and won. Then Crist set his sights on the governor's mansion, becoming the Republican nominee in 2006.

But Crist had some serious negatives on his résumé. Because he needed three tries to pass the bar exam, he had a reputation as something of a dim bulb, especially compared to Jeb Bush.

"You could fit Charlie's entire brain in Jeb's cerebellum," one *Orlando Sentinel* columnist carped.

Because Crist usually spoke in only the most glowing clichés, his critics tagged him as a lightweight. One Democrat complained that his policy statements were about as substantial as cotton candy. *Time* magazine said he was so perpetually chipper he was like "human Prozac." Some people wondered whether he got all of his ideas off bumper stickers.

Also, Crist was unable to play the role of the politician-as-family-man. While in college, Crist was married briefly. The couple had no children, and after the divorce Crist remained single. He lived alone, didn't own a house, didn't own a car. He was like a Republican Ralph Nader, a monk who had cast aside most of the usual distractions so he could focus on his crusade.

He had few hobbies. To stay fit, Crist swam laps every morning. To relax from the pressures of campaigning, he climbed aboard the twenty-five-foot Trophy sportfishing boat he kept tied up behind his parents' house. On weekends he often cruised around Tampa Bay in his boat, which he had named *Freedom*.

Boating meant a lot to Crist. When he was a state senator, colleagues noticed he carried a copy of *Florida Sportsman* around the way a recently converted

Christian might clutch a New Testament. They teased him that Karl Wickstrom must live in St. Petersburg because Crist always seemed to be carrying water for him. During Wickstrom's crusade for a net ban, Crist helped to lead the charge.

Florida is a big state, a fact that favors politicians not prone to airsickness. While running for governor, Crist turned to some wealthy friends who loaned him their corporate jets to get around. One was Harry Sargeant, owner of Sargeant Marine in Boca Raton and Crist's fraternity brother in Pi Kappa Alpha at Florida State. Another was Greg Eagle, a Cape Coral real estate developer. Crist insisted that the plane rides came with no strings attached.

"They adopt my agenda, not the reverse," he said. "Nobody's asked me for anything."

He raised a record-breaking forty million dollars for the campaign, which enabled him to flood the airwaves with advertising in a blitz the Rosen brothers would have admired. He flattened his primary opponent and beat the Democratic nominee in a walk—all in a year when Republicans nationwide came away the losers in elections, thanks to the unpopularity of the war in Iraq.

As one veteran political reporter noted, after eight years of Jeb Bush's hard-right ideology, the voters responded to Crist's "middle-of-the-road Republican philosophy that's easy to grasp and as upbeat as an Amway convention."

For environmental activists like Pat Rose, though, Crist seemed like he might wind up being worse than his predecessor. It wasn't just that he was a dedicated boater. While he was in the cabinet he had voted to approve the Swire Properties marina project in Miami that Governor Bush and nearly all the rest of the cabinet rejected. Worse, he had picked as his running mate none other than Representative Kottkamp, the Cape Coral Republican who had joined in the howling at Hankla in December 2002.

Then, to top it off, there were the people Crist picked to run the Fish and Wildlife Conservation Commission. He reappointed Commissioner Barreto, who had raised money for the Crist campaign in South Florida. Then Crist added three new members: a construction company executive, a developers' attorney, and a developer. Among the applicants Crist passed over: a biology professor from the University of South Florida, the conservation director of a privately owned wildlife preserve, and Pam McVety, Pat Rose's former boss. While the commission had long had more than its share of developers on the board, Crist had done what no other governor ever had: he had filled every seat with someone connected to the development industry.

"Looks like the developers have won again," said the biology professor, Henry Mushinsky. "I think his choices were extremely narrow and one-sided. Wildlife will not benefit from these sorts of actions."

Crist defended his selections by arguing that "just because somebody has business interests does not mean that they don't care about and have a deep love for natural Florida."

Thanks to Crist's appointments, the seven-member wildlife commission now consisted of

- Rodney Barreto, a Miami developer and lobbyist for developers
- Richard Corbett, a Tampa mall developer
- Brian Yablonski, a vice-president of the St. Joe Company, a developer
- Kathy Barco, a Jacksonville construction company executive
- Dwight Stevenson, NFL Hall of Fame player for the Miami Dolphins and now owner of a construction company
- Ken Wright, an Orlando development lawyer
- Ron Bergeron, a South Florida developer

The last two were particularly odd choices. Wright, fifty-nine, not only represented every big developer in Central Florida but also served as chairman of the Orlando-Sanford Airport Authority. The *St. Petersburg Times* had recently revealed that, as airport chairman, Wright had set up some cozy business deals that benefited himself and his friends. He steered an airport contract toward a company that employed two of his friends, who then collected commissions from the sale. Then Wright himself got hired to work as a salesman for the same company, collecting commissions on sales to other public agencies.

Wright insisted there was no funny business going on—no payoffs, no kickbacks.

"I'm a straight guy," he told a *Times* reporter. Taking a payoff would have endangered his lucrative law practice, he said, and "if you don't think I'm an honest guy, then I hope you deal with me enough to know that I'm not a stupid guy."

Bergeron, sixty-three, turned out to have even more baggage than Wright. He owned the largest road-contracting and site- development business in the state. He also owned cattle ranches in Broward and Hendry counties and frequently enjoyed competing as a rodeo cowboy. In fact, the arena in his hometown of Davie bore his name, and he usually wore cowboy hats and boots even when on business trips. But what he really liked to boast about was that he took his first airboat ride through the Everglades at age three.

"I've got a genuine appreciation for the environment," he said.

Bergeron also held the unique distinction of having been investigated by the same agency he had been appointed to oversee.

The cattleman relished giving acquaintances a tour of the wilder parts of his five-thousand-acre Hendry County ranch. In April 2006, Bergeron was leading just such a tour when he spotted an alligator sunning itself near a pond. Although the gator appeared to be at least seven feet long, Bergeron decided to demonstrate for his guests what he called "an old Cracker tradition."

He leaped on the gator and began wrestling with it. The big reptile wrapped its tail around Bergeron's leg, rolled him into the water, bit his left hand, "and proceeded to take him to the bottom of the pond," wildlife commission investigator Stephen Farmer wrote in his report on the incident. "Bergeron stated he began to strike the alligator on the nose as he was taught as a boy several times."

Finally the gator let go, and Bergeron swam to the surface. At a nearby hospital, a doctor informed him that the gator had broken two of his fingers.

Officer Farmer did not arrest Bergeron, but did recommend prosecution. After all, Bergeron admitted tackling the alligator, clearly violating the law. His X-rays confirmed the story.

But when the investigator met with Hendry County prosecutors in La Belle, they declined to pursue the case against the well-connected developer because "there was not enough evidence (i.e. sworn witness statements) to prosecute the subject," Farmer wrote.

Despite their questionable behavior, what appeared to count for more with Crist regarding his appointees was that, like Barreto, all three had been supporters of his campaign. Bergeron, for instance, happened to be among the crowd at Crist's million-dollar kickoff fund-raiser at the Tampa Airport Marriott in May 2005, the event that catapulted Crist to a financial lead he never relinquished. The Crist campaign reported receiving nine thousand from Bergeron and his network of businesses, in eighteen checks of five hundred dollars each, on one day in 2005.

Barco and Wright donated as well, and Wright—who had been one of the attorneys representing the Bush-Cheney campaign during the 2000 presidential recount—also served on Crist's transition team when he first took office as governor. Wright's responsibility as a transition team member was to see if anything needed fixing at the Fish and Wildlife Conservation Commission. He reported finding no problems.

The news coverage about Crist's developer-friendly appointments in August 2007 noted that the next big decision facing the wildlife commissioners would be the final step in downlisting manatees to "threatened." In addition, the commission—facing a major budget crunch—was considering slashing ninety positions from the division that enforced boating speed zones, as well as virtually eliminating statewide manatee rescue and recovery programs such as the one at the Lowry Park Zoo.

The final downlisting vote, and the vote on cutting enforcement and rescue, had been scheduled for the following month in Crist's hometown, at the St. Petersburg Hilton. It would also be the first meeting attended by Crist's new appointees—a fact noted in the first day's opening prayer, when the wildlife commission staffer asking God to bless the proceedings said, "Lord, join us in welcoming our newest commissioners, Ronald Bergeron and Ken Wright."

But there would be no downlisting vote. Two days before that September 2007 meeting, Crist sent a letter to Chairman Barreto officially asking him to postpone the downlisting vote. His staff then released the letter to the press to make sure everyone knew what had happened.

In his letter, Crist cited the record 416 manatees that had died in Florida the previous year. Because there was still no reliable way to count them, he wrote, "I believe a more prudent course of action at this time would be to postpone consideration of the proposed change in the status of this species."

Besides, the governor pointed out, those new state wildlife commissioners hadn't had a chance to become familiar with the whole manatee problem. Postponing the decision "will also allow the new members of the commission more time to evaluate this complex issue and ensure that they . . . are fully prepared to vote on an item of such gravity," he wrote.

"I want to be sure these wonderful, docile creatures are as protected as possible," Crist said in an interview with the *St. Petersburg Times.* He said he was not telling the commission how long to delay, or how to vote, but "I don't want to hurry to a decision. . . . I want to put the brakes on it."

What happened? Pat Rose said the news coverage of Crist's picks for the wildlife commission had for the first time focused the governor's attention on the downlisting issue.

"It helped to raise it on his radar screen," Rose said. "I think he was sensitive to the criticism he received about the appointments."

Rose met with Crist's top aides and urged him to at least delay the vote. Crist proved to be receptive, to say the least.

Unlike his predecessor, Crist had not lashed himself to an ideological mast, determined to stay the course no matter what happened. Instead, he took a more pragmatic view of politics, and generally he came out as more of a populist than anything else. If there was an underdog, he was for it. If there was a big business doing something questionable, he was frequently opposed. While he was a state senator, Crist had attacked the state's biggest utility, Florida Power and Light, for trying to burn an environmentally risky fuel imported from Brazil at its power plant in Manatee County. While he was attorney general he had gone after insurance companies and other corporations he said were gouging the public. Those kinds of stances built up his reputation, boosting his chances of winning the next election.

Despite his love for boating and his reputation as someone in the thrall of Wickstrom's magazine, Crist had already had an eye-opening experience with the boating industry.

When he was in the legislature, Crist had sponsored a bill to require all boat motors to be caged in a propeller guard in order to protect manatees. Although the majority of manatee deaths are caused by being clobbered by the hull or the skeg, Crist had seen pictures—photos just like the ones in Cathy Beck's computer, just like the ones Woodie Hartman and Pat Rose had used to get federal and state laws passed—showing how manatees were frequently sliced and diced by boat propellers. Requiring prop guards would fix at least that part of the problem, he reasoned.

Crist figured the boat manufacturers would, at worst, quibble about standards, but surely they could not oppose such a commonsense measure. Instead, he said, "the industry went crazy."

Putting guards on the boat propellers would cost too much money and would drive up the price to the customers; in short, it was bad for business, the industry's lobbyists said. They made sure Crist's pro-manatee bill sank like a stone.

Crist learned something he never forgot: the boating industry did not have manatees' best interest at heart, no matter how popular the animal might be. It was willing to put all its muscle into blocking measures that might hurt the industry's bottom line. To a populist like Crist, that made the choice about which side he was on a pretty easy one.

After hearing from the governor, Barreto, well aware of who had appointed him and a majority of his colleagues, immediately announced that the commissioners would be glad to do what the governor asked—although they would still go ahead with a truncated public hearing on the issue.

A day later, Crist himself dropped by the commission meeting to say thanks. When the governor strolled in, a waggish sound technician played the theme from *Jaws* over the loudspeaker system. Afterward, with a gaggle of reporters gathered around him in the hallway, Crist vowed to find the money in the budget to ensure that the wildlife commission would not have to make all those cuts.

Amid all the hoopla about Crist's intervention, there was one other startling development, announced with a frosty smile by Elizabeth Fleming of Defenders of Wildlife during the brief public hearing.

"Today the IUCN released its Red List of endangered species," she told the wildlife commissioners. The international organization where Lee Talbot got his start had spent a year reviewing the listing status of the Florida manatee— and ended up raising it, rather than lowering it, Fleming informed the commissioners.

"*That* is the application of good science," she told them sternly, then sat down, her eyes glittering in triumph.

Since 1982, the International Union for Conservation of Nature had listed the manatee as "vulnerable," and it kept that same designation during reviews in 1986, 1988, 1990, 1994, and even 1996, during the Red Tide epizootic. The species earned that designation because there were fewer than ten thousand mature adults when biologists added up both the Florida and Caribbean populations of the species. That number "was expected to decline at a rate of at least 10 percent over the course of three generations"—about sixty years—as a result of both habitat loss and manatees being killed by humans.

But now the scientists with the IUCN's "Sirenia" group decided that the listing for Florida manatees, and that segment alone, needed to be changed to "endangered."

They based their decision on Runge's 2004 computer modeling for the wildlife commission, the photos of scarred manatees in Cathy Beck's collection, the numbers of dead manatees compiled by Tom Pitchford's crew at the path lab, and, last but not least, the 2001 synoptic survey by Bruce Ackerman's scientific flying circus.

The Atlantic and southwest populations—which together made up 80 percent of the statewide population—both appeared to be stable at best, but just as likely were in decline, the IUCN reported.

Although Ackerman's count had found more than three thousand manatees in 2001, population calculations based on Beck's photos and Runge's models suggested that fewer than twenty-five hundred were adults, the IUCN reported. Meanwhile the number of boat-related deaths continued increasing—it was the number-one killer of adult manatees—as did the number of boats, the IUCN report noted.

Habitat continued to disappear due to development. Counties and cities continued to overpump the underground aquifer so people could water their lawns, which lowered the flows of the state's springs. If even a few of the power plants stopped spewing out hot water in the winter, the review noted, manatees would be in big trouble come the next hard freeze.

As a result, the IUCN's 2007 Red List said Florida manatees now deserved to be uplisted to "endangered" because they had "a population size of less than 2,500 mature individuals, and the population is estimated to decline by at least 20 percent over the next two generations . . . due to anticipated future changes in warm-water habitat and threats from increasing watercraft traffic over the next several decades."

That was exactly the same information the wildlife commission's staff had used in concluding that the manatee no longer fit the state's new definition of "endangered," a definition supposedly based on IUCN criteria. But now the IUCN itself was saying that the state's own data said they really *were* endangered, using the IUCN criteria.

The irony grew even deeper for anyone who checked the authorship of the IUCN's study, which had been evaluated and approved by Buddy Powell and Marine Mammal Commission chairman John Reynolds. The lead author was a scientist named Chip Deutsch, a manatee biologist whose employer just happened to be the Florida Fish and Wildlife Conservation Commission.

Deutsch, a New Yorker with curly blond hair, had previously worked with Cathy Beck and Bob Bonde at the U.S. Geological Survey. He said that in preparing the IUCN report he "used the same criteria, the same data, the same everything—it was just a matter of what the labels are."

Rose wrote an op-ed piece that the Save the Manatee Club circulated to the

Florida newspapers. The headline the club suggested was "Recent Confirmation of Manatee's Endangered Status Should Kill State Downlisting Plans."

But of course the IUCN listing did nothing of the sort. The only thing that had stopped the commission's vote was Crist.

To say the pro-boating and development forces were disappointed by Crist's intervention would be an understatement. Doug Rillstone, one of the phalanx of attorneys representing the Florida Chamber of Commerce and the Florida Home Builders Association, wrote to Barreto to complain that his clients feared that they "simply cannot be treated fair if any interest group who does not like the outcome of a species reclassification is allowed to delay the finality of the process simply by seeking to reconsider or change the process, especially where there is no substantive change in species protection."

The lawyer warned that if the commission did what the Save the Manatee Club and other environmental activist groups wanted, they would "push Florida to a system where wildlife management decisions will be made by courts and the legislature"—as if that wasn't already going on.

The boating-industry representatives who sat on Haddad's Manatee Forum denounced Rose for violating terms they had all agreed on three years before, terms that were supposed to lead to *Kumbaya*. They refused to attend another meeting with him.

"The purpose [of the forum] was to bring the situation forward and build decision making and consensus policy making, and avoid decisions being more politics driven," Buddy Powell said. "When Crist intervened, the boating groups said Save the Manatee Club has made this a political process again. According to them there was no need to meet anymore as a forum."

Rose shrugged off the complaints. "It's so childish," he said. "They didn't get their way so they took their ball and went home."

Ted Forsgren sent Crist a three-page letter strongly defending the idea of downlisting manatees. He conceded that his organization had gotten involved in the fight because it did not like how many areas would face regulation under the lawsuit settlement. However, Forsgren wrote, "substantial scientific evidence" supported the downlisting. As proof, Forsgren cited both the wildlife commission's own staff report (based on the misaligned IUCN criteria) and Hankla's five-year review. Strangely, he did not say a word about the Fraser report, which his own organization had paid for. For obvious reasons, he made no mention at all of the IUCN's uplisting.

"There will always be manatee and animal rights groups that will adamantly and emotionally oppose any manatee reclassification which removes the word endangered, no matter how large the population becomes," Forsgren wrote. "Science, not emotion, should be the foundation for the decision. . . . Upgrading the biological status from endangered to threatened is not anti-manatee."

By the time Forsgren sent the letter, though, Rose had launched his secret weapon.

•

When Rose saw the management plan that the wildlife commission staff had produced, he flipped. He said to himself, "I'm not taking this. This isn't right. People have got to listen. This is *wrong*."

Ken Haddad and his staff had kept telling everyone to wait until they saw the management plan before criticizing the downlisting. Now Rose had seen it, and it seemed more like a plan to produce a plan than an actual roadmap for helping manatees.

For instance, it called for developing a better method for estimating the manatee population within three years, without spelling out exactly how that could be done. Bruce Ackerman, who had tried in vain for more than a decade, had finally been pushed out of his job. He went back to counting land animals in Idaho, where there were fewer variables—and after he left, nobody else had come up with anything better.

The management plan also called for improving speed zone enforcement, but without including any specifics on where the money would come from. It did, however, call for a review of some of the existing speed zones to see if they needed alterations—something John Sprague had requested.

Rose felt like he was at the end of his rope. His appeal to Crist had bought some time, but not much—only three months. Barreto had announced that the vote would definitely take place at the wildlife commission's December meeting in Key Largo.

As the club faced its darkest hour yet, Rose had few allies to help him. Judith Vallee had resigned as executive director to devote herself to writing grant applications for the club, struggling to rebuild its funding in the post-9/11 economic doldrums. The board selected Rose to replace her—and he then fired his only rival for the job, Patti Thompson.

Rose knew he had to do something, but what? Every other alternative had produced a terrific backlash at best and actual setbacks at worst. The law had failed him. Science had failed him. Politics certainly didn't favor him.

So Rose turned to one of the most powerful forces in American society: celebrity.

This wasn't exactly a Hail Mary pass, an against-all-odds, so-crazy-it-might-work move. Governor Crist had repeatedly garnered headlines in his first year in office for hanging out with celebrities while discussing environmental issues. In the spring, he had appeared onstage with singer Sheryl Crow at a Gainesville concert to show that, like her, he was concerned about global warming. In the summer, he clowned for the cameras with action star-turned-California governor Arnold Schwarzenegger at a summit Crist had convened in Miami to discuss climate change. In the fall, Crist met with actor/director Robert Redford at a conference Redford had organized to talk about—what else?—global warming.

Although Schwarzenegger was a fellow Republican, Crow and Redford tended to back liberal Democrats. But Crist said he cared less about party affiliations than about passion.

"I'm reaching out to everybody," he said. "It's important to. We need to come together to do what's right."

Knowing how much Crist enjoyed basking in the glow of a big star, Rose made some phone calls and planted a suggestion or two. And thus it was that, on the night of Thursday, November 1, 2007, Charlie Crist got to meet Jimmy Buffett.

Buffett, though now sixty and as bald as a medieval monk, still played the role of the barefoot adventurer in his concerts. In truth he was more like the CEO of Jimmyworld Incorporated. He had raked in more than forty million dollars the previous year from his music, restaurant chain, books, clothing, and even toys.

He could still pack in the Parrotheads, too. His November 1 concert at Tampa's open-air Ford Amphitheatre, across the highway from the Seminole Tribe's Hard Rock Café and gambling casino, drew a sell-out crowd. As usual, those in attendance were decked out in various combinations of coconut shell bras, grass skirts, Panama hats, and Hawaiian shirts. Contingents of die-hard Parrotheads had flown or driven in from Michigan, Ohio, and Wisconsin.

"The tailgating started early in the afternoon," the *Tampa Tribune* noted, "and by the time Buffett took the stage many had that special glow that only comes from lots of beer and tequila." Fortunately, a steady breeze blew through the venue all evening, keeping the potentially rowdy crowd cooled down.

Crist showed up with a date, a wealthy brunette named Carol Rome who ran

Governor Charlie Crist met with Jimmy Buffett backstage prior to his Tampa concert, giving Buffett a chance to lobby him about downlisting. Then Crist got to introduce him, to the delight of the cheering crowd. Photo courtesy Florida Governor's Office.

a family-owned Halloween costume company in New York. She was getting divorced and had recently moved to a mansion on Miami's Fisher Island. Crist had met her just two months before, but the relationship had already taken on a serious tone. In a few months he would propose marriage.

Like Bob Graham before him, Crist was invited backstage. Unlike Graham, Crist got to see Buffett before the concert, while the Parrotheads out front were still tuning up their buzzes.

If some half-lit gambler from the Hard Rock had stumbled across the scene, he would have sworn that Crist was the one about to go to work, and Buffett the one relaxing with a ladyfriend. The governor wore a white shirt, a dark tie, dark slacks, and a pair of wingtips so highly polished they could have been used to flash messages across the desert. Buffett wore a yellow T-shirt, teal jams, and a pair of flip-flops—his *Margaritaville* uniform.

No journalists were allowed to sit in on their ten-minute confab, but afterward Crist confirmed that, just like Graham, he and the singer had chatted about manatees.

"He said, 'I just want to thank you for what you did for the manatees,'" Crist told an Associated Press reporter. "And I said, 'No, thank *you*. Thank you for doing so much for our state and looking out for our wildlife and our natural estuaries and caring so much about Florida.'"

Actually, Buffett had more to say to Crist than just a simple "thanks." At Rose's suggestion, the singer urged Crist to continue to resist the boaters and developers who wanted to downlist manatees. This meeting with a governor went far better than the one Buffett had had with Jeb Bush. When Buffett finished, Crist nodded: message received. Then Crist walked onstage to introduce his new friend to nearly twenty thousand cheering, boozy fans.

"He has Florida in his heart and he loves her like I do," Crist told the crowd. "God bless America. God bless Florida. And God bless Jimmy Buffett!"

Buffett shook Crist's hand and launched into a two-and-a-half-hour set that began with "Fruitcakes" and ended with a solo version of "Trying to Reason with Hurricane Season." One song he didn't play, though, was "Growing Older But Not Up."

With the wildlife commission meeting approaching, rumors about what Crist wanted his appointees to do floated this way and that, as if swept along by the breeze through the Ford Amphitheatre. One story said he wanted another delay. Another said he would let his commissioners do whatever they wanted. Reporters who asked Crist's staff got noncommittal answers.

Finally, on December 3, a reporter for the state's largest newspaper, the *St. Petersburg Times*, called up Crist himself to see what he would say. Throughout his years in public office, Crist had eagerly passed out his cell-phone number to reporters. Sometimes he would have a staff person return the calls, but frequently Crist himself would be on the line, usually beginning the conversation with, "Hi, this is Charlie Crist."

Sure enough, Crist called back and the reporter asked whether the commissioners he had appointed ought to vote on downlisting the manatee this time. Sure, Crist said.

Okay, the reporter said, and if it were you voting, would you vote yes on downlisting?

"I would not favor that," Crist said, suddenly sounding stiff and formal. "It would not please me. More importantly, it would disappoint the people of our state."

Crist went on to say that he had been talking to Chairman Barreto about what he wanted to happen. Despite all the things Barreto had said in the past about supporting downlisting, Crist said he had "great confidence" in his chairman to do the right thing now.

"He's a tremendous guy, and obviously his concern to manatees and to Florida is just fantastic," Crist said without an ounce of sarcasm in his voice.

When the reporter called Barreto, the normally boisterous lobbyist sounded somewhat subdued. He promised that he and his colleagues would give Crist's wishes "great weight."

In the end, what they did was find a middle path.

•

The last wildlife commission meeting of 2007 convened at a sumptuous Marriott resort on the Overseas Highway in Key Largo, not far from Barreto's second home. The hotel's conference center, where the meeting took place, had been built with tall windows offering a sweeping vista of the sea. But once the meeting room doors closed, it could have been a ballroom in Des Moines.

Barreto and four other commissioners wore fishing shirts like the ones Ted Forsgren favored, except theirs had the commission's own logo on the chest. The exceptions: Brian Yablonski, who wore a green plaid shirt, and Kathy Barco, who wore an orange turtleneck under a brown jacket.

They faced a room packed with more than two hundred people, many of them familiar faces from previous battles in the Manatee War. Ted Forsgren of the Coastal Conservation Association and John Sprague of the Marine Industries Association of Florida both looked grim. There was no sign of Wade Hopping this time, as if he couldn't bear to see what was about to happen.

Pat Rose wore his usual plain blue suit with a red, white, and blue tie that looked like he had swiped it from a used-car dealer. He sat quietly making notes on a legal pad, his black pen scratching away as he figured out what he would say to the commissioners when his turn came.

Nearly two hours after Barreto gaveled the meeting to order, the subject of manatees finally came up on the agenda. Kipp Frohlich stepped up to the lectern to talk about the management plan, which, he said, "seeks to eliminate any significant risk of extinction."

Yet no matter what happened in the future, he said, chances were that humans would always have to have special rules for dealing with this species.

"We will continue to manage this species in perpetuity," Frohlich said.

He acknowledged the plan had some shortcomings—noting, for instance, that while it sounded nice to say the state would come up with a better method for counting manatees within three years, "that's something we've been working on for as long as we've been working on manatees."

After the wildlife commission staff posted a copy of the management plan on its Web site for public comment, Frohlich told the commissioners, "We received twenty-eight thousand e-mails from around the globe. By far the greatest number of comments were not on the plan, but on the listing process."

Barreto asked him if the management plan would really be a step backward for manatees, as some newspaper editorials had contended. No, Frohlich said, "this plan is a step forward. Is it perfect? No. . . . But I think it's a darn good plan."

"It will *enhance* the protection of the manatee!" Corbett suddenly chimed in, his voice sounding higher than usual, as if he were imitating one of the Munchkins from *The Wizard of Oz*.

Barreto noted that more than thirty people had signed up to speak, and the first one he called was Pat Rose. Rose was surprised. His had not been the first name on the sign-up list. He figured Barreto was sending a message of some sort.

The Save the Manatee Club's new executive director strode to the microphone and did something befitting a diplomat. He announced quietly that the club now supported adopting the management plan—the same plan that Rose had previously said lacked any teeth.

"We'll work later on what our disagreements are," he said.

The big problem, he said, was the listing process, and he promised that his organization would "do anything we can do to get us out of this controversy we've found ourselves in."

Rose told the commissioners that he hoped they would approve the management plan but would not vote to downlist the species. He never mentioned Crist's name. He didn't have to.

Next came John Sprague, wearing a simple plaid shirt and jeans, his shoulders slumped a little more than usual, to say that the marine industry supported the management plan too.

"The downlisting is probably the big fight today," he said, sounding weary. "It's funny. It's all about a name."

He couldn't resist getting in a jab at Rose, though. "When Pat was in charge, we had twelve hundred manatees," he said, grinning. "We know that in 2001 we had thirty-three hundred. All these protection measures appear to be working to increase the number of manatees."

Sprague then made the most remarkable statement of the day: "We have no interest from the industry side in removing any protections. They've got to stay in place." No one remarked on his change of heart.

A few speakers later, a figure from the past stepped up: Thom Rumberger, the portly, garrulous attorney who had helped the Save the Manatee Club break free from the Audubon Society. Rumberger wobbled unsteadily to the microphone and mentioned that his first job had been milking venomous snakes for a Central Florida showman named Ross Allen. After that odd anecdote, Rumberger got to the point, telling the commissioners that if they voted to downlist the manatee, they would be making a serious mistake, because manatees were more than just an animal. They were an icon.

"The manatee is the face of Florida," the jolly Rumberger told them. "It represents the animal that all our children love."

A skinny woman, dressed mostly in black, then stood up and said she had driven down from Lake City, up near the Georgia border, and she didn't like coming all that way. In a sharp tone, she told the commissioners, "For all your talk of science, I doubt if you would know it if a textbook dropped in your laps." Vote to downlist the manatee, she warned them, and "you will be remembered as the signers of the death warrant for the manatee!"

In the past, hearing such an insult, Barreto might have snapped back some tart response. Not this time, though. This time all he said was, "Very cute." Then he called the next speaker.

One of Forsgren's board members complained about Crist's meddling with the commission vote. "This commission is being pressured to withhold the truth," he said. "Put the science first and tell the public the truth."

He was followed by Forsgren, who did little beyond read aloud the letter he had sent to Crist. After seven years of battling, he had no passion left to pump into his speech. He said his piece and sat down, then exhaled loudly.

Several people had driven down from Crystal River, Woodie Hartman's old stomping grounds. One was Tracy Colson, one of the Manatee Watch volunteers who had posted video clips on YouTube of tourists harassing manatees. Her gray hair was tied up in a braid, and she wore a purple fleece jacket, jeans, and sneakers. She came armed with big photos of Crystal River's manatees, which she showed to the commissioners.

"We call this 'The Survivors' Club,'" she told them, pointing out how they all had scars from being hit by boats. Unlike the attendees at Jeb Bush's manatee summit, though, nobody flinched at the carnage. They had seen it before.

Steven Webster of the dock builders' association, the onetime congressional witness, then told the commissioners that downlisting "is an overwhelming slam-dunk" according to all the scientific evidence he had seen (which evidently did not include the Runge report or the IUCN's Red List).

The speakers went on and on, and the commissioners just sat and listened to them vent. Finally, at 12:20 p.m., the last one sat down and it became the commissioners' turn to talk. It turned out they had a lot to say. Lunch would have to wait.

Barreto started things off. He praised the management plan, noted that both the Save the Manatee Club and the boating industry supported it, and called for its approval. The management plan passed without a single nay vote.

Under the listing process the commissioners had adopted in 2006, that should have been the end of the discussion. Manatees would be considered endangered no longer. They would be downlisted to threatened, effective immediately.

But Governor Crist's very public intervention had changed the rules. Barreto now opened the floor to yet another discussion of the listing process in general, and of downlisting manatees in particular—and he made it clear that he now viewed manatees as something special, something deserving special consideration.

"I believe," Barreto said, echoing Rumberger, "that the manatee is the icon for conservation in the state of Florida."

At that point, one of the new commissioners, Orlando lawyer Ken Wright, spoke up. He made a motion to defer the manatee downlisting decision again. He wanted it reviewed one more time by Ken Haddad's staff. In fact, Wright said, he wanted Haddad's staff to try again to come up with a better listing process.

Commissioner Corbett, working off an old playbook, suggested that the new commissioners still needed more time to understand the issue. Not true, said Wright: "I understand the issue now. I understood it in September."

And what was the issue? "I find myself in a box," Wright admitted with a rueful smile. He then explained to the crowd, "I find myself like the judge in the movie *Miracle on 34th Street*."

At the climax of that Christmas classic, Wright reminded everyone, a judge is asked to rule on an impossible question: whether Santa Claus really exists.

"Being put in the position of having to make a ruling that Santa Claus does not exist—I don't like that," Wright said. "This is not about science. This is about public policy. . . . This creature that we've got has become iconic in the state of Florida. It has a special place, regardless how science sees it."

In the movie, he said, the judge hears all kinds of testimony about how Santa's sleigh couldn't possibly go around the world in one night, and lots of other scientific evidence that would undercut belief in Kris Kringle's existence.

"But all that science makes no difference," Wright said, "if at the end of the day, public policy wants to recognize that Santa exists. . . . I don't want to endanger the credibility of this commission and our governor."

Corbett leaped in then to agree with him. He suggested postponing any decision for at least six months.

No, Barreto said, not six months. Instead, the chairman recommended they set no deadline for the wildlife commission's staff to figure out a new, improved listing process.

Wright's Santa Claus speech opened a floodgate of doubt. Yablonski said he, too, was now worried about the commission's credibility if it proceeded with downlisting. And Barco said that, although two years before she had been fine with the new listing process, now she had questions about it.

"As it started to get enacted, things came to light," she said. "What I saw, even before the governor threw in, was that people have a problem with the listing that has been consistent. They don't like the alignment."

What really got her attention, she said, was when she found out that land planners depend on the wildlife commissioners' listings to determine which habitats are in greatest need of preservation from development.

"That's when a lightbulb came on," the construction company CEO said. She figured out that endangered species get better habitat protection than other species.

"The biggest threat to this animal . . . is the loss of habitat by local or regional government," she said. "That's the part that concerns me. . . . That's what I've been grappling with, irrespective of the governor."

Now the rodeo cowboy leaped into the middle of the discussion. Ron Bergeron might wrestle alligators and ride bucking broncos, but he wasn't about to cross the governor.

"I am *definitely* for deferring the downlisting," Bergeron drawled.

Instead of calling wildlife "endangered" or "threatened," he suggested, "we should use some common sense. There are certain species that are in tremendous conflict with human activities." Manatees are one such species, Bergeron said, because "they have to maneuver around a million boats." Maybe it would be better to put manatees and other such wildlife into a category of "animals we care about," or "animals in conflict with humans," he said.

Stephenson the football player and Corbett the mall developer agreed. Then it was Barreto's turn again. He said that he supported what he called "Governor Crist's request that we take a pause"—although that wasn't actually what the governor had said he wanted.

"Certain people may say that's political," Barreto said. "To me, I don't see that as political. . . . We need to take the politics out of it."

Then he thanked Rose for agreeing to support the management plan—a nakedly political trade-off that Rose had been willing to make to get what he wanted—because "that set the tone for the meeting today."

At last, three hours and six years after they first started the discussion, the members of the Florida Fish and Wildlife Conservation Commission voted seven to zero to duck the manatee vote one more time. Instead, they asked for one more review of their listing process. They didn't set a date for making the final decision. Instead, they simply deferred it into thin air—not quite killing it, the way the governor had suggested, but still halting its seemingly unstoppable march forward, perhaps for as long as Crist continued to occupy the governor's office.

After the vote, Barreto joked with Frohlich that the staff now had "something to do for the next seven years." When Forsgren heard Barreto's joke about seven years, he blurted out, "I hope not!"

However, several months later, Haddad's staff suggested simply classifying as endangered all the species that were on the federal list that way. The commissioners immediately gave the staff another year to work on it.

Winning transformed Pat Rose from a man who was keeping his emotions tamped down to one who could not stop smiling. He stood outside the Key Largo meeting room grinning like the Cheshire Cat but (to Forsgren's chagrin) unlikely to disappear anytime soon.

When reporters crowded around him for quotes, Rose praised Crist, crediting him with turning the tide at the last minute and stopping the removal of manatees from the state's endangered list.

"This wouldn't be like this without the governor," he said, bouncing on his toes, his face lit up with obvious glee.

•

With all the publicity about manatees in 2007, and the state's economy starting its post-bubble nosedive, the number of manatees killed by boats that year dropped for the first time in three years. It fell to seventy-three—despite Fraser's contention that an increasing manatee population would lead inevitably to a higher death rate.

However, another number did go up: the number of boaters killed in 2007 totaled seventy-seven, up from the previous year's total of sixty-eight. Of the boaters who were killed, 85 percent had had no boater education courses prior to going out on the water.

So a *St. Petersburg Times* reporter asked Crist if—given all the praise he got for his courage on the manatee issue—he might next push for a law to require boaters to pass a licensing test.

Crist began laughing so hard he doubled over.

"Oh!" he said. "That's good! Anger a million people who vote!"

## The Dude Abides

BACK IN FRED MORSE'S ADOPTED HOMETOWN, in the place where Joe Moore made his crucial discovery, some people saw the long battle over the manatee's endangered status not as an object lesson about the conflict between science and politics, or even as an entertaining sideshow. They saw it as an opportunity.

After Pat Rose and Pam McVety persuaded Governor Martinez and the cabinet to require the thirteen coastal counties to draw up manatee protection plans in 1989, Miami-Dade County was one of the first to comply (the last ones, Palm Beach and Broward, finally got around to doing the job in 2007, eighteen years later).

Both Rose and Frohlich considered the Miami-Dade plan the best in the state, an example for other Florida counties to follow. The staff of the county's Department of Environmental Resource Management (DERM) had taken great care with how they put the plan together. DERM even hired experts from the University of Miami to analyze boating patterns in Biscayne Bay and poll boaters on their attitudes toward speed zones.

"The survey revealed that boaters overwhelmingly supported speed restrictions for boating safety and marine life protection," the 1991 study reported—a finding totally at odds with everything Karl Wickstrom would say.

How effective was the plan? It had helped persuade Governor Bush and the cabinet to reject the Swire Properties marina, despite the somewhat overblown promise that the development would halt the flow of drugs into Magic City. Yet the plan still allowed enough leeway for growth to continue. Between 1995, when the county approved the plan, and 2004, more than a thousand single-family docks and 315 multi-family and commercial docks had been okayed for construction along Miami-Dade's waterfront.

In fact, the Miami River had seen so many other alterations over the years that, by the time the twenty-first century arrived, Fred Morse and Kirk Munroe would have had a hard time recognizing it. The river now ran from the sprawling tarmac of Miami International Airport to the high-rise hotels and office towers that had turned the bayfront into a concrete canyon.

Bigger changes had occurred within the river itself. Its main tributary, Wagner Creek, had once been a natural stream fed by the Biscayne Aquifer. The city's growth had turned it into a six-foot-deep drainage ditch choked with trash. Biologists called it "one of the most polluted water bodies in South Florida."

Sewage dumping in the river and bay, first begun by Henry Flagler, finally stopped in the 1970s. But whenever the South Florida sky opened up during the rainy season, the river still collected all the contaminants that swept downhill from a sixty-nine-square-mile drainage area largely covered in pavement. Every year, thousands of tons of suspended solids, nitrogen, phosphorus, copper, lead, and zinc—not to mention so much fecal material that it repeatedly exceeded state pollution limits—rolled into the river.

By 1991, a grand jury report called the Miami River "a cesspool unfit to be utilized for drinking, fishing, or swimming."

Although the river gave the city its name, most of the residents barely noticed it as their cars rumbled across the bridge on the Dolphin Expressway. Yet the "sweet water" river where Seminoles once paddled to Brickell's trading post remained vital to the city's commerce. As of the late 1990s, more than sixty piers, wharves, and docks, as well as seven boat repair plants, lined its banks. The port brought in more than four billion dollars in cargo every year—yes, billion with a B—much of it shipped in from nations around the Caribbean.

But the riverbed contained nine hundred thousand tons of contaminated sediment, the accumulated pollution of six decades, dating back to the last major dredging in the 1930s. Studies connected the sediment's toxic qualities—which included PCBs, among other contaminants—with abnormalities cropping up among fish and crustaceans. Scientists had spotted creatures suffering from lesions, missing fins, scales that were reversed from the way they should grow.

This was more than just a biological nightmare. The buildup of crud made navigating the river difficult, if not impossible, for the largest cargo vessels. The ships could set sail at high tide or not at all, and then only with a partial load to avoid grounding. The Corps of Engineers calculated that the sediment was narrowing the river channel by a foot a year.

The Corps began the eighty-six-million-dollar job of dredging the sediment in 2004. Four years later the work was only halfway done. The Corps had had to suspend work twice after finding World War II munitions buried in the muck near where PT boats, designed by racing champion Gar Wood, had been built in the 1940s.

Rather than welcome the dredging, though, many of the river's users said they feared that making it easier to navigate might lead to further changes in the river's character.

Florida's speculation-fueled real estate bubble had swollen to astonishing proportions and—just as in Jim Kalvin's backyard in southwest Florida—began affecting what was being built along what had been a working waterfront. Between 2000 and 2008 nearly half the marine-industry land along the river had been gobbled up by residential rezonings approved by city officials who dismissed the watermen's complaints by arguing that the river was dead.

The runaway real estate market made multimillionaires out of developers who kept getting big loans from the banks to build more and more projects. Like the Rose brothers in Cape Coral, many didn't worry about such niceties as pulling permits or keeping financial records. Developers eager for new projects that would keep the money rolling in began buying up riverfront land, pushing out the marine industry, and launching the construction of more and more condos. And of course the builder of every new residential project wanted a lot more dock slips so the prospective buyers could tie up their speedboats.

But the prospective buyers didn't really want to live in the building and use the river. They only wanted to flip the property and make a big profit on the resale. They were convinced prices would keep soaring higher. They had all the confidence of Icarus flapping his wings and climbing nearer the sun.

In 2007, despite signs that the real estate bubble was about to burst, Miami-Dade County commissioners decided it was time to rewrite their manatee protection plan to accommodate more boats.

Although state wildlife commissioners and their staffers had repeatedly said downlisting the manatee would have no effect on its level of protection, the Miami-Dade decision showed that that was not true.

DERM's top official informed Kipp Frohlich that commissioners wanted a rewrite "in view of changes in the status of the manatee and . . . increasing demand for boating access."

In other words, since manatees weren't going to be classified as endangered anymore, it was time to build a lot more docks.

The push for a rewrite of the plan came from county commissioners who had a reputation for being unfriendly to the environment in general and manatees in particular. One commissioner made this very plain—to the point where a South Florida television commentator dubbed her "the Cruella De Vil of Biscayne Bay."

"I am not a lover of manatees," Miami-Dade commissioner Natacha Seijas announced during one meeting. She complained about manatees swimming in the canal behind her house. "As dumb as they always are," she said, "they keep floating back and forth."

Seijas said she wanted DERM employees "to come and pick them up," although she offered no suggestions about where they should be relocated. She added, "I want to know how big that herd is, because if that herd is way too big, it is time to find something else to do with it."

And during a discussion about taking steps to protect manatees in Biscayne Bay, Seijas said, "I don't see why we need to be creating an environment so they can continue."

None of her colleagues on the commission were quite as blunt as Seijas. However, Chairman Bruno Barreiro, during the same meeting where Seijas made her comments about the "dumb" manatees behind her house, complained that lately "there is a huge shortage of slips" in Miami, and as a result "slip prices are sky-high." Later he complained about state growth management officials, who he said were "very anti–any development."

When the commissioners informed Frohlich that they wanted to rewrite their manatee protection plan, he tried to convince them to leave it alone. They refused.

Instead, because they were certain the wildlife commission was on the verge of downlisting manatees, Seijas and her fellow commissioners approved spending seven hundred thousand dollars to rewrite their plan. They appointed a fourteen-member committee to oversee the rewrite.

Among the committee members the commissioners chose—in fact, the one picked by Seijas—was someone with more than a passing acquaintance with the laws governing manatee protection. He had a personal experience with them, sort of like Ron Bergeron's experience with the laws protecting alligators.

Dick Bunnell built docks for a living. In 2005—the year before he was tapped to sit on the manatee protection plan committee—a federal judge fined him $150,000 for building docks in manatee habitat without getting permits from the Corps of Engineers. The judge also sentenced him to fifteen hundred hours of community service and five years of probation.

While Bunnell was building the illegal docks, which lasted from 2001 to 2004, DERM staffers repeatedly warned him that he would need federal permits for what he was doing, but he ignored them.

Needless to say, Bunnell had some strong opinions about what was wrong with the county's manatee protection plan.

"There's way too much restriction and resistance to docks and boat ramps and boat slips, and that's a segment of our economy that's so strong in South Florida," he said, then reached for the Big John argument on manatee deaths: "I don't believe docks kill manatees. What hurts manatees is boaters that are not obeying the law."

By the time the committee began holding meetings, though, Miami's condo market had imploded. In some of the newly built high-rises, one out of every four condo units was in foreclosure. Miami lawyers who in the 1980s had raked in big bucks defending cocaine dealers now found lucrative work defending developers accused of fraud. There was such a glut of unsold condos that Miami topped the list of the United States' worst housing markets.

"We've gone from foreclosure to panic in a year," one developer, dubbed the Trump of the Tropics, told *Time* magazine.

Nevertheless, the manatee plan rewrite committee soldiered on, repeatedly asking the DERM staff for more data and even hiring Sarasota's Mote Marine Laboratory to conduct new studies.

On April 8, 2008, the committee held its first public hearing, a nighttime gathering at the University of Miami. Fifty people showed up. The majority said the county should not change its plan. Of those who did want a rewrite, several said they wished the plan could be made stricter, so manatees would get even more protection.

At least one committee member, Lynda Green, agreed with them. Green was a longtime volunteer with the manatee rescue network, like an amateur Tom

Pitchford. She had been one of the people who spoke against downlisting at the December 2007 wildlife commission meeting in Key Largo.

Yet Green was also, contrary to Karl Wickstrom's firm beliefs, an avid boater. In fact, she had been appointed to the committee to represent boating interests, not the environment.

Green had her own opinion about why the county commissioners wanted to push the rewrite along. "I think the commissioners want to reopen this because they want more development, they want more docks, and everything they want will be less protection for the manatee," she said.

At Green's suggestion, for their May 21, 2008, meeting the manatee plan committee members toured the Miami Seaquarium, the original home of Sewer Sam. They saw a pair of manatees named Romeo and Juliet that Craig Phillips had captured in the Miami River in 1958 to replace the dead Cleopatra. In 1975 the pair had produced the first manatee ever conceived in captivity, which the staff dubbed Lorelei. The Seaquarium's success persuaded the *New York Times* to (erroneously) report in a 1983 headline, "Captive Breeding May Be Last Hope of Sea Cow."

By the time the committee visited, Romeo had fathered sixteen calves, a dozen of them by Juliet, the rest by other females the Seaquarium had stocked. But what Green really wanted her colleagues to see were the injured manatees the aquarium staff had rescued. They saw one named Phoenix that had its tail cut off by a boat in 1993 and thus could not ever return to the wild. In another tank they saw Señora, brought to the Seaquarium in 2006 after being hit by a boat that not only fractured several ribs but also damaged the animal's lungs. Because of the lung damage, Señora had trouble remaining buoyant.

Green wanted to rub her fellow committee members' noses in what speeding boats were doing to the manatees. After all, she said, "how much data do you need when you see a manatee whose tail has just come off in your hands?"

For more than six decades, boats had been slamming and slicing manatees in Biscayne Bay, ever since that first one Dan Beard spotted back in the 1940s and wrote about in *Fading Trails*. Thousands of manatees swimming through Fred Morse's favorite body of water wound up wounded or killed, not to mention having to cope with the rampant pollution and the continuing loss of habitat.

In the last sixty years only one Miami manatee ever got away completely unscathed—but at a terrible price.

•

Before Craig Phillips ever dreamed of a Miami Seaquarium, there was the *Prins Valdemar*, a disaster that turned into a tourist attraction.

A steel-hulled, square-rigged Danish barkentine, the ship sank in Biscayne Bay in January 1926, right at the height of South Florida's last big speculation-crazed building boom. The wreck blocked the entrance to the port for weeks, preventing the delivery of lumber needed for all the homes under construction, putting a damper on the boom.

"We could see all these ships waiting to come into the port and they couldn't get in," recalled Alice Walters Wallace, who was a girl of three at the time. "They had to try to dredge around it and then get it out."

Finally a salvor dragged it to the city's waterfront. The ship, sans masts, was anchored at Bayfront Park, just an angler's cast from the foot of Flagler Street and the tourist hotels on Biscayne Boulevard. The park consisted of forty acres of land pumped from the bay bottom and landscaped with shrubbery (it's where the Miami Heat now play basketball in the American Airlines Arena).

No longer seaworthy, the *Prins Valdemar* became a struggling restaurant and even a hundred-room hotel for a while. Then Mrs. Wallace's father, R. J. Walters, turned it into the Miami Aquarium, the quintessential Florida tourist attraction.

"At the entrance girl artists do portrait sketches for a tip, and two monkeys, chained to a revolving iron ladder, swing round and round," *The WPA Guide to Florida* reported in the 1930s. "Live exhibits include sea turtles, stone crabs, Florida lobsters, shrimp, morays, sharks, stingrays, alligators, crocodiles, and two manatees, or sea cows, seldom seen in captivity. . . . On the upper deck are tables for eating and drinking, and seats for those who wish to sit and look out over Biscayne Bay."

The aquarium's exhibits were, of course, not nearly as sophisticated as those offered by modern aquariums. Walters made no effort to re-create an ecosystem. What he offered was, as one longtime Miami resident put it, "a glorified fish tank. . . . The darkened hold of the ship's huge white bulk was fitted with enormous, thick-glass aquarium tanks, lights, pumps, and fans." The result was "a dim undersea world that vibrated from the constant throb of pumps filtering salt water from the bay that surrounded it."

Still the tourists flocked to see this collection of curious specimens. The visitors included such celebrities as Amelia Earhart, Eleanor Roosevelt, even

After salvaging the *Prins Valdemar*, R. J. Walters converted it into the Miami Aquarium. Photo courtesy of Alice Luckhardt.

Ripley of "Ripley's Believe It or Not" fame, who anchored his own red Chinese junk at a nearby pier.

Walters's aquarium offered more than the average roadside attraction. On May 26, 1930, it became the scene of the first recorded birth of a manatee in captivity.

"Miami's population today was increased by a 40-pound baby," a wire service reported, noting that the mother's name was Maggie Murphy. "The calf was born yesterday and attracted crowds to the aquarium when its arrival became known throughout the city."

The joy over Sunny, as the calf was named, didn't last long. In November 1931 an aquarium employee trying to transfer Sunny to another tank accidentally dropped the calf, killing it.

Because R. J. Walters ran a construction business that occupied more and more of his time, he worked with various partners in operating the aquarium in his land-bound ship. In 1947 Samuel Stout took over the job, although the record is unclear about whether he owned the aquarium or merely operated it. Either way, he renamed the place the Miami Aquarium Tackle Company. Today aquariums have gift shops full of colorful knickknacks to supplement the income from ticket sales. Stout's idea: sell tackle to the area fishermen. The organization's new letterhead even said, "Live bait our specialty."

Stout had no experience at running either an aquarium or a tackle shop. He had previously made his living manufacturing women's wear in New York, then retired to Miami.

"Running an aquarium was his dream," said his granddaughter Paulette Carr.

Stout and Walters apparently decided they needed a new manatee exhibit to replace Maggie Murphy. Following Fred Morse's law to the letter, they obtained a permit from Dade County and from the state Board of Conservation to capture one manatee, then went hunting.

In 1947, according to *Sports Afield* magazine, a fisherman working for Walters found a big manatee and harpooned it through its fluke, believing that to be "a painless and practically bloodless operation since the tail is all gristle." Once Walters's crew got the manatee on board, the magazine said, "she was soon eating out of her keeper's hand."

But then Stout and Walters discovered that the manatee was pregnant and didn't like being held captive.

"Two weeks after her arrival," the magazine reported, "she suddenly lost interest in her food. The aquarium feared that the delivery could never take place in the tank's shallow confines, so they decided to give her a break." They released the pregnant manatee back into Biscayne Bay.

In early 1948 they got another chance. One day, Mrs. Wallace said, the aquarium crew spotted a large manatee that was "in close to shore. Her back had injuries. . . . She had been hit. . . . A motor on one of the boats had left deep lacerations on her back."

The crew trapped the injured manatee with a net and dragged it into their boat. They hauled it to Bayfront Park, then somehow lugged their captive aboard the *Prins Valdemar* and lowered it into the largest tank on board, which was belowdecks.

"They had a hard time getting her down in the hold," Mrs. Wallace said.

Someone on the staff concocted an ointment for the manatee's injuries, Mrs. Wallace recalled, "and I would get in the tank and rub it on her back. She liked that. She took to my sister and I right away. We'd get in the tank and hug her. For a manatee, she was a beautiful manatee."

This particular manatee was also, like the first one, female—and pregnant, although no one realized it for some months. When the aquarium staff did figure it out, instead of turning the manatee loose, they kept it. They named it Lady.

On July 21, 1948, Mrs. Wallace recalled, "my dad called and told us the little one was on the way. We knew it was due but we never knew when. When he knew she was giving birth, he called my sister and I. We came down because we wanted to see this new baby. He was such a little fella in comparison to his mom."

The calf turned out to be just as affectionate as Lady, Mrs. Wallace said. When she and her sister would climb into the tank—something none of the tourists could do, only the aquarium staff—"both liked to be loved and petted. They liked to give kisses."

The story Mrs. Wallace tells doesn't match up to the family stories that Paulette Carr has heard about Lady's calf. A story that ran in the *Miami Herald* when Stout died said Lady had no interest in the newborn calf, so he put the little one—then named Baby—into a separate tank. Stout said he put a cot next to Baby's tank so he could care for the calf around the clock. He said he refused to exhibit Baby until it was old enough to eat lettuce.

No matter which story is true, one thing is certain: for some reason, the Miami Aquarium did not announce the birth of this calf the way it had trumpeted the news about Sunny.

On June 25, 1949, about a month after Joe Moore started his new job at Everglades National Park, the pioneering biologist drove to Miami to see Lady. In a subsequent scientific paper, he cited Lady as an example of how manatees were smarter than most people assumed. He noted that Lady "came at call, rolled over, and curled its tail up to thrust the tip into the air. Each of these acts was separately requested by voice and gesture and rewarded with a lettuce leaf." According to a subsequent *Miami Herald* story, Lady's training was Stout's handiwork.

Moore just missed seeing Lady's calf do the same stunts. By the time he arrived, Lady was alone in the tank again, thanks to a manatee-related crisis on the other side of the state.

•

If you believe the historical marker on the grounds of the Manatee County Courthouse in Bradenton, Spanish explorer Hernando de Soto and his conquistadors first waded ashore there at the mouth of the Manatee River in 1539. If they were hungry, they might have captured a manatee and cooked some steaks.

You might think nobody would claim to be the starting point for a disastrous four-year search for gold through what would become the southeastern United States. De Soto's journey was so arduous that it would result in the leader's own death, not to mention the accidental extirpation of entire tribes of natives who had no immunity to the diseases brought by the white men. Yet there are a surprising number of other claimants around Florida for de Soto's starting point. However, only Manatee County has a National Park Service site to commemorate de Soto's landing.

Consequently, the annual De Soto Heritage Festival is a big deal in Bradenton, a spring fling that celebrates not only the landing by a bunch of heavily armed men in hot metal armor but also the subsequent settling of the region by Josiah Gates in 1842. The early settlers named the county after "the gentle sea cow, or Manatee, seen so frequently in the area's numerous waterways," according to the Manatee Chamber of Commerce.

The 1949 "De Soto Celebration," as it was known then, promised to be a really big postwar extravaganza. There was one problem. Nobody could find any of the county's namesake animals to put on display.

The Bradenton Chamber of Commerce, which organized the festival, had obtained a permit to catch one, but with just a week to go before the March 22 start of the celebration, no one could locate a single sea cow in local waters. They were apparently not quite as numerous as they had been in 1842.

"Our name will be MUD without the Manatee," one of the festival's organizers, a Bradenton real estate agent named Walter S. Hardin, wrote to a Miami politician who had offered to help.

The Miami politico, state senator R. Bunn Gautier, would later gain fame as the sponsor for bills that created Everglades National Park and the Florida Turnpike. The pipe-smoking Hardin, who would go on to become president of the state Board of Realtors, wanted Gautier's help persuading the Dade County Commission to grant Stout a permit to catch a manatee in Miami for Manatee County.

"After conferring with the County Commissioners," Senator Gautier replied, "they agreed to give Mr. Stout a permit to catch a Manatee for the purpose of displaying it in your county. . . . [Y]ou are definitely getting a Manatee for your celebration, and I hope the affair is a big success."

The senator offered one word of caution about Stout, however: "I was advised that his tactics in trying to catch the Manatee were not in accord with the Conservation Agent."

The *Sports Afield* story about harpooning had come back to haunt the Miami Aquarium, thanks to the Bradenton chamber's publicity man, T. L. Chryst, a Bradenton city councilman. He told reporters that Stout was going to catch Manatee County's manatee by harpooning it. Hardin later wrote someone that Chryst's reasoning went like this: "it being his thought that in developing interest in the exhibition of the Manatee, that it would make a more complete story to outline some procedure for capturing a sea cow."

When that story hit the papers, though, the Humane Society of Greater Miami and the Audubon Society protested such cruel treatment. This produced what the *Bradenton Herald* later called "a week of comic opera conflict."

Chryst didn't exactly apologize for stirring up the hoopla, explaining that "for our purposes this kind of publicity was fine." In fact, he condemned the Humane Society and "all such busybody organizations" that "decided to get their name in the papers with a great hullabaloo about protecting the manatees in the Miami River"—even though he had told the harpoon story for the sole purpose of getting Manatee County's name in the paper.

The Audubon and Humane Society complaints got the attention of the state conservation board, as Senator Gautier had warned. What really had the board upset, though, was not the harpooning. It was what appeared to be a clear violation of Stout's capture permit.

Just as the De Soto Festival got into full swing, helped along by the manatee that Stout had provided, the state board's supervisor, George Vathis, fired off a letter to Hardin via air mail. The letter said that the permit issued to Stout "has caused this department quite a bit of criticism and unfavorable publicity. It has been reported to this office that Mr. Samuel Stout of the Miami Aquarium . . . captured *two* Manatees or Sea Cows. . . . Of course you understand that your permit read for only *one* Manatee or Sea Cow to be taken."

Vathis ordered that as soon as the festival ended—which would be the next day—both of Stout's manatees should be "returned to the waters of Dade County (from where they were taken)" with the local conservation agent there as a witness.

Hardin, when he thanked Senator Gautier for his help getting the permit, said the harpooning controversy had actually helped the festival: "Certainly agree that the harpoon angle was unfortunate, for actually we understand that

Stout does not use a harpoon. However, considerable publicity was given, both to Miami and Dade County, and Bradenton and Manatee County."

But in replying to Vathis, the conservation board boss, Hardin took a humbler tone. He apologized for subjecting the board to any unfavorable publicity, adding that "any criticism that has arisen was due to misinformation and lack of understanding."

Hardin said Stout never harpooned any manatees for the celebration. Instead, he explained, the manatee they had displayed in a small concrete tank near the city pier was "approximately nine months old, and was born in captivity."

Therefore, Stout had not captured two manatees, just one pregnant one, he pointed out. Besides, Hardin told Vathis, putting Baby on display had proved to have "great educational value toward conservation. We still have a few in the Manatee River, but so many of our local people had never seen a Manatee, and when they did see one, they would probably try to shoot or harpoon it. However, now that they have seen one and realize that they are harmless—well, it's just good education."

According to Chryst the publicity man, Baby "gave pleasure to thousands of people who had a chance for the first time to see the animal this country was named for. It was a great favorite with children and hundreds of them petted it, fed it lettuce, and watched it roll over in a trick Mr. Stout had taught it."

When the festival was over, Stout picked up Baby and brought the calf back to the Miami Aquarium and to its mother, Lady. But the hullabaloo over harpooning had exacerbated permitting and financial problems already facing the aquarium-cum-tackle shop. City officials, who leased the *Prins Valdemar* its spot on the bayfront, considered the ship an eyesore they wanted to get rid of. Stout had proved such a poor businessman that he usually failed to show much profit.

Meanwhile, Vathis kept insisting that Stout's permit allowed him to keep only one manatee. Baby would have to be released back into Biscayne Bay. However, Stout feared that Baby had become too domesticated to live in the wild.

"If I had to turn that baby out into the bay now, it would die. It wouldn't know how to feed itself," he told the *Miami Herald*.

His solution: donate Baby to Manatee County permanently. All he wanted in return was to be reimbursed seventy-five dollars for the cost of trucking the calf back across Florida. The state conservation board approved Stout's idea.

Only then did anyone think to ask Manatee County officials if they wanted a full-time manatee mascot.

"Bradenton learned with some consternation today that it owns a sea cow," the *Bradenton Herald* reported on April 1, 1949. Four days later, though, Hardin wrote to Stout to accept the offer, explaining that city and county officials just needed time to figure out where to put their new municipal pet.

"At the moment sentiment is to install a tank inside the Chamber of Commerce Pier building and in that portion of the building now being used by the South Florida Museum," he wrote.

And that's what they did. The deal didn't trouble Miami officials at all, although the *Miami Herald*, in writing about Baby's imminent departure on April 29, 1949, conceded, "The youngster probably has an inferiority complex by now, the way she has been treated in recent months."

As for Stout, he claimed to be satisfied, despite losing such a star attraction from his aquarium: "I'm the happiest man in Miami because I am responsible for making thousands of people happy."

Manatee County's official mascot proved to be a continuing draw for tourists. They especially loved the tricks it could do. On April 15, 1950, after Baby had been living in Bradenton for about a year, Joe Moore drove over to see Lady's offspring at the South Florida Museum. In the same 1951 paper where he discussed Lady's performance, he mentioned the tricks the youngster had been taught by Stout as another example of how smart manatees are.

The two-year-old "came at call, rolled over, swam away toward the far end of the pool and back, offered its right flipper to shake hands, and reared up against the side of the pool standing on the ventral surface of its tail and holding its body 6 inches clear of the wall by means of its flippers, to 'rub noses' with its keeper. This meant thrusting its head about 18 inches above the surface of the water. . . . Each act was separately called for by voice and motion and rewarded with a lettuce leaf."

By the time Moore visited Baby, the Miami Aquarium had closed because of pressure from city officials. R. J. Walters accepted a refund of his seventy-five-hundred-dollar bond for leasing the site and agreed to let the city demolish the *Prins Valdemar*.

Some of the exhibits were shipped to other aquariums and museums, according to Walters's daughter. But the *Miami Herald* reported that many were simply released into the bay, with a sad-eyed Sam Stout looking on. Among the creatures the *Herald* said Stout had to turn loose into Biscayne Bay to take their chances with the pollution and the speeding boats: Lady, Baby's mother.

It's possible Lady joined the herd of manatees that Joe Moore studied on cold mornings from the Miami Avenue bridge, but no one knows for sure. R. J. Walters went on with his construction business. Stout went back to making women's wear, but he never really got over losing the aquarium, his granddaughter said.

The last remnant of the Miami Aquarium's menagerie remained in Bradenton. At some point, Manatee's manatee underwent a gender reassignment. Stout had somehow decided the calf was a female, so for the longest time that was what people in Manatee County thought too, until someone figured out it was actually a male.

The name changed too, going from "Baby" to "Baby Snoots" and finally, around 1970, becoming just plain "Snooty." There are several theories about where that name came from. One says that it's derived from Baby Snooks, a popular radio show character of the day. Another, which is endorsed by R. J. Walters's daughter, is that it came from how the calf would use its little snout to push things around. One way or the other, though, the manatee that is the official symbol of Manatee County came to be known as Snooty.

Snooty's continued survival became important to everyone in Manatee County. When Snooty caught the flu in 1967, it made headlines. In 1973, a clumsy tourist dropped a mechanical pencil in Snooty's tank. Snooty swallowed it and became badly constipated for more than a week. The local papers reported that "his handlers say the blockage eventually will kill him. . . . If he dies, the museum will have lost its main attraction. Manatee County will have lost the embodiment of its name, and Bradenton will have lost the attraction listed first in many tourist guides."

But Snooty survived the Great Pencil Scare, and Snooty's keepers declared the animal was delighted to be so well cared for.

"You can't find a manatee in Florida waters today that hasn't been cut up by the blades of motorboats," the museum's director told a reporter in 1977. "He's well off here."

Year after year, Snooty showed off for the thousands of schoolchildren and tourists who paraded past the little concrete tank, especially the crowds that flocked to the museum every July to celebrate Snooty's birthday. Year after year, Snooty kept surprising the audience by performing Sam Stout's tricks—rolling over for a treat, for instance.

Joe Moore wasn't the last manatee scientist to visit. In 1963, when Snooty was fifteen, Buddy Powell's parents brought their eight-year-old son to see Snooty. Decades later, Powell retained a vivid memory of standing on tiptoe to peer down into the water and see this mysterious creature that he still feared.

Woodie Hartman stopped by Snooty's tank in 1968. "I remember Snooty's keeper showing me some rudimentary Pavlovian tricks he could perform in his small circular tank," Hartman recalled in an e-mail decades later, "and voicing his embarrassment at Snooty's frequent 'auto-erotic' habits . . . in front of visitors."

Pat Rose visited Snooty sometime in the late 1960s while on a break from college. The edge of the tank had been built low enough that bolder visitors could reach down and touch Snooty. Frequently the star manatee would climb up on the edge of the tank and face the adoring audience. On this day, Snooty climbed onto the ledge and put a flipper over Rose's arm, then slid back into the water. A somewhat shaken Rose left with the distinct impression that the manatee had tried to pull him in.

"I think he was lonely," Rose said.

In the late 1970s, Snooty's visitors included Cathy Beck and Bob Bonde, fresh from California and looking for live manatees they could study to learn about the anatomy of the dead ones they were collecting. Snooty was the perfect specimen: not a single mark from a passing boat, lungs untouched by Red Tide toxins, never short of food, never affected by freezing temperatures.

On the other hand, that ten-by-eighteen-foot tank in the museum didn't give Snooty a lot of swimming room. And as Rose pointed out, despite seeing thousands of human faces every year, Snooty saw not a single other manatee.

The price for Snooty remaining perfect: celibacy and solitude.

•

Over the years, other manatees made the nightly news by showing up in unexpected places, like the one from Port Everglades that Tom Pitchford encountered in Virginia, leading him to move to Florida. Roving manatees showed up in the Bahamas and wandered over to the Texas coast. The most famous wanderer, Chessie, popped up in the Chester River on Maryland's eastern shore. Brought back to Florida, Chessie persisted in returning to the North, going as far as Rhode Island and garnering national headlines.

Year after year, though, Snooty stayed put, an unchanging example of the classic American roadside attraction. The passage of the Marine Mammal Pro-

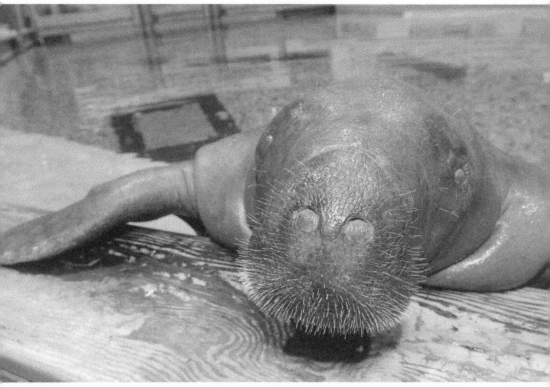

At age sixty, Snooty is the oldest captive manatee in the world—and still performing tricks he learned when Harry Truman was in the White House. Photo courtesy of the *St. Petersburg Times*.

tection Act and the Endangered Species Act had no impact on Snooty. Neither did Woodie Hartman's groundbreaking research in Crystal River. The Manatee Sanctuary Act, the creation of the Save the Manatee license plate, the deaths from Red Tide, the fights over the thirteen county manatee protection plans—none of it touched Snooty. If there were an animal kingdom equivalent to the lead character in the movie *The Big Lebowski*, whose motto is "The Dude abides," it would be Snooty: always the same, never different.

Then, in 1991, the year Snooty turned forty-three, some people started talking about making big changes in Snooty's life. Up until then, Snooty had been as solitary as Charlie Crist. But now the Save the Manatee Club—on the verge of breaking free from the Audubon Society and the state—demanded the museum move Florida's best-known manatee to Citrus County.

Judith Vallee wanted to turn Snooty loose in a much larger tank in the Homosassa Springs Wildlife State Park, where the middle-aged male could meet seven breeding-age females named Rosie, Amanda, Ariel, Best, Star, Adair, and Lydia, and possibly reproduce.

Snooty's solitary captivity is "the most depressing manatee story around," Vallee told the *St. Petersburg Times.* "Manatees are not domesticated animals. . . . I just think it's a tragedy."

Vallee urged club members to bombard Manatee County officials with letters about Snooty. "From Fremont, Calif., to Ten Mile, Tenn., the club's members have responded in force, flooding City Hall and the Manatee County Commission with letters," the *Orlando Sentinel* wrote.

One letter cited by the paper, written by a fifteen-year-old Massachusetts girl, told local officials, "Try for once to think of something other than your pocketbooks."

Vallee recruited the Humane Society—eight years before the two organizations would join forces to sue the state and federal government—to press the case for giving Snooty a chance to sire some offspring. But Manatee County resisted. New York had its Statue of Liberty, San Francisco its Golden Gate Bridge, St. Louis the Arch. Would anyone ask those cities to give up their symbols?

Snooty's chief keeper at the time, Carol Audette, warned that moving Snooty in with other manatees after so many decades alone might actually be bad for him.

"He's so acclimated to people," she said. "That's all he knows. His whole life people have been caring for him. . . . It's like having a pet."

Because Bradenton had acquired Snooty before either the Endangered Species Act or the Marine Mammal Protection Act had been passed, it turned out there was little all those letter writers could do to gain Snooty's freedom. Vallee's liberation campaign sputtered to a stop.

Snooty did eventually get some companions. By 1993 the museum had built a much bigger tank, sixty thousand gallons, big enough for three manatees. In 1998, a few months before Snooty turned fifty, the federal government granted permission for another manatee to join the show.

The manatee that finally shattered Snooty's solitude was another male, a four-and-a-half-year-old from the Miami Seaquarium named Newton. Newton had been found in July 1993 in a Miami inlet, a seven-day-old calf dehydrated and starving—in short, an orphan on the verge of becoming a statistic.

Getting Newton to eat had required bottle feeding around the clock, which meant the calf had gotten far too comfortable around people.

As a result, Seaquarium officials considered Newton too tame to cut it in the wild, and the orphan stayed in their tanks for more than four years. But now they needed to move Newton out to make room for more recently injured Miami manatees in need of treatment, and the South Florida Museum eagerly accepted the gift.

After some initial hesitation, the two manatees became like brothers. Snooty alone had been eating 60 pounds of lettuce, cabbage, broccoli, sweet potatoes, carrots, and apples a day. Adding Newton required boosting the feedings to 150 pounds a day. They frequently ate side by side, like a pair of Early Bird Special customers bellying up to the counter in their favorite diner. But Snooty kept the spotlight, not only by virtue of seniority but also because Sam Stout wasn't around to teach the new kid any tricks.

Seven months later, on a Saturday afternoon in August 1998, aquarium employees noticed that Newton seemed sluggish, hanging back while Snooty entertained the crowd. After the 4 p.m. show, they noticed Newton hadn't surfaced for air in quite a while, and didn't appear to be moving at all. Alarmed, they hauled the manatee out.

Newton was dead. Pitchford's crew at the necropsy lab found that a recurring bacterial infection in Newton's shoulder had suddenly spread throughout the manatee's blood system.

"The bacteria, when it gets a chance to go systemic, kills quite rapidly," said Dr. David Murphy, the Lowry Park Zoo veterinarian who frequently drove down from Tampa to care for Snooty and Newton.

Aquarium staffers kept a close eye on Snooty, but their star attraction never got sick. The old boy did appear to miss having a tankmate, though. This time, though, solitude didn't last long.

Over the next ten years aquarium officials brought in a string of young manatees—nearly one a year—to keep Snooty company. Most were injured or ill, needing time to recuperate from what had happened to them before returning to the wild. Not one was brought in to breed with the aging manatee.

Every year the aquarium threw a big party to celebrate Snooty's birthday, the largest one-day event on the South Florida Museum's calendar. Hundreds of children made Snooty birthday cards, competing to see whose was best. Snooty got no cake, but the museum's manatee keepers fed him treats like strawberries and pineapple slices. Then a big crowd gathered by Snooty's tank to sing "Happy Birthday." Everyone wondered if Snooty would make it another year.

"Because Snooty is a geriatric animal," Dr. Murphy told the *Sarasota Herald-Tribune* after Newton died, "each day he lives, he is setting a record."

•

Two weeks before Snooty turned sixty, Buddy Powell met me in front of the South Florida Museum. The museum sits about a block from a marina on the Manatee River where signs warn "Caution: Manatee Area."

On this July morning the crepe myrtles were blooming to beat the band. As we walked to a coffee shop nearby, we had to push our way through humidity so thick it was like being wrapped in a wet blanket.

Powell seemed weary, his eyes tired. He had recently quit his post with the environmental group Wildlife Trust after seven years there. He had been trying to launch a new organization that would allow him to continue his scientific work, but so far he had been unable to raise sufficient funding. The Boy Wonder Biologist who had grown up to travel the globe studying sirenians, the man who had once headed up the manatee science program for both the feds and the state, one of the most preeminent marine mammal experts in the world, was at the moment unemployed.

After thirty minutes of chatting and looking at some old photos, we walked back, paid our admission, and climbed the stairs past an enormous set of megalodon jaws to see the Snooty Show.

We stood together on the upper observation deck with several other adults. Below us, on the lower deck, chattering elementary-age children craned their necks to see the star swimming in circles with its latest recuperating companion. Snooty looked good for sixty, probably the result of a healthy diet and plenty of exercise, not to mention lots of checkups from Dr. Murphy.

Powell said there were still people who wanted Snooty to have a chance to mate. After all, Snooty's genes dated back to 1940s Miami, back in Joe Moore's day. But it seemed highly unlikely anything would ever come of it, he said. Not even the Save the Manatee Club was clamoring for Snooty's freedom anymore.

"This is a situation that is unique," Pat Rose told me later. "And we're certainly not advocating we release him on his sixtieth birthday."

When the two women running the Snooty show asked for questions, a boy named Vince—a slender boy with shaggy brown hair who resembled a young Buddy Powell—raised his hand.

"Why do manatees have to watch out for boats if they hear danger?" Vince asked.

One of the women explained that manatees usually live in murky water, not mentioning why it's usually so murky.

"People are often driving too fast, and so people don't see them," she said in a slow, patient tone.

Another kid asked how long manatees live.

"We don't know with Snooty," the curator replied, which prompted a mild snort from Powell. "It's kind of just a waiting game," the woman added with a shrug.

The kids were part of a science camp the museum sponsored during the summer. The brochure featured a cartoon Snooty wearing a pith helmet and a Hawaiian shirt—a typical Parrothead outfit. Snooty had become not just Manatee County's mascot but a valuable fund-raiser for the museum. Someone dressed up in a Snooty costume for an annual fund-raising picnic by the river, and there was a ball in his honor as well. As a result, the museum had paid to have Snooty's name trademarked.

For a while Snooty's tank had a live webcam, so anyone with an Internet connection could watch him splashing around. Snooty also had a MySpace page, as if a manatee needed to do some social networking with other web-savvy mammals. But that turned out to be the handiwork of some volunteers who had failed to get proper authorization for using Snooty's trademarked image, so the museum told them to shut it down and then disabled the webcam.

Forget all that high-tech modern stuff, though. The old tricks still play best for the live crowd. One of the women conducting the show waved her hand, and on cue Snooty rolled over and took a carrot as a reward. The kids all leaned in close, their eyes wide.

After the show, Powell and I walked downstairs to the first floor, where a window in the side of Snooty's tank offered everyone an underwater view. The kids all trooped downstairs too, to sit and eat their lunches and talk about what they had seen. As Snooty swam back and forth past the window, the sight reminded Powell of another old manatee he had seen recently, as well as the mystery of how long manatees might live.

"I was in Crystal River last winter," he said. "Piety was there with a calf. That's a manatee I could still recognize from the early days with Woodie. It was a really moving experience for me. She was really one of my favorite manatees. I've got a photo of her as a calf, being suckled by her mom."

Snooty zoomed by the window again, and Powell spotted something that a casual observer would have missed—something that Sam Stout was probably responsible for, just like the tricks.

"His paddle," Powell said, pointing at Snooty's tail. "It's disproportionately bigger. He's a small manatee. He should be huge. It's probably because he was kept in such a confined space when he was young, so he didn't grow as much."

Nevertheless, Powell predicted Snooty could live another twenty years, long enough for an eightieth-birthday party.

"A lot of these creatures live longer than we think they can," he explained. He pointed out the example of Sadie, another of the Crystal River manatees that he and Hartman had studied. Sadie was probably the same age as Snooty—and unlike the star of the South Florida Museum's water tank, the old girl had spent all sixty years in the wild, dodging boats and algae blooms and harassing divers. Sadie had the shredded tail to prove how rough life could be in the wild. Yet like Snooty, Sadie knew how to abide.

"Sadie was a big female having calves in 1967," Powell said. "She was probably twenty at the time. It's just a testament to their ability to survive. Look at all the changes in Florida in the past forty years. They are incredibly resilient."

We chatted for a few minutes with the women leading the science camp, and watched as they quizzed the kids on what they had learned. Sure enough, the children remembered that Snooty ate lettuce, carrots, and potatoes and weighed thirteen hundred pounds.

"See?" one of the teachers joked. "Diets don't work."

Then Powell and I wandered back up the stairs to the front of the museum. I was ready to leave, but he wasn't. He stopped by the ticket counter up front to talk with the woman behind the desk. She handed him a clipboard and a pen.

When I left, Buddy Powell was applying to be a museum volunteer. He wanted to work with Snooty.

# Acknowledgments

BECAUSE THEY LOOK SO ODD, manatees tend to fascinate people. But what I have always found fascinating is the effect that manatees have on people. Quite a few of those people helped me get this book done, and I want to thank them all. Unfortunately, I don't have room for that, so I'll only single out a few.

Among the many who generously opened their files to me, foremost among them was Cathy Beck of the U.S. Geological Survey's Sirenia Project in Gainesville. Academic papers, newspaper clippings, photos—you name it, she found it. And she never got impatient with my many requests for help.

Larry Wiggins and Susan Markley helped me with the history and geography of Miami, a city I have visited but cannot claim to know. Similarly, my colleague Barbara Behrendt shared her tremendous expertise regarding Crystal River. Any errors about either place resulted from my carelessness, not theirs.

My good friend Craig Waters of the Florida Supreme Court did some crucial legwork for me on the records, such as they are, of the 1893 legislative session.

Many biologists spent time helping me understand the subtleties of their research. Particularly helpful were Bruce Ackerman, Bob Bonde, Tom Pitchford, and Jim Valade—but again, the conclusions I have drawn are my own, not theirs.

Alice Luckhardt and Paulette Carr very kindly shared with me their research into the history of the Miami Aquarium, even though they don't agree on what the evidence shows.

My colleagues Paul Jerome and Matt Waite proved invaluable in helping me turn some old images into a digital format that could be reproduced in this book.

My executive editor at the *St. Petersburg Times*, Neil Brown, gave me permission to plumb the archives of the state's largest paper for this book, for which I will be forever grateful. Also, researchers Caryn Baird, Angie Drobnic Holan, and John Martin aided me tremendously in tracking down some more obscure sources.

All the folks at University Press of Florida have been wonderful, particularly John Byram, Stephanie Williams, Nevil Parker, Michele Fiyak-Burkley, and Jonathan Lawrence.

Last but by no means least, I want to thank my wife, Sherry—not just for reading the manuscript and catching all the stuff I had missed, but also just for putting up with all the effort I had to put into this book. She's a true gem, and I thank God for her every day.

# Notes

*Author's note*: When these notes cite interviews, that means they are from interviews I conducted with the subject either while reporting on environmental issues for the *St. Petersburg Times* or while researching this book.

## Prologue: The Sirens' Song

*As the sun dipped* . . . : Author's personal observations; interview with Mike McCartney; Kim D'Agostino background from http://www.melking.com/agents_bio.php?id=58.

*At the back of* . . . : Description of meeting arrangements, the problem with the partition and the effects of the cold from interviews with Dave Hankla and public information officer Chuck Underwood, as well as author's observations.

*When Hankla finished* . . . : Author's observations; interview with Lindsay Harrington.

*Up front, Hankla's expression* . . . : Author's observations; interview with Cynthia Frisch.

*The manatee might seem* . . . : Jeff Brazil, "First Year of the Last Decade: A Special Report," *Orlando Sentinel*, December 16, 1990.

*The manatee's vaguely feminine* . . . : Hartman, "Florida Manatees," 343; for a comprehensive account of manatees' anatomy, life history, reproduction, and other biological characteristics, see Hartman, *Ecology and Behavior of the Manatee*, and Reep and Bonde, *Florida Manatee*.

*Manatees have been classified* . . . : For details on how manatees wound up listed as endangered, see chapter 4. Information on the difficulty of finding a Florida panther from the Florida Fish and Wildlife Conservation Commission's own longtime panther hunter, Roy McBride, who's been tracking them since the 1970s.

*But at the end of the twentieth century* . . . : Population figures from U.S. Census Bureau; interview with Bob Bonde.

*As with the duckbill platypus* . . . : The story about the false teeth comes from Barbara

Behrendt, "Two Homosassa Springs Manatees Moving to Epcot," *St. Petersburg Times*, April 5, 1988.

*The image of the manatee* . . . : The array of manatee-related merchandise is truly staggering, as anyone who has ever visited the gift shop at the manatee viewing center at Tampa Electric Company's Big Bend power plant in Apollo Beach can attest. On the NBC-TV network, *Late Night* host Conan O'Brien featured a recurring comedy sketch called "The Horny Manatee." The two murder mysteries are the award-winning private eye yarn, *Hour of the Manatee* by E. C. Ayres (1994), and *Naked Came the Manatee*, a comic tale put together a chapter at a time by a committee of writers including Dave Barry, Elmore Leonard, Edna Buchanan, Les Standiford, and Carl Hiaasen.

*Like dolphins and whales* . . . : Information on manatee mortality from http://research. myfwc.com/features/category_sub.asp?id=2241; information on manatees' bones, skin, and blood from interview with manatee biologist James "Buddy" Powell.

*The Lowry Park Zoo* . . . : Author's personal observations. For an exhaustive behind-the-scenes look at the operation of this institution, including further information on its manatee hospital, see Thomas French's nine-part series "Zoo Story," published in the *St. Petersburg Times* between December 2 and December 16, 2007, available at http://www.sptimes. com/2007/webspecials07/special_reports/zoo/.

*At least two-thirds* . . . : Estimates from Bob Bonde and Cathy Beck of the U.S. Geological Survey's Sirenia Project.

*In a cluttered classroom* . . . : My thanks to Lee Winograd (now Murphy) and her preschool class of three-year-olds at the Lutheran Church of the Cross Day School for letting me sit in and observe their discussion of manatees.

*After all, Florida has* . . . : To see the "Let Us Alone" state flag, see http://dhr.dos.state.fl.us/ facts/symbols/flags.cfm?page=2.

*More than a million* . . . : Florida Fish and Wildlife Conservation Commission, "Boating Accidents Statistical Report 2007," 3, http://myfwc.com/law/boating/2007stats/intro.pdf.

*As I covered Florida's war* . . . : Andrew C. Revkin, "How Endangered a Species?" *New York Times*, February 12, 2002.

*But that word* . . . : "Mermaid," *Encyclopedia Mythica*, available at http://www.pantheon. org/articles/m/mermaid.html; Shakespeare's lines about the mermaid are spoken by Oberon, King of the Fairies, in act 2, scene 1 of *A Midsummer Night's Dream*; "Sirens," *Encyclopedia Mythica*, available at http://www.pantheon.org/articles/s/sirens.html.

*The Sirens, however* . . . : Thomas Bullfinch, *The Complete and Unabridged Bullfinch's Mythology*, Modern Library Edition (New York: Random House, 1998), 224.

## Chapter 1. Sweet Water, Dirty Water

*In the 1980s, Miami* . . . : James Kelly, "Trouble in Paradise," *Time*, November 23, 1981. The 2006 documentary *Cocaine Cowboys*, directed by Billy Corben, offers an intriguing and even entertaining look at the era, thanks to interviews with police, prosecutors, drug dealers, and smugglers.

*It was also a remarkably* . . . : Wiggins, "Birth of the City of Miami," 5–6; R. M. Munroe and Gilpin, *The Commodore's Story*, 69–70, 79.

*Back then, one early* . . . : The settler was Kirk Munroe, quoted in Leonard, *Florida Adventures of Kirk Munroe*, 27.

*But that was all . . .* : Reilly, *Tropical Surge*, 71–72.

*"Panthers were still to be . . ."* : R. M. Munroe and Gilpin, *The Commodore's Story*, 82. Ralph Munroe, a boat builder and amateur photographer, and Kirk Munroe, a children's book author, were both northern transplants who settled in Coconut Grove in the 1880s. Although they became friends, they were not related.

*While the tourists might . . .* : Cory, *Hunting and Fishing in Florida*, 24–26; LeBaron, "The Manatee, or Sea Cow"; Canova, *Life and Adventures*, 82–83.

*Those South Florida pioneers . . .* : M. B. Munroe, "Pioneer Women of Dade County," 52.

*In late 1884, a swell named . . .* : Blackman, *Miami and Dade County*, 125–26; *Makers of America (Florida Edition*, 121–22; Rerick, *Memoirs of Florida*, 630; Gilpin, "To Miami, 1890 Style," 91; Wilson, "We Choose the Sub-Tropics," 23; in 1880 the U.S. Census Bureau pegged Florida's population at 269,493, while the population of Boston was 362,839, according to the 1884 Fifteenth Annual Report of the Massachusetts Bureau of Labor Statistics, available at http://historymatters.gmu.edu/d/5753/.

*Still, the area had its . . .* : R. M. Munroe and Gilpin, *The Commodore's Story*, 79.

*Morse could see the sort . . .* : "Frederick S. Morse," *Florida Times-Union and Citizen*, South Florida and Christmas edition, December 1897; Blackman, *Miami and Dade County*, 125; Peters, *Biscayne Country*, 172–73.

*Now when boats landed . . .* : Wilson, "We Choose the Sub-Tropics," 20.

*Living in a land . . .* : R. M. Munroe and Gilpin, *The Commodore's Story*, 166–67, 169; McIver, "Boats on Biscayne Bay."

*The Peacock Inn was . . .* : Burnett, *Florida's Past*, 47–49.

*Because there were so . . .* : Kirk Munroe letter, "They Have Manatee in Florida," *New York Times*, September 13, 1891.

*An expert manatee-hunter . . .* : Gregg, *Where, When, and How*, 7; "From Florida in a Tank: Arrival of Largest Sea-Cow Ever Caught," *New York Times*, July 30, 1879; letter to the editor from C. H. Townsend, "The Aquarium's Sea Cow," *New York Times*, August 11, 1906.

*Dead manatees could double . . .* : LeBaron, "The Manatee, or Sea Cow."

*Scientists were so eager . . .* : Roberts, *Unnatural History of the Sea*, 5–15, LeBaron, "The Manatee, or Sea Cow."

*Some scientists speculated . . .* : True, "The Sirenians, or Sea-Cows," 123; Frederick William True Papers, Smithsonian Institution Archives, http://siarchives.si.edu/findingaids/FARU7181.htm.

*Some of Florida's settlers . . .* : Bangs, "Present Standing of the Florida Manatee."

*Even the tourists took . . .* : William Drysdale, "At Florida's Front Door: A Hasty Look at Jacksonville and Its Suburbs," *New York Times*, April 7, 1889.

*In 1892, a publisher put out . . .* : Wright, *Sea-side and Way-side No. 4*, 291–96; Wright background from Susan Mitchell Yohn, *A Contest of Faiths: Missionary Women and Pluralism in the American Southwest* (Ithaca, N.Y.: Cornell University Press, 1995), 32.

*Wright was not the only . . .* : K. Munroe, *Canoemates*, 284–92, available at http://freepages.genealogy.rootsweb.ancestry.com/~fassitt/canoe_mirror/munroe/munroe_00.html.

*By 1893, Morse, like many . . .* : Blackman, *Miami and Dade County*, 125–26.

*The legislature that year . . .* : Church, *Life of Henry Laurens Mitchell*, 83–85, 86; Barnett, *Mirage*, 18. I am indebted to Craig Waters of the Florida Supreme Court for his research into the conflicts and accomplishments of the 1893 legislature as reflected in the Senate and House journals in the supreme court's collection.

*On the first day* . . . : House Bill No. 295, *House Journal*, 1893 Legislature, pp. 451 and 1030; House Bill No. 295, *Senate Journal*, 1893 Legislature, pp. 1026 and 1175; "An Act for the Protection of the Manatee," chapter 4208, *Laws of Florida*, 1914, p. 144.

*Morse's manatee bill could* . . . : Gary White, "Florida Women Key to Forming Conservation Groups," *Lakeland Ledger*, March 5, 2004, available at http://www.everglades.org/030504.html; Dieterich, "Birds of a Feather"; Kirk Munroe, "A Forgotten Remnant," *Harper's Weekly*, November 21, 1891, reprinted in Leonard, *Florida Adventures of Kirk Munroe*, 163.

*There is another intriguing* . . . : Betz, "Sea Cow Deception."

*Whatever Morse's motives* . . . : "A Sea-Cow for Central Park," *New York Times*, May 7, 1896; *Miami Metropolis*, August 28, 1896, quoted in Chesney et al., *Miami Diary*, 130. One of the best early accounts of capturing wild manatees alive—complete with photos—is in A. W. and Julian Dimock's *Florida Enchantments* (New York: Outing, 1908), 29–59. The brothers waited until *after* they had successfully caught one to get the necessary county permit, but did not have any legal problems as a result.

*More than twenty years* . . . : David Fairchild (writing anonymously), "A New Food Mammal," *Journal of Heredity* 8, no. 8 (1917): 344. Fairchild's main purpose in writing this piece was to pass along an idea from famed inventor Alexander Graham Bell for creating a captive breeding herd of manatees to use "for an important food supply for Florida and the world. There is no reason to doubt that herds could easily be kept in the lagoons of Florida, as private property." Needless to say, this scheme, like the one proposed for Card Sound back in 1893, went nowhere.

*However, when wealthy playboy* . . . : Cory, *Hunting and Fishing in Florida*, 25–26.

*In 1894, Morse was* . . . : St. Augustine correspondent of the *Jacksonville Sun*, "Southern Part of Dade: Fred S. Morse Talks of the Biscayne Bay Region," reprinted in the *Tropical Sun*, November 29, 1894.

*Around this time Morse* . . . : Flagler's role in turning Florida into a tourist mecca, and Miami into a city, is well told in a number of books. I pieced it together from Gail Clement, "Everglades Timeline: Reconstruction Era Comes to the Everglades (1865–1900)," available at http://everglades.fiu.edu/reclaim/timeline/timeline5.htm; Henry Morrison Flagler biography, http://www.flaglermuseum.us/html/flagler_biography.html: R. M. Munroe and Gilpin, *The Commodore's Story*, 253–56; Wiggins, "Birth of the City of Miami," 23–26; Shappee, "Flagler's Undertakings in Miami"; Burnett, *Florida's Past*, 18–19.

*Morse himself died in 1920* . . . : "Well Known Miami Man Answers Call: Frederick Morse, One of Miami's Oldest Inhabitants, Is Dead," *Miami Herald*, July 3, 1920; R. L. Townsend, "To Frederick S. Morse, a Tribute," *Miami Herald*, July 18, 1920.

*In 1930, ten years after* . . . : Wilson, "Miami: From Frontier to Metropolis," 42; R. M. Munroe and Gilpin, *The Commodore's Story*, 83.

*Five days a week* . . . : Moore, "Observations of Manatees in Aggregations"; interview with Melliny Lamberson; "About the Author: Joseph C. Moore," *Everglades Natural History* 1, no. 1 (1953): 38; Moore, "A Mysterious Encounter," 7.

*After all, no less an authority* . . . : Moore noted Allen's inclusion of the manatee in "Status of the Manatee," 22.

*But Moore's new boss* . . . : Beard et al., *Fading Trails*, 96–97; Stephen Trumbull, "Sea Cows Making Comeback," *Miami Herald*, April 29, 1949, reprinted in *Audubon Magazine*, September–October 1949, 337.

*Despite Fred Morse's law* . . . : Moore, "Range of the Florida Manatee," 10–11; Moore, "Status of the Manatee," 23.

*Of course, as another Florida* . . . : Barbour, *That Vanishing Eden*, 166 and 98–99.

*But there were more intriguing* . . . : Moore, "Range of the Florida Manatee," 3–4; Barbour, *That Vanishing Eden*, 99; Bangs, "Present Standing of the Florida Manatee."

*Still, the Miami River seemed* . . . : The Miami River Commission's history of the river is available at http://www.miamirivercommission.org/river3.htm; Barbour, *That Vanishing Eden*, 166.

*A big reason for* . . . : Katrinka Vander Linden, "The Miami River: Past, Present and Future," 7, an internship report submitted to the faculty of University of Miami Rosenstiel School of Marine and Atmospheric Science in partial requirement for the degree of Master of Art, Miami, November 27, 1996.

*One of the first things* . . . : Moore, "Observations of Manatees in Aggregations," 2–3; Moore, "A Mysterious Encounter," 7–8.

*The first outboard boat* . . . : Bernard B. Redwood, "A Short History of Motor Boating," *Journal of the Society of Arts*, March 23, 1906, 512–20, http://www.lesliefield.com/other_history/a_short_history_of_motor_boating.htm; "National Marine Manufacturers Association Hall of Fame: Ole Evinrude," http://www.nmma.org/awards/?WinnerId=79.

*Just as the invention of* . . . : "Gar Wood Shatters Own Speed Mark," *Miami Herald*, February 6, 1932; Rex Saffer, "Gar Wood Goes Over Century Mark in Three Runs," Associated Press, March 20, 1931; George E. Van, "Powerboat King Gar Wood Dies at 90 in Miami," *Detroit News*, June 20, 1971.

*By the 1940s, Florida's* . . . : Beard et al., *Fading Trails*, 96–97.

*Just six months after Moore* . . . : Sprunt, "Mystery Mammal."

*Moore sketched an outline* . . . : Moore's sketches appear only in his final academic paper on manatees, "Observations of Manatees in Aggregations"; interview with Melliny Lamberson.

*In a tiny U.S. Geological Survey* . . . : Interview with Cathy Beck and tour of the U.S. Geological Survey Sirenia Project office in Gainesville; Thomas J. O'Shea, Lynn S. Lefebvre, and Cathy A. Beck, "Florida Manatees: Perspectives on Populations, Pain, and Protection," in Dierauf and Gulland, *CRC Handbook of Marine Mammal Medicine*, 33–35.

## Chapter 2. When Woodie Met Buddy

*Buddy Powell loved nothing* . . . : Interviews with James A. "Buddy" Powell Jr. and Pat Purcell; Crystal River history from http://www.crystalriverfl.org/index.asp?Type=B_BASIC&SEC={C17B62BA-C55F-4E93-B546-57022F60B2E5}; Hartman, *Ecology and Behavior of the Manatee*, 2; Allan, Kuder, and Oakes, *Promised Lands*, 292.

*There was only one thing* . . . : Interview with Powell; Powell, *Manatees*, 7.

*One day in 1967* . . . : Interviews with Powell and Daniel "Woodie" Hartman.

*The stranger's name* . . . : Interviews with Powell and Hartman; Eric Atkins, (headline missing), *St. Petersburg Times*, April 1, 1971.

*Hartman earned a biology* . . . : Interviews with Hartman and James "Jim" Layne.

*Most of the time, manatees* . . . : Interview with Hartman; Hartman, "Florida Manatees," 342. Jim Valade of the U.S. Fish and Wildlife Service, who has been studying manatees since

1978, told me the story about witnessing the manatee necrophilia incident while recovering a carcass. He also told me a much funnier story about something he witnessed during the inauguration of the manatee exhibit at Epcot's "Living Seas" exhibit in June 1988. Various dignitaries stood on a stage in front of the tank's glass wall to give speeches. During a speech by a Fish and Wildlife Service official, Valade said, one of the male manatees swam up to the wall and, to the amazement and amusement of the crowd, began masturbating. Apparently those flippers are good for more than just swimming.

*"It didn't take long for us . . ."* : Powell, *Manatees*, 8.

*The more Hartman watched . . .* : Interview with Hartman; Hartman, *Ecology and Behavior of the Manatee*, 126.

*He also saw visiting anglers . . .* : Hartman, "Florida Manatees."

*Having gotten acquainted . . .* : Reep and Bonde, *Florida Manatee*, 45; interviews with Hartman and Powell.

*Although the grant did not require it . . .* : Hartman, "Florida Manatees"; National Geographic Society history from http://press.nationalgeographic.com/pressroom/index.jsp?pageID=factSheets_detail&siteID=1&cid=1047675381100.

*By the time the story appeared . . .* : Interview with Hartman; "Wild Kingdom," Museum of Broadcast Communications, http://www.museum.tv/archives/etv/W/htmlW/wildkingdom/wildkingdom.htm.

*Cousteau first gained fame . . .* : Gordon Chaplin, "Jacques Cousteau, Drowning in His Own Legend," *Washington Post Magazine,* January 11, 1981, 8; Madsen, *Cousteau*, 130–43; Munson, *Cousteau*, 109–11; "Cousteau to Hunt Atlantis," *St. Petersburg Times*, October 8, 1975; "Sea People Predicted," *St. Petersburg Times*, October 10, 1964.

*Thanks to Cousteau . . .* : Gerald Jonas, "Jacques Cousteau, Oceans' Impresario, Dies," *New York Times*, June 26, 1997.

*Cousteau had become an avowed . . .* : Madsen, *Cousteau*, 163.

*In this battle of . . .* : Interview with Woodie Hartman; Nancy Lesnett, "To Study the Manatee," *St. Petersburg Times*, January 18, 1971.

*While they waited for . . .* : Interviews with Woodie Hartman and Buddy Powell.

*In 1969, a twelve-hundred-pound . . .* : Zeiller, *Introducing the Manatee*, 25–34; Associated Press, (headline missing), *St. Petersburg Times*, March 16, 1971; Nancy Lesnett, (headline missing), *St. Petersburg Times*, March 21, 1971; Eric Atkins, (headline missing), *St. Petersburg Times*, April 1, 1971.

*Titled "Forgotten Mermaids," . . .* : John J. O'Connor, "TV: With Cousteau and His 'Forgotten Mermaids,'" *New York Times*, January 24, 1972; *St. Petersburg Times* area TV listings for same night; "Cousteau Show Moving," *St. Petersburg Times*, January 25, 1972; all quotes from the show are from a videotape of "Forgotten Mermaids" that I purchased via amazon.com.

*By the time the show . . .* : Interviews with Hartman and Powell; Munson, *Cousteau*, 170. Powell notes that, since Sewer Sam's release, biologists have learned that captive manatees need far more than two weeks to be reconditioned to living in the wild.

*Powell and his college buddies . . .* : Madsen, *Cousteau*, 171; Munson, *Cousteau*, 111; interview with Powell.

*After the show aired . . .* : Interview with Hartman.

*So this time Hartman let . . .* : Interviews with Hartman, Powell, and Pat Purcell.

*Hartman and his helpers . . .* : Betty Alexander, "Research Finds Drop in Manatee Number," *St. Petersburg Times*, December 17, 1973.

## Chapter 3. Selling the Sea Cows

*Buddy Powell couldn't believe* . . . : Interview with Buddy Powell; editorial, "Slow, Manatee Crossing," *St. Petersburg Times*, December 31, 1978.

*Powell's mentor, Woodie Hartman* . . . : Rick Ballard, "Manatee Authority Seeks Practical Refuge Regulations," *Citrus County Chronicle*, January 17, 1971.

*But once America saw* . . . : Interviews with Pat Purcell and Buddy Powell.

*Five months after the Cousteau* . . . : Rick Ballard, "Manatee Refuge Sought," *St. Petersburg Times*, May 25, 1972; Betty Alexander, "Research Finds Drop in Manatee Number," *St. Petersburg Times*, December 17, 1973.

*Hartman's young protégé ran* . . . : Pete Wolfe, (headline missing), *St. Petersburg Times*, March 4, 1979; interviews with Buddy Powell and Pat Purcell.

*All these manatee fans needed* . . . : Interviews with Buddy Powell, Pat Purcell, Pearl Dick, and Helen Spivey; Miriam Cohen, "Kings Bay Boardwalk Draws Fire, Praise from Citrus Outdoorsmen," *St. Petersburg Times*, June 28, 1979.

*As soon as Powell heard* . . . : Kevin P. Mulligan, (headline missing), *St. Petersburg Times*, July 17, 1979; *Federal Register* notice, vol. 45, no. 220, November 12, 1980, pp. 74880–83; United Press International, "Conservation Group to Buy 14 Kings Bay Islands," *St. Petersburg Times*, December 16, 1981.

*Bob Dick had made his fortune* . . . : Interview with Pearl Dick; Jeffrey Good, "Activist Fights to Keep Developers Away from Unspoiled Waters," *St. Petersburg Times*, January 6, 1983; Ann Marie Laskiewicz, (headline missing), *St. Petersburg Times*, February 28, 1982.

*Over two years Pearl Dick* . . . : Interviews with Pearl Dick and Helen Spivey; Ann Marie Laskiewicz, "Fund Drive for Manatee Sanctuary Is Short of Goal," *St. Petersburg Times*, October 5, 1982.

*Spivey was the daughter* . . . : Jim Ross, "Helen Spivey Is More Than the 'Manatee Lady,'" *St. Petersburg Times*, November 20, 1994; Amylia Wimmer, "William 'Bear' Spivey, Spouse of Activist, Dies," *St. Petersburg Times*, November 18, 1997; interview with Spivey.

*Spivey and the Dicks had* . . . : Editorial, "North Suncoast Residents Should Support Drive to Provide Sanctuary for Manatees," *St. Petersburg Times*, February 24, 1982; Grunwald, *The Swamp*, 255–59.

*Soon, though, the drive* . . . : "Burt Reynolds Supports Drive to Buy Sanctuary for Manatees," *St. Petersburg Times*, June 8, 1982; editorial, "Don't Betray Our Manatees," *St. Petersburg Evening Independent*, June 12, 1982; Ann Marie Laskiewicz, "Residents Urged to Help Buy Islands for Manatees," *St. Petersburg Times*, September 1, 1982.

*By 1982, the drive had* . . . : Ann Marie Laskiewicz, (headline missing), *St. Petersburg Times*, December 16, 1982; Crystal River National Wildlife Refuge brochure, U.S. Fish and Wildlife Service, May 2001.

*How much had the fund-raising* . . . : Barbara Behrendt, "Manatee Fest Goes from Fundraiser to County Identity," *St. Petersburg Times*, January 12, 2001.

*Fifteen years later* . . . : Interviews with Buddy Powell and Woodie Hartman; Hartman, "To Save a Sea Cow." Powell's plan for Hartman to review the status of manatees twenty years after his book was published seemed at first like a brilliant move. "The original plan was for us to coauthor the report," Hartman said in 2008. "He would take what I'd written, flesh it out, and edit it." But Powell's state job "required far too much diplomacy and discretion" for the report to tell the whole story, Hartman explained, and before they could finish it, Powell quit. As a result, Hartman said, "the report became just another dust-gathering manuscript with no eye-opening revelations." Powell says he still hopes to someday publish an updated version. He very generously shared Hartman's original draft with me.

*Everywhere he looked . . .* : Interview with Hartman; Hartman, "To Save a Sea Cow," 23 and 49; Bridget Hall Grumet, "Sea Cow Souvenirs," *St. Petersburg Times*, January 11, 2002; author's personal observations during tour of Crystal River and review of phone book; tourist quoted in the documentary *Manatees: Florida's Gentle Giants* (George Stover Adventure Productions, 1999).

*"Today, if we did not . . ."* : Barbara Behrendt, "Manatees Mean Big Business," *St. Petersburg Times*, February 14, 2001; Barbara Behrendt, "County a 'Poster Child' of Manatee Protection," *St. Petersburg Times*, November 1, 2002.

*The annual Manatee Festival . . .* : Kim Gilmore, "Manatee Festival Still Hot," *St. Petersburg Times*, February 11, 1994; Barbara Behrendt, "Manatee Fest Goes from Fundraiser to County Identity," *St. Petersburg Times*, January 12, 2001.

*To Hartman, the transformation . . .* : Interview with Hartman; Hartman, "To Save a Sea Cow," 71.

*Just as Powell had once . . .* : Barbara Behrendt, "Winter Bringing Manatee Worries," *St. Petersburg Times*, December 18, 1999.

*The sanctuary had expanded . . .* : Alex Leary and Barbara Behrendt, "Federal Purchase of Springs Proposed," *St. Petersburg Times*, July 13, 2001.

*There were other changes . . .* : Barbara Behrendt, "Crystal River Sewer Plant a Sign of Change," *St. Petersburg Times*, December 3, 1992; Jim Ross, "Helen Spivey Is More Than the 'Manatee Lady,'" *St. Petersburg Times*, November 21, 1994. Spivey was the only Democrat in the United States to take what had been a Republican seat in the 1994 election, the year the GOP enjoyed a landslide victory across the nation. She served only one two-year term before losing to a Republican challenger, in an election in which Republicans took control of the state House for the first time since Reconstruction.

*While there were more . . .* : Barbara Behrendt, "More Boaters Taking to Water," *St. Petersburg Times*, January 23, 2007.

*And despite all the protections . . .* : Data on manatee mortality, including individual necropsy reports, from http://research.myfwc.com/features/category_sub.asp?id=2241.

*Then there were the divers . . .* : Hartman, "To Save a Sea Cow," 49–50; Barbara Behrendt, "A Meeting of the Minds on Manatees," *St. Petersburg Times*, March 23, 2007.

*In 2006, two former volunteers . . .* : Barbara Behrendt, "Manatee Petting: Just Good Fun, or Marine Harassment?" *St. Petersburg Times,* March 20, 2006; Barbara Behrendt, "Dive Tour Operators Feeling the Heat," *St. Petersburg Times*, April 6, 2006; letter from Timothy J. Ragan of the U.S. Marine Mammal Commission to Sam Hamilton, U.S. Fish and Wildlife Service, March 14, 2007; the YouTube video by Kingery and Colson can be viewed at http://www.youtube.com/watch?v=BbCPiD1NjeQ.

*Beyond what was happening . . .* : Interview with Pat Purcell; Southwest Florida Water Management District, "Crystal River/Kings Bay Surface Water Improvement and Management Plan," July 10, 2000, pp. 3–6; K. M. Hammett, C. R. Goodwin, and G. L. Sanders, "Tidal-Flow, Circulation, and Flushing Characteristics of Kings Bay, Citrus County, Florida," U.S. Geological Survey and Southwest Florida Water Management District, 1996, pp. 59–60.

## Chapter 4. Making the List

*As he waited his turn . . .* : Interview with Hartman.

*Hartman was scheduled to . . .* : Karen McPherson, "Dingell Marks 50 Years Representing His Michigan district in Congress," *Toledo Blade*, December 18, 2005.

*At last Dingell called . . .* : Statement of Daniel Hartman to the House Subcommittee on Fisheries and Wildlife Conservation, September 9, 1971, pp. 129–32, from the files of the U.S. Marine Mammal Commission; interview with Hartman.

*That Congress would even consider . . .* : "Lacey Act—Feather Trade," in Animal Welfare Institute's Endangered Species Handbook, http://www.endangeredspecieshandbook.org/legislation_lacey.php; Price, *Flight Maps*, 84.

*Gradually, though, the idea . . .* : Clark, Reading, and Clarke, *Endangered Species Recovery*, 19–21.

*Leopold's theme of valuing all . . .* : Beard et al., *Fading Trails*, ix.

*Rachel Carson's 1962 best-seller . . .* : Linda Lear, "Rachel Carson and the Awakening of Environmental Consciousness," http://nationalhumanitiescenter.org/tserve/nattrans/ntwilderness/essays/carsonf.htm.

*Federal biologists were not . . .* : Mann and Plummer, *Noah's Choice*, 150.

*A Pennsylvania native, Gresh . . .* : Interior Department press release, "Gresh Appointed as FWS Regional Director in Atlanta," February 3, 1954, http://www.fws.gov/news/historic/1954/19540203b.pdf; Interior Department press release, "Career Employee Named New Southeast Regional Director for Federal Wildlife Agency," September 25, 1967, http://www.fws.gov/news/historic/1967/19670925b.pdf.

*Gresh fired off a memo . . .* : I obtained copies of the September 2, 1965, memo to Walter Gresh from Lansing Parker, the September 20, 1965, letter from O. Earle Frye Jr. to Gresh, and Gresh's October 6, 1965, letter to Gottschalk from Jim Valade of the U.S. Fish and Wildlife Service. Regrettably, the original Gresh memo of August 18, 1965, questioning why manatees were not included in the Redbook, was not in Valade's file.

*Earle Frye was no . . .* : Spillan, "O. Earle Frye, Jr."; David L. Lansford, United Press International, (headline missing), *St. Petersburg Times*, July 23, 1973; Associated Press, "Sciences Academy Seats O. E. Frye as President," *St. Petersburg Times*, March 14, 1965.

*As for manatees, one . . .* : Moore, "Mammals from Welaka."

*Gresh's recommendation worked its . . .* : Parker, who apparently was not quite as concerned about manatees as Gresh was, died of a heart attack while hunting in October 1965. He was thus not around to object to adding them to the endangered list.

*Phillips had designed . . .* : Interview with Craig Phillips; Paul Davis, "Press Phillips Looks Back," *St. Petersburg Times*, June 2, 1961; Dick Bothwell, "Youthful Craig Phillips Building Brilliant Career as Naturalist-Illustrator," *St. Petersburg Times*, January 6, 1952.

*He named her Cleopatra . . .* : Phillips, *The Captive Sea*, 171–83.

*Decades later, Phillips said . . .* : Interview with Phillips.

*"According to Craig Phillips . . ."* : "Florida Manatee or Florida Sea Cow," Sheet M-22, January 1966, by Rare and Endangered Fish and Wildlife of the United States, U.S. Department of the Interior, Bureau of Sport Fisheries and Wildlife, from the files of Mark Plummer, coauthor of *Noah's Choice*.

*The first official endangered . . .* : Doc. 67–2758, *Federal Register*, vol. 32, no. 48, March 11, 1967, p. 4001; "Secretary Udall Names 78 Endangered Wildlife Species," Department of the Interior press release, March 12, 1967, http://www.fws.gov/news/historic/1967/19670312a.pdf.

*On the staff of Nixon's Council . . .* : Interview with Lee Talbot; Talbot biography, http://mason.gmu.edu/~ltalbot/talbotcv.html; Mann and Plummer, *Noah's Choice*, 159–62.

*When he arrived at . . .* : Interview with Lee Talbot; Weber, *From Abundance to Scarcity*, 100, 126.

*In December, Dingell's committee . . .* : Ninety-second Congress, Report no. 92-707, House Committee on Merchant Marine Fisheries, December 4, 1971, from the files of the U.S. Marine Mammal Commission. The Senate's Committee on Commerce issued its own report (no. 92-863) six months later, on June 15, 1972, which said manatees' future was "jeopardized by new forces—development, pollution, and watercraft."

*Talbot viewed the Marine Mammal . . .* : Interview with Lee Talbot.

*Once or twice a week . . .* : Interviews with Lee Talbot and Nathaniel Reed.

*"Nothing is more priceless . . ."* : Richard Nixon Statement on Signing the Endangered Species Act of 1973, December 28, 1973, from John T. Woolley and Gerhard Peters, The American Presidency Project, Santa Barbara, California: University of California (hosted), Gerhard Peters (database), available at http://www.presidency.ucsb.edu/ws/?pid=4090.

*Thanks to the idealistic Talbot . . .* : Mann and Plummer, *Noah's Choice*, 161–63; Weber, *From Abundance to Scarcity*, 129, 156–58.

*"The absence of information . . ."* : Weber, a former special assistant to the director of the National Marine Fisheries Service, made this statement in his book *From Abundance to Scarcity*, 157.

*The man the agents arrested . . .* : William Nottingham, "Man Will Admit Killing Porpoise If He Can Escape Jail," *St. Petersburg Times*, October 5, 1977; Frank DeLoache, "Man Who Shot Porpoise Gets Suspended Sentence," *St. Petersburg Times*, October 25, 1977.

*"The Fish and Wildlife Service . . ."* : Interview with Lee Talbot.

*The Tennessee Valley Authority . . .* : Interviews with Zygmunt Plater and Nathaniel Reed; Mann and Plummer, *Noah's Choice*, 164–75; Plater, "Endangered Species Act Lessons."

*In June 1978, the Supreme . . .* : The case is styled *TVA v. Hill*, 437 U.S. 153 (1978).

*While the snail darter controversy . . .* : Manatee mortality statistics from http://research.myfwc.com/manatees/search_summary.asp.

*The man Talbot had handpicked . . .* : Twiss's biography from the *Society for Marine Mammalogy Newsletter* 12, no. 1 (2004): 9; John Twiss to Lynn Greenwalt, March 8 and August 23, 1978, and John Twiss to Robert L. Herbst, assistant secretary, Department of the Interior, November 9, 1978, all from the files of the U.S. Marine Mammal Commission.

*Still, one of the big issues . . .* : Minutes of the Sixteenth Meeting of the U.S. Marine Mammal Commission, February 23, 1978, p. 25–26.

*Even better, the Florida Legislature . . .* : Interview with Pat Rose; Florida Manatee Sanctuary Act, ch. 78-252, 1978 Fla. Laws 725; Keith Rizzardi, "Toothless? The Endangered Manatee and the Florida Manatee Sanctuary Act," *Florida State University Law Review* 24 (1997): 377–405, available at http://www.law.fsu.edu/journals/lawreview/downloads/242/rizzardi.pdf.

*Rose was tall and gap-toothed . . .* : Interview with Pat Rose, who also shared a copy of his extensive résumé.

*Meanwhile, though, things . . .* : Rizzardi, "Toothless?"

## Chapter 5. Barnacle Brains and Parrotheads

*Bob Graham had a problem* . . . : Boyle and Mechem, "There's Trouble in Paradise," 84 and 93; Grunwald, *The Swamp*, 271–72; interviews with Estus Whitfield, Ron Book, and Bob Graham.

*Just in case anyone* . . . : Boyle and Mechem story reprinted under the headline "Florida's Booming to Some, but It's Bombing to Others," *Tallahassee Democrat*, February 11, 1981.

*The governor's own fourteen-year-old* . . . : Interviews with Bob Graham and Ron Book.

*When that February 17, 1981, concert* . . . : Buffett played two concerts in Tallahassee that month, with a day in between for the field house to play host to a basketball game. No one knows for sure which concert Graham and his daughter attended, but the second, on February 19, was on a school night. It seems a safe bet that the concert Graham took his daughter to was the weekend one.

*Florida's most famous troubadour* . . . : Eng, *Jimmy Buffett*, 12, 27, and 33; Eve Zibart, "The Peg-Leg Pirate with the Tunes of Gold; Humor's Key to the Songs of Jimmy Buffett; Jimmy Buffett: Humorist with a Sense of Song," *Washington Post*, July 13, 1978; Steve Persall, "Are You a Parrothead?" *St. Petersburg Times*, January 25, 1991; Richard Harrington, "Jimmy Buffett," *Washington Post*, July 11, 1980; Elizabeth Willson, "Making Millions in Margaritaville," *Florida Trend*, May 1991.

*At the end of January 1981* . . . : The LP of *Coconut Telegraph* was released January 31, 1981, according to http://www.amazon.com/Coconut-Telegraph/dp/B000W15CAA.

*Sometimes I see me* . . . : Lyrics from "Growing Older but Not Up," by Jimmy Buffett, reprinted by permission of Coral Reefer Music.

*After the concert ended* . . . : Interviews with Bob Graham and Ron Book; Eng, *Jimmy Buffett*, 220–21; Kelly Scott, "Jimmy Buffett Doing His Part for the Florida Manatees," *St. Petersburg Times*, March 27, 1981; Buffett testimony from *Save the Manatee Committee et al. v. Florida Audubon Society*, Seminole County Circuit Civil Court case no. 92-1019-CA-16G. I tried repeatedly to get an interview with Buffett, requesting access to him via both the Save the Manatee Club and his Margaritaville lobbyist in Tallahassee, Jeff Sharkey, with no success. Although he is a former journalist, Buffett tends to avoid reporters.

*Did Johnny Jones's criticism* . . . : Interviews with Book, Whitfield, and Graham.

*"I volunteered my services . . ."* : Buffett testimony, *Save the Manatee Committee v. Florida Audubon Society*.

*Just like Buddy Powell* . . . : "Rumble in Manateeville," *People*, May 18, 1992.

*"What we're seeing now . . ."* : Eng, *Jimmy Buffett*, 221.

*During their backstage chat* . . . : Buffett testimony, *Save the Manatee Committee v. Florida Audubon Society*; interviews with Graham and Book.

*But a few weeks after* . . . : Interviews with Book and Pat Rose; memo from Ron Book to Duane Bradford, April 14, 1981, regarding formation of the Save the Manatee Committee, and Book's notes from the meeting from Save the Manatee Club archives.

*That was fine with Buffett* . . . : Buffett testimony, *Save the Manatee Committee v. Florida Audubon Society*.

*Except, of course, it wasn't* . . . : List of original Save the Manatee Committee members provided by Pat Rose; "Buffett, Graham Join Forces on Save the Manatee," *St. Petersburg Times*, May 27, 1981; Michael Ludden, "Tallahassee Takes Note of Manatee Pal Buffett," *Orlando Sentinel*, May 27, 1981; Florida DNR press release announcing first Save the Manatee Committee meeting,

May 22, 1981, from Save the Manatee Club files; interviews with Bob Graham, Ron Book, and Pat Rose; Buffett testimony from *Save the Manatee Committee v. Florida Audubon Society.*

*Over the next twenty years . . .* : Eng, *Jimmy Buffett*, 216 and 313; Date, *Quiet Passion*, 237–38; Associated Press, "Singer Buffett Cheers Chiles on Environmental Record," *St. Petersburg Times*, October 23, 1994; interview with Ron Book.

*Over the next several years . . .* : "Group Seeks to Save Manatees," Associated Press, September 27, 1981; Eng, *Jimmy Buffett*, 222.

*Letters poured in from . . .* : Interviews with Pat Rose, Judith Vallee, and Estus Whitfield.

*Then, in 1984, Buffett came . . .* : Interview with Judith Vallee; Lynn Phillips, "Flood of People Want to Adopt Manatee," *Orlando Sentinel*, November 26, 1984; Steven Drummond and Barbara Behrendt, "Manatees Have Friends All Over," *St. Petersburg Times*, May 13, 1990.

*By the time the . . .* : Interviews with Pat Rose and Judith Vallee; Gannon, "The Last of the Manatees?" 24.

*Some of the older, more . . .* : Interviews with Judith Vallee and Charles Lee.

*In 1986, to raise money . . .* : Ed Birk, "Challenger License Plates Go on Sale in Florida," Associated Press, January 2, 1987; "Space Shuttle Plates Raise $5-million," United Press International, May 16, 1988; Dahlia Lithwick, "Poetic Licenses," *Slate*, February 6, 2003, http://www.slate.com/id/2078247/.

*Vallee could see what . . .* : Interviews with Judith Vallee, Pat Rose, and Pam McVety; Kevin Spear, "Manatee Plate Designer Pleased by Popularity," *Orlando Sentinel*, July 14, 1990; "A New Look for an Old Favorite," *Florida Wildlife*, January/February 2008, 18.

*One of the first people . . .* : Kendra Brown, "Singer Tags New License Plates to Save Manatees," *St. Petersburg Times*, March 13, 1990.

*Only later did Vallee . . .* : Bill Moss, "Manatee Battle Takes Shape as a Pirate Looks at Rebellion," *St. Petersburg Times*, April 8, 1992; interviews with Judith Vallee and Pat Rose.

*With the Save the Manatee . . .* : Clark, Reading, and Clarke, *Endangered Species Recovery*, 132; letter from MTAC vice-chairman Daryl Domning to Florida Department of Environmental Protection Secretary David Struhs, May 20, 1999.

## Chapter 6. The Breakup

*Jimmy Buffett never recorded . . .* : Description of Buffett and the scene at the Audubon protest from a photo by Joe Burbank of the *Orlando Sentinel* that appeared in *People* magazine, May 18, 1992, 89; William Booth, "Squabble in Margaritaville over the Manatee; Conservation Club's Fate Has Songwriter Buffett, Florida Audubon Society at Odds," *Washington Post*, May 3, 1992.

*"Bernie came here . . ."* : Interview with Judith Vallee.

*Yokel contended he was . . .* : Interview with Bernie Yokel; Booth, "Squabble in Margaritaville Over the Manatee," *Washington Post*, May 3, 1992; Bill Moss, "Manatee Battle Takes Shape as a Pirate Looks at Rebellion," *St. Petersburg Times*, April 8, 1992.

*As far back as 1987 . . .* : Interviews with Pat Rose and Estus Whitfield.

*In the meantime, though, Audubon's . . .* : Mary Beth Regan, "Audubon Board Agrees to Finish Battle in Court," *Orlando Sentinel*, May 18, 1992; interview with Bernie Yokel.

*Then, in 1989, came the first . . .* : Interviews with Pat Rose and Bernie Yokel.

*Gissendanner had been a veterinarian . . .* : Eliot Kleinberg, "Everglades Visionary Takes Another Shot at State House," *Palm Beach Post*, July 26, 2008; interview with Pat Rose.

*But in 1987, Gissendanner . . .* : David Ballingrud, "Florida Resources Official Is Indicted," *St. Petersburg Times*, June 23, 1987; Jon Nordheimer, "Top Florida Official Is Charged with Taking a Bribe in Drug Case," *New York Times*, June 23, 1987; digest item on Gissendanner sentencing, *St. Petersburg Times*, March 24, 1988.

*The Gissendanner scandal . . .* : Date, *Quiet Passion*, 156–81; Graham official U.S. Senate biography, http://graham.senate.gov/biography.html.

*To replace him in the governor's . . .* : Colburn, *From Yellow Dog Democrats*, 123–26.

*Rather than maintain the tradition . . .* : David Ballingrud, "Democrats Spring DNR Surprise on Martinez," *St. Petersburg Times*, June 3, 1987; Martin Dyckman, "Cabinet's DNR Caper: An Exercise in Florida Intrigue," *St. Petersburg Times*, June 14, 1987.

*Gardner turned out to have some . . .* : Diane Rado, "State Park Plans Are Developing," *St. Petersburg Times*, February 28, 1988; "Parks Official Resigns over Policy Dispute," *St. Petersburg Times*, November 29, 1988.

*Then there was the time . . .* : Diane Rado, "DNR Head Acknowledges Gifts, Scrambles for His Job," *St. Petersburg Times*, August 1, 1989.

*When top jobs came open . . .* : Charlotte Sutton, "DNR Chief Gardner Resigns," *St. Petersburg Times*, August 6, 1991; interviews with Pat Rose and Pam McVety; Associated Press, "Legislator Takes Job She Voted to Create," *St. Petersburg Times*, August 14, 1988; Associated Press, "Former Official to Pay Fines," *St. Petersburg Times*, June 15, 1991; "Utility Lobbyist Details His Dealings with Lawmakers," *St. Petersburg Times*, March 25, 1992; Lucy Morgan, "Ethics Charges to Stand," *St. Petersburg Times*, December 4, 1992.

*Gardner's methods for dealing . . .* : Charlotte Sutton, "DNR Chief Gardner Resigns," *St. Petersburg Times*, August 6, 1991; "DNR Chief Takes Over Manatee Protection Plan," *St. Petersburg Times*, October 14, 1988; interviews with Pat Rose and Pam McVety.

*Fortunately, Gardner's attention soon . . .* : Interviews with Pat Rose and Pam McVety; Jeff Brazil, "First Year of the Last Decade: A Special Report," *Orlando Sentinel*, December 16, 1990.

*Exactly what happened next . . .* : Interviews with Bernie Yokel and Pat Rose; Mary Beth Regan, "Manatee Dispute Tied to Personal Friction," *Orlando Sentinel*, June 2, 1992.

*In the meantime, Rose . . .* : Interviews with Pat Rose and Pam McVety.

*At a spring 1989 meeting . . .* : Final Report, "Recommendations to Improve Boating Safety and Manatee Protection for Florida Waterways," October 24, 1989; Associated Press, "Manatee Deaths Rising, Cabinet Told," *St. Petersburg Times*, May 12, 1989; Jeffrey Schmalz, "Florida Seeks Boating Limits for Its Congested Waterways," *New York Times*, August 30, 1989; interviews with Pat Rose and Pam McVety.

*On October 24, 1989, they presented . . .* : Interviews with Pat Rose and Pam McVety; Tim Nickens, "Cabinet Approves Boat Speed Limits, Licenses," *St. Petersburg Times*, October 25, 1989; David Cox, "State to Let County Devise Own Manatee Plan," *St. Petersburg Times*, October 25, 1989; Final Report, "Recommendations to Improve Boating Safety and Manatee Protection for Florida Waterways," October 24, 1989.

*The plan won cabinet approval . . .* : Interview with Pam McVety.

*The target was broader . . .* : Interview with Bob Martinez.

*"Below 30 mph, high-performance . . ."* : Linda Kanamine, "Florida Boaters Resent Speed Limits," *USA Today*, March 4, 1993.

*"Look, you've got to put . . ."* : Jeff Brazil, "First Year of the Last Decade," *Orlando Sentinel*, December 16, 1990.

*Those heated exchanges could . . .* : Interview with Pam McVety.

*Rose's iron determination . . .* : This description comes from page 81 in a book by Tom McGill, one of the founders of Citizens for Florida Waterways. The title alone should suffice to give the full flavor of the prose: *The Florida Manatee Conspiracy of Ignorance*. It comes with an enthusiastic cover blurb from Representative Bob Allen, who made headlines in 2007 when he was arrested for trying to pick up a man in a public restroom, then claimed he had done so only because he was intimidated by the undercover officer because he was black.

*Rose, in an interview . . .* : Jeff Brazil, "First Year of the Last Decade: A Special Report," *Orlando Sentinel*, December 16, 1990. The Hopping quote comes from the same series of stories, a remarkably in-depth examination of the status of the dispute over manatee protection in that year.

*By far the strongest opposition . . .* : Craig Quintana, "DNR Wants Stricter Boat Rules," *Orlando Sentinel*, January 10, 1990; Craig Quintana, "Boating Speed Plan Hits Dead End," *Orlando Sentinel*, February 7, 1990; Craig Quintana, "Volusia OKs State Boat Speed Limits," *Orlando Sentinel*, February 9, 1990; Craig Quintana, "3 Foes Say Big John Has Said Enough," *Orlando Sentinel*, April 13, 1992

*But the battle wasn't . . .* : Craig Quintana, "The Issue of Manatee vs. Man," *Orlando Sentinel*, June 24, 1991; Polly Dean, "Hawgin' on the St. Johns," *Florida Game and Fish*, October 7, 2002, http://www.floridagameandfish.com/fishing/bass-fishing/FL_1007_02/index.html; for Highland Park Fish Camp see http://www.hpfishcamp.com; interview with Rick Rawlins.

*Rawlins launched a group . . .* : Rick Rawlins, "Boaters Are Battling Unreasonableness, Not Speed Limits," *DeLand/West Volusia Beacon*, November 30, 1994; Chase Squires, "Despite Setbacks, Boaters Continuing Speed Limit Fight," *Daytona Beach News-Journal*, March 21, 1992; Linda Kanamine, "Florida Boaters Resent Speed Limits," *USA Today*, March 4, 1993.

*Privately, the Save the Manatee . . .* : Interview with Patti Thompson; Chase Squires, "Despite Setbacks, Boaters Continuing Speed Limit Fight," *Daytona Beach News-Journal*, March 21, 1992.

*The controversy grew so nasty . . .* : Interview with Patti Thompson; Jeff Brazil, "Manatee Debate Fires Up Volusia; Hostility Includes Death Threats," *Orlando Sentinel*, May 22, 1991; Denise O'Toole, "State Agrees to Relax Boat Speed Limits," *Daytona Beach News-Journal*, July 16, 1993.

*While Volusia was the most contentious . . .* : Interviews with Patti Thompson and Pat Rose.

*In the state capital . . .* : Julie Hauserman, "A Lobbyist Not Afraid to Take On Manatees," *St. Petersburg Times*, April 23, 2000; Cynthia Barnett, oral history interview with Wade Hopping, July 22, 2003.

*When a legislator helped out . . .* : Martin Dyckman, "Tallahassee Arm-twisting," *St. Petersburg Times*, October 16, 1994.

*At the marine manufacturers' behest . . .* : Jeff Brazil, "Manatee Measures Make Waves," *Orlando Sentinel*, March 10, 1991.

*Meanwhile, top DNR officials began . . .* : Interviews with Pam McVety and Pat Rose.

*Yet the Save the Manatee . . .* : Interviews with Judith Vallee and Patti Thompson; Jeff Brazil, "Manatee Measures Make Waves," *Orlando Sentinel*, March 10, 1991; Patty Shillington, "Murdering the Manatees," *Houston Chronicle*, September 5, 1994.

*To keep an eye on the creation . . .* : Interviews with Patti Thompson and Judith Vallee, and author's tour of Save the Manatee Club offices, April 2003.

*When Governor Martinez ran* . . . : Colburn, *From Yellow Dog Democrats*, 133–39; Eng, *Jimmy Buffett*, 312; Tim Nickens, "Chiles Leaves Footprints in Many Parts of Florida," *St. Petersburg Times*, December 13, 1998; Lucy Morgan, "Mourning with Joy for a Life Well-Lived," *St. Petersburg Times*, December 17, 1998.

*Although a progressive on social issues* . . . : Julie Hauserman, "Cabinet Approves State Land Sale Plan," *St. Petersburg Times*, February 12, 1997; Julie Hauserman, "Nominee for Game Post Withdraws," *St. Petersburg Times*, April 29, 1997; interviews with Pat Rose, Pam McVety, and Patti Thompson.

*Gardner resigned from the DNR* . . . : Charlotte Sutton, "DNR Chief Gardner Resigns," *St. Petersburg Times*, August 6, 1991; Associated Press, "New Director Says She Can Handle DNR," *St. Petersburg Times*, December 29, 1991; David Olinger, "Protecting Business or the Environment?" *St. Petersburg Times*, July 28, 1994.

*Politics even affected personnel* . . . : Interviews with Pam McVety and Pat Rose.

*Wetherell and her deputies* . . . : Memorandum from Pat Rose to Virginia Wetherell, July 16, 1992; letter from Pat Rose to Philip Claypool of the Florida Commission on Ethics, July 15, 1992; letter from Florida Commission on Ethics director Bonnie Williams to Pat Rose, September 8, 1992, and attached Ethics Commission decision CEO 92-045, all provided courtesy of Pat Rose.

*Save the Manatee had become* . . . : Interview with Bernie Yokel.

*Once again, there are two* . . . : Interview with Pat Rose.

*But Yokel contends it was* . . . : Interviews with Bernie Yokel and Pat Rose; letter from Jimmy Buffett and Pat Rose to Bernie Yokel, February 25, 1991.

*But in February 1992* . . . : Mary Beth Regan, "Manatee Club Wins Ruling against Audubon," *Orlando Sentinel*, June 27, 1992; interviews with Judith Vallee, Bernie Yokel, and Pat Rose.

*Yokel changed the locks* . . . : Bill Moss, "Manatee Battle Takes Shape as a Pirate Looks at Rebellion," *St. Petersburg Times*, April 8, 1992.

*Allegations flew back and forth* . . . : Carol Joy Bice, "Better Together," *Orlando Sentinel*, April 26, 1992.

*They predicted that this fight* . . . : Charles Jaco, "Singer Buffett Wrangles with Audubon over Sea Creature," CNN transcript, May 28, 1992.

*Buffett accused Audubon officials* . . . : William Booth, "Squabble in Margaritaville over the Manatee," *Washington Post*, May 3, 1992; Heather Dewar, "Big Bucks Breed Distrust between Buffett, Audubon," *Miami Herald*, April 12, 1992.

*Buffett hired two attorneys* . . . : Mary Beth Regan, "Audubon Official: Money Matters in Manatee Fight," *Orlando Sentinel*, May 29, 1992; Mary Beth Regan, "Audubon, Club Like Manatees but Don't Care for Each Other," *Orlando Sentinel*, May 8, 1992.

*While the battle raged* . . . : Interview with Patti Thompson.

*Under the circumstances* . . . : Letter to Save the Manatee Club from Melanie Waite, Gulf Breeze Middle School, June 9, 1992, from Patti Thompson's files.

*People with no love for* . . . : Rick Pierce, "Political Notes" column, *Fort Lauderdale Sun-Sentinel*, April 12, 1992.

*To make matters worse* . . . : Mary Beth Regan, "Manatee Dispute Tied to Personal Friction," *Orlando Sentinel*, June 2, 1992; interviews with Bernie Yokel and Pat Rose.

*"It was horrible* . . ." : Interview with Pat Rose.

*But money is the fuel* . . . : Mary Beth Regan, "Audubon, Club Like Manatees but Don't Care for Each Other," *Orlando Sentinel*, May 8, 1992; Mitchell Smyth, "He's in Love with the Manatee," *Toronto Star*, October 25, 1992; Buffett testimony from *Save the Manatee Committee et al. v. Florida Audubon Society*, Seminole County Circuit Civil Court case no. 92-1019-CA-16G.

*As a result, Seminole County Circuit . . .* : Mary Beth Regan, "Manatee Club Wins Ruling against Audubon," *Orlando Sentinel*, June 27, 1992.

*Months passed, and the case . . .* : Mary Beth Shanklin, "Save the Manatee Club, Audubon Society Make Up," *Orlando Sentinel*, March 19, 1993; interviews with Karsten Rist, Pat Rose, Judith Vallee, and Patti Thompson.

*Governor Chiles selected one . . .* : Interviews with Pat Rose, Judith Vallee, and Patti Thompson.

## Chapter 7. Flying Blind

*Lenisa Tipton stuck her head . . .* : Author's observations while riding with Tipton and Rich Castle on February 23, 1999..

*When Hartman, Buddy Powell, and . . .* : Interviews with Woodie Hartman and Buddy Powell.

*In 1976, a new team tried . . .* : Interview with Blair Irvine; Irvine and Campbell, "Aerial Census of the West Indian Manatee."

*Nevertheless, nine years later . . .* : Interview with Bruce Ackerman.

*But people in the boating industry . . .* : Herhold and Lowe quotes from Jeff Brazil, "State Tries to Get an Accurate Head Count on Its Manatees," *Orlando Sentinel*, January 25, 1991.

*Finally the DNR agreed . . .* : Interviews with Pat Rose and Bruce Ackerman.

*Marine-industry lobbyist Wade Hopping . . .* : Jeff Brazil, "Manatee Census Takes to the Skies," *Orlando Sentinel*, January 24, 1991; interview with Pam McVety.

*A month later, Ackerman's volunteers . . .* : Jeff Brazil, "1,465 Manatees Counted—Biologists Think This Is Right," *Orlando Sentinel*, February 20, 1991.

*Ackerman's crew flew another count . . .* : Interview with Bruce Ackerman.

*But in 1993, the temperature . . .* : Interviews with Bruce Ackerman and Pat Rose.

*Thanks to that mandate . . .* : Craig Quintana, "413 Fewer Manatees Counted," *Orlando Sentinel*, January 26, 1995; Craig Quintana, "Recount Finds 379 More Manatees," *Orlando Sentinel*, February 10, 1995.

*The basic problem . . .* : Interview with Bob Bonde.

*After every count, Ackerman . . .* : Interview with Bruce Ackerman and author's tour of his office.

*Perhaps, some scientists thought . . .* : Craig Quintana, "Manatee Study Stirs Controversy," *Orlando Sentinel*, March 14, 1994; interview with Patti Thompson; Miriam Marmontel, "Florida Manatees Are Still Endangered," *Save the Manatee Club Newsletter*, May 1994. For the final version of Marmontel's study, see Marmontel, Humphrey, and O'Shea, "Population Viability Analysis of the Florida Manatee."

*While Marmontel dealt with . . .* : Interviews with Pam McVety, Bruce Ackerman, and Brad Weigle; Tim Roche, "Things That Go Bump in the Night . . . ," *St. Petersburg Times*, May 1, 1996.

*"The numbers counted only . . ."* : Interview with Pam McVety.

*Ackerman himself, writing in 1995 . . .* : Bruce Ackerman, "Aerial Surveys of Manatees: A Summary and Progress Report," in O'Shea, Ackerman, and Percival, *Population Biology of the Florida Manatee*, 22.

"*Manatees have been so . . .*" : Interview with Bruce Ackerman.

*Then the manatee's advocates . . .* : Author's personal observations, verified by Patti Thompson and Bruce Ackerman. For one notable example of the use of "only," see Luis Lopez Portillo, "Waters Grow More Deadly for Manatees," *Fort Lauderdale Sun-Sentinel*, November 15, 1996.

*Then, in January 1996 . . .* : Elizabeth Levitan Spaid, "Florida Flap Over the Sea Cow Count," *Christian Science Monitor*, February 23, 1996.

*Rather than satisfying the boating . . .* : Craig Quintana, "Count Finds Lots of Manatees," *Orlando Sentinel*, January 13, 1996.

*Ackerman himself, buoyed by . . .* : Elizabeth Levitan Spaid, "Florida Flap Over the Sea Cow Count," *Christian Science Monitor*, February 23, 1996.

*Wade Hopping completely agreed . . .* : Craig Quintana, "Manatees Lumber toward Safer Status," *Orlando Sentinel*, February 23, 1996.

## Chapter 8. Growing Bananas with Curious George

*Florida's largest estuary . . .* : Description from Tampa Bay Estuary Program and author's personal observations.

*Bob Smith loved Tampa Bay . . .* : Interviews with Bob Smith and Pete Zuazo.

*A day later, the dead . . .* : Interview with Tom Pitchford; review of records at Marine Mammal Pathology Laboratory in St. Petersburg for field ID no. MNW0113; Save the Manatee Club press release, "Ragtail the Manatee Becomes the Latest Victim of a Boat Collision," March 27, 2001.

*Pitchford stood six foot one . . .* : Interviews with Tom Pitchford, Meg Pitchford, and Alex Costidis, and tour of pathology lab. Costidis gleefully showed me the video of the British television report, then e-mailed me the clip to enjoy over and over. I still have it on my computer.

*While Pitchford and other colleagues . . .* : Interview with Kristen Fick.

*Among the three hundred or so manatees . . .* : Interviews with Patti Thompson and Judith Vallee; Save the Manatee Club press release, "Ragtail the Manatee Becomes the Latest Victim of a Boat Collision," March 27, 2001.

*Pitchford was the fifth of ten . . .* : Interviews with Tom and Meg Pitchford; obituary, "Charles F. Pitchford," *The Virginian-Pilot*, December 10, 1996.

*Then one day a manatee . . .* : Interviews with Pitchford and Cathy Beck. Like Sewer Sam, PE176, the manatee that got Pitchford interested in the subject, has never been seen again.

*Back in Woodie Hartman's day . . .* : Interviews with Blair Irvine, Dan Odell, Cathy Beck, Bob Bonde, and Tom Pitchford; review of early necropsy records in files of the Marine Mammal Pathology Laboratory, St. Petersburg.

*Beck, Bonde, and a third biologist . . .* : Bonde, O'Shea, and Beck, *Manual of Procedures*, 48; Scott D. Wright, Bruce B. Ackerman, Robert K. Bonde, Cathy A. Beck, and Donna J. Banowetz, "Analysis of Watercraft-Related Mortality of Manatees in Florida, 1979–1991," in O'Shea, Ackerman, and Percival, *Population Biology of the Florida Manatee*, 259; Bruce B. Ackerman, Scott D. Wright, Robert K. Bonde, Daniel K. Odell, and Donna J. Banowetz, "Trends and Patterns in Mortality of Manatees in Florida, 1974–1992," in O'Shea, Ackerman, and Percival, *Population Biology of the Florida Manatee*, 224.

*Every day as he drove . . .* : Interviews with Tom Pitchford and Bruce Ackerman. One January day Pitchford and I met for lunch at a soul food restaurant called the Harbor Club in the Tampa neighborhood of Sulphur Springs. He and his staff had discovered that the restaurant overlooks a small spring bubbling up from under the Hillsborough River, where manatees often bask in the warmth. After polishing off a plate of pork chops, Pitchford began snapping pictures of a pair of manatees that had settled into the boil. Suddenly, the River Odyssey Eco-Tour boat sponsored by the Lowry Park Zoo rumbled up, scaring them off. Just as the manatees began easing back into the boil, the tour boat backed up until it was nearly on top of them. The manatees fled. Normally as mild as milk, Pitchford sputtered with outrage on the ride back to St. Petersburg. He called zoo officials to complain, and as a result the zoo's president fired off a letter to the tour boat operator, Sun Line Cruises, calling the captain's actions "unacceptable." The cruise line promised to be more careful.

*Statewide, the record for dead . . .* : Mortality records from http://research.myfwc.com/manatees/search_summary.asp.

*"If we have some kind . . ."* : Mike Frankel, "201 Manatee Deaths in 1995 Not Linked to Cold Conditions," *Tampa Tribune*, January 4, 1996.

*That year, Pitchford stumbled . . .* : Interview with Pitchford; information on Red Tide from http://research.myfwc.com/support/view_faqs.asp?id=13. It should be noted that the research done by FWRI expert Karen Steidinger on Red Tide has been so important that the species was renamed in her honor. It is now known as *Karenia brevis*.

*In 1982, Red Tide killed . . .* : David Olinger, "What Is Killing the Manatees?" *St. Petersburg Times*, April 9, 1996.

*Then, on the evening of March 5 . . .* : David Olinger and Jeff Klinkenberg, "The Manatees Are Dying and No One Knows Why," *St. Petersburg Times*, April 17, 1996.

*By mid-month, Pitchford had hauled . . .* : Interviews with Pitchford and Ken Haddad.

*By the end of the month . . .* : Craig Quintana, "Manatee 'Epidemic' a Deadly Mystery," *Orlando Sentinel*, March 29, 1996; David Olinger and Jeff Klinkenberg, "The Manatees Are Dying and No One Knows Why," *St. Petersburg Times*, April 17, 1996.

*CNN and* People *magazine ran . . .* : John Zarrella, "Mystery Epidemic Kills over 100 Manatees in Florida," CNN transcript, April 3, 1996; David Olinger and Jeff Klinkenberg, "The Manatees Are Dying and No One Knows Why," *St. Petersburg Times*, April 17, 1996; Marla Cone, "Epidemic Hits Rare Manatees," *Los Angeles Times*, April 11, 1996.

*By early April, the die-off . . .* : David Olinger and Jeff Klinkenberg, "The Manatees Are Dying and No One Knows Why," *St. Petersburg Times*, April 17, 1996.

*As the mystery continued, Pitchford . . .* : Interviews with Tom Pitchford and Ken Haddad.

*Complicating matters was the . . .* : Interviews with Tom Pitchford and Steve Klett; author's observations on visiting Crocodile Lake National Wildlife Refuge in June 2003.

*Toward the end of April . . .* : Interview with Tom Pitchford.

*Englewood and two other . . .* : Kathleen Beeman, "Manatees Dying Less Frequently," *Tampa Tribune*, May 2, 1996; Nanette Woitas, "Zoo Cares for Sick Manatees," *Tampa Tribune*, April 25, 1996; editorial, "Not-so-Mysterious Manatee Epidemic," *Tampa Tribune*, July 15, 1996.

*On May 13, Ginger Wetherell . . .* : David Olinger, "Manatee Die-off Appears to Be Over," *St. Petersburg Times*, May 14, 1996; Sue Landry, "Red Tide Caused Manatee Die-off," *St. Petersburg Times*, July 3, 1996; Linda Kanamine, "'Red Tide' Cited in Deaths of Manatees," *USA Today*, July 3, 1996; "Scientists Say Toxin in Red Tide Killed Scores of Manatees," *New York Times*, July 5, 1996.

*The Miami Seaquarium's veterinarian . . .* : Craig Quintana, "Manatee 'Epidemic' a Deadly Mystery," *Orlando Sentinel*, March 29, 1996.

*Some time later . . .* : Interview with Tom Pitchford.

*With all the worldwide attention* . . . : Luis Lopez Portillo, "Waters Grow More Deadly for Manatees," *Fort Lauderdale Sun-Sentinel*, November 15, 1996.

*The following year boats* . . . : Mortality figures from Florida Fish and Wildlife Conservation Commission's Web site; interview with Tom Pitchford and tour of the pathology lab.

*One of the most vocal critics* . . . : McGill's *Florida Manatee Conspiracy* drips with contempt for all of the state's biologists at the path lab, including Pitchford, referring to him and his staff as "biocrats," "butchers," and "second-rate scientists who employ junk science."

*Boaters even hired a retired* . . . : Interviews with Tom Pitchford and Ross Burnaman; Jim Waymer, "Judge Denies Boaters' Witness in Manatee Case," *Florida Today*, October 24, 2001.

*As with Ackerman's surveys* . . . : Interviews with Ackerman, Pitchford, Patti Thompson, and Jim Kalvin.

## Chapter 9. The Man in the Krispy Kreme Hat

*The twenty-two-foot boat* . . . : Author's personal observations while riding with Lieutenant Kiss and Officer Riley, March 2002; the photo of Deputy Erb appeared with Andrew C. Revkin, "How Endangered a Species?" *New York Times*, February 12, 2002.

*Federal wildlife officers patrolling* . . . : Interview with Special Agent Vance Eaddy.

*Yet enforcement of the laws* . . . : Letter from John Twiss to Lynn Greenwalt, March 8, 1978; letter from John Twiss to Lynn Greenwalt, August 23, 1978.

*John Burton, a wildlife officer* . . . : Jeff Brazil, "A Deadly Year for Manatees," *Orlando Sentinel*, December 22, 1991.

*In 1994 there were* . . . : Boat registration figures from Florida Fish and Wildlife Conservation Commission's Office of Boating Safety.

*One Connecticut couple* . . . : Jeffrey Schmalz, "Florida Seeks Boating Limits for Its Congested Waterways," *New York Times*, August 30, 1989.

*Although other states had* . . . : Comparative boating accident figures from Florida Fish and Wildlife Conservation Commission's Office of Boating Safety.

*Scientists at the state's marine* . . . : Ken Haddad and Frank Sargent, "Scars Under the Water," *The Florida Naturalist*, Winter 1994; F. J. Sargent, W. B. Sargent, T. J. Leary, D. W. Crewz, and C. R. Kruer, "Scarring of Florida's Seagrass: Assessment and Management Options," Florida Marine Research Institute Technical Report TR-1, 1995; interview with Ross Burnaman, author of seagrass memo.

*Lawyers and scientists weren't* . . . : Dave Barry, "Manatee Insanity: Brain-challenged Boaters Can't Steer Clear of Lovable Lugs," *Fort Worth Star-Telegram*, April 26, 1998.

*"Most people on the river . . ."* : Associated Press, "Legislators to Consider Boat Licensing, Speed Limits," *St. Petersburg Times,* October 29, 1989.

*"This is why people go . . ."* : Jeffrey Schmalz, "Florida Seeks Boating Limits for Its Congested Waterways," *New York Times*, August 30, 1989.

*"Why license people if . . ."* : Keith Morelli, "Fla. Boaters Log Most Accidents, but Operator Licensing Shunned," *Tampa Tribune*, March 31, 2003.

*Complicating the situation further* . . . : Patrick May and Trish Power, "Fast and Fun, Water Bikes Have Their Dangerous Side," *Miami Herald*, September 26, 1995; Rick Jervis, "Accidents Up along with Water Bikes' Popularity," *Miami Herald*, February 11, 1996.

*On the afternoon of Sunday* . . . : Wendy Melillo and Avis Thomas-Lester, "Howard Student Dies after Hitting Pop Star's Boat," *Washington Post*, September 25, 1995; Knight-Ridder Newspapers, "Estefans Not Negligent in Miami Boating Death of Barrington Native," *Providence Journal-Bulletin*, September 26, 1995; Patrick May and Trish Power, "Fast and Fun, Water Bikes Have Their Dangerous Side," *Miami Herald*, September 26, 1995.

*In the 1980s, when . . .* : Jonathon King, Stuart McIver, and Matt Schudel, "The 25 People Who Made Florida," *Fort Lauderdale Sun-Sentinel*, February 26, 1995; Peter Castro, "Little Glorita, Happy at Last," *People*, August 12, 1996.

*The crash upset Estefan . . .* : Rick Jervis, "Singer's Newest Gig: Safe Boating Lobbyist," *Miami Herald*, February 6, 1996; Larry Kaplow, "Estefan Urges Boat, Water Safety," *Palm Beach Post*, February 8, 1996; Diane Hirth, "Singer Advocates Safe Boating Bill," *Orlando Sentinel*, February 8, 1996.

*When she talked to members . . .* : "Gloria Estefan Leaves Legislators Tongue-tied," *Miami Herald*, February 8, 1996; Kit Troyer, "Political Support Goes for a Song," *St. Petersburg Times*, March 20, 1996; Michael Van Sickler, "Lawmaker Says a Song May Help Calm the Waters," *Florida Times-Union*, March 20, 1996; "Keeping a Promise," *Florida Times-Union*, May 21, 1996; Lucy Morgan, "For Them, Law on Boating Too Little, Too Late," *St. Petersburg Times*, May 27, 1996; Dantzler, *Under the Panther Moon*, 280–81; interview with Rick Dantzler; Michelle Genz, "Golden Girl," *Miami Herald*, May 31, 1998. In *Under the Panther Moon*, Dantzler identifies another senator as making the song request. However, all the stories about the bill signing identify King as the one to whom Estefan promised to sing "Cuts Both Ways."

*The Florida Marine Patrol . . .* : Ludmilla Lelis, "Many Boaters Ignore Manatee Signs," *Orlando Sentinel*, August 6, 1998; Susan Cocking, "All's Calm in Wake of Merger," *Miami Herald*, July 4, 1999.

*The state routinely spent . . .* : Interviews with Lieutenant Kiss and Officer Riley; Willie Howard, "Poor Pay Thins FWC Patrol Ranks," *Palm Beach Post*, July 7, 2002.

*Federal officers faced more . . .* : Sandra Cleva, "Enforcing the Law for Endangered Species," *Endangered Species Bulletin*, November/December 1999; Robert Bryce, "Protection of Wildlife Threatened," *Christian Science Monitor*, July 2, 1991; Jessica Speart, "War Within: Illegal Wildlife Traders and the Division of Law Enforcement of the U.S. Fish and Wildlife Service," *Buzzworm*, July 1, 1993.

*Every year, twelve thousand legitimate . . .* : Craig Pittman, "Struggling to Stop the Smuggling," *St. Petersburg Times*, September 5, 2002; Manuel Roig-Franzia, "Undercover to Bust Wildlife Smugglers," *Washington Post*, July 19, 2004; interviews with Terry English and Jorge Picon.

*Some deaths, like Ragtail's . . .* : Jeff Brazil, "Manatee's Death Causes Heartaches," *Orlando Sentinel*, March 7, 1993.

*Usually state and federal wildlife . . .* : Interviews with Dan Odell, Tom Pitchford, Cathy Beck, Bob Bonde, and Blair Irvine.

*Even when the killer's identity . . .* : Jeff Brazil, "First Year of the Last Decade: A Special Report," *Orlando Sentinel*, December 16, 1990.

*Occasionally, state or federal . . .* : Press release, "Broward Men Sentenced to Prison for Illegal Attempt to Harass, Capture, and Kill Protected Manatee," U.S. Attorney's Office for the Southern District of Florida, January 18, 2008; "Men Sentenced to Prison Time for Abusing Manatee," Associated Press, January 19, 2008.

*Through the first half . . .* : Author's personal experiences covering Destin in 1981 and subsequent visits, as well as occasional coverage of Tarpon Springs from 1989 to 1994; interview with Jerry Karnas, a former Save the Manatee Club lobbyist from Cortez. For more on this subject see Ben Green, *Finest Kind: A Celebration of a Florida Fishing Village* (Macon, Ga.: Mercer University Press, 1985).

*Yet through the 1980s* . . . : Lyman E. Barger, Herman E. Kumpf, and H. Charles Schaefer, "The Driftnet Fishery in the Fort Pierce–Port Salerno Area Off Southeast Florida," *Marine Fisheries Review,* U.S. Department of Commerce, January 1, 1989.

*In 1984, the Port Salerno* . . . : My reconstruction of the Malmsten case comes from records of *U.S. v. Malmsten et al.,* U.S. District Court, Southern District of Florida, Case no. 84-CR-8052, and from the following news accounts: Betsy Gunders, "Manatee Killing Results in Court Date for 3 Port Salerno Men; Fourth Sought," *Stuart News,* May 25, 1984; "4 Fishermen Plead Not Guilty to Charges of Killing Manatee," *Stuart News,* June 2, 1984; Chris Kelly, "State Dropping Manatee Charge for 1 Fisherman," *Palm Beach Post,* July 7, 1984; Tracy Kolody, "2 Fined for Butchering Manatee," *Stuart News* July 10, 1984; Tracy Kolody, "4 Face U.S. Charges in Manatee Kill," *Stuart News,* August 25, 1984; "Three Men Plead Innocent in Case of Butchered Sea Cows," *Stuart News,* September 13, 1984; Lisa Hoffman, "Angler Gets Jail in Death of Manatee," *Miami Herald,* August 1, 1985; editorial, "Manatees and Justice," *Miami Herald,* August 1985. I also reviewed the Florida Department of Corrections inmate locator Web site to find the information on James Michael Hughes.

*Four years after Jimmy Malmsten* . . . : Don Wilson, "Speeders Often Leave Manatees in Their Wake," *Orlando Sentinel,* October 8, 2000.

*Leading the charge, as usual* . . . : Cathy Vaughn, "River Speed Limits Lose Court Fight," *Orlando Sentinel,* October 8, 1992; Craig Quintana, "Manatee-Protection Law Suffers Another Setback in Volusia Ruling," *Orlando Sentinel,* January 30, 1993; Blake Fontenay, "Boat Activist's Ticket Dismissed," *Orlando Sentinel,* February 16, 1995; Mike Archer, "Judge: Activist Guilty of Speeding in Zone," *Orlando Sentinel,* April 26, 1996.

*While Rawlins battled on* . . . : Final order in *Bonita Bay Properties Inc. v. Department of Environmental Protection,* Florida Division of Administrative Hearings Case no. 95-002552RP; Kevin Lollar, "Lee Tied for Most Deaths of Manatees by Boats," *Fort Myers News-Press,* January 7, 1999; Kevin Lollar, "Approval Nears for Manatee Zones," *Fort Myers News-Press,* February 20, 1999.

*Under a law called* . . . : *Zabel v. Tabb,* 430 F.2d 199 (5th Cir. 1970); *Deltona v. United States,* 657 F. 2d 1210 1184 (Ct. Cl. 1981), cert. denied, 455 U.S. 1017 (1982). For more details on the Corps' administration of wetlands protection laws, see Pittman and Waite, *Paving Paradise.*

*From 1975 to 1981, the Florida* . . . : Interview with former Corps regulator Haynes Johnson and retired colonel James W. R. Adams.

*As a result, permit denials* . . . : Ludmilla Lelis and David Cox, "'Enforce the Law,' Lawsuits Demand," *Orlando Sentinel,* January 14, 2000; letter from Corps of Engineers to Eric Glitzenstein.

*By the end of the 1990s* . . . : Hartman, "To Save a Sea Cow," 68; interview with Patti Thompson.

## Chapter 10. Pegasus Rising

*As Patti Thompson traveled* . . . : Interviews with Patti Thompson and E. F. "Fran" Stallings; Chad Gillis, "Whatever Happened To: Former Bonita Springs Environmentalist Fran Stallings," *Naples Daily News*, December 31, 2003; Laurin Sellers, "Changes in Attitude: Manatee Club Leaves Docile Image in Wake," *Orlando Sentinel*, July 15, 2001; Chris W. Colby, "Reactions to News of Norris Plea Agreement Vary Widely," *Naples Daily News*, January 7, 2004.

*Vallee kept the door . . .* : Author's personal observation from visit to Save the Manatee Club office, April 2003; interviews with Judith Vallee, Patti Thompson and Fran Stallings.

*In April 1996, the assertive Stallings . . .* : Interviews with Fran Stallings and Pat Rose; Steve Persall, "Are You a Parrothead?" *St. Petersburg Times*, January 25, 1991.

*Although Cynthia Frisch hailed . . .* : Interview with Cynthia Frisch.

*Pegasus billed itself as . . .* : Pegasus Foundation, http://www.pegasusfoundation.org, including the 1998 annual report, http://www.pegasusfoundation.org/1998_annual_report.htm.

*Not long after Frisch's encounter . . .* : Interview with Cynthia Frisch; review of Frisch's notes from her research, provided by Frisch.

*Birdsey was a soft-spoken . . .* : Interviews with Cynthia Frisch, Fran Stallings, and Patti Thompson; Shawn McCarthy, "Easy and Breezy, but Not So Beautiful: Why Some Residents of Cape Cod Refuse to Plug in to Offshore Wind-energy Project," *Toronto Globe and Mail*, May 20, 2006; Sally D. Swartz, "Mass. Woman Wants to Help Martin Start Land Trust" *Palm Beach Post*, August 21, 1997; Tyler Treadway, "For Home-Based Hobe Sound Dealer, Art Is Everywhere (Really)," *Stuart News*, January 28, 2001; Barbara Birdsey with George Cadwalader, *Moving Heaven and Earth: A Personal Journey into International Adoption* (Washington, D.C.: Francis Press, 2000), 23–24.

*Rose had stuck to his . . .* : Interviews with Pat Rose and Judith Vallee.

*Finally, reluctantly, Rose agreed . . .* : Interviews with Pat Rose and Cynthia Frisch.

*In his crusade to . . .* : Interviews with Fran Stallings and Cynthia Frisch; news advisory, "Everglades Coalition 13th Annual Conference Set for Jan. 15–18," U.S. Newswire, January 9, 1998; author's observations from covering four Everglades Coalition meetings.

*But to join forces with other . . .* : Interviews with Fran Stallings, Patti Thompson, Judith Vallee, and Cynthia Frisch.

*To most of the public, the Humane . . .* : Mahalley D. Allen, "Laying Down the Law? Interest Group Influence on State Adoption of Animal Cruelty Felony Laws," *Policy Studies Journal* 33, no. 3 (2005): 443–57; David Ward, "Bold Approach Helps Humane Society Gain Coverage," *PR Week*, June 7, 2004; Larry Copeland, "Animal Rights Fight Gains Momentum," *USA Today*, January 28, 2008; Shawn Zeller, "Pet Causes," *The National Journal*, January 1, 2000; Edward T. Pound, "One Nonprofit's Woes," *U.S. News and World Report*, October 2, 1995; Tracy Thompson, "Fur Is Flying at the Humane Society; Animal Protection Group Rattled as Feud Renews a 7-Year-Old Battle," *Washington Post*, August 14, 1996; Kim North Shine, "Humane Society Exec Stole Funds; Ex-Michigan Director Pleads Guilty to Theft," *Detroit Free Press*, June 17, 1999; Associated Press, "Former Anti-Iditarod Crusader Sentenced for Embezzling," August 7, 1999.

*With the Humane Society on board . . .* : Interviews with Cynthia Frisch and Pat Rose; description of meeting based on the agenda for meeting and photos from Frisch's files; David Dahl and Jean Heller, "Amid Rubble, Clinton Offers Help," *St. Petersburg Times*, February 26, 1998. When I interviewed Graham in 2008, he had no memory of giving this 1998 speech or getting an award from Frisch.

*That that particular firm's . . .* : Interview with Eric Glitzenstein; Kim Eisler, "Need a Good Lawyer?" *Washingtonian*, April 2002; Kim Eisler, "Babar's Best Friend," *Washingtonian*, September 2003; biographies of Meyer and Glitzenstein are at http://www.wildlifeadvocacy.org/who.html.

*Although the couple kept . . .* : Interviews with Cynthia Frisch and Eric Glitzenstein; description of SeaWorld visit from Frisch and from snapshots she shared with me.

*Stallings, not an easy . . .* : Interview with Fran Stallings and Cynthia Frisch.

*In June 1998, Frisch . . .* : Interviews with Cynthia Frisch and Eric Glitzenstein.

*Before any suit could be . . .* : Interviews with Fran Stallings, Pat Rose, and Eric Glitzenstein.

*"Fran and I started to . . ."* : Interview with Patti Thompson; Craig Pittman, "Plans Abound to Fix the Ooze of Okeechobee," *St. Petersburg Times*, February 26, 2006.

*By early 1999 the big . . .* : Interviews with Cynthia Frisch, Eric Glitzenstein, Judith Vallee, and David Guest; Earthjustice Legal Defense Fund, http://www.earthjustice.org/about_us/offices_staff/staff/david_guest.html.

*Stallings really wanted Guest . . .* : Interviews with Fran Stallings, Cynthia Frisch, and David Guest.

*Still, Guest wasn't all . . .* : Interview with David Guest.

*Fortunately, another Florida case . . .* : Ludmilla Lelis, "Activists Try to Save Manatees with Suit," *Orlando Sentinel*, May 22, 1999; Ludmilla Lelis, "Manatee Safety Goes to Court," *Orlando Sentinel*, January 13, 2000; Craig Pittman, "Turtles, Tradition Collide in Daytona," *St. Petersburg Times*, June 1, 1999.

*Before filing any lawsuit . . .* : Interview with Cynthia Frisch.

*One of the people hesitant . . .* : Interview with Fran Stallings and Pat Rose.

## Chapter 11. The Time Has Come

*John Ellis "Jeb" Bush . . .* : Colburn, *From Yellow Dog Democrats*, 145–48 and 158–62; Sydney Freedberg, "Jeb Bush: The Son Rises Away from Dad's Shadow," *Miami Herald*, August 15, 1994; Jim Saunders and Randolph Pendleton, "Four Years after His Close Defeat, Republican's Victory Not in Doubt," *Florida Times-Union*, November 4, 1998; "Two Jebs and Ajax," *Miami Herald*, August 20, 1998; Julie Hauserman, "A Stand for the Manatees," *St. Petersburg Times*, July 24, 2000. I repeatedly requested an interview with the former governor, but he did not respond.

*Although Jimmy Buffett had . . .* : Interviews with Pat Rose and Fran Stallings.

*In yet another promising . . .* : Interviews with Buddy Powell and Nat Reed.

*Rose set up an appointment . . .* : Interview with Pat Rose; Lesley Clark, "Buffett Talks to Bush on Manatee Safety," *Miami Herald*, May 20, 1999; David Royse, "Jimmy Buffett Urges Bush to Help Decrease Manatee Deaths," Associated Press, May 19, 1999; Margaret Talev, "Manatee Supporter Buffett Aims to Kill Tampa Zoo Project," *Tampa Tribune*, May 20, 1999.

*Still, Bush gave the manatee . . .* : Interview with Fran Stallings.

*The day after Buffett's botched meeting . . .* : Interviews with Eric Glitzenstein and David Guest; letter from Manatee Coalition to U.S. Army Corps of Engineers and U.S. Fish and Wildlife Service, May 20, 1999.

*As for the state, it . . .* : Letter from Manatee Coalition to Florida Department of Environmental Protection, May 20, 1999; interview with Pat Rose; Craig Pittman, "Groups Plan to File Suits over Manatees," *St. Petersburg Times*, May 21, 1999.

*Yet hardly anyone at . . .* : Interviews with Patti Thompson, Pat Rose, and Buddy Powell.

*That's not the way Powell's* . . . : Ludmilla Lelis, "Activists Try to Save Manatees with Suit," *Orlando Sentinel,* May 22, 1999.

*The sense of outrage over* . . . : Interview with Fran Stallings and Bush environmental adviser Allison DeFoor. In an e-mail, DeFoor confirmed the confrontation with Stallings but said he preferred to call it "a passionate discussion in public between two people of differing views (horrors!)."

*The letter to the Corps* . . . : Interview with Eric Glitzenstein; letter from Manatee Coalition to U.S. Army Corps of Engineers and U.S. Fish and Wildlife Service, May 20, 1999.

*The boss of the Fish and Wildlife* . . . : Interviews with Dave Hankla, Pat Rose, and Fran Stallings.

*That standard was lower* . . . : Author's review of biological opinions issued on projects affecting panther habitat, 1984 to 2009.

*The keen-eyed Woodie Hartman* . . . : Hartman, "To Save a Sea Cow," 58; interview with Dave Hankla.

*Representing the Corps in the* . . . : Between 2003 and 2005, I interviewed John Hall seven times, and exchanged e-mails with him more times than that, for a series of stories in the *St. Petersburg Times* about Florida's vanishing wetlands. After the first stories ran, he stopped returning my calls or responding to my e-mails. He is now retired from the Corps and working as a developer's consultant.

*In negotiating with Glitzenstein* . . . : Interviews with Eric Glitzenstein and Fran Stallings.

*Meanwhile, despite the big splash* . . . : Interviews with Eric Glitzenstein and David Guest; Wade Hopping memo to members of the Boating Coalition's Manatee Task Force, September 3, 1999.

*Wade Hopping, doing some investigating* . . . : Wade Hopping memo to members of the Boating Coalition's Manatee Task Force, September 3, 1999.

*Hopping's memo found a welcome* . . . : Letter from George Reynolds to Wade Hopping, September 10, 1999.

*Unfortunately for Hopping* . . . : Julie Hauserman, "Trade Group Will Fight Manatee Protections," *St. Petersburg Times,* September 30, 1999.

*Hauserman's scoop, picked up* . . . : Sally D. Swarz, "Manatees' Endangered Status Questioned," *Palm Beach Post,* October 6, 1999.

## Chapter 12. Oh No, Mr. Bill!

*Pursuing a pair of major* . . . : Save the Manatee budget from 1999 IRS Form 990, accessed via the nonprofit watchdog Guidestar Web site; interview with Judith Valle.

*After all, the organization's major* . . . : Interview with Judith Vallee; author's visit to the 2003 Manatee Ball; interview with Harry Fink and various other Parrotheads.

*Paying the bills being racked* . . . : Interviews with Fran Stallings and Pat Rose.

*Still, even Pegasus couldn't* . . . : Interviews with Cynthia Frisch, Fran Stallings, Patti Thompson, and Judith Vallee; James E. Lalonde, "The Wizard of OS/2," *Seattle Times,* March 27, 1988; Notebook, "25 Years Ago at Microsoft," *Time,* March 1, 2000. My attempts to contact the Letwins drew no response.

*Now the two suits could* . . . : The Washington case is styled as *Save the Manatee Club et al. v. Ballard* and can be accessed at http://www.savethemanatee.org/newslfedlawsuitdoc.htm;

the so-called state case is styled as *Save the Manatee Club et al. v. Egbert* and can be accessed at http://www.savethemanatee.org/newslstatelawsuitdoc.htm.

*Even those Save the Manatee* . . . : Interviews with Judith Vallee, Cynthia Frisch, and Fran Stallings.

*The Save the Manatee Club faxed* . . . : January 13, 2000, Save the Manatee Club press release, http://www.savethemanatee.org/newsprlawsuitannouncement.htm; interview with Patti Thompson.

*Glitzenstein took a more measured* . . . : Craig Pittman and Vanita Gowda, "19 Groups Sue, Say Manatees' Protection Poor," *St. Petersburg Times*, January 14, 2000.

*Over at the U.S. Fish and* . . . : Craig Pittman and Vanita Gowda, "19 Groups Sue, Say Manatees' Protection Poor," *St. Petersburg Times*, January 14, 2000.

*Two months after the suits* . . . : Interviews with Eric Glitzenstein and David Guest.

*Then, in mid-April, the* . . . : Cyril T. Zaneski, "Manatee Litigation Seeks Marina Curb," *Miami Herald*, April 24, 2000; Save the Manatee Club press release, "Army Corps Issues License to Kill Manatees: Manatee Advocates File Request for Injunction," April 18, 2000, http://www.savethemanatee.org/newsprinjunction.htm; interview with Eric Glitzenstein.

*The agenda for the July 25, 2000* . . . : Cabinet meeting agenda, July 25, 2000, http://www.myflorida.com/myflorida/cabinet/agenda00/0725/agenda_botiitf.html; Cabinet meeting transcript, http://www.myflorida.com/myflorida/cabinet/agenda00/0725/trans.html; interview with Patti Thompson; Julie Hauserman, "A Stand for the Manatee," *St. Petersburg Times*, July 25, 2000; Jackie Hallifax, "Bush Sends Message on Manatees," Associated Press, July 26, 2000; editorial, "The Manatee's Best Friend?" *Lakeland Ledger*, July 27, 2000.

*Jeb Bush was no Fran Stallings* . . . : Craig Pittman and Diane Rado, "Cabinet Reverses Stand on Marina," *St. Petersburg Times*, November 30, 2000; Craig Pittman and Julie Hauserman, "An Unnatural Silence," *St. Petersburg Times*, October 14, 2002.

*Something similar happened with* . . . : Mark Hollis, "Manatees Get Push from Bush," *Orlando Sentinel*, August 25, 2000.

*On October 19, Bush convened* . . . : Interviews with Julie Hauserman, Pat Rose, Jim Kalvin, Dave Hankla, and Buddy Powell; agenda and summary of October 19, 2000, Manatee Summit, courtesy of Pat Rose and Save the Manatee Club archives; Julie Hauserman, "Summit's Charge: Protect State's Manatees," *St. Petersburg Times,* October 20, 2000.

*Sprague, then in his* . . . : Mike Vogel, "Manatee-minded," *Florida Trend*, August 2006; Brian Bandell, "Marine Industry Grapples with Space, Storm Issues," *South Florida Business Journal*, October 22, 2004.

*When Rose and Sprague finished* . . . : Interviews with Pat Rose and Julie Hauserman; Julie Hauserman, "Summit's Charge: Protect State's Manatees," *St. Petersburg Times,* October 20, 2000.

*Smirking, Bush reached into* . . . : Interview with Julie Hauserman; Mr. Bill information from http://www.mrbill.com/mbbio.html.

*Because Bush left early, he* . . . : Julie Hauserman, "Summit's Charge: Protect State's Manatees," *St. Petersburg Times*, October 20, 2000.

*Not only did Bush's summit* . . . : Tom McGill, "Manatee Summit Playing with a 'Stacked Deck,'" press release from Citizens for Florida Waterways, October 2000; Julie Hauserman, "Summit's Charge: Protect State's Manatees," *St. Petersburg Times*, October 20, 2000.

*With his shaggy blond hair* . . . : Interviews with Jim Kalvin, Ron Pritchard, Rick Rawlins, and John Sprague. The reporter who tagged along on Kalvin's tour of Port of the Islands—and witnessed the woman telling him to slow down—was me. That was for a story headlined "Boater's Rights: Captain of a Cause," *St. Petersburg Times*, September 9, 2002.

*The others listened to Kalvin . . .* : Interviews with Dave Hankla and Jim Kalvin.

*First, Rose lost a race . . .* : Interview with Pat Rose.

*With Rose unavailable . . .* : Interviews with Eric Glitzenstein and Patti Thompson.

*As Thompson regained her . . .* : Interviews with Patti Thompson and Fran Stallings.

*During settlement negotiations . . .* : For Facciola see http://www.dcd.uscourts.gov/facciola-bio.html; interview with Eric Glitzenstein.

*On Wednesday, January 5, 2001 . . .* : Settlement of *Save the Manatee Club v. Ballard*, http://www.eswr.com/mansett.pdf; Save the Manatee Club press release, "Landmark Settlement Reach in Federal Manatee Case," http://www.savethemanatee.org/newsprfedsettlement.htm; Ludmilla Lelis, "New Rules Settle Suit to Protect Manatees," *Orlando Sentinel*, January 5, 2001.

*In announcing the settlement . . .* : Dan McCue and Jennifer Sergent, "Lawsuit over Manatee Rules Settled," *Jupiter Courier*, January 7, 2001.

*"Today is a good day . . ."* : Dan McCue and Jennifer Sergent, "Lawsuit over Manatee Rules Settled," *Jupiter Courier*, January 7, 2001; Barbara Behrendt, "Manatee Lady Has New Outlet for Her Fight," *St. Petersburg Times,* November 6, 2000.

*Not everyone was quite . . .* : Interview with Dave Hankla.

*As it happened . . .* : Interview with Bruce Ackerman; Craig Pittman and Alex Leary, "2001 Manatee Count Sets Record," *St. Petersburg Times*, January 11, 2001.

*This was the day of . . .* : Interview with Patti Thompson.

## Chapter 13. Eat Umm

*On the day Bruce Ackerman . . .* : Interviews with Jim Kalvin and Tom Pitchford; Kevin Lollar, "Record Manatee Counted," *Fort Myers News Press*, January 11, 2001.

*Other boating advocates took . . .* : Interview with Ron Pritchard.

*Columnists at several newspapers . . .* : Frank Sargeant, "Realities Should Decide Manatee Regs," *Tampa Tribune*, January 14, 2001; Sam Cook column, *Fort Myers News-Press*, January 14, 2001.

*Cook's column resonated well . . .* : Author's personal observations from visits to Fort Myers and Cape Coral; Kevin Lollar, "Boaters Humor Adds Dark Taste to Manatee Debate," *Fort Myers News-Press*, October 7, 2001; Kevin Lollar, "DMV Can't Stomach Manatee Tag," *Fort Myers News-Press*, October 19, 2001.

*Leonard and Julius Rosen had already . . .* : Barnett, *Mirage*, 25–27; Mormino, *Land of Sunshine, State of Dreams*, 53; Waitley, *Best Backroads of Florida*, 170–72; Allan, Kuder, and Oakes, *Promised Lands*, 117–57; Board, *Remembering Lee County*, 113–15. Nat Reed, who got his start in public service working for Governor Kirk, told me that he was one of Kirk's aides assigned to find a way to shut down the Rosens. Among the others: Wade Hopping.

*Still, slowly, people came . . .* : Peter S. Goodman, "This Is the Sound of a Bubble Bursting," *New York Times*, December 23, 2007.

*As Cape Coral boomed . . .* : Interview with Craig Manson; Dick Hogan and Jeff Cull, "Dock Permits Upset Boaters," *Fort Myers News-Press*, June 7, 2001; Jeff Cull and Kevin Lollar, "Corps Exerts Power over Boat Dock," *Fort Myers News-Press*, June 30, 2001.

*Although Cape Coral residents* . . . : Jill Tyrer, "Dock Squeeze: The Shortage of Public Marina Space Is Getting Critical, Says Ken Stead," *Gulfshore Business*, December 2004; boat registration figures from Florida Fish and Wildlife Conservation Commission.

*The downside to cramming* . . . : Interview with Jay Gorzelany, Mote Marine Laboratory.

*In 2000, Lee tied Brevard* . . . : Manatee mortality figures and 2000 boating accident figures from Florida Fish and Wildlife Conservation Commission.

*"It's just not worth . . ."* : Interview with Ben and Lori Nelson.

*Still, for many Lee* . . . : Byron Stout, "Manatee Rules Need Correcting," *Fort Myers News-Press*, November 27, 2002.

*The personification of the disdain* . . . : Interview with Ross Burnaman; *Fish and Wildlife Conservation Commission v. William D. Wilkinson et al.*, Lee County Case no. 00-8661MM; *Wilkinson v. Florida Fish and Wildlife Conservation Commission*, Lee County Circuit Court Case no. 00-3899-CA; Mike Hoyem, "Judicial Circuit Official Fighting Manatee Rules in Court," *Fort Myers News-Press*, August 29, 2002; Mike Hoyem, "Judge Rejects Manatee Zones," *Fort Myers News-Press*, November 13, 2002; Betty Parker, "Manatee Zones Still in Effect," *Fort Myers News-Press*, November 14, 2002.

*Because of Wilkinson's extensive* . . . : The attorney who was supposed to take over the case from Burnaman for the Fish and Wildlife Conservation Commission missed the deadline for filing the appeal, and so the judge's decision stood. As a result, the state's taxpayers got stuck with the bill for the defendants' court costs, nearly forty thousand dollars. But the win backfired on Wilkinson and his buddies. Once the state speed zones had been tossed out, the U.S. Fish and Wildlife Service stepped in and slapped federal speed zones on those areas. The state speed limit had been thirty-five miles per hour. The federal limit was twenty-five.

*It didn't help that rumors* . . . : Jennifer Maddox, "Environmentalists, Government Not Agreeing about Manatee Issues," *Vero Beach Press-Journal*, March 18, 2001.

*People upset about what* . . . : Jim Saunders, "Crackdown Urged to Aid Manatees," *Florida Times-Union*, March 27, 2001; Byron Stout, "Boaters Balk at Manatee Laws," *Fort Myers News-Press*, March 2, 2001; House Memorial 1177, "Open Access to the Waterways of the State," sponsored by Representative Jeff Kottkamp; Steve Bousquet and Deirdre Morrow, "Friend, 'Fighter' Joins Crist," *St. Petersburg Times*, September 13, 2006.

*"We're tired of the federal . . ."* : Harrington's comments at Fish and Wildlife Conservation Commission public hearing in Punta Gorda, July 11, 2002; interview with Harrington.

*Since Harrington at that point* . . . : Harrington entry in *2001–2002 Florida House of Representatives Clerk' Manual*; Rodney Carouther, "Boaters Criticize Manatee Zones," *Sarasota Herald-Tribune*, March 3, 2001; Byron Stout, "Boaters Balk at Manatee Laws," *Fort Myers News-Press*, March 2, 2001; Frank Sargeant, "CCA Says Manatees Are Not in Crisis," *Tampa Tribune*, February 11, 2001; Alison LePolt, "Manatee Suit Talks Will Be in Public," *Fort Myers News-Press*, March 14, 2001; interview with Dave Hankla.

*Many of the people who attended* . . . : Interview with Ted Forsgren; information on the Coastal Conservation Association of Florida from http://www.ccaflorida.org.

*The first signs of trouble* . . . : Julie Hauserman and Craig Pittman, "Manatees Trump Miami Marina Plan," *St. Petersburg Times*, March 14, 2001; Lesley Clark, "Cabinet Rejects Marina Plan," *Miami Herald*, March 14, 2001; Kathleen Krog, "What's Good for the Bay Can Be Good for Business," *Miami Herald*, March 14, 2001; transcript of March 13, 2001, Florida Cabinet meeting, http://www.myflorida.com/myflorida/cabinet/agenda01/0313/trans.html; Carlos

Miller, "Miami: A Young but Turbulent History," Magic City Media, http://www.magiccity-media.com/HistoryofMiami.html. As Miller notes, 2001 was not a great year for the Magic City: "The fact that Mayor Joe Carollo was arrested for domestic violence in February 2001 . . . prompted the *New York Times* to say that Miami was 'the epicenter of embarrassment.' It didn't help that five months later, former city manager Donald Warshaw was sentenced to a year in prison for stealing nearly $70,000 from a children's charity while serving as Miami's police chief."

*When one newspaper reported . . .* : Jennifer Maddox, "Environmentalists, Government Not Agreeing on Manatee Issue," *Vero Beach Press Journal*, March 21, 2001.

*Glitzenstein could see that . . .* : Interview with Eric Glitzenstein.

## Chapter 14. Bad Boys

*During the presidential campaign . . .* : McClellan, *What Happened*, 72–73.

*A prime example was . . .* : Tim Kenworthy, "Interior Secretary Norton Submits Resignation," *USA Today*, March 10, 2006; "Ethics Scandal Didn't Prompt Resignation, Norton Says," *Seattle Times*, March 11, 2006; Edmund L. Andrews, "Interior Official Assails Agency for Ethics Slide," *New York Times*, September 14, 2006; Jeff Woods, "Norton vs. the Environment," *Defenders of Wildlife*, Summer 2002, http://www.defenders.org/newsroom/defenders_magazine/summer_2002/norton_vs_the_environment.php; Martin Kettle, "Echoes of Slavery as Bush Nominees Back Confederacy," *The Guardian*, January 12, 2001, http://www.guardian.co.uk/world/2001/jan/12/worlddispatch.usa.

*On March 26, 2001, the . . .* : Byron Stout, "Manatee Refuge, Sanctuary Locations to Be Revealed May 2," *Fort Myers News-Press*, March 27, 2001.

*Glitzenstein's clients agreed . . .* : Interview with Eric Glitzenstein.

*Getting to the point . . .* : Interviews with David Guest and Patti Thompson.

*State wildlife officials made it . . .* : Interview with Kipp Frohlich; Craig Pittman, "Safe Havens, Legal Turmoil," *St. Petersburg Times*, March 25, 2001.

*For the pro-boating groups . . .* : Craig Pittman, "Safe Havens, Legal Turmoil," *St. Petersburg Times*, March 25, 2001.

*But Judith Vallee . . .* : Kevin Lollar, "War on the Water: The Manatee Debate," *Fort Myers News-Press*, March 18, 2001.

*The final say on the settlement . . .* : Author's personal observations from ten years' covering the wildlife commission.

*They were supposed to take . . .* : Craig Pittman, "Some Say Manatee in Danger No More," *St. Petersburg Times*, April 7, 2001.

*As it happened, someone . . .* : Interview with Ted Forsgren; Thomas Fraser, "Manatees in Florida: 2001," March 2001, http://www.ccaflorida.org/updates/Mar26_manatee.htm; Conservation Association of Florida press release, "CCA Florida Releases Revealing Report Scientific Report about Manatees," March 27, 2001, http://www.fmca.us/issues/cca.html; Craig Pittman, "Some Say Manatee in Danger No More," *St. Petersburg Times*, April 7, 2001.

*In other words, he wasn't . . .* : Interview with Cynthia Frisch. The word "biostitute," a combination of "biologist" and "prostitute," is commonly applied to scientists whose expertise appears to be for sale to the highest bidder. When I covered criminal courts, prosecutors and defense attorneys had a similar term for a particular psychologist whose expert testimony usually suited whoever paid him. They called him "Dr. Jukebox": put in a coin and he'd play whatever tune you wanted.

*In July 2001 the MTAC*...: Minutes from July 23–26, 2001, meeting of the Manatee Technical Advisory Committee.

*But Forsgren argued that*...: Curtis Morgan, "Too Many Manatees?" *Miami Herald*, April 1, 2001.

*Actually, a panel of manatee*...: Interviews with Buddy Powell, Lynn Lefebvre, Bruce Ackerman, and Dave Hankla.

*A week after the Fraser report*...: Jim Waymer, "Summit Targets Manatee Protection," *Florida Today*, April 7, 2001.

*Then came the Fish and Wildlife*...: Author's personal observations from covering hearing; Craig Pittman, "Manatee Accord Hailed as Lifesaver," *St. Petersburg Times*, April 20, 2001; Ludmilla Lelis, "Manatee Suits Settlement May Downshift Boats to Idle," *Orlando Sentinel*, April 20, 2001; Jim Waymer, "New Boating Rules Top Manatee Settlement," *Orlando Sentinel*, April 20, 2001.

*After making her public statement*...: Interview with Colleen Castille.

*But to some of the people*...: Michelle Hudson, "Agency OKs manatee Suit Settlement," *Fort Myers News-Press*, April 20, 2001.

*That prospect greatly concerned*...: Interview with Karl Wickstrom; Kevin Lollar, "Boaters Climb Aboard Opposition to Restrictions," *Fort Myers News-Press*, March 18, 2001; Jeff Klinkenberg, "Both Sides of the Net," *St. Petersburg Times*, October 23, 1994; Ken Cogburn, "Fishing, Boating Bolster Economy," *Treasure Coast Business Journal*, July 1, 2001.

*Wickstrom said he had actually*...: Interview with Karl Wickstrom.

*Wickstrom didn't confine his*...: Author's personal observations while covering this event.

*Wickstrom's readers responded*...: Between 1999 and 2005, I visited the Florida Sportsman online message boards repeatedly and printed out messages that I thought might be useful for stories; this section comes from that file full of printouts. Laura Combs of the Save the Manatee Club told me the vandalism story and showed me printouts of the messages regarding where she lived. The thread regarding who had hit manatees began with the posting by Captain Chris on May 20, 2002, at 4:10 p.m.

*While his aide was cutting deals*...: Craig Pittman, "Some Say Manatee in Danger No More," *St. Petersburg Times*, April 7, 2001.

*Now, with the state settlement*...: Letter from Governor Bush to Sam Hamilton of the U.S. Fish and Wildlife Service, May 29, 2001.

*That was good enough*...: Pamela Smith Hayford, "Wildlife Service Drops Dock Fees as Funds Found," *Fort Myers News-Press*, August 15, 2001.

*Meanwhile, again and again*...: Interview with Eric Glitzenstein.

*But a lot of the delay*...: Interviews with Eric Glitzenstein and Craig Manson.

*With Norton's department kowtowing*...: Interview with Eric Glitzenstein; *Federal Register* notice, August 10, 2001 (66 FR 42318).

*On October 24, 2001, Glitzenstein*...: Letter from Eric Glitzenstein to U.S. Department of Justice, October 24, 2001; U.S. Newswire, "Gale Norton, Other Federal Officials Charged with Flagrant Breaches of Landmark Manatee Settlement Agreement," October 24, 2001.

*If the federal agencies*...: Andrew Revkin, "How Endangered a Species?" *New York Times*, February 12, 2002.

*When the Save the Manatee Club* . . . : Ludmilla Lelis, "Manatee Dispute Heats Up," *Orlando Sentinel*, October 25, 2001.

*However, the state hadn't* . . . : Interviews with Eric Glitzenstein and Craig Manson.

*Governor Bush treated the wildlife* . . . : Curtis Morgan, "Florida Governor Raises Eyebrows by Naming Miami Lobbyist to Wildlife Panel," *Miami Herald*, September 12, 2001; Curtis Morgan, "Miami Lobbyist/Angler Shows His Wild Side," *Miami Herald*, November 9, 2006.

*Barreto's passion for fishing* . . . : When Roberts left the wildlife commission board in 2004, he rejoined the CCA-Florida board. Full background at http://www.voterfocus.com/ws/ws-cand/candidate_pr.php?op=cv&e=5&c=escambia&ca=129&rellevel=4&committee=N.

*Another commissioner appointed* . . . : Interview with John Rood and review of the bio at http://www.vestcor.com/executive-team/john-d-rood; Carl Hiaasen, "Manatees Remain Threatened," *Miami Herald*, November 16, 2003.

*At one meeting, a closed-door* . . . : Transcript of Florida Fish and Wildlife Conservation Commission executive session, March 28, 2003.

*Even when the state wildlife* . . . : Interview with David Guest; Jim Waymer, "Court Battles Could Delay Enforcement of Manatee Zones for Quite Some Time," *Florida Today*, September 29, 2001; Jim Waymer, "Judge Upholds Manatee Zones," *Florida Today*, April 18, 2002.

*For instance, they argued* . . . : Nanette Woitas, "Manatee Testing: 'Now Hear This,'" *St. Petersburg Times*, January 26, 1992; McGill's *Florida Manatee Conspiracy* offers repeated praise for Gerstein's work; interviews with Ross Burnaman, David Guest, Kipp Frohlich, and Buddy Powell; Manatee Technical Advisory Council, "Recommendations on Acoustic Technology as a Manatee Protection Strategy," November 30, 2000; B. L. Weigle, I. E. Wright, and J. A. Huff, "Responses of Manatees to an Approaching Boat: A Pilot Study," presentation at the First International Manatee and Dugong Research Conference, Gainesville, Florida, March 1994. Perhaps the definitive word on this subject is Calleson and Frohlich, "Slower Boat Speeds Reduce Risks to Manatees," available at http://www.int-res.com/articles/esr2007/3/n003p295.pdf.

*Kalvin was ready to bail* . . . : Interviews with Jim Kalvin, Ross Burnaman, and David Guest.

*In October 2001, the devastating* . . . : Dara Kam, "Lawmaker Raises Ante in Manatee Zone Fight," *Florida Today*, October 31, 2001.

*The recovery plan had been* . . . : Interviews with Dave Hankla, Buddy Powell, and Eric Glitzenstein; Craig Pittman, "Expert Opinions on Manatees Ignored," *St. Petersburg Times*, July 21, 2001; Craig Pittman, "Plan Has Manatees off Endangered List," *St. Petersburg Times*, November 1, 2001.

*Early the following year* . . . : Interview with Glitzenstein.

*Now the battle moved to* . . . : Judge Emmet Sullivan's biography, http://www.dcd.uscourts.gov/sullivan-bio.html.

*On April 17, 2002* . . . : Author's personal observations from covering press conference; interviews with Cynthia Frisch, Helen Spivey, and Susannah Lindberg (now Susannah Randolph).

*Sometimes, though, her job* . . . : Interviews with Susannah Lindberg (Randolph) and Cynthia Frisch; description of Grim Reaper protest from photo provided by Cynthia Frisch.

*Another time she unleashed* . . . : Interview with Susannah Lindberg (Randolph); Paige St. John, "'Manatee Body Bags' Left at Lobbyist's Office," *Florida Today*, December 13, 2001.

*Props like the body bags* . . . : Interviews with Susannah Lindberg (Randolph) and Helen Spivey.

*Another of Lindberg's initiatives* . . . : Interviews with Susannah Lindberg (Randolph), Cynthia Frisch, Fran Stallings, and Eric Glitzenstein.

*Tallulah's appearance marked* . . . : "O.J. Contests Boat Speeding Ticket," Associated Press, September 25, 2002; Luisa Yanez, "Arrest Warrant Issued, Then Rescinded for O.J. Simpson," *Miami Herald*, November 6, 2002; "O.J. Simpson Pays Boat Speeding Fine," Associated Press, November 22, 2002; Patrick Hruby, "Dubious Achievement Awards of 2002," *Washington Times*, December 26, 2002; Frank Cerabino, "O.J. Squeeze Play Pits Manatees vs. National Security," *Palm Beach Post*, November 8, 2002.

*Simpson wasn't the only* . . . : Craig Pittman, "Manatee Rules Crimp Super Bowl Plans," *St. Petersburg Times*, July 14, 2002.

*While O. J. Simpson tangled* . . . : Julie Hauserman, "Manatees No Threat to $60-million Film," *St. Petersburg Times*, August 1, 2002; David Royse, "Film Makers Get Break from Manatee Rules for Boat Scene," Associated Press, August 1, 2002; Curtis Morgan, "Manatee-Protection Speeds Waived for Hollywood Chase," *Miami Herald*, August 2, 2002; Julie Hauserman, "Cut! Manatees Keep Cameras from Rolling," *St. Petersburg Times*, August 3, 2002.

*During the hearing, Glitzenstein* . . . : Transcript of July 31, 2002, hearing; interview with Eric Glitzenstein.

*An editorial in the* . . . : Editorial, "Bad Boys vs. Manatees," *St. Petersburg Times*, August 9, 2002.

*For his next trick* . . . : Interview with Eric Glitzenstein; Larry Wheeler, "Judge Orders Manatee Protection Measures, Criticizes Agency Foot Dragging," Gannett News Service, July 31, 2002; Jennifer Sergent, "Official Denies Deliberately Violating Manatee Order," *Fort Pierce Tribune*, November 19, 2002.

*The day after Sullivan's* . . . : Jeff Cull, "Bush Makes Campaign Stop in Cape: Manatee Ruling Disappoints Governor," *Fort Myers News Press*, August 2, 2002.

*Instead of appealing, Norton's* . . . : Interviews with Eric Glitzenstein and Craig Manson; transcript of hearing, November 5, 2002.

*Manson had been a judge* . . . : Interview with Craig Manson; Interior Department press release, "Secretary Norton Announces Resignation of Craig Manson, Commends His Stewardship of Nation's Parks and Wildlife," November 16, 2005, http://www.doi.gov/news/05_News_Releases/051116a.htm.

*Glitzenstein, however, is* . . . : Interview with Eric Glitzenstein.

*As with all of the* . . . : Amanda Grissom, "Craig's List," *Grist*, April 15, 2004, http://www.grist.org/news/maindish/2004/04/15/griscom-manson/.

*But Manson now threw himself* . . . : Interviews with Craig Manson and Eric Glitzenstein; Craig Manson, "Florida Treasure Needs a Florida Solution," *Fort Lauderdale Sun-Sentinel*, December 16, 2002.

## Chapter 15. Down with the Manatee

*Ted Forsgren's love affair* . . . : Interview with Ted Forsgren; Steve Waters, "Manatee Crisis Over," *Fort Lauderdale Sun-Sentinel*, April 8, 2001.

*So on August 20, 2001* . . . : Petition from Ted Forsgren to Florida Fish and Wildlife Conservation Commission, dated August 17, 2001, http://www.floridaconservation.org/imperiledspecies/petitions/Manatee-Petition.pdf; Craig Pittman, "Group Wants Manatees off Endangered List," *St. Petersburg Times*, August 21, 2001.

*Patti Thompson strongly disagreed . . .* : Interview with Patti Thompson.

*Still, manatee biologists said that . . .* : Interviews with Bob Bonde and Bruce Ackerman.

*One study, done by Tom Pitchford's . . .* : Interviews with Meg Pitchford and Bruce Ackerman; Lynn Lefebvre, "Manatee Population Ecology and Management Workshop Held in Florida," *Sirenews*, April 2002, http://www.sirenian.org/sirenews/37APR2002.html.

*For instance, Asian elephants . . .* : National Zoo, http://nationalzoo.si.edu/Animals/Asian-Elephants; National Park Service, "Status of Cape Sable Seaside Sparrow 2007 Survey Report," http://www.nps.gov/ever/parknews/status-of-cape-sable-seaside-sparrow-2007-survey-report.htm.

*After Forsgren turned in . . .* : David Fleshler and Neil Santaniello, "Manatee Protection Faces Review," *Fort Lauderdale Sun-Sentinel*, November 1, 2001.

*One of the first stops . . .* : Interview with Dan Odell.

*To understand why, turn . . .* : David Olinger, "Ibis at Center of Fiscal Dispute," *St. Petersburg Times*, April 5, 1995; "A Bird on the Head," *St. Petersburg Times*, April 22, 1995; John Kennedy, "Senate Lets the Ibis Off the Hook," *Orlando Sentinel*, April 21, 1995; Rob Chepak, "Bid to Clip Ibis Funds Doesn't Fly," *Tampa Tribune*, May 3, 1995.

*The rewrite took four years . . .* : Craig Pittman, "Money a Factor in Species Protection," *St. Petersburg Times*, March 22, 1999.

*But the way the state wildlife . . .* : Bruce Ritchie, "State Retools Protection Process," *Tallahassee Democrat*, April 16, 2004.

*"When I saw those . . ."* : Interview with Patti Thompson; Craig Pittman, "Species' Endangered Status at Risk," *St. Petersburg Times*, December 9, 2001.

*The Florida Ornithological Society did . . .* : Craig Pittman, "Woodpecker's Status Lowered," *St. Petersburg Times*, September 4, 2003.

*Species of special concern didn't . . .* : Craig Pittman, "A License to Kill Gopher Tortoises," *St. Petersburg Times*, May 7, 2007.

*Despite the strong protests . . .* : Craig Pittman, "Species' Endangered Status at Risk," *St. Petersburg Times*, December 9, 2001.

*The law that Woodie Hartman . . .* : Interview with Dave Hankla; "U.S. Fish and Wildlife Service Seeks Public Comment on Proposed Regulations for the Florida Manatee," U.S. Fish and Wildlife Service press release November 6, 2002, http://www.fws.gov/northflorida/Releases-02/014-02-FWS-Proposes- MMPA-ITRs-110602.htm.

*As if to underline the . . .* : Information on manatee mortality from http://research.myfwc.com/features/category_sub.asp?id=2241.

*What did that mean? . . .* : Jeff Cull, "Manatee Plan Could Dock Development," *Fort Myers News-Press*, November 7, 2002; Wendy Fullerton, "Property Rights vs. Manatee Protection," *Fort Myers News-Press*, November 24, 2002; *Federal Register* notice, "Florida Manatees; Incidental Take during Specified Activities; Proposed Rule: Notice of Public Hearings," November 29, 2002, http://www.epa.gov/EPA-IMPACT/2002/November/Day-29/i30374.htm.

*Jim Kalvin quickly condemned . . .* : Jeff Cull, "Manatee Plan Could Dock Development," *Fort Myers News-Press*, November 7, 2002.

*Although the wildlife service . . .* : Interviews with Eric Glitzenstein, Pat Rose, Judith Vallee,

Dave Hankla, and Patti Thompson; Jim Waymer, "Fish & Wildlife Proposes Rule to Regulate Marine Construction in Manatee Areas," *Florida Today,* November 7, 2002.

*On November 23, 2002, about . . .* : Wendy Fullerton, "Cape Coral Rallies to 'Unlock Docks,'" *Fort Myers News-Press*, November 24, 2002.

*Two weeks later came the first . . .* : Author's observations of hearing; interviews with Dave Hankla, Jim Kalvin, Cynthia Frisch, Laura Combs, and Susannah Lindberg (Randolph); Jeff Cull and Don Ruane, "Manatee Plan Hearing Draws 2,500-plus Foes," *Fort Myers News-Press*, December 3, 2002. My estimate of the size of the crowd came from the Lee County deputy working security.

*The following night . . .* : Author's observations from covering the second hearing.

*The rest of the hearings . . .* : Interview with Dave Hankla; David Fleshler, "Bush Blames Manatee Protection Plan," *Fort Lauderdale Sun-Sentinel*, December 13, 2002.

*By then, though, Judge Manson . . .* : Interview with Craig Manson; Jeff Cull, Larry Wheeler and Betsy Clayton, "New Plan Benefits Manatee," *Fort Myers News-Press*, January 25, 2003.

*Nevertheless, a week after Bush . . .* : I covered Goss's first campaign for Congress and interviewed him several times about his background. While he did show me his belt and suspenders, I could get no details from either him or the CIA about his agency work; Suzanne Goldenberg, "The Guardian Profile: Porter Goss," *The Guardian*, August 13, 2004.

*"The idea of not allowing . . ."* : Larry Wheeler, "Jeb Bush, Congressman Step into Manatee vs. Dock Debate," Gannett News Service, January 30, 2003; interview with Craig Manson.

*Meanwhile, the U.S. Marine . . .* : Letter from David Cottingham to Dave Hankla, 2002; interview with Craig Manson.

*In an effort to shore . . .* : Interviews with Dave Hankla and Mike Runge.

*The answer Runge came up . . .* : Michael C. Runge, "A Model for Assessing Incidental Take of Manatees Due to Watercraft-Related Activities," released by the U.S. Fish and Wildlife Service as Appendix 1 of the Final Environmental Impact Statement on Incidental Take Regulations, April 4, 2003; interview with Runge.

*But it was impossible . . .* : E-mail from Patti Thompson to author, April 4, 2003; Save the Manatee Club press release, "Long Term Prospects for Manatee Recovery Look Grim, According to New Data Released by Federal Government," posted online April 4, 2003.

*"The Runge report is . . ."* : Interview with Judith Vallee, April 17, 2003.

*Glitzenstein told reporters . . .* : Associated Press, "Report Warns of Fla. Manatee Extinction," April 25, 2003; Kevin O'Horan, "Manatees' Future in Doubt," *Tallahassee Democrat*, May 3, 2003.

*Years later, Runge said . . .* : Interview with Mike Runge.

*While environmental advocates . . .* : Frank Sargeant, "Numbers Get Twisted in Incessant Manatee Debate, but They're Fine," *Tampa Tribune*, May 4, 2003.

*Although the Fish and Wildlife . . .* : Ivona Lerman, "Manatee Groups Fear New Rule Feds Would Allow Boat-Related Deaths," *Daytona Beach News-Journal*, May 3, 2003; interviews with Dave Hankla, Mike Runge, and Craig Manson.

*On May 5, 2003, the day . . .* : Jeff Cull, "Limits on Dock Permits May Ease," *Fort Myers News-Press*, May 6, 2003; interviews with Craig Manson, Dave Hankla and Eric Glitzenstein.

*The end of the year brought . . .* : Manatee mortality figures from Florida Fish and Wildlife Research Institute.

*A week after the regulations* . . . : Don Ruane and Jeff Cull, "Dock Builders Get Relief from Agency," *Fort Myers News-Press*, May 14, 2003.

*"The walls of Harborside Convention Center . . ."* : Online Casts column, "Federal Hearings Draw Angry Anglers from across the State," May 16, 2003, http://www.floridasportsman.com/casts/030516/.

*In August 2003, both the Florida Marine* . . . : Jeff Cull, "Agencies Feel Heat over Cape Docks," *Fort Myers News-Press*, August 13, 2003.

*Soon the manatee madness had spread* . . . : Scott Carroll, "County Poised to Sue over Restrictions," *Sarasota Herald-Tribune*, October 8, 2003; Scott Carroll, "Dock Permit Ban Likely to Remain," *Sarasota Herald-Tribune*, October 22, 2003.

*In some places the problem* . . . : Editorial, "What Manatee Protection Plan? Sarasota County Commission Muddied the Waters," *Sarasota Herald-Tribune*, February 15, 2004.

*Rather than condemning local* . . . : Jeff Cull, "Agencies Feel Heat over Cape Dock Permits," *Fort Myers News-Press*, August 13, 2003; interview with Craig Manson.

*The proposal came from* . . . : Diana Voyles-Pulver, "Feds Going Slow on Manatee Rules," *Daytona Beach News-Journal*, November 20, 2003; interview with Ken Haddad.

*At this point the Manatee War* . . . : Rush Limbaugh quoted in Jason F. Shogren, ed., *Private Property and the Endangered Species Act: Saving Habitats* (Austin: University of Texas Press, 1998), 81.

*With Republicans running the lower* . . . : Bettina Boxall, "Foe of Endangered Species Act on Defensive over Abramoff," *Los Angeles Times*, February 14, 2006; Webster testimony from transcript of April 28, 2004, hearing of the House Resources Committee.

*This form of practical extortion* . . . : Byron Stout, "Manatee Club Pays for Actions," *Fort Myers News-Press*, April 23, 2003.

*During a closed-door meeting* . . . : Transcript of Florida Fish and Wildlife Conservation Commission executive session, March 28, 2003.

*It didn't take long for* . . . : Author's notes from covering the April 14, 2004, Fish and Wildlife Conservation Commission meeting in Tallahassee.

## Chapter 16. Political Science

*In January 2003, the state wildlife* . . . : Fish and Wildlife Conservation Commission meeting agenda, January 23–25, 2003; author's personal observations.

*"The manatees . . . according to . . ."* : David Fleshler, "Florida Wildlife Officials to Decide If Manatee Keeps 'Endangered' Status," *Fort Lauderdale Sun-Sentinel*, December 30, 2002.

*Yet taking the manatees down* . . . : Standing Watch, http://www.standing-watch.org/shutdown.html, accessed January 13, 2003. As soon as the wildlife commission staff recommended delaying the vote, the "civil disobedience" note was taken down from the site, but I kept a printout.

*Before the meeting, the* . . . : Kenneth J. Haddad, "Preliminary Biological Status Review of the Florida Manatee (Trichechus manatus latirostris)," Florida Fish and Wildlife Conservation Commission, September 2002.

*In accordance with the state's* . . . : Fleshler, "Florida Wildlife Officials to Decide If Manatee Keeps 'Endangered' Status," *Fort Lauderdale Sun-Sentinel*, December 30, 2002; Haddad, "Preliminary Biological Status Review."

*Ken Haddad, the preacher's kid . . .* : David Fleshler, "State Delays Decision on Status of Manatees," *Fort Lauderdale Sun-Sentinel*, January 24, 2002; Chad Gillis, "Wildlife Commission Delays Decision on Reclassifying Manatees," *Naples Daily News*, January 24, 2003.

*Because of the recommended delay . . .* : Author's personal observations from covering the meeting.

*Pat Rose, still not completely . . .* : Interview with Rose; Patrick M. Rose, "State Plays Games; Manatees in Trouble," *Jupiter Courier*, March 12, 2003.

*"It's killing us . . ."* : David Fleshler, "State Delays Decision on Status of Manatees," *Fort Lauderdale Sun-Sentinel*, January 24, 2002.

*The sponsor was a Manatee County . . .* : Senator Mike Bennett's member page, http://www.flsenate.gov/Legislators/index.cfm?Members=View+Page&District_Num_Link=021&Submenu=1&Tab=legislators&chamber=Senate&CFID=134582461&CFTOKEN=62346743; Steve Bousquet, "Riding a Soft Money Train," *St. Petersburg Times*, January 6, 2008; Mike Salinero, "Bill Emptying Manatee Trust Fund Survives," *Tampa Tribune*, April 22, 2003; Kevin O'Horan, "Bennett Keeps Focus on Sea Cow Trust Fund," *Bradenton Herald*, April 25, 2003.

*Haddad had arranged for two . . .* : Interviews with Patti Thompson and Judith Vallee.

*So in May 2003, the wildlife commissioners . . .* : Author's personal observations from covering the meeting; e-mail from Buddy Powell to the author, May 27, 2003.

*Corbett, the mall developer . . .* : Richard Corbett's background from Florida Fish and Wildlife Conservation Commission; interview with Gil McRae.

*To Cynthia Frisch, the attitude . . .* : Interview with Cynthia Frisch.

*In September 2003, while meeting . . .* : Author's observations while covering the November 19, 2003, wildlife commission meeting.

*Then, in November 2003, the wildlife . . .* : David Fleshler, "Wildlife Panel May Downgrade Manatees' Status," *Fort Lauderdale Sun-Sentinel*, November 6, 2003.

*Rood's blithe comment ticked off . . .* : Carl Hiaasen, "Manatees Remain Threatened," *Miami Herald*, November 16, 2003.

*Meanwhile, manatee deaths were again . . .* : Manatee mortality statistics from Florida Fish and Wildlife Research Institute.

*"It's not a scientific decision . . ."* : Interview with Tom McGill.

*Only months earlier, Rood . . .* : Interview with John Rood.

*During the year delay, the legislature . . .* : Lawmakers filed several manatee-related bills, but the main one was CS/SB 540, which passed and was signed into law June 23, 2004, by Governor Bush. See also the Senate Natural Resources Committee staff analysis of the bill, April 19, 2004.

*Ted Forsgren especially liked . . .* : Craig Pittman and Toni James, "Easing of Manatee Rules Nears Passage," *St. Petersburg Times*, April 30, 2004.

*Outraged environmental advocates . . .* : Paul Flemming, "Bill Would Require Manatee Studies," *Florida Today*, April 20, 2004; Victor Hull, "Manatee Measure Drawing Criticism: Environmentalists Say Sponsors Are Pro-Development," *Lakeland Ledger*, April 25, 2004.

*Had Bennett checked, he . . .* : Sally Swartz, "Save the Manatees, Governor," *Palm Beach Post*, May 5, 2004.

*In the meantime, as members rotated . . .* : Profiles of Brian Yablonski and Kathy Barco from the Florida Fish and Wildlife Conservation Commission; further details on Yablonski from Lucy Morgan, "The New Breed," *St. Petersburg Times*, March 7, 2004.

*In mid-2004 President Bush named* . . . : Interview with Kathy Barco; Craig Pittman, "Choice for Wildlife Post Alarms Environmentalists," *St. Petersburg Times*, October 17, 2004; Don Plummer, "Conservative Foundation's Leader Quits, Denies Charges," *Atlanta Journal-Constitution*, October 5, 2000.

*A month after the end of the* . . . : Interview with Jim Kalvin.

*One of the groups that had* . . . : Interview with Dan Odell.

*In its place, Haddad* . . . : Ken Haddad, September Executive Director's Report, August 30, 2004; interviews with Buddy Powell, Judith Vallee, Patti Thompson, and Helen Spivey.

*By December 2004, Haddad and* . . . : Interviews with Manley Fuller and Pat Rose.

*In the weeks leading up to* . . . : Author's personal observations from Haddad's visit to the *St. Petersburg Times* editorial board.

*As the April 2005 meeting date* . . . : Information on Defenders of Wildlife from http://www. defenders/org; interview with Elizabeth Fleming.

*One of the experts she contacted* . . . : Georgina M. Mace and Russell Lande, "Assessing Extinction Threats: Toward a Reevaluation of IUCN Threatened Species Categories," *Conservation Biology* 5, no. 2 (1991): 148–57; Lande's initial comments on Florida's listing process are contained in *Florida Field Naturalist* 31, no. 4 (2003): 80–81, available at http://www.fosbirds. org/FFN/Articles/FFNv31n4p81–82Cox.pdf.

*On April 14, 2005, the commissioners* . . . : Author's personal observations from covering this meeting.

*A few days later, in an e-mail* . . . : Lande's e-mail to Perran Ross was copied to Pat Rose, who gave it to me. Two years later, Lande was still boiling about how the wildlife commission ignored his advice. When I e-mailed him to verify that he did indeed send this steaming snot-gram to Ross, the IUCN expert replied yes and added that, given the mismanagement by the state, "the best hope for the Florida manatee may be that if . . . it does manage to survive the coming decades, subsequent flooding of south Florida by rising sea levels due to global warming may allow it to recover."

*The news got worse for Glitzenstein's* . . . : "Service Seeks Public Input for Manatee Five-year Review," U.S. Fish and Wildlife Service news release, April 14, 2005; Laurin Sellers, "Manatees Teeter as Endangered, State and Federal Agencies May Bump It off List," *Fort Lauderdale Sun-Sentinel*, April 15, 2005.

*Runge worked with the state* . . . : Interview with Michael Runge.

*But 2005 turned out to be* . . . : Information on manatee mortality from the Florida Fish and Wildlife Research Institute; Craig Pittman, "Red Tide, Boats Take a Grim Toll," *St. Petersburg Times*, January 7, 2006.

*Two weeks after those numbers* . . . : Elsa M. Haubold, Charles Deutsch, and Christopher Fonnesbeck, "Final Biological Status Review of the Florida Manatee (*Trichechus manatus latirostris*)," Florida Fish and Wildlife Conservation Commission, April 2006; interview with Patti Thompson.

*Now at last it was time for* . . . : Author's personal observations from covering this meeting.

*The downlisting vote brought the* . . . : Editorial, "Manatees in the Fast Lane," *Lakeland Ledger*, April 14, 2007; Steven Webster, "Executive Director's Report," *FMCA Advocate*, April 2007, 7.

*While Runge had been helping* . . . : Interview with Michael Runge; Michael C. Runge,

Carol A. Sanders-Reed, Catherine Langtimm, and Christopher J. Fonnesbeck, "A Quantitative Threats Analysis for the Florida Manatee (*Trichechus manatus latirostris*)," U.S. Geological Survey Open-File Report 2007-1086; interview with Dave Hankla.

*One newly hired Interior Department official* . . . : Interviews with Michael Runge, Todd Willens, and Dave Hankla; Willens background from http://www.washingtonstrategies.com/html/todd.html; "U.S. Fish and Wildlife Service: Endangered Species Act Decision Making," GAO-08-688T, May 21, 2008, http://www.gao.gov/new.items/d08688t.pdf.

*Someone inside the Fish and Wildlife* . . . : Joint Save the Manatee Club–PEER press release, April 9, 2007; Peter Whorisky, "Manatees' Status May Change," *Washington Post*, April 9, 2007; the PEER press release had the unsigned memo attached, headed as "White House Report R4:03/26/07."

*Underlining Runge's results, Pitchford's* . . . : Information on manatee mortality from Florida Fish and Wildlife Research Institute.

*The results of the five-year review* . . . : Interviews with Michael Runge, Dave Hankla, Buddy Powell, and David Laist; "Service Announces Availability of the West Indian Manatee Five-Year Review and Its Staff Recommendation to Reclassify the Species," U.S. Fish and Wildlife Service press release, April 9, 2007; "U.S.G.S. Releases Threats Analysis for Florida Manatees," U.S. Geological Survey press release, April 9, 2007.

*Newspaper opinion-makers from* . . . : Editorial, "Doom the Manatee: That's What New Species Status Will Do," *Bradenton Herald*, April 13, 2007; editorial, "Manatees in the Fast Lane," *Lakeland Ledger*, April 14, 2007; Dave Hankla, "Manatee Success Is Ignored," *Florida Today*, May 3, 2007.

## Chapter 17. When Jimmy Met Charlie

*If a team of scientists* . . . : Steve Bousquet, "A Fuzzy Line Divides Personal and Political Lives: Charlie Crist," *St. Petersburg Times*, August 27, 2006; Adam C. Smith, "So, Tell Us about Yourself, Mr. Crist," *St. Petersburg Times*, November 8, 2006; Steve Bousquet, "Crist Is Going Places, with Help," *St. Petersburg Times*, October 28, 2006; Steve Bousquet, "Either Way, Expect Change," *St. Petersburg Times*, November 5, 2006; Steve Bousquet and Alex Leary, "New Governor Will Have Familiar Face," *St. Petersburg Times*, October 25, 2006; Mike Thomas, "Charlie's Luck Trumps Jeb's Brainpower in Big Sugar Deal," *Orlando Sentinel*, June 26, 2008; Michael Grunwald, "Is Florida the Sunset State?" *Time*, July 10, 2008, http://www.time.com/time/magazine/article/0,9171,1821648,00.html.

*Boating clearly meant a lot* . . . : Interview with former senator Rick Dantzler; "Governor Elect Charlie Crist Is a Strong Supporter of Marine Protections," CCA-Florida *Seawatch*, December 2006, http://www.ccaflorida.org/seawatch/december06.html#governor.

*Then, to top it off, there were* . . . : Craig Pittman and Matthew Waite, "Wildlife Board: Friends or Foes?" *St. Petersburg Times*, August 9, 2007.

*The last two were particularly odd* . . . : For more details about Ken Wright's dealings as airport chairman, see chapter 16, "Banking on Phony Numbers," in Pittman and Waite, *Paving Paradise*.

*Bergeron, sixty-three, turned out to have* . . . : Bergeron's biography is from his application for appointment to Governor Charlie Crist; Florida Fish and Wildlife Conservation Commission Report no. 06-SR-26-4415.

*Despite their questionable behavior . . .* : Steve Bousquet and Craig Pittman, "Wildlife Appointees All Crist Boosters," *St. Petersburg Times*, August 21, 2007.

*The final downlisting vote, and . . .* : Author's personal observations from covering meeting.

*But there would be no downlisting . . .* : Letter from Governor Charlie Crist to FWC chairman Rodney Barreto, September 10, 2007, http://www.floridaconservation.org/imperiledspecies/petitions/Crist-letter.pdf; Craig Pittman, "Governor: Slow Down Manatee Decision," *St. Petersburg Times,* September 12, 2007; interviews with Governor Crist, Rodney Barreto, and Pat Rose.

*Despite his love for boating . . .* : Interview with Governor Crist.

*A day later, Crist himself . . .* : Author's observations from covering September 2007 Fish and Wildlife Conservation Commission meeting.

*Since 1982, the International . . .* : 2007 IUCN Red List, http://www.iucnredlist.org/search/details.php/22103/summ.

*The irony grew even . . .* : Interviews with John Reynolds, Buddy Powell, and Chip Deutsch.

*Rose wrote an op-ed piece . . .* : Patrick Rose, "Recent Confirmation of Manatee's Endangered Status Should Kill State Downlisting Plans," Save the Manatee Club, November 20, 2007, http://www.savethemanatee.org/news_oped_downlisting_11-07.html.

*To say the pro-boating and development . . .* : Letter from Doug Rillstone to FWC chairman Rodney Barreto, November 30, 2007.

*The boating-industry representatives . . .* : Interviews with Buddy Powell and Pat Rose.

*Ted Forsgren sent Crist a three-page . . .* : Letter from Ted Forsgren to Governor Crist, November 19, 2007.

*When Rose saw the management plan . . .* : Interview with Pat Rose; "Florida Manatee Management Plan," December 2007, Florida Fish and Wildlife Conservation Commission, http://myfwc.com/docs/WildlifeHabitats/Manatee_MgmtPlan.pdf.

*This wasn't exactly a Hail Mary pass . . .* : "Governor Crist Joins Stop Global Warming Virtual March," governor's office press release, April 17, 2007, http://www.flgov.com/release/8872; "Governor Crist Highlights Florida's Steps to Address Climate Change at National Conference for Mayors," governor's office press release, September 9, 2007, http://www.charliecrist.com/news.php?id=46; Craig Pittman and David C. Adams, "How Gov. Crist Became Gov. Climate," *St. Petersburg Times*, July 21, 2007.

*Knowing how much Crist enjoyed . . .* : Interview with Pat Rose.

*He could still pack in . . .* : Walt Belcher, "Buffett's Fans Revel in Safe Harbor at Amphitheatre," *Tampa Tribune*, November 2, 2007; set list from http://www.buffettworld.com/set-lists/sl-2007/#28.

*Crist showed up with a date . . .* : Brendan Farrington, "Fla. Gov. Charlie Crist Proposes to Girlfriend," Associated Press, July 5, 2008, http://ap.google.com/article/ALeqM5jqT5UNKqtL-8fre8UFBQJFFdw7vEAD91NGPGOo.

*Like Bob Graham before him, Crist was . . .* : Brendan Farrington, "Jimmy Buffett and Governor Talk Manatees," Associated Press, November 2, 2007, http://ap.google.com/article/ALeqM5gzxcuIgXUCv1feyFFLrHbIcKtsjQD8SLJ52Oo; description from official governor's office photo.

*Actually, Buffett had more to say . . .* : Interviews with Governor Crist and Pat Rose.

*Finally, on December 3 . . .* : I was the *St. Petersburg Times* reporter who called Crist.

*The last wildlife commission meeting . . .* : Author's personal observations from covering the meeting. In August 2009, Hopping, seventy-seven, died of complications from a stroke and esophageal cancer.

*With all the publicity about* . . . : Manatee mortality and boating statistics from Florida Fish and Wildlife Conservation Commission.

*So a* St. Petersburg Times *reporter* . . . : Me again.

## Chapter 18. The Dude Abides

*After Pat Rose and Pam* . . . : Records of the Miami-Dade Department of Environmental Resources Protection and the Manatee Protection Plan Review Committee, http://www.miamidade.gov/derm/manatee_agendas_and_information.asp; interviews with Pat Rose and Kipp Frohlich.

*"The survey revealed . . ."* : University of Miami Rosensteil School of Marine and Atmospheric Science, "Final Report, Boat Use Patterns and Boat Traffic Study, Biscayne Bay, Dade County, Fla.," August 12, 1991, p. 1, http://www.miamidade.gov/derm/library/conservation/boat_use_patterns.pdf.

*How effective was the* . . . : Transcript of March 13, 2001, Florida Cabinet meeting, http://www.myflorida.com/myflorida/cabinet/agenda01/0313/trans.html; Miami-Dade DERM PowerPoint presentation, "Manatee Protection in Miami-Dade County," http://www.miamidade.gov/derm/library/mpprc/Informationalpresentation_MPP.pdf.

*In fact, the Miami River had* . . . : Records of the Miami River Commission, http://www.miamirivercommission.org/dredge.htm.

*The Corps began the eighty-six-million-dollar* . . . : U.S. Army Corps of Engineers press release dated May 30, 2008, headlined "U.S. Army Corps of Engineers Suspends Work after Military Munitions Dredged from Miami River."

*Rather than welcome the dredging* . . . : Coralie Carlson, "Miami River Dredging Promises to Clean Up Pollution, Downtown," *Naples Daily News*, November 29, 2004; Matthew Pinzur and Michael Vasque, "Not So Fast on Westward Sprawl, State Tells Dade," *Miami Herald*, July 19, 2008.

*The runaway real estate market* . . . : Michael Grunwald, "Is Florida the Sunset State?" *Time*, July 10, 2008, http://www.time.com/time/magazine/article/0,9171,1821648-1,00.html.

*In 2007, despite signs that the* . . . : Miami-Dade County Commission ordinance 07-144, creating the Miami-Dade Manatee Protection Plan Review Committee, approved October 2, 2007, http://www.miamidade.gov/derm/library/mpprc/Ordinance_07-144_Creating_the_Manatee_Protection_Plan_Review_Committee.pdf.

*DERM's top official informed* . . . : Letter from Carlos Espinosa of Miami-Dade DERM to Kipp Frohlich, September 5, 2007, http://www.miamidade.gov/derm/library/mpprc/05-09-07-MPPRC_letter_to_frohlich.pdf.

*The push for a rewrite* . . . : Jim Defede, "Natacha Seijas Is Downright Mean," CBS4-Miami, December 18, 2006; Daniel A. Ricker, "'Dumb' Manatees Get a Drubbing," *Miami Herald*, November 22, 2004; Matthew I. Pinzur, "Barreiro Proposes Permanent Line," *Miami Herald*, May 14, 2008.

*When the commissioners informed* . . . : Letter from Kipp Frohlich to Carlos Espinosa of Miami-Dade DERM, September 18, 2007, http://www.miamidade.gov/derm/library/mpprc/18-09-07-MPPRC_letter_to_derm.pdf.

*Dick Bunnell built docks for . . .* : "Miami Contractor Sentenced for Building Illegal Structures," U.S. Army Corps of Engineers press release, August 1, 2005, http://www.saj.usace.army.mil/cco/newsReleases/archive/2005/nr0550.htm.

*Needless to say, Bunnell had . . .* : Interview with Dick Bunnell.

*By the time the committee began . . .* : Grunwald, "Is Florida the Sunset State?"

*On April 8, 2008 . . .* : Draft minutes, April 8, 2008, public hearing of Miami-Dade Manatee Protection Plan committee; interview with Lynda Green.

*At Green's suggestion . . .* : Draft minutes, May 21, 2008, meeting of Miami-Dade Manatee Protection Plan Committee; United Press International, "Birth Makes History," *St. Petersburg Times*, May 4, 1975; Jane E. Brody, "Captive Breeding May Be Last Hope of Sea Cow," *New York Times*, March 22, 1983; interview with Lynda Green.

*Before Craig Phillips ever . . .* : History of the *Prins Valdemar* courtesy of Alice Luckhardt and her godmother, Alice Walters Wallace, daughter of the ship's owner, R. J. Walters.

*"At the entrance girl artists . . ."* : Federal Writers' Project, *The WPA Guide to Florida* (1939; reprint, New York: Pantheon Books, 1984), 215.

*The aquarium's exhibits were . . .* : Murrell, *Miami*, 108–9.

*Walters's aquarium offered more . . .* : "40 Pound Baby Not on Census," *Danville (Va.) Bee*, May 27, 1930; Thomas Barbour, "The Birth of a Manatee," *Journal of Mammalogy* 18, no. 1 (1937): 106–7.

*Because R. J. Walters ran . . .* : Samuel Stout obituary, "Sea Cows Were His Good Friends," *Miami Herald*, January 26, 1955; interview with Stout's granddaughter Paulette Carr. Most of the documents on this case from the files of the Manatee County Historical Society were first uncovered by Ms. Carr, who then passed them on to the U.S. Geological Survey's Sirenia Project staff, which is where I got them. I should add, too, that Ms. Carr strongly disagrees with my interpretation of events, because it does not give her grandfather sole credit.

*In 1947, according to . . .* : Harwood, "The Sea Cow Is a Tourist."

*In early 1948 they got another . . .* : Interview with Alice Walters Wallace.

*The story Mrs. Wallace tells . . .* : Interview with Paulette Carr; Samuel Stout obituary, "Sea Cows Were His Good Friends," *Miami Herald*, January 26, 1955.

*On June 25, 1949, about . . .* : Moore, "Status of the Manatee," 31; Samuel Stout obituary, "Sea Cows Were His Good Friends," *Miami Herald*, January 26, 1955.

*The 1949 De Soto Festival promised . . .* : Letter from Walter S. Hardin to Senator R. Bunn Gautier, March 14, 1949, from Manatee County Historical Society files; "Looking Back: Manatee County 1900–2007," *Bradenton Herald*, May 15, 2007.

*The Miami politico, state senator . . .* : R. Bunn Gautier background from obituary, "Deaths Elsewhere," *St. Petersburg Times*, February 10, 1989, and from "University of Miami—Named Buildings History," Fall 2001, 32–33, http://www6.miami.edu/advancement/NamedBuildings-Medical.doc.

*"After conferring with the . . ."* : Senator R. Bunn Gauthier to Walter Hardin, March 18, 1949, from Manatee County Historical Society files.

*The* Sports Afield *story about harpooning . . .* : Letter from Walter S. Hardin to George Vathis, March 28, 1949, from Manatee County Historical Society files.

*When that story hit the papers . . .* : Betty Kohlman, "After 28 Years, the Truth Comes Out about Baby Snoots," *St. Petersburg Times*, January 24, 1977.

*Chryst didn't exactly apologize . . .* : Letter from T. L. Chryst to Walter Hardin, March 29, 1949, from files of Manatee County Historical Society.

*Just as the De Soto Festival got into . . .* : Letter from George Vathis to Walter Hardin, March 25, 1949, from files of Manatee County Historical Society.

*Hardin, when he thanked Senator Gautier . . .* : Letter from Walter Hardin to Senator J. Bunn Gautier, March 21, 1949, from files of Manatee County Historical Society.

*But in replying to Vathis . . .* : Letter from Walter Hardin to George Vathis, March 28, 1949, from files of Manatee County Historical Society.

*When the festival was over . . .* : "Live Manatee Drops into Lap of Bradenton," *Bradenton Herald*, April 1, 1949; Samuel Stout obituary, "Sea Cows Were His Good Friends," *Miami Herald*, January 26, 1955.

*Meanwhile, Vathis kept . . .* : Samuel Stout obituary, "Sea Cows Were His Good Friends," *Miami Herald*, January 26, 1955; letter from George Vathis to Manatee County Commission, March 31, 1949, from files of the Manatee County Historical Society; terms of the deal from letter from Walter Hardin to Representative J. Ben Fuqua, April 4, 1949, from files of the Manatee County Historical Society.

*"Bradenton learned with some consternation . . ."* : "Live Manatee Drops into Lap of Bradenton," *Bradenton Herald*, April 1, 1949; letter from Walter Hardin to Samuel Stout, April 5, 1949, from files of the Manatee County Historical Society.

*And that's what they did . . .* : Lawrence Thompson, "Miami's Sea Calf Going to Bradenton," *Miami Herald*, April 29, 1949.

*As for Stout, he claimed . . .* : Betty Kohlman, "After 28 Years, the Truth Comes Out about Baby Snoots," *St. Petersburg Times*, January 24, 1977.

*The two-year-old "came at call" . . .* : Moore, "Status of the Manatee," 32.

*By the time Moore visited Baby . . .* : Interview with Alice Walters Wallace; Samuel Stout obituary, "Sea Cows Were His Good Friends," *Miami Herald*, January 26, 1955.

*Snooty's continued survival . . .* : "Baby Snoots Has the Flu, Sore Throat," *St. Petersburg Times*, December 31, 1967; Robert Kyle, (headline missing), *St. Petersburg Times*, March 7, 1973; Thomas Oldt, (headline missing), *St. Petersburg Times*, July 25, 1977. Snooty was popular fodder for newspaper features over the years, but one of the odder stories ran in the *St. Petersburg Times* on June 5, 1966. It's about moving the manatee to a larger tank. The byline says the story is "By BABY SNOOTS as Told to Pat Piper."

*Joe Moore wasn't the last manatee scientist . . .* : Interviews with Buddy Powell, Woodie Hartman, Pat Rose, Cathy Beck, and Bob Bonde.

*Over the years, other manatees made . . .* : For a rundown on Chessie's travels, see http://www.sirenian.org/chessie.html; the U.S. Geological Survey has tracked plenty of other wanderers, such as this one: http://soundwaves.usgs.gov/2006/09/research2.html.

*Then, in 1991, the year Snooty turned . . .* : Barbara Behrendt, "Museum No Place for a Manatee, Some Say," *St. Petersburg Times*, June 28, 1991; Jeff Brazil, "Snooty the Manatee and His Sad Saga," *Orlando Sentinel*, September 1, 1991.

*The manatee that finally shattered . . .* : Dale White, "New Roomies: Snooty, Meet Newton," *Sarasota Herald-Tribune*, February 3, 1998; John DeSantis, "Manatee Matchup: Sea Cows Cavort," *Sarasota Herald-Tribune*, February 5, 1998; Kathleen Beeman, "Snooty, Newton Making Nice-Nice," *Tampa Tribune*, February 10, 1998; Dale White, "Sibling Rivalry? Back Seat Not for Snooty," *Sarasota Herald-Tribune*, February 24, 1998; Dale White, "Museum Seeks Help with Water Bill," *Sarasota Herald-Tribune*, February 26, 1998.

*Seven months later, on a Saturday* . . . : Gretchen Parker, "Bacteria Can Kill Rapidly, Vet Says," *Sarasota Herald-Tribune*, August 25, 1998; Morgan Stinemetz, "Doctor Keeps Watch Over Snooty," *Sarasota Herald-Tribune*, September 21, 1998.

*Over the next ten years aquarium* . . . : Brett Barrouquere, "Mo to Move in with Snooty," *Sarasota Herald-Tribune*, November 12, 1998; Brian Neill, "Odd Job: Manatee's Manatee Maintenance," *Bradenton Herald*, June 3, 2007.

*Two weeks before Snooty turned* . . . : Author's personal observations; interview with Buddy Powell; interview with Pat Rose.

*For a while Snooty had* . . . : Interview with Marjory Margold of the South Florida Museum and Parker Manatee Aquarium; Tiffany St. Martin, "Wish Snooty a Happy 58th birthday," *Bradenton Herald*, July 20, 2006.

*After the show, Powell and I walked* . . . : Interview with Buddy Powell; author's personal observations.

# Selected Bibliography

Allan, Leslie, Beryl Kuder, and Sarah Oakes. *Promised Lands*. Vol. 2, *Subdivisions in Florida's Wetlands*. New York: INFORM, 1977.

Bangs, Outram. "The Present Standing of the Florida Manatee, *Trichechus Latirostris* (Harlan) in the Indian River Waters." *American Naturalist*, September 1895, 783–87.

Barbour, Thomas. *That Vanishing Eden: A Naturalist's Florida*. Boston: Little, Brown, 1944.

Barnett, Cynthia. *Mirage: Florida and the Vanishing Water of the Eastern U.S.* Ann Arbor: University of Michigan Press, 2007.

Beard, Daniel B., Frederick C. Lincoln, Victor H. Cahalane, Hartley H. T. Jackson, and Ben H. Thompson. *Fading Trails: The Story of Endangered American Wildlife*. New York: MacMillan, 1942.

Betz, Joseph J. "Sea Cow Deception." *Sea Frontiers* 14, no. 4 (1968): 204–9.

Blackman, E. V. *Miami and Dade County, Florida: Its Settlement, Progress, and Achievement*. Washington, D.C.: Victor Rainbolt, 1921.

Board, Prudy Taylor. *Remembering Lee County: Where Winter Spends the Summer*. The History Press, 2006.

Bonde, Robert K., Thomas J. O'Shea, and Cathy A. Beck. *Manual of Procedures for the Salvage and Necropsy of Carcasses of the West Indian Manatee (Trichechus manatus)*. Gainesville: U.S. Geological Survey, 1983.

Boning, Charles R. *Florida's Rivers*. Sarasota: Pineapple Press, 2007.

Boyle, Robert H., and Rose Mary Mechem. "There's Trouble in Paradise." *Sports Illustrated*, February 9, 1981, 82–96.

Burnett, Gene M. *Florida's Past: People and Events That Shaped the State*. Vol. 1. Tampa: Hillsboro Printing, 1986.

Calleson, Scott, and R. Kipp Frohlich, "Slower Boat Speeds Reduce Risks to Manatees." *Endangered Species Bulletin* 3 (2007): 295–304.

Canova, Andrew P., assisted by L. S. Perkins. *Life and Adventures in South Florida*. Tampa: Tribune Printing Company, 1906.

Chesney, Ann Spach, Frances G. Hunter, Harriet Stiger Liles, Ann Josberger McFadden, Eliza Phillips Ruden, and Larry Wiggins. *Miami Diary, 1896: A Day by Day Account of Events That Occurred the Year Miami Became a City*. Miami: privately printed, 1996.

Church, George B., Jr. *The Life of Henry Laurens Mitchell, Florida 16th Governor*. New York: Vantage Press, 1978.

Clark, Tim, Richard P. Reading, and Alice L. Clarke, eds. *Endangered Species Recovery: Finding the Lessons, Improving the Process*. Washington, D.C.: Island Press, 1994.

Colburn, David R. *From Yellow Dog Democrats to Red State Republicans: Florida and Its Politics since 1940*. Gainesville: University Press of Florida, 2007.

Cory, Charles B. *Hunting and Fishing in Florida*. New York: Arno Press, 1970. Reprint of 1896 edition.

Dantzler, Rick. *Under the Panther Moon and Other Florida Tales*. Port Salerno: Florida Classics Library, 2001.

Date, Shirish V. *Quiet Passion: A Biography of Senator Bob Graham*. New York: Penguin/Tharcher, 2004.

Dierauf, Leslie A., and Frances M. D. Gulland, eds. *CRC Handbook of Marine Mammal Medicine*. Boca Raton: CRC Press, 2001.

Dieterich, Emily Perry. "Birds of a Feather: The Coconut Grove Audubon Society, 1915–1917." *Tequesta* 45 (1985): 5–27.

Eng, Steve. *Jimmy Buffett: The Man from Margaritaville Revealed*. New York: St. Martins Press, 1996.

Gannon, Frank. "The Last of the Manatees?" *Philip Morris Magazine*, September–October 1990, 22–25.

Gilpin, Mrs. John R. "To Miami, 1890 Style." *Tequesta* 1 (1941): 89–102.

Gregg, W. H., with Captain John Gardner. *Where, When, and How to Catch Fish on the East Coast of Florida*. Buffalo: The Matthews-Northrup Works, 1902.

Grunwald, Michael. *The Swamp: The Everglades, Florida, and the Politics of Paradise*. New York: Simon & Schuster, 2005.

Hartman, Daniel S. *Ecology and Behavior of the Manatee (Trichechus manatus) in Florida*. Special Publication no. 5, American Society of Mammalogists, 1979.

———. "Florida Manatees, Mermaids in Peril." *National Geographic*, August 1968, 342–53.

———. "To Save a Sea Cow: The Story of Manatee Conservation in the United States." Unpublished study, Florida Department of Environmental Protection, 1999.

Harwood, Kitty. "The Sea Cow Is a Tourist." *Sports Afield*, November 1947, 50, 89.

Irvine, Blair, and Howard W. Campbell. "Aerial Census of the West Indian Manatee, *Trichechus manatus*, in the Southeastern United States." *Journal of Mammalogy* 59, no. 3 (1978): 613–17.

LeBaron, J. Francis. "The Manatee, or Sea Cow." *Forest and Stream* 13 (1880): 1005–6.

Leonard, Irving A. *The Florida Adventures of Kirk Munroe, Narrative and Biographical*. Chululota, Fla.: Mickler Brothers, 1975.

Madsen, Axel. *Cousteau: An Unauthorized Biography*. New York: Beaufort Books, 1986.

*Makers of America (Florida Edition): An Historical and Biographical Work by an Able Corps of Writers*. Vol. 3. Atlanta: A. B. Caldwell, 1909.

Mann, Charles C., and Mark L. Plummer. *Noah's Choice: The Future of Endangered Species.* New York: Knopf, 1995.

Marmontel, Miriam, Stephen R. Humphrey, and Thomas O'Shea. "Population Viability Analysis of the Florida Manatee (*Trichechus manatus latirostris*), 1976–1991." *Conservation Biology* 11, no. 2 (1997): 467–81.

McClellan, Scott. *What Happened: Inside the Bush White House and Washington's Culture of Deception.* New York: Public Affairs, 2008.

McGill, Tom. *The Florida Manatee Conspiracy of Ignorance.* Merritt Island, Fla.: RALCO, 2004.

McIver, Stuart. "Boats on Biscayne Bay." *South Florida History* 27, no. 3 (1999): 10–13.

Moore, Joseph C. "Mammals from Welaka, Putnam County, Florida." *Journal of Mammalogy* 27, no. 1 (1946): 49–59.

———. "A Mysterious Encounter." *Chicago Natural History Museum Bulletin*, November 1964, 7–8.

———. "Observations of Manatees in Aggregations." *American Museum Novitiates* no. 1811 (1956): 1–24.

———. "The Range of the Florida Manatee." *Quarterly Journal of the Florida Academy of Science* 14 (1951): 1–19.

———. "The Status of the Manatee in the Everglades National Park, with Notes on Its Natural History." *Journal of Mammalogy* 32 (1951): 22–36.

Munroe, Kirk. *Canoemates: A Story of the Florida Reef and Everglades.* New York and London: Harper & Bros., 1892.

Munroe, Mary Barr. "Pioneer Women of Dade County." *Tequesta* 3 (1943): 45–56.

Munroe, Ralph Middleton, and Vincent Gilpin. *The Commodore's Story.* Miami: Historical Association of Southern Florida, 1974.

Munson, Richard. *Cousteau: The Captain and His World.* New York: William Morrow, 1989.

Murrell, Muriel V. *Miami: A Look Back.* Sarasota: Pineapple Press, 2003.

O'Shea, Thomas, Bruce Ackerman, and Franklin H. Percival, eds. *Population Biology of the Florida Manatee.* Information and Technology Report 1, Department of the Interior, August 1995.

Peters, Thelma. *Biscayne Country, 1870–1926.* Miami: Banyan Books, 1981.

Phillips, Craig. *The Captive Sea: Life Behind the Scenes of the Great Modern Oceanariums.* Philadelphia: Chilton Press, 1964.

Pittman, Craig, and Matthew Waite. *Paving Paradise: Florida's Vanishing Wetlands and the Failure of No Net Loss.* Gainesville: University of Florida Press, 2009.

Plater, Zygmunt J. B. "Endangered Species Act Lessons over 30 Years and the Legacy of the Snail Darter, a Small Fish in a Porkbarrel." *Environmental Law* 34, no. 2 (2004): 289–308, http://ssrn.com/abstract=617581.

Powell, James. *Manatees: Natural History and Conservation.* Stillwater, Minn.: Voyageur Press, 2002.

Price, Jennifer. *Flight Maps: Adventures with Nature in Modern America.* New York: Basic Books, 2000.

Reep, Roger L., and Robert K. Bonde, *Florida Manatee: Biology and Conservation.* Gainesville: University Press of Florida, 2006.

Reilly, Benjamin. *Tropical Surge: A History of Ambition and Disaster on the Florida Shore.* Sarasota: Pineapple Press, 2005.

Rerick, Rowland H. *Memoirs of Florida.* Vol. 2. Atlanta: Southern Historical Association, 1902.

Roberts, Callum. *The Unnatural History of the Sea.* Washington, D.C.: Island Press, 2007.

Shappee, Nathan D. "Flagler's Undertakings in Miami in 1897." *Tequesta* 19 (1959): 3–13.

Spillan, Trisha. "O. Earle Frye, Jr. Moves on after 31 Years of Service." *Florida Wildlife*, May–June 1977, 38–39.

Sprunt, Alexander, Jr. "Mystery Mammal—The Florida Manatee." *Audubon Magazine*, September–October 1949, 286–88, 337.

True, Frederick W. "The Sirenians, or Sea-Cows." In *The Fisheries and Fishery Industries of the United States*, ed. G. Browne Good, 114–36. Washington, D.C.: Government Printing Office, 1884.

Waitley, Douglas. *Best Backroads of Florida.* Vol. 2, *Coasts, Glades, and Groves.* Sarasota: Pineapple Press, 2001.

Weber, Michael L. *From Abundance to Scarcity: A History of U.S. Marine Fisheries Policy.* Washington, D.C.: Island Press, 2002.

Wiggins, Larry. "The Birth of the City of Miami." *Tequesta* 55 (1995): 5–37.

Wilson, F. Page. "Miami: From Frontier to Metropolis: An Appraisal," *Tequesta* 14 (1954): 25–49.

———. "We Choose the Sub-Tropics." *Tequesta* 12 (1952): 19–45.

Wright, Julia McNair. *Sea-side and Way-side No. 4.* Boston: D.C. Heath, 1892.

Zeiller, Warren. *Introducing the Manatee.* Gainesville: University Press of Florida, 1992.

# Index

Craig Pittman is a native Floridian. Born in Pensacola, he graduated from Troy State University in Alabama, where his muckraking work for the student paper prompted an agitated dean to label him "the most destructive force on campus." Since then he has covered a variety of newspaper beats and quite a few natural disasters, including hurricanes, wildfires, and the Florida Legislature. Since 1998 he has reported on environmental issues for Florida's largest newspaper, the *St. Petersburg Times*. In 2004 he won the Waldo Proffitt Award for Distinguished Environmental Journalism in Florida for revealing a secret plan by the state's business leaders to transfer water from sleepy north Florida to booming south Florida. Pittman shared the 2006 Waldo Proffitt Award for the series "Vanishing Wetlands" written with colleague Matthew Waite. The series, which found that federal and state wetland protection programs did little to save swamps and marshes, also won a national award, the Kevin Carmody Award for Outstanding Investigative Reporting, from the Society of Environmental Journalists. Pittman and Waite shared a second Proffitt Award and a second Carmody Award in 2007 the series "When Dry Is Wet," which exposed the flaws in the wetland mitigation banking industry. He is coauthor, with Waite, of *Paving Paradise: Florida's Vanishing Wetlands and the Failure of No Net Loss* (University Press of Florida, 2009).

THE FLORIDA HISTORY AND CULTURE SERIES

Edited by Raymond Arsenault and Gary R. Mormino

*Al Burt's Florida: Snowbirds, Sand Castles, and Self-Rising Crackers*, by Al Burt (1997)

*Black Miami in the Twentieth Century*, by Marvin Dunn (1997; first paperback edition, 2016)

*Gladesmen: Gator Hunters, Moonshiners, and Skiffers*, by Glen Simmons and Laura Ogden (1998)

*"Come to My Sunland": Letters of Julia Daniels Moseley from the Florida Frontier, 1882–1886*, edited by Julia Winifred Moseley and Betty Powers Crislip (1998; first paperback edition, 2020)

*The Enduring Seminoles: From Alligator Wrestling to Ecotourism*, by Patsy West (1998)

*Government in the Sunshine State: Florida Since Statehood*, by David R. Colburn and Lance deHaven-Smith (1999)

*The Everglades: An Environmental History*, by David McCally (1999; first paperback edition, 2000)

*Beechers, Stowes, and Yankee Strangers: The Transformation of Florida*, by John T. Foster Jr. and Sarah Whitmer Foster (1999)

*The Tropic of Cracker*, by Al Burt (1999; first paperback edition, 2009)

*Balancing Evils Judiciously: The Proslavery Writings of Zephaniah Kingsley*, edited and annotated by Daniel W. Stowell (2000)

*Hitler's Soldiers in the Sunshine State: German POWs in Florida*, by Robert D. Billinger Jr. (2000; first paperback edition, 2009)

*Cassadaga: The South's Oldest Spiritualist Community*, edited by John J. Guthrie Jr., Phillip Charles Lucas, and Gary Monroe (2000)

*Claude Pepper and Ed Ball: Politics, Purpose, and Power*, by Tracy E. Danese (2000)

*Pensacola during the Civil War: A Thorn in the Side of the Confederacy*, by George F. Pearce (2000; first paperback edition, 2008)

*Castles in the Sand: The Life and Times of Carl Graham Fisher*, by Mark S. Foster (2000)

*Miami, U.S.A.*, by Helen Muir (2000)

*Politics and Growth in Twentieth-Century Tampa*, by Robert Kerstein (2001)

*The Invisible Empire: The Ku Klux Klan in Florida*, by Michael Newton (2001)

*The Wide Brim: Early Poems and Ponderings of Marjory Stoneman Douglas*, edited by Jack E. Davis (2002)

*The Architecture of Leisure: The Florida Resort Hotels of Henry Flagler and Henry Plant*, by Susan R. Braden (2002)

*Florida's Space Coast: The Impact of NASA on the Sunshine State*, by William Barnaby Faherty, S.J. (2002)

*In the Eye of Hurricane Andrew*, by Eugene F. Provenzo Jr. and Asterie Baker Provenzo (2002)

*Florida's Farmworkers in the Twenty-first Century*, text by Nano Riley and photographs by Davida Johns (2003)

*Making Waves: Female Activists in Twentieth-Century Florida*, edited by Jack E. Davis and Kari Frederickson (2003; first paperback edition, 2003)

*Orange Journalism: Voices from Florida Newspapers*, by Julian M. Pleasants (2003)

*The Stranahans of Fort Lauderdale: A Pioneer Family of New River*, by Harry A. Kersey Jr. (2003)

*Death in the Everglades: The Murder of Guy Bradley, America's First Martyr to Environmentalism*, by Stuart B. McIver (2003; first paperback edition, 2009)

*Jacksonville: The Consolidation Story, from Civil Rights to the Jaguars*, by James B. Crooks (2004; first paperback edition, 2019)

*The Seminole Wars: America's Longest Indian Conflict*, by John and Mary Lou Missall (2004; first paperback edition, 2016)

*The Mosquito Wars: A History of Mosquito Control in Florida*, by Gordon Patterson (2004)

*Seasons of Real Florida*, by Jeff Klinkenberg (2004; first paperback edition, 2009)

*Land of Sunshine, State of Dreams: A Social History of Modern Florida*, by Gary R. Mormino (2005; first paperback edition, 2008)

*Paradise Lost? The Environmental History of Florida*, edited by Jack E. Davis and Raymond Arsenault (2005; first paperback edition, 2005)

*Frolicking Bears, Wet Vultures, and Other Oddities: A New York City Journalist in Nineteenth-Century Florida*, edited by Jerald T. Milanich (2005)

*Waters Less Traveled: Exploring Florida's Big Bend Coast*, by Doug Alderson (2005)

*Saving South Beach*, by M. Barron Stofik (2005; first paperback edition, 2012)

*Losing It All to Sprawl: How Progress Ate My Cracker Landscape*, by Bill Belleville (2006; first paperback edition, 2010)

*Voices of the Apalachicola*, compiled and edited by Faith Eidse (2006)

*Floridian of His Century: The Courage of Governor LeRoy Collins*, by Martin A. Dyckman (2006)

*America's Fortress: A History of Fort Jefferson, Dry Tortugas, Florida*, by Thomas Reid (2006)

*Weeki Wachee, City of Mermaids: A History of One of Florida's Oldest Roadside Attractions*, by Lu Vickers (2007)

*City of Intrigue, Nest of Revolution: A Documentary History of Key West in the Nineteenth Century*, by Consuelo E. Stebbins (2007)

*The New Deal in South Florida: Design, Policy, and Community Building, 1933–1940*, edited by John A. Stuart and John F. Stack Jr. (2008)

*The Enduring Seminoles: From Alligator Wrestling to Casino Gaming, Revised and Expanded Edition*, by Patsy West (2008)

*Pilgrim in the Land of Alligators: More Stories about Real Florida*, by Jeff Klinkenberg (2008; first paperback edition, 2011)

*A Most Disorderly Court: Scandal and Reform in the Florida Judiciary*, by Martin A. Dyckman (2008)

*A Journey into Florida Railroad History*, by Gregg M. Turner (2008; first paperback edition, 2012)

*Sandspurs: Notes from a Coastal Columnist*, by Mark Lane (2008)

*Paving Paradise: Florida's Vanishing Wetlands and the Failure of No Net Loss*, by Craig Pittman and Matthew Waite (2009; first paperback edition, 2010)

*Embry-Riddle at War: Aviation Training during World War II*, by Stephen G. Craft (2009)

*The Columbia Restaurant: Celebrating a Century of History, Culture, and Cuisine*, by Andrew T. Huse, with recipes and memories from Richard Gonzmart and the Columbia restaurant family (2009)

Lightning Source UK Ltd.
Milton Keynes UK
UKHW012056210622
404775UK00003B/54